Commanding Wellington's Horse Artillery

Commanding Wellington's Horse Artillery

Letters of Colonel Sir Augustus Simon Frazer, K.C.B. Commanding the Royal Horse Artillery in the Peninsular War & Waterloo Campaigns

ILLUSTRATED

Edward Sabine

Commanding Wellington's Horse Artillery
Letters of Colonel Sir Augustus Simon Frazer, K.C.B. Commanding the Royal Horse Artillery in the Peninsular War & Waterloo Campaigns
by Edward Sabine

ILLUSTRATED

First published under the title
Letters of Colonel Sir Augustus Simon Frazer, K.C.B. Commanding the Royal Horse Artillery

Leonaur is an imprint of Oakpast Ltd
Copyright in this form © 2018 Oakpast Ltd

ISBN: 978-1-78282-720-7 (hardcover)
ISBN: 978-1-78282-721-4 (softcover)

http://www.leonaur.com

Publisher's Notes

The views expressed in this book are not necessarily those of the publisher.

Contents

Preface 7

LETTERS DURING THE PENINSULAR CAMPAIGNS
1812 11
1813 31
1814 260

LETTERS DURING THE WATERLOO CAMPAIGN
1815 330

Preface

The writer of the following letters was the son of Colonel Andrew Frazer, of the Royal Engineers, and of Charlotte, daughter of Stillingfleet Durnford, Esq., of the Ordnance Office. He was born on the 5th of September, 1776, at Dunkirk, where his father was at the time Assistant Commissary for the demolition of the works of that fortress. He received his early education at the High School of Edinburgh, where he was a contemporary of Lord Brougham, Francis Horner, and Professor Pillans, although their junior. Through the kindness of an introduction from Leonard Horner, Esq., I am indebted to John Russell, Esq. (grandson of the historian Robertson), both for his own recollections, and for those of George Ross, Esq., and Dr. Alexander Gillespie, of Augustus Frazer at this period of his life. These three gentlemen were his contemporaries at the High School, and the two last were his class-fellows. They are all still living, (1859), and concur in describing him as a lively boy, fond of boyish sports, clever, and, for his years, accounted a good scholar.

He must, however, have left the High School soon after he was thirteen years of age, as in August, 1790, he was admitted as a Gentleman Cadet into the Royal Military Academy at Woolwich; from whence he obtained the commission of Second Lieutenant in the Royal Regiment of Artillery, on the 18th of September, 1793, and in December of that year joined the army in Flanders, commanded by His Royal Highness the Duke of York. In January, 1794, he was promoted to First Lieutenant, and was attached with two field-guns to the 3rd Regiment of Foot Guards, with whom he served until the return of the army to England in May, 1795; having during that period been present at the affair of Mouvaux, April 14th, 1794, the Battle of Cateau Cambresis, April 26th, the affairs of the 10th, 17th, 18th, and 22nd of May, near Tournay, the affair of Boxtel, in September, and the recapture of Fort St. Andre, in the November of the same year. In May, 1795, Lieut. Frazer was appointed to the Royal Horse Artillery, and in September, 1799, received the commission of Captain-Lieutenant, being still continued in the Horse Artillery, with a troop of which he embarked the same month for North Holland; and was present at the affairs of September 19th, near Bergen, and of the 2nd and 6th of October, near Egmont and Alkmaer. In November, 1799, he returned to England with the troops employed in the service in North Holland.

In September, 1803, Captain Frazer received the commission of Captain of Artillery, and was appointed to the command of a troop of Horse Artillery, with which in March, 1807, he embarked for South America, where he commanded the Artillery of the expedition against Buenos Ayres, and was present at the assault of that city in July, 1807. In June, 1811, Captain Frazer received the brevet rank of Major; and in November, 1812, joined, in the Peninsula, the army under His Grace the Duke of Wellington, having made a temporary exchange of troops with Major Bull, who was under the necessity of returning to England from severe illness. The letters in this volume commence from this date.

In April, 1813, Major Frazer was appointed to command the Horse Artillery of the Duke of Wellington's army, and was present at the affairs of Salamanca and Osma in May and June; at the Battle of Vitoria (on which occasion he received the brevet rank of Lieut.-Colonel); at both operations of the siege of St. Sebastian, where he commanded the batteries of the right attack; at the passage of the Bidassoa, on the 7th of October; of the Nivelle, on the 10th of November; at the affairs on the Nive, on the 9th, 10th, 11th, 12th, and 13th of December, 1813; at the crossing of the Adour, on the 23rd of February, 1814; at the investment of Bayonne, on the 27th of February (where he received a severe wound); and at the Battle of Toulouse on the 10th of April, 1814.

Hostilities then ceasing, Lieut.-Colonel Frazer returned to England, receiving for his services with the Peninsular Army a medal and two clasps, and the distinction of a Knight Commander of the Bath. Soon after his arrival in England, Lieut.-Colonel Sir Augustus Frazer, K.C.B., was appointed to command the Artillery in the eastern district of England; and on the 20th of December, 1814, was promoted to a Regimental Lieut.-Colonelcy in the Royal Artillery.

Hostilities having broken out afresh on the return of the Emperor Napoleon from Elba, Sir Augustus Frazer joined the Allied Army in Flanders, under the Duke of Wellington, in March, 1815, and resumed the command (which he had previously held in the Peninsula) of the

Horse Artillery of the army. On assuming this command, the high reputation which Sir Augustus Frazer enjoyed as an Artillery officer, combined with his firmness of character, prevailed on the Duke of Wellington, who was at first not favourable to the exchange, to permit him to substitute 9-pounders for 6-pounders in the troops of Horse Artillery serving with the army. To this exchange, which preceded the Battle of Waterloo, may justly be ascribed much of the success of that memorable day, in the far heavier loss which the case-shot of the 9-pounders, stationed in front of the British line, inflicted upon the enemy advancing to the attack, and in the consequent saving of life to the allied troops by whom the attack was repulsed.

The advantage of such a substitution will not be doubted in the present day, when the importance of the employment of heavier field ordnance than was then customary, has become a matter of universal recognition. A lively narrative of the subsequent events of the Waterloo campaign, together with the march to Paris, and the surrender and occupation of that Capital, will be found in the letters nearer the close of the volume.

Whilst serving with the army of occupation, Sir Augustus Frazer was appointed British Artillery Commissioner, for receiving over from the French the fortresses to be occupied by the Allied Army pursuant to the treaty of peace. On the return of the army to England, he was appointed to the command of the Horse Artillery at headquarters (Woolwich), which he retained until promoted to a regimental colonelcy in January, 1825. In October, 1827, he received the appointment of assistant inspector of the Ordnance Carriage Department, and in July of the following year, that of director of the Royal Laboratory, which last appointment he retained until his death, which took place on the 11th of June, 1835. Sir Augustus Frazer was elected a Fellow of the Royal Society on the 21st of June, 1816.

Sir Augustus Frazer married, in 1809, Emma, youngest daughter of James Lynn, Esq. of Woodbridge, in Suffolk, and had issue two sons. The eldest, Augustus Henry, born in August, 1810, obtained a commission in the Royal Artillery, and retired from the service after attaining the rank of second captain; he died unmarried while travelling in Syria, in July, 1848. The younger son, Andrew James, born in October, 1812, obtained a lieutenant's commission in the Rifle Corps, from which he retired after a short service, and died unmarried at Ramsgate, in July, 1845. Sir Augustus Frazer had an only sister, Maria Ernestine, who was married to M. Huber, since deceased; she is still living, (1859), in Vienna.

The letters contained in this volume were addressed partly to Lady Frazer, and partly to her brother-in-law and sister, Major-and Mrs. Moor, of Great Bealings, in Suffolk. Lady Frazer survived both her sons, and died at Woolwich in November, 1856: Major and Mrs. Moor are also deceased. The letters have lately come into the possession of their two children, the Rev. Edward Moor, of Great Bealings, and Charlotte, married to the Vice-Chancellor Sir William Page Wood. The late Captain Augustus Henry Frazer had contemplated the publication of his father's life, but his own premature death arrested this design. It appeared, however, to the present possessors of the correspondence, that the letters possessed an interest of their own apart from the important military events to which they relate, and the distinguished position occupied by the writer.

The letters are remarkable for their lively, and at the same time simple, exhibition of the first impressions made on a mind of more than ordinary vigour, by the stirring events of the period. They placed the letters, therefore, in my hands to arrange for publication, and to edit. I believe that any artillery officer might have been glad and proud to have paid this tribute to the memory of one who had been so great an ornament to the corps; but to myself the office has been peculiarly agreeable. I had the advantage of being a subaltern officer of Sir Augustus Frazer's troop from 1807 to 1812, and was honoured by his friendship, for which, and for the benefits of his counsels and example, I have ever cherished a deep sense of gratitude. More than any other officer whom I have known, he possessed the faculty of impressing on those who served with him a sense of their responsibility to the country which maintains them in an honourable position, and of inspiring them with a desire on all occasions to prefer the interests of the public service (whether in or beyond the strict line of duty) to their own personal comfort, convenience, or advantage.

The volume is indebted to General Sir John Burgoyne, Bart., G.C.B., for the plan of the attack on St. Sebastian, which has been copied, by his permission, from an original in the War Office. The two original maps by which the progress of the army from Portugal through Spain into France may be traced, and in which are inserted the names of most of the places referred to in the letters, have been drawn expressly for the work by Mr. Arrowsmith.

Edward Sabine.

13 Ashley Place, London. March, 1859.

Letters During the Peninsular Campaigns

1812

Letter 1

Ordnance Office: 1 p. m. 12th Nov. 1812.

I have been out of luck this rainy morning, having found no one in the way; General Macleod is at Woolwich, and till I shall have seen him I know nothing. I now write while waiting to see Col. Chapman, the master-general's secretary; and I am to see Torrens about 2 p.m. at the Horse Guards. Bloomfield has left town with the prince two days ago, I shall therefore lose the opportunity of seeing him. All these things delay progress, and no place is more uncomfortable at all times to me, and particularly so at present, than London.

3 p.m. 13th Nov.

P.S.—I have at last seen General Macleod, and received his orders to proceed forthwith to Portsmouth.

Letter 2.

Portsmouth: 25th Nov. 1812.

You desire me to do what I cannot do just yet—*viz.* to determine the term of our separation; this must be dependent, not on ourselves, but, even humanly speaking, on a thousand little contingencies beyond our foresight and control. Of this rest assured, that I have no wild ambition to gratify, nor any great thirst for applause; that I have neither the desire nor intention to do more than my duty; and that I no longer consider myself at liberty to run the risks I may formerly have done. Let this acknowledgment, with all the reflections to which it may, and doubtless will, give rise, content you; and let us both trust that a merciful Providence will soon re-unite us,

I have secured a passage on board the *Loire* frigate, going as a single ship with General Rebow. Captain Brown commands her; quite a stranger to me, but a very gentlemanly man. My getting into the *Loire* has been chiefly from the friendly offices of General Rebow, who has been more than usually attentive. A horse transport takes in artillery horses on Thursday. Mine will go comfortably in this vessel.

LETTER 3

Portsmouth: 26th Nov. 1812.

I set off for Spithead in the boat of Mr. Spencer, ordnance storekeeper, taking Close, (Capt. Charles Close, Royal Artillery, A. D. C. to General Rebow), with me. We went to the *Loire*, a noble frigate, mounting forty-eight guns, and well-manned; from thence we paid our respects to the *Sea Horse*. I have a further treat in expectation, that of going to the *Victory*, and seeing where Nelson fell.

I am glad to hear that your friend has been prevailed upon to lay his hand once more to the labouring oar, and that he will again settle steadily to his profession. Few of us, I believe, possess sufficient versatility of talent to justify a change of profession; and when he compares his mode of life with the rest of us, he must surely be convinced that, although all have their share of inconveniences, he is in no way worse off than others.

Watch-box in the Dockyard: 11 a.m.

The horses are embarking in the *Hawkesbury*, No. 378, a fine transport. After seeing this, I shall proceed to the *Loire* or *Sea Horse*. Forty horses, all artillery, are going in the *Hawkesbury*, and two lieutenants of drivers, so that Smith will be in clover. The bustle is increasing: three ships taking in horses at the same time; a couple of hundred fellows roaring, and twice that number working on the *Dreadnought* in a dock just by. I feel as quiet amidst all this bustle as if I were quite unconcerned; and this I find often the case, my mind being frequently never more tranquil than when surrounded by all from which the reverse might be expected.

Many thanks to Moor, for his letters to the Marquess and Marshal: I trust in time to know them both. I feel here, though strange, yet satisfied that I am where I ought to be, and in the path of duty; I shall want no urging to return whenever it may be right. I have no wish but to be restored to my family. I had today letters from Stace, (Mr. Commissary Stace), and Gold, (Col. Gold, R. A.), and a very warm one from Jasper Nicolls, (Lieut.-General Sir Jasper Nicolls), going to India: he is well known to the Moors, and is an excellent soldier and man.

★★★★★★

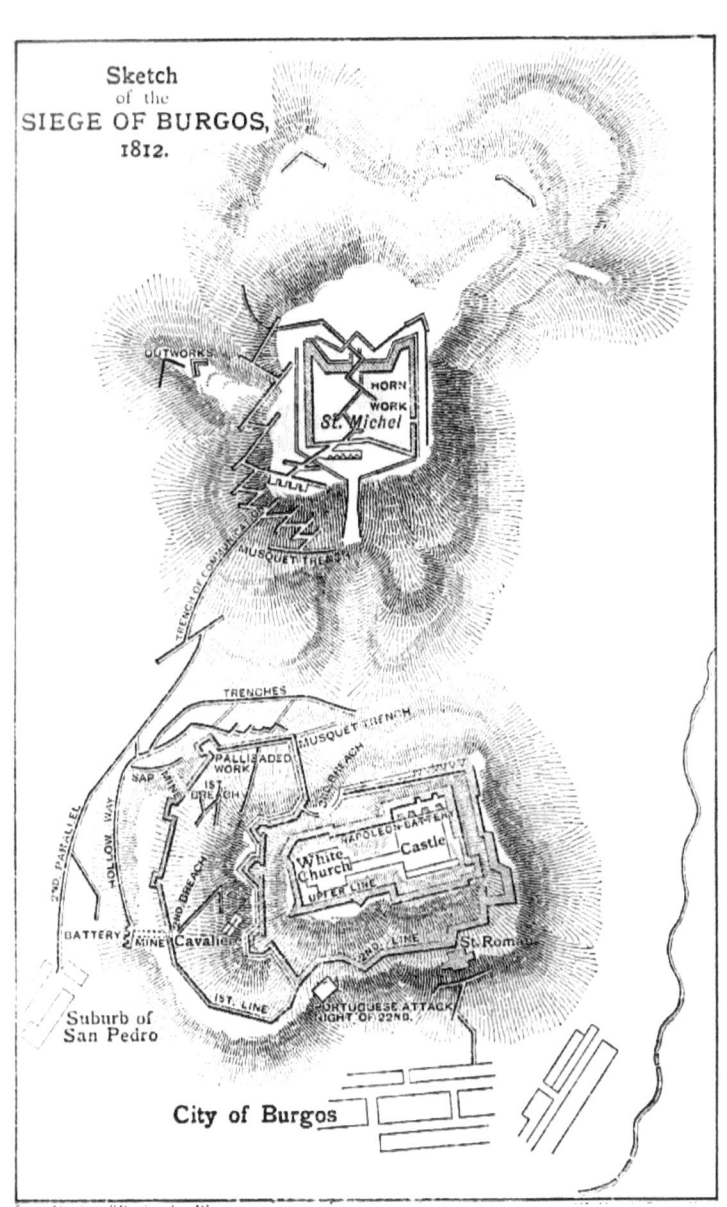

Notes to above:—Major Edward Moor, F. R. S., of Bealings, near Woodbridge; married to Lady Frazer's sister. Major Moor had served with the "Marquess" (of Wellington), then Sir Arthur Wellesley, in India: the "Marshal" is Marshal Beresford.

✶✶✶✶✶✶

Letter 4

H.M.S. *Sea Horse*, Spithead:
8 a.m. 27th Nov. 1812.

I mentioned yesterday that this ship has received orders to proceed to the West Indies. Nothing can be more beautifully fitted up than Gordon's cabins, nor anything more comfortable and even elegant, except a little corner on shore with a wife whom one loves. The ship is now unmooring,—that is, in plainer English, a couple of hundred fellows are stamping over one's head, and rudely dancing to a shrill pipe, whilst the anchor is getting up. Charles Gordon, (then Captain in the Royal Artillery), goes to Gibraltar in the *Iphigenia* frigate, Captain Pellew, the captain with whom, a few days ago, I expected to have sailed to Lisbon.

We are in the midst of interesting scenes: the *Victory* on one quarter, the *Loire* on the other, the buoy of the unfortunate *Royal George* just astern, and the *Antelope*, arrived from Newfoundland with Sir J. Duckworth, within two cables' length. How many associations, how many recollections, come at once in the contemplation of these objects. We are at breakfast, and making comparisons, not much to the advantage of Gordon's breakfast, with those at Bealings, which are enough to spoil any soldier in the kingdom.

When you can spare it, you will oblige me by giving some little donation from yourself to our little school, to which I wish well from the bottom of my heart. How amiable are Sabine's attentions to it, and how comfortable is the thing for our men and their children.

Letter 5

H.M.S. *Loire*, Lisbon:
9 a.m. 14th Dec. 1812.

We have just anchored safe and well, but I have not yet been on shore. The packet sails today, as well as the *Lavinia* frigate. Nothing can be more striking than the entrance into the Tagus; Fort Saint Julian on the one side, and Fort Saint Bugio on the other, with a tumbling sea over the bar. The forts are a mile asunder. The country is wild and arid, dark mountains forming the background; no trees visible, except here and there a scattered pine. Houses without roofs attest the seat of war, and give a foretaste of its miseries.

Captain English, of H.M.S. *Impétueux* (the flag-ship of Admiral Martin), has just been on board; from him we hear that Sir Edward Paget has been taken prisoner and sent to Paris, and that the army has fallen back from Salamanca. I will write to you again when I know more.

8 p.m. 14th Dec. 1812.

I have rambled all day up and down this wonderful city; this scene of past grandeur, and present mixture of hurry and indolence. We landed about ten, left our cards at General Peacock's, the commandant, from thence waited on Sir Charles Stuart, the minister, who invited us to dine at three; thence to the town-major's to procure billets: mine is at No. 159, Calçada de los Bardhinos Italianos; where, after walking for at least two hours, preceded by a guide, I at last arrived and introduced myself, billet in hand, to the family, consisting of five ladies, two little children, and one man announcing himself as uncle to one of the ladies. We all talked at once, none understanding the other, with the exception of the uncle, who had a smattering of French, and through whom I made the common assurances of giving no trouble, &c. &c. &c., and took possession of two very elegant rooms richly ornamented, overlooking a vineyard, and the Tagus opening to a great breadth; above which rose abruptly the hill on which the house stood.

Thus—and finding out, and sitting by the bedside of Colonel Robe, (Sir William Robe, of the Royal Artillery), arrived last night from the army (on men's shoulders)—the time for dining at the minister's slipped away. I therefore walked over the city, uphill and downhill, visited the artillery hospital (clean and admirable in the highest degree), stables, &c., got a fresh guide, and reached with difficulty the artillery mess at five, just before dinner, and sat down in a superb room to an excellent dinner, served with every delicacy, in the confiscated palace of a Count de Louie, who has joined the French Army.

In the interim I had despatched a cart in search of William (my servant) and the baggage, and fully purposed sleeping at my billet, the name of which, in mercy to your eyes and my own fingers, I avoid repeating: but alas, no William, no baggage to be heard of. Accordingly, I started again to the inn where James, (Dr. James Lynn, Lady Frazer's brother), and some of my fellow-passengers were to dine, and, by great good luck, discovered not only James, but William and all my baggage;—joyful sight! having worn the soles of my boots quite through:

footworn and tired, I am now going to sleep in James' room.

General Rebow and Close are also here, and the general furnishes the paper on which I write. I say nothing of the filth of the streets, nor of two dead jackasses partly eaten by dogs in the public streets, nor of palaces and convents really beautiful without, nor of 100 women washing skins in a pool of water in a retired square, whom with tucked up garments my unlucky stars stumbled me upon; nor of fifty other unaccountable mixtures of filth, splendour, and misery, which salute the senses at every corner: thanks to Providence for the steep declivities of most of the streets here; nothing but their sharp descents could guard against the plague in a city where cleanliness seems unknown.

Sir Stapleton Cotton, who sails by the *Lavinia* frigate tomorrow, affords the opportunity of sending this letter. Headquarters of the army are at Freneda. Lord Wellington had a most narrow escape when Sir Edward Paget was taken, and owes his not being a prisoner to the fleetness of his horse. I shall not remain here, I imagine, above four or five days.

Letter 6

Lisbon: 16th Dec. 1812.

I write from a large room in the arsenal, where I am receiving a camp-kettle, water-bucket, nosebags for my horses, and a multitude of useful articles; a little tent, a wooden canteen, and luxuries of all kinds.

In another room artificers are making a stretcher for my bed, and a great canvas cover for my bedding; and all this with an alacrity which would flatter even the Shah Abbas himself. I meet at every step some old acquaintance or friend among the men and artificers, who strive to repay former attentions to their comforts. These returns gratify me very peculiarly: their value at present is really great. So true is it, that all have it in their power, at some time or other, to return good. *Apropos* of the *Shah*, Sharpe, (attached to the Persian Embassy under Sir Gore Ouseley; married to Lady Frazer's sister), has indeed conferred on me the favour of all others most pleasing, in his present of a sword; he knows, I see, how to take the weak side of a soldier in touching the foible, which we, who are said to live by the sword, possess.

I shall write to Sharpe by this mail, that I may not be ungrateful for his very great attention. I am now vexed that I had not (as I really intended) written to him on my leaving England. I never in my life delayed anything without seeing cause afterwards to be sorry for it; and seldom without remarking that opportunities once lost can seldom be regained. The *Hawkesbury* transport, with my horses, arrived yesterday, after a very boisterous passage. I learned that my horses are well, though nine died out of forty. Today has been squally, with torrents of rain; but with transitions of sunshine and storm, which at first surprise a stranger: not a cloud to be seen one moment, and before another you are drenched with rain. This season is said to last from ten days to three weeks, after which spring begins, and the flowers appear.

Meat is scarce—sixteen pence a pound for beef, a dollar for a fowl, and six dollars for a turkey. This sounds alarming; but the army is allowed a ration of one pound of meat and one and a half pound of bread, which the messman takes. Our mess is half a dollar daily for dinner, and wine is paid for as drank. Madeira four shillings and sixpence per bottle, red wine of the country about one shilling and ten pence, and white wine one shilling and sixpence per bottle; but excellent of their kind. The messman must be a conjurer; nobody has a dollar, consequently he is never paid; but all live well. This, except the want of coin, may be called the golden age, everything good being within reach, without the trouble of carrying money. But by the general orders of yesterday, strengthened by government proclamation today, guineas of England are to be received in all public contracts and private money transactions throughout the Portuguese dominions.

I have forgotten the number of thousands of *reis* (a little Portuguese coin) for which the guinea is to pass; but it is on the scale of one pound one shilling English. You would smile to see my writing-table with two nice little girls of six or seven years old laughing by my side: we are already the best friends imaginable. I find my host is captain in the Portuguese Navy, and that every Monday there is a rout at the house. This accounts for an invitation I had last Monday from "*la belle compagnie*" as he styled it. Nothing can be more civil than the people are. I went this morning over several of the inhabited rooms in the palace of Count Louie, in part of which our mess is: nothing can be more splendid than the decorations, nor more chaste than the proportions, of several of these apartments.

I purpose tomorrow calling on General Rebow, General Nugent, and Sir Charles Stuart; while in the interim I trust the horses will be landed, and my new mules arrived; a few days will suffice to stretch their legs, and then we shall set off. I shall take in charge a young officer, Lieutenant Baynes, and some five or six horse artillerymen and two horses. The routes are prescribed, and the journey, I understand, will be of ten or twelve days.

Lieutenant-Colonel Fisher is now the commanding officer of the Artillery, having left Lisbon a fortnight since to join the army. Among other officers named in today's orders as having obtained leave, is Robert Macdonald, (Lieut.-Colonel Robert Macdonald, of the Royal Artillery), for four weeks to Ciudad Rodrigo; he received a severe wound on the 17th, but is in no danger.

I should like to have dear Augustus in the room in which I now write, (his son, subsequently an officer of the Royal Artillery, died when travelling in Syria): the lofty walls are covered with painted cloth, in which the story of Joseph and his brethren is told in a coarse but bold manner, as large as life: seven half-length paintings, also as large as life, obscure all the figures of Joseph except the legs, and present for your admiration Cleopatra with her asp, Herodias with John the Baptist's head just cut off, Herodias again with the head in a charger, the far-famed Grecian daughter giving milk to her aged father, Dalilah cutting off Samson's hair, and a lady with a gold cup in her hand and the pyramids of Egypt in the background, the exact subject of which I have not yet made out: between these paintings, and to the further exclusion of Joseph, are twenty-two engravings, in the old tawdry French style, of the marriage and actions—that is, journeys and feasts—of Henry IV. of France; the queen making a very prominent figure in most.

Three pairs of folding doors, a great mirror, a harpsichord, a kind of dulcimer, a couple of windows opening to a balcony, and a painted ceiling, make up the decorations and outlets of the room. I sleep in another, and behind a great screen which obscures the subject of the tapestry with which the walls are hung. *Adieu.*

Letter 7

Lisbon: 18th Dec. 1812.

I now write at Sir Charles Stuart's, whilst waiting for dinner (such is the ease, the very enviable ease, of foreign manners), so that the portion of the day which Addison somewhere describes as the most irksome of the twenty-four hours becomes to me one of the most delightful, since I shall hold converse with an absent sister and friend. I went yesterday to look at the house of the Marquis Louie, in part of which we mess. Nothing can be more elegant than the suite of apartments. I believe I have already mentioned that the marquis, having joined the French, has been outlawed, and his estates confiscated; nevertheless, the *marchioness* lives in some splendour in part of the hotel.

The lower storey of all houses of any distinction here is appropriated to the courtyard and stabling; above this storey, in a little low kind of intermediate storey called the *entresol*, are accommodated the humble connections and dependents, not absolutely servants; above this is the suite of rooms inhabited by the family, and above those are the lodging rooms of the servants, who seem to live more on terms of familiarity and almost equality with their masters, than we are used to. This, however, I take as yet on report, for I pretend not to the intuitive faculty of discovering at a glance the manners and habits of strangers.

Letter 8

Lisbon: 19th Dec. 1812.

I have as yet learned too little of the real state of affairs of this country to authorise my forming any opinion. I have, nevertheless, had some interesting conversations with persons capable of judging; it is however necessary, and more especially so at first, to be on one's guard, and not to make known all one hears. I trust I have formed a very valuable acquaintance in General Nugent, through whom it is said a great deal of the secret correspondence of several of the continental courts friendly to the politics of England passes. I have just introduced the general to Lieut. Colonel Jones of the engineers, by whose bed we have been sitting for the last two hours. Colonel Jones (who has been severely wounded in the Burgos affair) was with Maitland's force at Alicant, and, from his situation and information, prominent in all the discussions relative to the landing of the force. (Colonel Jones is the author of the account of the War in Spain, Portugal, and the South of France, from 1808 to 1814 inclusive).

It appears clear that Maitland has acted very wisely, and though, from his temperament and zeal, peculiarly alive to the sarcastic remarks made on the delay of his expedition, was in no ways to blame. The force consisted of 6100 men, all infantry, of which, from 3000 to 3500 were British, the rest Calabrese and other uncertain descriptions of troops. The force under Baron d'Eroles, not more than 2000 men, other troops in the province amounting to between 4000 or 6000 men, but none on whose remaining together above three days any dependence could be placed: the enemy having 4000 men in the field, with a disposable force in neighbouring garrisons of 13,000 or 14,000 men, exclusive of 4000 left in Barcelona; these numbers were confirmed by returns of each particular corps, deserters from each of which further corroborated the statement.

Portuguese Infantry Police Guard Lisbon

The event you know to be, that our force (now, from different reinforcements, of 18,000 men) is at Alicant, which is described as naturally strong, and capable, if the works be effectively strengthened, of permanent defence. On the whole, it appears that a spirit of vigorous resistance still remains in Catalonia, but in that province alone; and that this is so, from the hope that England will at some time send thither an army of unquestionable force; but that the spirit would evaporate if any efforts should be made which might fail: further, that the first step must be the siege of Barcelona, the failure of which, even if it should fail, would not materially affect other parts of the province; though success in obtaining that, and one other permanent fortress, would be indispensable for further operations.

It further appears that the French troops depend for their sustenance solely on the fortresses; that their efforts are consequently confined to three days' march outwards, three days' return, and their receiving rations on the moment of their return, the whole produce of the harvests having been swept into the garrison towns; there is in some (as Barcelona) two years' supply, and in most more than one year. The point to the immediate westward of Tarragona is mentioned as the most eligible for debarkation and securing a place of arms; the promontory offering on both sides safe anchorage for transports in any wind, with the safe transition from the one side to the other on change of wind.

Colonel Jones subsequently made his way across from Alicant to Madrid, joining the Marquess just previous to his moving from the capital in advance. Lord Wellington is convinced that the hovering on the coast for so long a time of the Alicant expedition was of essential use in distracting the attention of the enemy, and that, considering the paucity of force (the real evil), everything that could be expected was done.

With respect to the Burgos failure, the want of will to employ sufficient artillery, with the amplest power of having done so, and the selection, contrary to repeated suggestions, of ineligible pieces for breaching, appear to have been the principal causes of want of success. Rest assured there has been no want of skill or zeal in either of the corps to whom sieges must be confided, and that the true error is acknowledged in its fullest extent. On the whole aspect, little reliance is to be placed, in the opinion of those competent to form an opinion, on either the spirit or efficiency of the Spaniards; while the difficulty of financial arrangements seems admitted by all, though necessarily

SIEGE OF BURGOS

less understood except by few.

In this capital, as in all others removed from the immediate vicinity of armies, though used to the common reports of the incidents of the war, little is known, and less thought about the matter; in vain do you attempt to obtain information from the multitude of commonplace idlers who swarm in the streets. Lord Wellington is gone to Cadiz, the object of course unknown, though believed to be finance. Headquarters at Freneda, with the advanced and other posts nearly as before the commencement of the late brilliant though indecisive campaign.

The troops here have one pound of meat and one and a half pound of bread daily, and in all other quarters a pint of wine is added. Fresh or salt provisions are issued according to the supply. At this moment salt provisions only. Veal is prohibited. Beef sells at sixteen-pence per pound; to the inhabitants it is the principal meat. To get mutton it is necessary to send some way into the country, and to buy a whole sheep.

Yesterday was the queen's birthday. The cannon of the ships fired a salute at 1 p. m., and a partial illumination took place at night. I did not go to the opera, having employment at home. *Adieu.* I shall write from time to time.

Letter 9

Lisbon: 21st Dec. 1812.

You will have a shoal of letters at once, the two last packets being on shore, and much damaged. The gale on Saturday was unusually violent; much mischief has been done, and many lives lost: it is considered a very unusual tempest. I yesterday went with James Lynn across the Tagus, about two miles wide, to Almada, and rode with Bolder, of the Engineers, round all the lines and works of defence on the Alentejo side of the river. These works were necessary to prevent the enemy bombarding Lisbon from the opposite side, in case of their getting so far. The day was beautiful, the scenery perhaps the finest in the world.

The castle of Almada is the spot from which Barker's Panorama of Lisbon was taken. It stands on very high rocky ground, immediately above the Tagus, the view extending from Fort Julian at the river's mouth on the one side, to many miles up the river on the other. Lisbon in the foreground, with its beautiful buildings, the Cintra Mountains in the distance on the Alentejo side. Abrupt rocks and points of land crowned with redoubts, and intersected with vineyards, olive-trees, and aloes, slope imperceptibly towards a more plain country, covered with pine forests, joining to the chain of mountains running from Setubal (St. Ube's), where are the great salt pans which supply much of the salt used in England.

After riding over roads, rugged at one step and up to the horses' bellies in another, for five hours, we descended, crossed the Tagus, and dined at the Artillery mess; from thence the doctor came home with me, and joined "*la belle compagnie*;" that is, the rout which I formerly mentioned. We were covered with mud from our excursion, but were made very welcome. I danced one reel. The company played high. We looked on till past twelve. I had ordered my cot for myself, meaning the doctor to sleep in the bed I usually do; but our hostess would not allow it, and had a bed brought for James, whom through William, I suppose, they learnt to be my brother-in-law. They made a thousand inquiries about you: whether you were coming to Lisbon; how glad they should be to have you with them whilst I should be with the army; and how many, and how old, the children are which I had left behind. All these little attentions are very pleasing; and however, some folks doubt the sincerity of the protestations of the Portuguese, civility is always welcome.

Letter 10

Lisbon: 23rd Dec. 1812.

I write at General Rebow's while breakfast is preparing, and after returning from one of the most interesting rides imaginable. I got up at daybreak, and scrambled my way to see the celebrated aqueduct, which conveys the water to a great part of Lisbon. The aqueduct is carried on stone arches over all the inequalities of the different valleys which it meets with between the mountains near Cintra and Lisbon. The valley, about a couple of miles from hence, which, I believe, is called that of Alcantara, is most abrupt. The width of the principal arch, I am told, is sixty feet; the height I could not determine. The channel for the water is covered in with a stone footpath, of four feet wide, on each side; at intervals are turrets for giving air, to which side windows also contribute.

Unluckily, there is no going from one footpath to the other; a very little more labour might have made a good carriage-road on the top. From the aqueduct, I made a trip to the celebrated church of Estrella, which is beautiful, both without and within. The architecture is chaste and the paintings are fine. The whole of the interior is of different coloured marbles, except the doors, which are of mahogany, and the frames of the paintings, which are, as usual, gilt. High mass was performing, but very few people in the church,—not above a couple of dozen.

My going from hence is fixed for tomorrow, by way of Santarem, Abrantes, Castel Branco, and so on. We form a cavalcade of ten men and as many horses, asses, and mules. I have chosen that road to avoid a multitude going by way of Coimbra. It is always an object to have a clear road in a country of war. I dined yesterday with poor Robe. It is a charity to sit with him; the society of old friends enlivens him; and he has a thousand good anecdotes, both instructive and amusing. After breakfast, I am to meet Robe's son, and am going with him to the church of San Juan, the mosaic decorations of which are described as most beautiful. I have made all, or nearly all, my little purchases; lined the cape of my coat with oilskin; got blankets for my horses and mules, and a little tea, coffee, sugar, and salt; which last is very scarce with the army. The bread here is generally very bad, with a bitter taste. Much bad flour is made into bread. All the flour used comes from America, the ships of which country crowd the port. They are, of course, licensed by us.

Captain Brown of the *Loire* tells me that the two strange sail (frigates) with which we kept company for a week, are made out by the *Pique* to have been enemies. The *Pique* was near them two days after we lost sight of them. Captain Brown describes the storm of Saturday to have been tremendous, and his frigate in very great danger, and at one time momentarily expecting to have been dashed against the rocks of this ironbound coast. Captain Brown declares that in twenty-three years' service he never saw a real gale of wind before.

Lisbon: 24th Dec.

I am now on the eve of starting. I was up at two this morning packing up and settling trifling matters. My route is made out for Abrantes only, where it will be renewed. It is today for Saccavem; 25th, Villa Franca; 26th, Azambuja; 27th, Santarem, and halt on the 28th; 29th, Golegao; 80th, Punhete; 31st, Abrantes. I hardly know how or when I may write again, but of course wherever there are commissariat stations, there must be the means of getting letters conveyed per post.

The chapel of Saint Juan which we looked at yesterday in the Church of St. Roque (I won't answer for the orthography), is inexpressibly beautiful. It is entirely in mosaic except the table of the altar, the cornices of which are cornelian, the front *lapis lazuli,* and the horizontal part jasper inlaid with porphyry and amethyst. Three very beautiful pictures in mosaic represent the Annunciation, the Baptism of St. John, and the Pentecost. The colours are vivid, and the expression admirable. This chapel is much the most worth seeing of anything I have yet met with, and is justly esteemed the wonder of Lisbon.

Letter 11

Under an old olive tree between Saccavem and Villa Franca: 9 a. m. 25th Dec,

We were to have marched yesterday at ten, but the usual incidents, of the baggage proving too much for the mule, of its tumbling off, of one man running one way and one another, &c., delayed us till past one. But our march was short, called two leagues, and we were housed before dark. In future we shall manage better: I now write by the roadside whilst waiting for the little party, and, with a clothes-brush for my table, manage very well. There are two roads from Lisbon to Saccavem, a higher and lower; we came the latter, which, like all others here, is paved, in many parts bad enough, or rather too bad, and seldom a mile from the Tagus. The country is beautiful though rugged and rocky, with vineyards, olive and orange trees, and the common (not the medicinal) aloe growing on all sides. Yet houses unroofed or in ruins grieve and surprise the mind not yet used to the misery which war, indolence, and bad government occasion.

On reaching Saccavem or any other billet, you show your route to the *Juiz de Fora* (equivalent to our constable or billet master, or, I believe. Justice of the Peace), who gives a billet on the house of an inhabitant, who shows you the room allotted for your reception. By an order of Lord Wellington, the inhabitant is merely bound to furnish the four walls, but the style of building is favourable for quartering men. The rooms are generally within each other, that is, one leads into another; so that the masters lay down their beds in the inner, and the servants in the outer ones.

26th Dec.

We marched yesterday to Villa Franca, four leagues from Saccavem, passing from Saccavem through Povor, Alverca, where the first lines (or rather, reckoning from the front, the third) rest on the Tagus and Alhandra; immediately behind which were our advanced lines, while Massena's advanced corps occupied Villa Franca, distant a short league from Alhandra. Tell Major Moor these lines are strong redoubts, closed in rear, in many cases revetted, and occupying, at the distances prescribed by the ground, the tops of a very mountainous range extending from Alhandra by Torres Vedras to the sea on the left; and that as far as I could see they were connected by an abattis (felled trees), in many cases running in front of the works. They are undoubtedly very formidable.

The ordnance still remain in the works, but the ammunition has been removed. From Lisbon, houses on both sides of the road deserted and unroofed mark the scene of war. Alverca is much ruined, but Alhandra more; and it is a mortifying truth (to ascertain which I made many inquiries), that this town suffered more from the British Army than Villa Franca did from the French; both towns are in a deplorable state of ruin, but Alhandra much the worst of the two. From Saccavem to Villa Franca is three leagues, the scenery, with the Tagus on the right and the mountains on the left, very wild and beautiful.

We dined well at a kind of sutler's inn, and were charged most exorbitantly; but being Christmas Day, we resolved to have a good dinner. We drew rations here for two days, receiving for each person one pound of salt meat, a pound and a half of bread, and a pint of wine, all good of their kind: seven pounds of wood for fuel, and for each horse twelve pounds of corn, and twelve pounds of straw. These are issued by commissaries, stationed at convenient places for the purpose.

We had yesterday a little drizzling rain, but the weather is generally very fine; the mornings and evenings somewhat cold, but when the sun is out, like our fine April days. We left Villa Franca at eight this morning (26th), and marched three leagues to Azambuja, passing through Castanhero, Caregada and Villa Nova, all with many ruined houses; the country becoming on our left more mountainous, though we still remain in the low country, by the side of the Tagus.

We passed many orange groves, which looked beautiful, but the fruit is not yet ripe for eating, though much is already packed for England. In an olive grove we passed many carts laden with oranges, and some with glass from Leyria, the bullocks of which were unyoked and feeding, while their drivers were regaling themselves with bread and onions under the trees, quite in the style which *Gil Blas* mentions. The muleteers one meets with make a singular appearance in a kind of great coat made entirely of cords, which hang in loose rows, connected by strings passing horizontally. This is a most clumsy description of coat, made of the fibre of the aloe, but will turn any rain.

We parted company at Caregada with twenty officers and 150 artillery horses, going to Coimbra, and it was partly to avoid march-

ROYAL HORSE ARTILLERY

ing with them, and partly to see Abrantes, that I chose to have my route made out for this road, instead of joining the army by way of Coimbra. Tomorrow we march four leagues to Santarem, and I shall pass the very spot represented in the drawing you have. In the midst of ruined towns, the inhabitants make no complaints, and, as far as I have yet seen, are extremely civil and kind; which I wonder at the more, as they must on this road be harassed by the continual passing of troops to and from the army.

It is necessary, however, to be much on your guard, since marauders come down from the mountains, and carry off saddles, bridles, or any other article left carelessly about. Wood is abundant, but the transporting it to the towns is difficult, both from the want of people and of industry. It is true that these three days of our march have been holidays; but I have not yet observed one soul at work. The leagues here are of very uncertain length, and mean any distance from three miles to nearly five. There is nothing new with the army, where I wish myself arrived. When I get a little nearer, I shall push on; but having no non-commissioned officer, and none but very young soldiers, I do not choose to risk leaving them to their wits in a country where there are prowlers enough to play tricks with the unwary. I shall write to you from Santarem. From Lisbon to Saccavem, and indeed to Villa Franca, you see at every couple of hundred yards pyramids of salt thatched over with reeds, by the side of the salt pans, where the salt is obtained from the water of the Tagus.

Letter 12

Santarem: 28th Dec. 1812.

I have little news for you, indeed none, for I have not yet, at 2 p.m., left the house, which is a very cold one, with neither doors nor windows, and there is today a keen searching wind. The Tagus is overflowed, and our route is accordingly to be changed. I hope, however, to go by Abrantes. This place is the dirtiest of the dirty. Fifty Hercules, with a dozen rivers like Alpheus, would be puzzled to clean it in a twelvemonth. I never saw filth heaped together in such profusion. This is an hospital station; Abrantes and Coimbra, and latterly, I believe, Ciudad Rodrigo, are the same. I have yet seen few whom I know; but sick officers and soldiers abound. I am called away to go to the upper town, and I shall be glad of the walk to make me warm.

Since I wrote the above, I have been taking a long walk over the range of hills, on which was Massena's position previous to his retiring. A finer prospect or stronger position can hardly be imagined. Abrupt rocks, rugged mountains, and hills clothed with olives, with orange groves and vineyards in the valleys, and the majestic Tagus rolling at one's feet, form a scene highly picturesque. *If*—but how comprehensive is the word—if but industry and peace were here, instead of indolence and war, what a paradise might be made of parts of this country!

When I wrote this morning, I observed that in the whole of the country I had not yet seen one soul at work; but in my rambles today I discovered three ploughs, each drawn by four oxen, driven by one man and guided by another. This town is full of beautiful buildings, but all in some state of ruin. There are five or six convents and churches of more than ordinary size; but the squares are overgrown with weeds, marking the total want of care. I was assured today by the *commandant*, that a whole estate of a countess of his acquaintance in the neighbourhood, has been untilled last year for want of husbandmen; and that this want of men is severely felt all over the kingdom.

It seems unaccountable that, with a river teeming, as I am assured the Tagus is, with fish, nothing but sardines should be brought to market; and with a daily communication with Lisbon there is almost nothing to be bought.

We were to have marched tomorrow for Golegao, and from thence through Punhete to Abrantes; but the overflowing of the Tagus has rendered that road ineligible, and we march tomorrow for Pernes, and from thence through Torres Novas, Thomar, and Martinchel to Abrantes, which we shall reach on January 2nd. I had wished to see Abrantes from the strength of its position. It is, you know, the place from which Junot takes his title of duke. By the way, it is fair to remark that during his reign at Lisbon, all agree that he did much good; and that the police was well regulated. Hundreds of the otherwise idle poor were by his orders employed, at the expense of the rich, in cleaning the streets; and many other wholesome regulations were made, all of which were suffered to revert to their original confusion the moment we became masters of the city.

It is an evil in some degree attendant on our system of supporting our ally, that in upholding the existing government we uphold existing abuses, and appear to have neither ability nor inclination to ameliorate the condition of the people, nor to correct abuses which, without any indiscreet zeal or attempt at reform, might, in many cases of common sense, be attended to with success.

1813

Letter 13

Thomar: 1st Jan. 1813,

We quitted the main road on the 29th of December, and marched through wild paths to Pernes, seeing all around marks of the late gale, which has blown down olive trees without number. Pernes is a pretty little town, placed romantically in a valley between two rocky hills, on the side of one of which the town stands. We were lodged in an excellent house, of which the owner had fled at the approach of the French, leaving his steward in possession. We had a good fireplace in our room, and a handsome dessert of oranges, raisins, and figs sent by the host after dinner. The town, however, is in ruins.

I walked before dinner to the summit of the hill on which the church stands; it was desolate: tombs broken open and altar prostrate; all which religion and reason point out as most sacred violated; a broken inscription on a monument placed to the "eternal" memory of someone whose name I could not decipher, afforded one of those mortifying recollections on the perishable nature of everything here below. In the course of the day we saw for the first time numbers of cork-trees recently barked, and at Pernes several of the larger earthen jars made to contain oil: these reminded me of the old story of the *Forty Thieves*. A squadron of German cavalry came into the town after our little party; some of them had lost their way in the mountains.

On the 30th I set off early, attended by Smith, to get to Torres Novas before the German Cavalry should have occupied all the billets. The distance was said to be three leagues. We rode, however, for five hours, rather fast, sometimes following one path, sometimes another, and frequently through a wild forest country, where neither human being nor track were to be seen. It began to be very dubious whether we should get to Torres Novas at all. After tumbling down our horses, jumping over walls, and other occurrences more like hunting than marching, we reached at length Torres Novas, a very considerable town situated as usual in a valley, and on the banks of a romantic stream. There is a fine Moorish castle here, of course in ruins.

There had been a considerable manufactory of some kind of stuffs here—I could not make out what—but it, too, had been utterly ruined by the French. In my scrambling ride I had passed through three villages, one utterly desolate; not a vestige of a human being: another, with three or four persons only, yet there were in each 200 or 800 houses. The third, which was called Bugalios, seemed to have escaped unhurt. In our way through them we had zigzagged terribly. I now learn that the poor peasantry, afraid of being pressed as guides, are willing to get rid of inquiries about the way, either by denying any knowledge of it, or by giving any answer which they imagine most likely to induce the inquirer to pass on. I shall in future recollect this—it will spare me many turnings.

In Torres Novas the *Juiz de Fora* spoke French, and lodged us in his own house very comfortably. We took in Captain Keytes of the 51st regiment, going to join the army, and with whom I had formed an acquaintance on board the *Loire* in our passage from England. Yesterday we set out for Thomar, said to be three leagues from Torres Novas, but certainly twenty miles at least, through a more cultivated country than I have seen. We passed one village in ruins, and one town, Sisara, not much better. The country occasionally wild and heathy, but generally laid out in olive grounds. White clover and rye, pretty forward, and some wheat, were seen this day, and two and a half brace of partridges, the first I have seen in this country. They were red-legged, which is the more common kind here.

Thomar is a beautiful town: it is on a little plain at the foot of rocky hills. The Alva runs with rapidity close to the streets, which are clean; it is regularly built, and has an air of comfort more than any Portuguese town I have seen. In the house opposite the one in which I write, Marshal Ney had his headquarters in the retreat from Santarem. Just above Thomar, on the summit of a hill, stands a noble convent of the military order of Christ (I will obtain some account of it), in which 500 French were quartered for some time. The convent is in ruins; fine paintings in the chapel torn in pieces, and many carried away; the organ broken, the altars thrown down, fireplaces made in all the cloisters, and everything broken and defaced, not to afford shelter or comfort for the troops, but in wanton barbarity. The architecture of this convent is so fine, and the whole pile of buildings so noble, that I wonder I had never heard it mentioned.

I had been struck with the majestic appearance of the building, and of an aqueduct which led to it, on our approaching Thomar, and determined to stroll up to it. Previous to setting out, I asked a well-dressed young man, who spoke French tolerably, if there was anything in Thomar worthy the observation of a stranger, to which he said really, he did not know; and such is the unaccountable indolence of these people, that I dare say he said nothing but truth. The generality of the people really seem to know nothing beyond the very street in which they are; you ask in vain the name of the river at their doors, or the distance to the next town.

We rambled near the cloisters of the convent for a couple of hours, and in coming down to the town were most agreeably surprised on meeting Charles Blachley, (then Captain Charles Blachley of the Royal Artillery), on his way from Bull's troop to Lisbon on promotion. He left the troop three days ago; we have in consequence changed our route and halted today, previous to taking the mountain road tomorrow towards Espinal. I hope, by Blachley's advice, to reach the troop in four days' march. It is now at Midors or Villa da Coja, the one on the left and the other on the right of the road leading from Coimbra to Celorico. We shall get into this road at or near Pocos, and shall leave it between Penalva and Galices. You will find all these places in the map of Portugal. Today we rest our beasts, and regale on fish caught in the Alva. Blachley has saved us a long and very needless march, by way of Abrantes, Niza, and Castello Branco.

After joining the troop, I shall go to headquarters to pay my respects there; this I shall easily manage singly, as distance is then no object: with baggage, one's movements are circumscribed. *Adieu* for the present. I am going to look about and take a stroll.

Seven p.m.:

Blachley and I took a long walk to the most favourable points for seeing the town to advantage. There is a considerable cotton manufactory here; the Portuguese proprietor is married to an English lady, who was very civil to some of our party. I did not go. We have been drawing 'two days' more provisions, to last us to Espinal. The wine here costs about two pence a pint; on the Douro, about three half-pence. It is very good red wine, and, if nicely bottled, would be excellent. Oranges are selling here forty for a *rial*, that is three halfpence; so, I am assured. I have hitherto avoided eating any, as they are hardly yet ripe.

Letter 14

Espinal: Jan. 4.

My last letter to you was written on New Year's Day, and sent by Charles Blachley to Lisbon. On the 2nd, I marched to Cobacos, called four leagues, but about twenty-four miles. This village you will find in the map (Eliot's), in which it looks well enough; but in reality, when in a bleak valley you have passed half a dozen hovels, most without roofs, and inquire how far you are from Cobacos, you are told you have just passed it. So it was with us, and I was glad to take up my quarters in an unfinished house, with the laths,—but not the plaster, which I hope some future traveller may find,—as a shelter from the wind, which at morning and evening is cold and searching.

The country this day was wild and beautiful, the road generally a bleak track on a mountainous ridge, with rich valleys on either side, and the view on both terminated by the distant and higher mountains. The day, whilst the sun was out, was warm; violets in full blossom; wheat, rye, and white clover to be seen on all sides, and olive groves in profusion. A great tract was of pine forest, which extended beyond the bounds of our prospect. The road lay directly northward, so that the sun was a sure guide to prevent our losing it. It was occasionally rugged, but in general very good.

At Cobacos I found myself alone for the first time, and, after making myself a comfortable retreat, by nailing up blankets round a corner of the hovel, had just finished a good dinner on my ration of meat, cooked again with a little rice, and was putting my paper in order to write to you, when the trampling of horses and an English voice made me send to inquire who was there. It proved to be an English commissary benighted, after losing his way in the mountains we had passed in the morning. Of course, I invited the poor man to partake of the remnants of my fare, which he joyfully accepted. He was very thankful, and very conversable, and soon took his leave to lie down in a neighbouring hovel, where his interpreter had procured him shelter.

I should mention that we have suddenly lost our orange groves; not an orange tree now to be seen, nor a single orange to be had. At Thomar they were to be bought, as I believe I mentioned, at forty for three half-pence. Yesterday morning we set off early, and reached Espinal about 2 p.m. The road in general good, though with occasional patches of rock, and lying now and then through, and sometimes along the edges of, little rivers. For a mile or two here and there, the road in the valleys is made on fir-trees laid close to each other, which make a very good road for horses, though rather a jolting one for carriages. The morning was very cold and frosty, ice in the shade thicker than a shilling.

At a distance we see the ever frozen and snowy tops of the Sierra de Estrella, a part of which, judging from the map, we seem to have crossed. Though the country for the last two days has been wilder, yet it has less the air of having been ruined by the war, than that I had before passed. Most of the houses are unroofed, but in most are inhabitants. The soil, where cultivated, appears a very red mould. Whether this is good or bad, I am not farmer enough to determine; but the valleys seem abundant, though, as they form a very small tract when compared with the mountains they divide, and which are absolutely barren except of fir-trees, this district is probably poor.

Yesterday, although Sunday, was a kind of fair here; the town swarmed with pigs, and with women selling out of hampers rice, peas, beans, and bread. There were at least ten women to one man; the men had each a rude kind of pike. The wine here is bad, but of strength, I suppose, sufficient to answer the common purpose of wine, since, hearing a monstrous noise under my window, I looked out and saw a scramble, occasioned, as I imagine, by the joint endeavours of two ladies to get home one of the gentlemen, whom I suppose to be husband to one. However, all this was in vain; he seemed to prefer the endearments of his flagon to those of either Helen, and after pulling both their caps off, struck some good-humoured fellow who came to appease matters. The latter returned the blow, and in an instant fifty fisticuffs were given and received, and the battle became general.

Men, women, children, and pigs joined in with the scramble, and hats and caps and boots and shoes flew about. I believe none of the party were either sober or hurt, and the fray ended by each picking up a dirty hat or cap, and being somewhat worse off (as the combatants in all wars are) than before the squabble.

You will be glad to hear, for the honour of the sex, that the ladies carried off their man in triumph. This row put me into a good humour, which I had lost in endeavouring to get billets for my horses and people. The *Juiz de Fora* was sick; then he was gone out; then his house was at the bottom of the valley below the mountain on which Espinal stands; in short, there were twenty reasons why no billets were to be had. However, by persevering, first in one any and then in another, I at last detected a very placid-looking old gentleman at the foot of the mountain, sitting very quietly under his own vine, superintending the killing of (I hope) his own pig. His sickness was only like one of those dreadful headaches of a friend of ours on field-day mornings, and I could not persuade him to do what perhaps he had never been taught,—I mean to write out billets; yet he sent a boy with me, by whose assistance we soon got housed.

I met here a corporal (Miller), formerly of my troop, but now of Macdonald's, returning from Abrantes with a remount of horses and mules for that troop. This was very apropos, one of my horses having lost a shoe, which is a serious matter in these stony regions. Three days more will, I hope, bring me to the troop, which I learn from an officer of the 5th Dragoon Guards, whom I met yesterday, has marched from Midors to Villa da Coja. Both are in the neighbourhood of Galices, which is on the high road from Coimbra to Celorico, and towards which I shall in the first instance direct my steps. We shall set out early for Miranda de Corvo, and have drawn our three days' rations, there being no commissariat station further on our route till we join the troop. I shall remain only two days at Villa da Coja with the troop, and shall push on to headquarters, see and hear what it affords, and then run down to Coimbra, so as to see as much as I can. Fresh horses and a little exertion will easily manage this. *Adieu.*

Letter 15

Villa Coja, on the Alva: Jan. 7.

I arrived here yesterday. My last letter was dated the 4th, from Espinal, which I left on the same day, and reached easily the little, beautiful, but, as usual, ruined town of Miranda de Corvo, a quarter of a league out of the road. On the 5th I passed through more rugged roads than I have yet seen, to a little village a league beyond the Puente de Murcella. It was called San Martinhos, and looked very tempting, embowered in trees, and with a nice white steeple; but on approaching there was nothing but wretchedness. We had then marched from seven in the morning till past three, and were too tired to dispute about quarters, so I took up my abode in an uninhabited house, of which the outside walls alone remained.

The day was very cold, and there was literally nothing eatable to be had, so there was only the old resource of wrapping oneself up warm in all one's cloaks and blankets, and going to sleep, which I did till yesterday morning. Between Miranda de Corvo and the Puente de Murcella, and about two long leagues from either, is the Foz d'Aronce, a miserable village, with a very narrow bridge over the rapid Ceira, which rolls with rapidity through a rocky chasm. It was here that Marshal Ney, who had posted a considerable body of his troops with the village and river in their rear, was overtaken and attacked two years ago by Lord Wellington, when the marshal paid dearly for his injudicious position.

Between the Foz d'Aronce and the Puente de Murcella, the road, after winding through valleys and occasional hills, mounts the side of a very rugged mountain, on reaching the rocky summit of which the Sierra de Estrella broke on our view in frozen majesty. It was impossible not to exclaim, "How noble! how sublime!" The heights of Busaco terminated our view to the left, the Sierra in our front and nearly round the horizon, the rolling Alva rushing at our feet. Nothing less like a road can be imagined than our descent to the Puente de Murcella, which was concealed from our view by the winding of the mountains; nor should we have had any chance of discovering its direction but for the fortunate occurrence of meeting a peasant who was going to the little village near the bridge, and who very obligingly conducted us thither.

The bridge, like all others here, has been blown up, and is now repaired in a temporary manner. I never recollect having been more willing to leave any place than San Martinhos yesterday morning. Tomorrow, leaving servants and horses here, I proceed on fresh horses towards Mealhada Sorda and Freneda. The first is the village in which are the artillery headquarters; the last that in which Lord Wellington's are. I shall be three days on my journey to either; they are a league asunder. *Adieu.*

Letter 16

Alverca: 5 p.m. Jan. 9.

I take up my pen after a very tedious and weary ride. My last letter was dated the 7th, from Villa Coja, where it informed you that I had found Bull's troop on the preceding day. (This letter is missing). I had secured, as I thought, Henry Blachley's company along the most dreary road towards Mealhada Sorda, the artillery headquarters; however, at daybreak yesterday, I heard he was not well, and that I must set out alone. I had previously sent out a fresh horse to Sampayo, where Macdonald's troop was said to be; and I set out about nine, after very heavy rain, to reach that town. The road was said to be most direct from Coimbra, and so straight that I could not miss it.

It was straight and plain at first, but afterwards became so rugged and intricate that I lost my way repeatedly, and towards evening found my shadow lengthening, and evening coming on far from any abode of man. After imagining it not unlikely that I might pass the night on horseback alone, and on a jaded beast, I suddenly, to my great comfort, found myself within a quarter of a mile of a town which rocks and some wild trees had concealed. I had no doubt but this was Sampayo, but it was not; nor was another little place a league further. Still urging on my tired horse, at length I reached Sampayo, which I found occupied by Portuguese troops, and that no horse artillery were there.

I had, before I set out, heard that Captain Dyneley had applied to be sent to Mello, on account of the scarcity of forage at Sampayo, and I determined to push on for Mello, said to be one league further, but under the Sierra. Accordingly, after again twice losing my way and passing through two or three wretched places, just before dark my heart was cheered by seeing two of our men. I had then given up all hopes of seeing the troop. These men had been pressing bullocks for one of the wains required for looking for forage next day, and they soon conducted me to Dyneley's quarters, where I was received with the utmost hospitality.

One must have ridden all day through some of the wildest countries imaginable, must have expected to have irretrievably lost one's way, and have felt the uncomfortable sensation which being solitary, under such circumstances, cannot fail to produce, to have known how light my heart felt when I found myself surrounded by friends. Dyneley's hospitality arranged everything, and after a night's rest in his excellent bed, I set out this morning, attended by an orderly of Macdonald's troop, who escorted me hither on my way to Mealhada Sorda, still six or seven leagues distant.

We have today ridden about six leagues, which has taken us the whole day. About midway we passed through Celorico, situated on a craggy rock, with an old castle on the. summit. It is a wild, wretched-looking place, now more dreary than ever, from being one of the stations for the sick of our army. I had passed yesterday (though at some distance from the road) the cantonments of two or three divisions of the army, but with the exception of a few sick stragglers had seen no British soldiers. Both yesterday and today my route has been through the valley of the Mondego. Nothing can be more barren than what I have passed through today; no trees, no verdure, alternate sand and loose rocks, and the view on both sides bounded by rocky hills, stretching on the right to the frozen Sierra, and on the left towards a tract of country exhibiting no signs of cultivation. In the whole way the scenery was wild and desolate without being romantic.

We have today passed through several little towns in ruins, and mostly deserted. The little village or town of Mello is at the foot of the Sierra, and romantic. I saw at Mello some old troop friends among the men, *viz*.: Quarter-Master Baynes, Bombardier Stewart, and Driver Brownhill, and also Bombardier Roebuck, who had received on Christmas-Day the letter I brought from England from his wife. I write in a cold and dirty room of a wretched and partly deserted town. Tomorrow I shall set off early, and having again to travel alone shall lose no time, and I hope to reach Mealhada Sorda by one or two o'clock. I shall endeavour to bring Ross back with me. I understand he wishes to go to Coimbra, and it is really unpleasant travelling here alone.

One meets, however, occasionally something droll. I thought yesterday I saw several zebras coming towards me, and although I knew the thing was impossible, could not divest myself of the idea till a drove of asses, with striped blankets over them, approached near enough to clear up the mistake. I find these striped blankets very common among the muleteers. These are a most hardy race; they sleep all the year round in the open air on the mountains, with their mules. At Coja our surgeon had in vain endeavoured to persuade some of those attached to the commissariat mules of Bull's troop, who were really ill, to sleep under cover. They heard what he had to say, but though houses, both inhabited and uninhabited were to be had, left the town at sunset to sleep on the foggy banks of the Alva.

I like our quarters at Coja better than those at Mello, where the men are more harassed in procuring forage than at Coja. This duty, however, is severe everywhere, and renders the winter no season of rest for cavalry. I see much around me here which calls for serious reflection, and nothing which does not inspire me, in common I hope with all my countrymen, with gratitude to the Almighty, who is pleased to spare our happy land from the scourge which desolates this.

Letter 17

Mealhada Sorda: Jan. 11.

I reached this village last night; it is the headquarters of the Artillery, and one league from Freneda, the headquarters of the commander-in-chief. I am now going to Major Ross's troop of Artillery, near Fort Conception, and shall then retrace my steps to Coimbra, and push on to Oporto before I settle and report myself to the general officer commanding the division to which Bull's troop is attached. Indeed, if practicable, I shall cross the Tagus, and visit Badajos and Abrantes on my return. I find, however, that travelling alone in this country requires strength both of body and mind; nor is it altogether safe.

On my way from Villa Coja to Mello, I lost my way very uncomfortably; and from thence to Alverca the same thing occurred repeatedly. The country is there wild, barren, and rocky; it is, in fact, nothing but rocks devoid of verdure or of any signs of cultivation; and the dead carcases, both of men and animals, which are occasionally met with, together with the kites, vultures, and wild dogs prowling about, give the whole an aspect of horror which appals the mind. There is nothing to relieve the wretchedness of the scene. When you approach a village, all is ruin and misery. I have never yet seen war wear so savage an appearance.

In riding yesterday, from Alverca to this place, I crossed the Pinhel by a ford, and the Coa by the Almeida bridge, and, leaving Almeida to the left, scrambled over the rocky ravines on the banks of the Coa, and, after repeatedly losing my way, came hither by Castello Bom and Freneda. The wildness of the country is far beyond what I had expected. The poor orderly who accompanied me yesterday had such a roll down a precipice, in following me, that I really thought he and his horse would have reached the Coa before they stopped. Both were much cut by the rocks; but no bones broken.

From the Puerto de Murcella, I skirted the cantonments of several divisions of the army. They are on both sides of the road, though generally on the southern side, and under the Sierra, which term seems here to be applied almost exclusively to the Sierra de Estrella. I have accordingly seen much of the army in detail, and a most wretched appearance it makes; certainly, much worse in personal appearance (and decidedly so as to clothing) than the Portuguese troops. I do not yet see why this should be. The privations of the troops during the late retreat are admitted by reasonable men to have been sufficiently severe. Bread for seven, and meat for four days, and forage for about as many, seem to have been wanting. A considerable portion of both men and animals in consequence subsisted on acorns, of which, I am told, an abundance, of a sweet kind, resembling bad chestnuts, is generally to be had.

We were getting on very well yesterday, and had reached the deserted village of Junça, two leagues from hence, when, unluckily, we met a Frenchman, mounted and clad in one of our men's jackets. He announced himself as one of the corps of guides, and directed us to take a turning which led us utterly wrong, and we soon lost all road, and got entangled in the rocky ravines on the Coa, the wildest I have yet seen. There was no time for irresolution; the horses tired, and day declining, among rocks where there was not a soul from whom to inquire what direction to pursue. So, at hazard, we bolted down a very rough ravine, and it was then that I thought the orderly, though a resolute horseman, would have rolled into the river beneath.

This episode took us to Castello Bom, which we otherwise should not have seen; it is situated on the summit of a craggy rock. From thence to Freneda the country is sandy, and suddenly flat. A great many stone walls divide fields in which there is not the smallest sign of verdure or cultivation; but I am told that a good deal of hay is made here. The enemy continues quiet; and probably both sides find their account in keeping in repose during this very cold weather. General Alten's cavalry are on and in front of the Agueda, between which and the Tormès both sides make the usual patrols.

Letter 18

Aldea-de-Bispo: Jan. 13.

I wrote yesterday to say I had been both at the headquarters of the army and of the Artillery. The marquis is supposed to be at Lisbon. I left Mealhada Sorda yesterday, and rode with Colonel May to Villa Formosa, where Ross and Captain Cairnes had come to meet me. Our road lay across a very open country, and the position of the action of Fuentes Onoro. Ross's troop is in the little town of Aldea-de-Bispo, just under the ruined Fort Conception. This fort is on the Spanish frontier (for I write in Spain), and was intended as a counter fort to Almeida, which is the advanced Portuguese fort. The little River Turones here divides the two kingdoms.

Fort Conception has been blown up, and is in the usual ruinous condition. It was a very beautiful work of masonry. I can hardly believe myself to be in the same country as lately: an open country, good roads, houses comparatively clean, rooms with windows, and the habitable part of the houses on the ground floor, are all so unlike the rugged country I have lately struggled through, that it seems a sort of dream. I feel, I hardly know why, a reluctance to return to Portugal, and would fain go on to Madrid. Perhaps, in due time, I may; yet the speculations as to the next campaign are very various. With great exertions on the part of England, much may be done; but there must be no want of means, no half measures.

The present sick list is 22,000; the total British force 58,000; these are round numbers; but, I believe, near the truth. The sick decrease about 100 daily, and, in a few weeks, the sick list will be even more decreased. I have heard of General Stewart; he is at Vezin, in command of the first division of infantry. A letter, which he had written to me in answer to one I wrote from Lisbon, has been forwarded to Coja, where I shall find it. I have secured Captain Jenkinson's return with me to Coja; he will accompany me to Coimbra, and, I hope, to Oporto, whither I am resolved to go. I shall take a peep at Busaco by the way. Robert Macdonald is here, walking on crutches, and remarkably well. I shall see him safe to Coja, and take care of him by the way. Travelling back with friends will be pleasant to all; travelling alone is really the reverse, and now that it is over I confess it to have been, to say the least, very ineligible. *Adieu* for a while!

LETTER 19

Mello: Jan. 17.

I have been scrambling about so much that I hardly know when or of what I have written. I believe my last was from Aldea-de-Bispo, when with Ross's troop. I left Aldea two days ago, and revisited Almeida with Jenkinson. The morning was cold and frosty, and, in riding on the frozen edges of the glacis, down slipped my Spanish steed. This is the only adventure worth recounting of one of the dirtiest towns in Portugal. It is now wretched in appearance: you recollect the works were blown up by the French. The magazine had previously been blown up, either by accident or design; and, last week, a wine-house, in which five stolen barrels of gunpowder had been concealed, blew up.

All these occurrences have added to the desolation of this wretched fortress. Its situation is, however, on the banks of the romantic Coa; and if industry and cleanliness, rarely separated, were to replace filth and indolence, Almeida might be a delightful place. From Almeida we proceeded to reconnoitre some adjacent ground, the scene of interesting actions; and after examining the ford of the Coa, which was not altogether practicable, crossed by the bridge. This bridge is carved, and is in the most romantic glen: the green water, the purple rocks, the din of dashing waves, the wildness of the scene, and the abruptness of the craggy cliffs, give a character of terrific grandeur which is indescribable.

From the bridge, leaving my former route towards Alverca, we turned to the left, and pursued our journey to the town of Guarda; and soon afterwards, in an attempt (by the advice of a peasant) to find a short way, got entangled in some rocky dells, near the source of the River Pinhel, which we twice crossed and recrossed by fording. The day, which had been unusually cold, was also at intervals very foggy. Now and then we saw Guarda, occasionally above the clouds. Towards afternoon we reached, in fine sunshiny weather, the foot of the mountain. Soon after we began to ascend we were enveloped in fog so thick that nothing could be seen.

At last, about 8 p.m., we reached one of the paved roads which on four sides of the mountain approach Guarda. On getting within a quarter of a mile of the town, we suddenly lost our fog, and found ourselves riding by moonlight. The transition seemed like enchantment. Jenkinson's horse had fallen on the paved road, and we entered on foot, and stopped in the first open place till a servant should run forward to the house where, about a year before, Jenkinson had been lodged for six weeks. We had reckoned all day on being comfortably lodged here, the owner being a respectable inhabitant, in easy circumstances.

Our old enemy the fog, however, returned before the servant, and we were cold and comfortless. At last the man came with the account that the house was in ruins, (Marmont had made an irruption into this province during our siege of Badajos), and the owner, in one corner, as willing, but less able, to receive us as formerly; and the servant had accordingly procured a billet elsewhere. We were very glad to get housed anywhere, and sat over a charcoal fire till the baggage arrived, which at last it did; so that by ten at night we had an excellent dinner, and, with some hay and a cloak, I slept well.

Next morning, we rose early, determined to see the lions of Guarda; but the fog returned with increased density, and I literally left the town without having seen it. We walked, however, through the streets, ran our heads against the bishop's palace, a very poor-looking building; and looked at the cathedral, really a fine building, but mutilated by the French; the organ broken to pieces, the altars thrown down. Guarda is said to be the highest town in Portugal. If I mistake not, Laborde says it is somewhat lower than Madrid, and about 3000 feet above the sea.

We left the town about 10 a.m., rather chagrined that we were denied the noble views it affords. After walking slowly down one of the paved roads, and again ascending a little, the fog began to clear away among some rocky scenery; and just as we reached the top of the mountain, before descending in good earnest, the volumes of mist rolled away, and discovered the rich valley of the Mondego. Nothing can surpass, and I have seen nothing in any part of the world I have yet been in to equal, the majestic, the noble, the magnificent prospect which here broke on my view. I will not attempt what I cannot perform—to describe the varied scenery which presented itself, from the frozen Sierra to the rugged craggy cliff; the valley softened to all the laughing luxuriance of cultivated beauty.

We walked in silent admiration of the charms which nature had thrown around us in boundless profusion. Jenkinson, who had frequently been on the spot, ascertained the time of our descent to be forty minutes; for my own part, I thought only on all around me, and how happy I should have been to have had a companion to whom I could impart my sensations. At length we reached the valley, where the houses in ruins, and the beautiful country-seats deserted, reopened to our view the real misery which distance had served to conceal. Still cultivation remained, and the sound of numerous cascades, the trees, chiefly chestnuts interspersed with cedars, and the vineyards, were highly charming.

In about two hours we forded the Mondego, and, leaving Celorico about two leagues to our right, struck again into the second chain of the Sierra, at the opposite foot of which we knew we should somewhere find Mello. Knowing my taste for scrambling, Jenkinson permitted me to lead, and, after passing the village of Lagiosa, we turned short to our left, and followed the track of a bullock wain, which seemed to lead in the wished-for direction.

Soon afterwards we discovered that, in the earnest admiration of the surrounding beauties, we had lost the wain track, and, indeed, all other tracks. However, we pushed on, and were soon obliged, in mercy to our horses, to dismount, and clamber up the sides of the mountain, the top of which we reached, with much panting, in a hot sun. We were again on a level with Guarda, and again in the regions of cold. It had snowed during the night, and the air was piercing. We therefore postponed taking our glass of wine, as we had proposed to do on reaching the summit of the mountain, and pushed on.

The path we took was, as usual, scrambling, always on the edge of the declivity; but the country horses are so sure-footed, that one rides with the most perfect confidence within an inch of rolling down, one can hardly see how far.

We found ice on the mountain of sufficient strength to bear ourselves and horses, and, being now on the shaded side of the Estrella, found the cold very uncomfortable. At our feet lay my former road by Celorico. At length, after much slipping, laughing, and sliding, we reached Mello. Today is the 18th of January. Tomorrow we shall again set off, though we shall not attempt to reach Coja in one day; it is eight leagues distant.

Letter 20

Coja: Jan. 21.

I returned to Coja yesterday in two days from Mello. I have described this place to you, as well as told you my further intention of visiting Oporto, where I hope to find the governor. Sir Nicholas Trant, with whom I am acquainted. I had the pleasure of receiving two very friendly, nay, affectionate letters: one from General Stewart, the other from General Alten. General Stewart is at Guinalde; General Alten, for the moment, at Lisbon. I shall soon manage to see both, and to cultivate my friendship with two men whom I have reason to esteem.

I have been minutely inspecting the horses of Bull's troop; having just seen those of two other troops here, I could more justly appreciate the admirable condition and state of those of Bull's. Their order does him, and Ramsay in Bull's absence, the greatest credit. I augur well of his other arrangements. I have already seen enough of the unfortunate sick of this army to authorise the conviction that there is great room for improvement in the arrangements for the sick, and that more medical aid is much required. Humanity and policy equally dictate the necessity of care and tenderness towards sick men; I fear, in many cases, both have been wanting.

I have no fear of tiring you, though I can say little but repetitions of similar adventures. I have not yet lost my relish for the magnificent scenery which surrounds us. From Mello to Coja the road lies on what is known by the term (expressive enough) of "hog's back;" but what I think cannot tire in reality, may be tedious in description. Expressions cannot vary as the beautiful tints of nature do. *Adieu*, I am called away.

Letter 21

Convent of Santa Cruz, Coimbra: Jan. 26.

I begin to forget the last place and time of my writing. I believe the last letter was from Coja, on my way hither. We left Coja on the 22nd, and after crossing the pass of the Puerto de Murcella, slept at the village of Foz d'Aronce, which I formerly mentioned as the place where our army overtook and surprised Marshal Ney. We slept in the house in which Massena, Ney, and Junot were at the time of the surprise. Macdonald had set out with us, but, owing to bad roads and long leagues, could not come on with us. It was a rainy cold afternoon; our mules did not come up till after dark. We had previously quartered ourselves on the great house of the village, partly by persuasion, partly by force.

This was the first instance of incivility on the part of the natives which I had witnessed. It was, however, of little consequence, as we were in want of nothing but house room. The next morning, we had the pleasure of receiving a note from Macdonald, who had determined to go to Miranda de Corvo; and not to push on to Coimbra until the 24th. This set our minds at ease; we had before been uneasy about him. We had come round by Foz d'Aronce to avoid ferrying across the Ceira, which would have been difficult. After seeing our mules and baggage safely over the mountains between Foz d'Aronce, and ferrying over the Deuca, we rode through most beautiful scenery to Coimbra.

This is a fine city on the Mondego, over which there is a stone bridge 600 yards in length. There are, I believe, eight colleges in Coimbra, besides many convents and other public buildings, which give an air of grandeur to the city; nothing can be more beautiful than the approach: the Mondego, about the breadth of the Thames at Richmond, rolling through a rich valley perfumed with orange groves; crowds of people coming to and from market; roads hardly passable from the number of commissariat mules going to the army with supplies—all these reminded us that we were returning to the haunts of men. The streets are full of students wearing caps not unlike those to be seen at our own universities.

These students are said to learn nothing but how to be idle, and to avoid joining the army. There are a thousand of them. Downman, (Lieutenant-Colonel Downman, R.H.A.), had provided quarters for us in this spacious convent, the richest, as we are told, in Portugal, since the destruction of the more celebrated one of Mafra. The gardens of the convent are very extensive, and though in the formal taste which we call Dutch, very beautiful. Orange and lemon trees in full beauty, and the finest cedar trees I have seen. *Jets d'eau* abound, both in the squares of the numerous cloisters and in the gardens. There are aviaries and fish-ponds, and a terraced vineyard of extent enough to produce wine for I know not how many rosy-faced monks. The gardens, too, are in nice order.

Tomorrow, or next day at farthest, we proceed towards Oporto, four days' journey from hence. Downman and Colonel Cathcart (son to Lord C. and Quartermaster-General of the cavalry division) will accompany us. Macdonald will go towards Lisbon when we set out for Oporto; he bears his journey well. Coimbra is one of the hospital stations. I have not yet ascertained the number or state of the sick. Yesterday we rode to Busaco, and spent the whole day in examining the position of the contending armies in the hard-fought action of Busaco. I must write an account of our day to you. I must first acquaint you that this is one of the lions of the country, and formed one inducement to my visit to Coimbra.

The mountain of Busaco is said to be four leagues distant. There is no village of that name, nor any other building than the convent. This is in a very romantic garden in which are trees of uncommon size and beauty. Every variety of oak, cedar, cypress, and pine, and all in profuse luxuriance. To enter this paradise, you climb up a steep ascent through a long forest of fir trees. All in the garden, which is surrounded by a high wall, is peace and silence: little chapels at each turning and projecting point invite meditation, and I was only roused from a brown study, by the barking of a large convent dog, who seemed jealous of any intruder. Soon after, by the assistance of a man from the convent who opened a gate, we were conducted out of the garden, and found ourselves on part of Lord Wellington's position; and in five minutes stood, with our map before us, on the very spot where his lordship remained during the whole action.

This is a projecting rocky point, called ever since Wellington Knoll. Beneath our feet lay the medley of lesser mountains, on which Massena's army was posted, and, directly opposite, the spot where the rival general was placed. Nothing can be conceived more formidable than the position of the British Army, nor can one avoid wondering at, and admiring the daring bravery which the enemy showed in his attack. Captain Jenkinson, who had been engaged, explained everything most fully. I should not forget to mention that the sea is distinctly visible from Busaco. The rock of Lisbon has been said to be so, but I doubt the fact.

Coimbra is a great hospital station; the daily deaths are fourteen, but sickness is decreasing as spring advances. I shall not be at Coja for ten or twelve days. My troop must soon leave that place, but whither to go we know not. The same want of forage prevails everywhere; the poor peasants hide, and our people waste it; and between both causes there is now and then considerable want.

Letter 22

Oporto: Sunday, Jan. 31.

We have just arrived here. We left Coimbra on Thursday, and slept that night at Avelans. On Friday we slept at Pinhero, and yesterday at Carvallos. I now write in such a confused place, (the one room of an hotel in which ourselves, our servants, and baggage are tumbled together,) that I can hardly recall my ideas to sufficient order to write a collected letter. We left at Coimbra the country and most of the traces of warfare, and immediately observed greater cultivation, greater signs of industry, better houses, and all the pleasing marks of that composure which indicates that property is in some measure secure.

Between the Mondego and the Vouga, the country was more than usually beautiful; from the Vouga to the Douro more wild, and again inclining to sterility. Nothing can be more striking than the approach to Oporto: it would make a panorama of uncommon interest. The view bursts on one by surprise. There is a suburb called Villa Nova, built in a straggling manner, through the narrow streets of which you descend by a steep and very ill-paved road, till on turning a corner you suddenly find yourself on a spacious quay, the Douro just before you, and Oporto, on beautiful rocky varieties of ground, immediately in front.

The river is about 250 yards wide, over which is a bridge built on boats, of which there are thirty-four. There are contrivances for separating parts of this bridge, when it is wished that vessels should pass. I have as yet observed no masted vessels above the bridge; there are many brigs immediately below it. Downman accompanied us on a visit to the governor. Sir Nicholas Trant, who received us with the most friendly attention. With difficulty we escaped from the apartments he wished us to occupy in his house, on the just plea of not leaving our companions in the lurch.

Trant's house is superb, both in decoration and size. He sent two Portuguese officers with us to show us the way to the best hotels, gave us billets in case we should find them occupied, and showed us news just received of the miseries of the French army, the convention between the Prussians and Russians, and news from Spain, just received, and forwarded to Lord Wellington. It appears that 600 cavalry, chiefly gendarmerie, and 3000 infantry, have very lately left the neighbourhood of Madrid for France; that Joseph Buonaparte was undoubtedly to go (or had gone) from Madrid on the 23rd December; that the neighbouring districts have been ransacked for horses, mules, and all means of transport, to enable the French to carry off as much as they could lay hands on.

The French have re-occupied Santander, and have levied there 5000 rations. They have changed the governor and garrison of Santoña, which they have strengthened and provisioned for four months. The intelligence is from my friend Colonel Bourke, who is governor of Corunna. Trant showed me Bourke's letter, which he was enclosing to Lord Wellington, who reached Freneda on the 25th of December. We shall leave Oporto on Wednesday. Our gipsy mode of life is quite whimsical: I am become a complete wanderer without a home, or rather equally at home in all places.

Letter 23

Oporto: Feb. 2.

I wrote two days ago concerning our arrival at this place. Nothing can exceed the very friendly attentions we have met with from Sir Nicholas Trant. His house, boxes at the theatre, carriage and horses, all at our service. We went to the theatre the night of our arrival. The house pretty enough, though ill-lighted, and the performances dull; so much so that we left in the middle of some piece intended to represent a story of old Frederick of Prussia yielding to the entreaties of a lady in behalf of her husband, who had been sentenced to death for some military misdemeanour which we could not exactly make out. This piece is in high favour at present.

Yesterday we rambled over the city, more and more pleased with its beauty, its cleanliness, the width of the streets, the foot pavements, and the numerous shops, into which, in spite of ourselves, we continually strolled. We dined at Trant's. Our party was large. The rooms and feast elegant. It seemed the more so to us from the reverse scenes we had lately witnessed. In the evening Downman and I accompanied the governor in his carriage to the house of a Donna Rossi. Nothing can be steeper than some of the streets of Oporto, nothing more jolting than the governor's carriage, nor more wild than his Excellency's mules. The coachman, who could not find his way to a house at which he had been twenty times, declared as usual that the mules were drunk; there was clearly a little want of sobriety on the outside of the carriage.

However, we arrived safe, and found a very pleasant party of thirteen ladies, and I know not how many men. There are eight Mesdemoiselles Rossi, of whom six were in the room. The other ladies were cousins. All sang and danced well—all spoke French. We had *bravuras*, and glees, and country dances; said all conceivable, and, I suppose a few inconceivable, gallantries; and at last found ourselves a second time under the auspices of the sober coachman.

Today is a saint's-day, and in consequence (most luckily for us) the shops are shut. The town major is coming to show us the lions, and I shall be able to say I have seen the thousand pipes of port wine, the Bar of Porto (the proper name of this city, the "O" which we add being merely the article "the"), the convent, and twenty other lions of the place, of which I shall only now repeat, that nothing I have seen in this country can in any degree vie with it, and all my fellow-travellers agree that it is superior to Madrid. Today we shall hear all the particulars of the late good news from Russia; of all this we have had but hurried and indistinct accounts. Nothing is yet known of the opening of the campaign here; the spring will very soon be sufficiently advanced. *Adieu.*

Letter 24

Oporto: Feb. 3.

I stand up (not sit down) in a window, to write a few lines before we leave this nice place. We rode yesterday over all the remarkable places in the neighbourhood. After seeing where the English army crossed the Douro when the French retired before them, we rode to the public seminary for the education of young men intended for the Church. It is a noble building, with a beautiful octagonal chapel. From this we looked at a very handsome hospital; near it is a jail, also handsome, and the only finished building of the whole. It appears that all here is conducted in a style of magnificence beyond their means; in consequence, many edifices remain unfinished. This may rather be called, by an inversion of speech, building *with*, than *for* posterity; however, the fault is a good one, or, at least, a splendid one. After viewing the city from the top of the highest steeple, which is on the church called Clericos, we rode to see the Bar of Oporto, about a league off, by a paved road through very clean suburbs, and with elegant *Quintas* (country houses) on each side, having gardens, bowers, and arbours, and all that looked luxurious.

Close by the sea is the little bathing town of St. John's, with lodging-houses in the English style, all of which, we were told, let very dear in the bathing season. There was some surf, and some little swell on the bar; but the wind, which was along shore, prevented our seeing the bar in its usual state of agitation. The shore near it is very rocky, and the soil not good, but in high cultivation. The river is there perhaps half a mile wide, or hardly so much. There is a little fort to guard the entrance of the Douro, with three pretty ladies but no guns in it. In returning, we took what is called the lower road, which is close to the water's edge. It was nearly one continued quay the whole way. The day was propitious, that of St. —— I have forgotten whom.

The people, all in their Sunday clothes. Many *Quintas*, which the cliffs had concealed from our view in going towards the sea, now burst upon us at every winding of the river. I never saw a more gay, animating scene. All seemed joyous and smiling; the water as smooth as glass; vessels with colours flying; ladies at all the windows. The shores are very bold, like those of the Avon below Clifton, but more beautiful, or rather, more grand. From all this you will perceive we have had great reason to be pleased with our Oporto trip.

On returning, Jenkinson and I went to pay our respects to the governor, whom we knew to be unwell. Nothing could exceed his attention. We had previously declined dining with him, and now merely left our cards without asking to see him. On getting to the hotel, we found he had sent us a very fine pineapple. He had also marked out a new route for our return to Coimbra. In consequence, we shall strike off to the right at Carvalhos, and sleep tonight at Ovar. Tomorrow, we shall go four leagues by water (with all our mules and horses), to Aveiro, a town close by the sea, and out of the common beat. We shall afterwards scramble as far by land as daylight will admit, and shall reach Coimbra on Friday, the 5th.

LETTER 25

Convent of Santa Cruz, Coimbra: Feb. 8.

I will now resume an account of our return from Oporto, where my last letter was dated. I believe it informed you of our intention of returning hither, at the recommendation of Trant, by way of Ovar and Aveiro. We reached Ovar, a nice clean fishing-town, full of laughing children, just before sunset on the 3rd. We had in some measure lost our way, and made six or seven leagues of what we had been told were but four. Our route, like the general ones of Portugal, lay through low, sandy plains, with pine forests: the scenery much resembling Dutch Flanders. Fields cultivated and manured (a rare sight) with great apparent industry.

Our baggage reached Ovar an hour after ourselves; servants all growling at the length of the way and the misery of the house into which we were poked; the whole party required this change to wean them from the luxuries of Oporto. From Ovar, on the following morning, we rode a mile and a half to the place of embarkation on the Lake of Aveiro. The straggling houses near the wharf are, I believe, called Alonça. After much screaming of men, and kicking of horses and mules, we embarked in three vessels, previously provided by the *Juiz de Fora* of Ovar. The day was serene and fine, at first without a breath of air. Two men, with long poles, pushed each boat along.

The novelty of the scene, its stillness and repose, were indescribably beautiful. The contrast of the opposite shores of the lake, on one side of which we heard, beyond the sandhills, the distant roaring of the sea, whilst on the other, pine forests formed the foreground of a view finally bounded by the Sierra de Aluba and Busaco, gave a variety of character which absolutely enchanted us. Some fishermen chanting at a little distance, and the busy throng of boats employed in collecting weeds from the bottom of the lake (as we suppose for manure) filled up the pleasing picture of peace and industry. In an hour a breeze sprung up, and sails were hoisted; the sun was before this very inconvenient.

We soon lost sight of Ovar, and came to the broadest part of the lake, which is, I should think, about ten miles wide. The quantity of wild fowl we here saw exceeds all I could have imagined. They rose by thousands, the rushing of their wings on leaving the water more resembling a cataract than anything to which I can compare it. The lake, after receiving the streams of the Vouga, was interspersed with low reedy islands, between which we steered, every moment rousing flights of wild fowl.

After a passage of five hours, we reached Aveiro, a very clean, fine, and large town, in the Dutch style. There are several canals with bridges over them. The canal by which we entered was sixty feet wide, and half a mile long; with a good stone wall on either side, and convenient places at intervals to land or embark at. After waiting on the *Juiz de Fora*, and getting an excellent billet at one of the best houses in the place, we mounted our horses, which had passed an idle morning, and rode round the place; which, from its contrast to the other towns lately seen, appeared to great advantage. The houses, the churches, the gardens, all in excellent order, would have told us, even without our otherwise knowing it, that this happy town has escaped the miseries of war.

No enemy has ever visited it: all is tranquil and free, even from soldiery. On the green sod, under some sycamore trees, we could have fancied ourselves in England, in which no town is more clean than Aveiro. At dinner, our host (as is the Portuguese custom), paid us a long visit, without joining in our plentiful feast. He brought a present of some fine fruit, and all the common civilities passed, which are usual between people prepared to be pleased with each other. He informed us there were seven convents in the town, which was to have been a city, and to have been called Braganza Nova; that its trade had declined, owing to the war, but that he yet hoped it would revive.

On the following morning we bade *adieu* to Aveiro, and galloped to Coimbra. The distance is said to be about nine leagues, but in Portugal no idea of real distance can be formed by the reported one; a league appears to mean anything, from three miles to six. The road from Aveiro is excellent, a hard sand almost all the way.

LETTER 26

Coimbra: Feb. 9.

I have little to add to the incidents contained in my late letters. There is not much military information to be picked up in our present scattered state. All seem to agree that it is not likely that we should take the field for a few weeks. There is a kind of rainy season yet to be expected, and the green forage, which in the spring is the chief support of the cavalry, will not be fit to cut for four or five weeks. In the meantime, the want of long forage, that is, of straw, is felt a great deal. The cavalry is now changing cantonments, and taking up fresh ones in the vicinity of the Soure River, to the southward of Coimbra, with the exception of General Anson's Brigade, which is, or is to be, at and round Agueda, near the Vouga.

Bull's troop of Horse Artillery marches today from Coja towards Anadia, (also near the Vouga,) which cantonment has been assigned to it at my request. That part of the country is yet untouched, and, as far as we can learn, and from all we could observe on our late trip to Oporto, is plentiful and abundant. Considerable ordnance depots are forming here, and are to be formed at Oporto. I have yet no means of conjecturing the probable operations of the ensuing campaign. It is obvious, however, that much remains to be done before this army shall be fit to take the field.

Sickness is at present the greatest evil. Fever, the effect of fatigue, of want of clothing and of cleanliness, is the principal disease. The 4th Regiment has lost seventy-nine men, and had an increase of 187 sick within a few days. The Guards have suffered in nearly the same proportion. There are ninety-three sick artillery in this army hospital, and fifteen have died within the last fortnight. These details, which have accidentally come within my observation, give an unfavourable idea of what the number and state of the sick may be. The climate is, I should think, unfavourable to health at this season; a very hot sun, and cold and keen air.

I write in the din of I know not how many score of convent bells, which peal incessantly. Whether meditation or indolence be the intended employment of the inhabitants of these cloisters, they would do wisely to confine the bellringing to stated times. After three ineffectual attempts to see the museum, Colonel Cathcart has arranged that it shall be open for our inspection at three o'clock today. In this seminary of the arts and sciences, not a thermometer could be found two days ago; we wanted, but in vain, to find one for the warm bath of Colonel Elley, our adjutant-general. *Adieu.* I shall in future write more regularly, and in a more connected manner.

Letter 27

Quinta de Gracioso: Feb. 13.

My last was from Coimbra. We visited the museum, as I told you we should, previously attending, for half an hour each, two halls of instruction, where professors read (in clear and audible voice to about 100 students in each room) lectures, on what subject we could not discover. However, we were naturally much edified, and as all eyes were fixed upon us, and not on their books, it is reasonable to suppose the students were equally so. There seemed to be a difficulty and a favour made of showing us the museum, which we could not account for.

It had been, we were told, much more worth seeing than at present, but many of the most valuable specimens had been removed to the museum at Lisbon. There remained, however, shells, fossils, and minerals in abundance; these occupied several rooms. In another were stuffed birds, beasts, and fishes, many very well executed, and some which I had never before seen. From these rooms we went almost reluctantly to those appropriated to models of instruments and machines connected with natural philosophy. All the instruments were English. There was a thermometer, notwithstanding what I have said of our having been unable to procure one for Colonel Elley.

There were two small paintings, reminding me of one I may have told you I had seen at Paris, painted on canvass, not stretched but mounted thus ~~~~~~~: and the subject varied as viewed from different points. A queer little figure of an old lady was produced, to demonstrate the centre of gravity. To recover us from the laughter and confusion into which the exhibition of the little lady had thrown us, we were electrified, and then took our leave of the professor, who had obligingly shown us this part of the museum.

On the 10th we left Coimbra for Martagoa, expecting to meet there Bull's troop, which was to have crossed the Mondego on its route to Anadia. Downman and Harding traversed Busaco by the convent gardens. Jenkinson and I purposely took another way, to examine a different part of the attack on our position there. Having now crossed the mountain three times, I have formed a good idea of Massena's attack, of which the boldness is more and more surprising the more it is considered.

After proceeding to Bailie, a quarter of a league beyond Martagoa, where we dined and slept, I determined to leave my companions, and go to Avelans de Cima, on the route to Anadia, and, as the sequel will show, only a league from it. Accordingly, on the 11th, the rest of the party set off on their route to Mello; and I procured a guide, and with my batman. Driver Terry (picked up at Lisbon), two mules and my horse, took the mountain road to Avelans, by what is called the Caramula Pass. This is the road by which Massena turned our Busaco position, which he had been unable to force. I believe the guide took us some short cuts on the mountains; Massena must otherwise have been much to be pitied.

I never saw any road so bad. Water quite underneath one's feet seemed now and then to invite a false step over the precipices, and I expected to have to pick up the broken remains of my baggage. However, we managed to reach Avelans just before dark. From Martagoa the distance is said to be only four leagues, and at all openings on the mountains, Busaco is close at one's elbow. I left Avelans and went half a mile further to the house of the prior, near a nice little church.

The prior's hospitality produced sausages, eggs, rice, pumpkins and apples; and I dined like a lord. He would receive no money for these good things, nor for straw for our beasts. We talked for three hours, and passed in review the whole politics of Europe. All this in Portuguese. His housekeeper was a sun-burnt, shrivelled old woman like Petrarch's. You recollect his reflection, (which you will see quoted in Zimmermann's *Solitude*), on the shrivelled charms of his attendant (he whose sufferings from love had been so acute), "that had Helen or Lucretia possessed such a face, Troy had not been burnt, nor Tarquin driven from the empire of the world."

I had heard of the *Quinta de Gracioso,* and first established my quarters in the magnificent room in which I write, and then sallied forth to Anadia, a mile from hence. It rained all yesterday. The minister of Anadia, the Juiz being absent, is now with me; we are going to look at quarters for the troops. He talks French badly, but writes it better; and we have already exchanged two or three notes. *Adieu*! I am called away.

Letter 28

Coimbra: March 10.

You will have heard from my last letters that my late employment has been confined to the tedious and painful investigation of offences brought before the general court-martial of which I am a member. We have no very particular news. Nothing remarkable has occurred in either army. A partial affair of outposts near Bejar, in the vicinity of the mountain pass of Puerto de Baños, took place some days ago; General Foy having attacked our outposts with a squadron of cavalry and some 1200 or 1500 infantry. The enemy was repulsed with a loss of twenty men on each side. One French *aide-de-camp* and two other officers were taken: one Portuguese officer was wounded.

The 50th British Infantry and the 6th Portuguese Caçadores were the troops engaged. On our side they were under Lieutenant-Colonel Harrison, and behaved gallantly. The Puerto de Baños and the Puerto de Pico are the only convenient, or indeed practicable, passes for troops over the Sierra between Coria and Plasencia: accordingly, their possession is of value to either party.

Our 4th Division has moved, and is on the other side of the Coa: others are ready, but no movement of consequence will, according to probability, take place yet. The enemy has retired from Salamanca towards Rueda, but is collecting 7000 or 8000 men in order to levy contributions and plunder the towns in the mountainous district of the Sierra de Francia, in front of Ciudad Rodrigo; this we may find it necessary to prevent. Soult has gone to France; twelve men per company, and a proportion of officers, have also quitted the enemy to join the cohorts in France. Count Reille now commands the opposing army. Maucune is second in command. Lord Wellington is expected at Lamego, for what purpose I know not.

The hospitals here are understood to be preparing for a move; but these reports are common, and may possibly be unfounded. The last campaign cost the cavalry 4000 horses and 1100 men out of 7000 of each. I cannot yet learn the losses of infantry and artillery so correctly as to state them; but a truce to such subjects.

I found yesterday, at the end of a long walk in the gardens of a convent, a kind of alcove, with a *jet-d'eau*, spouting up its columns of water in an arbour surrounded by myrtle, privet, cypress, and almond trees, all growing in profusion. All around were seats placed for the indolent fraternity to lounge on. The tiles forming them had on them the representative of every species of hunting: the elephant, the tiger, the wild boar, and twenty others, down to the little rabbit. I am disturbed by the hum of the ladies coming to market under the little back window of my apartment, which looks into the street. Nothing can be more simple than the market here. Women bring everything on their heads; leather, wood, saltfish, poultry, grass, and straw, and down they squat in the middle of a dirty street, and there's the market. Poultry of all kinds, tied together in whimsical confusion. If you wish to buy a woodcock, you must also take a robin, a crow, or a thrush, or any game which chance may have thrown into the bunch.

There is a fine plain near Coimbra, inviting a gallop. The Mondego runs rapidly over it, having here and there fords over the sandy channel. Downman and I were debating the other evening whether we should cross over for the sake of returning from our ride by a different road, when a party of men arrived with their oxen, which they were driving home; they all plumped in with the beasts, partly swimming, and gained the opposite bank; immediately afterwards came a lady, who crossed with equal simplicity, leaving us ashamed of our indecision. There is a confusion of justice here, which to our ideas is strange: people accused of all crimes, and those accused of none, are all huddled together in the same cell.

At Coja, a woman had confessedly murdered her husband; she had for her companion an old woman, whose son, having been drawn for the militia, had absconded. This is the common practice; on the absconding or desertion of any man from the army, his female relations are imprisoned until he is heard of. This may be politic; of the justice, we, in our happy country, should be apt to doubt. Many of the common prisons in the towns have trapdoors in the ceiling to let the prisoners down by; but no doors by which they can escape.

Here there seems an odd custom: a certain number of prisoners are let out every day, though heavily chained, to take the air in front of the prison, which is just by the riverside, and close to the principal entrance of the town by the bridge. They talk gaily to all passers-by, and seem no ways disconcerted.

Adieu! I am not without hopes that I shall yet, in the course of the morning, receive your letters. Perhaps the postman may have encountered a stream of mules going in a wrong direction; in this case there is no remedy, no resource, but patience; no alternative but that of sailing some little way with the multitude, till the beast can be persuaded to proceed in the original road, which is often a work of some time.

Letter 29

Quinta de Gracioso: March 14.

Today is Sunday, and I write at my window in a clear, frosty, fine morning, without a cloud or a breath of air to stir the leaves; all is quietness and repose, such as the day should be. I found, on joining Bull's troop, that he had been in the habit of reading prayers to the troop, whenever the duties of the field would permit; and I have with pleasure followed so good an example. Our Divine service is generally attended by twenty or thirty peasants, who come to wonder at what they cannot understand; but they behave with decorum, and we endeavour to make the service as serious and solemn as we possibly can.

I well know, and the idea has often flashed across my mind, that you would consider my frequent applications for articles to be sent from England, as indicating too plainly that my return would not probably be so near as you had hoped. Let me be honest with you.

I ever have had, and can ever have but one wish, to which all others are very minor; it is to return to you and to my children, and this I trust I shall do. I have no longer a wild course of ambition to run, or to chase fancied happiness in those paths in which I know it is not to be found. Under the conviction that to home I am to look for the real happiness of this life, it is my intention to return whenever duty will allow me; and sooner than this I know your regard for my honour will never lead you to wish that I should return.

I do not imagine that I shall remain in my present situation, but even if I should, I shall have no hesitation in requesting leave of absence whenever the approaching campaign shall be over. That campaign will, in all probability, be rather one of fatigue than danger; but even if the dangers of it should be more than common (which we have not the least reason to expect), I trust to the same merciful Providence to which I have owed my former protection.

I am persuaded that your prayers will place additional security round me. You know that I should never have applied to be sent abroad, and that from the moment I married, I formed the resolution to court no risks or dangers, equally determining never to shun them when they presented themselves in the line of duty. I wish we had Bell here: I yet hope to have him, and if I succeed Downman, to make him my adjutant. This will afford him means of information, more than if he were tied to a troop. I have written home on the subject, and shall write this mail to General Lloyd. They fill up the vacancies with boys who have the very beginnings of duty to learn, instead of sending men to support the honour of the corps.

I hope to carry this point, as well as several others which appear to me to be required. In the correspondence both at home and with superiors here, which this entails, I have full employment; but I meet everywhere with attention to my remarks, though I do not imagine that all I wish may be acceded to.

Bell once away from my troop, what a change there will have been! all new faces and new systems, of which every man has, of course, a little one of his own. I miss my old friend Hall, (quartermaster serjeant of his own troop), very much; he would be the very man here; it is his spirit of readiness and cheerful devotion to the service, which is in times of exertion so valuable.

I have arranged with Downman that the men who shall replace others sent from this troop as unserviceable, shall be men lately sent from my own troop. I like old faces and friends, and they will be willing to come to me, as knowing my ways.

One of the points which I hope I have carried is, to send away from all the troops such men as, though not now sick or unserviceable, are sure of becoming so if taken into the field. It is clear there are many, whom to expose to hardship would be to doom to death, though they are capable of much service at depots, where they can be taken care of.

I am going to Coimbra, to meet Downman and Major Dyer. I am in daily intercourse with Downman, who is exerting himself to bring forward the Horse Artillery. I am going on Thursday to Figueira, a little seaport town at the entrance of the Mondego. I go there on a bathing party with Downman: a day or two's idleness by the seaside will do us both good.

Letter 30

Coimbra: 5 a.m. March 15.

I was at Quinta de Gracioso yesterday, and wrote to you from thence, but arrived here in the afternoon in time to see a very curious procession, which is an annual one, as I am told, on the second Sunday in Lent. A figure of our Saviour, as large as life, and carrying his cross, was supported on a platform, carried by six men, clothed in purple silk gowns; these were preceded by the Roman banner, with S.P.Q.R. (denoting the senate and people of the old Roman republic), accompanied by the other banners of the present Roman Catholic Church.

Immediately behind the platform followed, one by one, but accompanied by men in purple gowns, and carrying tapers, six little children, fantastically dressed out with hoops and stuffed petticoats, puffed out with every variety of gaudy ribbons. They had great plumes of different colours on their heads, and were covered with rings, necklaces, and medals. Besides a kind of circular band of crimped silk, which stood out from their shoulders, each had a pair of wings. I believe they were meant to represent angels.

The first carried a cup, the second a dish with three dice in it, the third a sponge, the fourth a spear, the fifth a crown of thorns, and the sixth another spear or reed, all expressive of some part of the crucifixion.

These were followed by all the monks and clergy. The procession was closed by a regiment of militia, the band of which played very solemn airs. The soldiers had their arms in one hand and their hats in the other. All spectators uncovered and silent.

I mixed with the crowd, and was accosted by one of the supporters of the angels: he was muffled up in silk, but I recognised him to be a saddler of Coimbra, whom I had occasionally employed. He told me that one of the little figures was his daughter. She was a nice little girl of about five years, staggering under the awkward suit which encumbered her.

My friend further informed me that this procession took place annually, and alternately by day and night. It stopped at every church for some time. Our officers and men took off their hats, and showed

Mounted Officer of the
Royal Horse Artillery

respect, which was pleasing. Indeed, a crowd or mob in this country, from whatever cause collected, exhibits none of those marks of noise or disturbance which so generally accompanies ours in England. *Adieu!* My horse is waiting to carry me to Anadia.

Letter 31

Quinta de Gracioso: 2 p.m. March 15.

I got here to breakfast, and always enjoy the quiet walks about the Quinta after the bustle of Coimbra. I have been lately much amused by several mules I have met, not merely sheared, but absolutely filigreed in the most whimsical manner. There are people whose trade it is to shear and to cut their hides in the fantastical manner admired in this country. All the trees are coming into leaf; and amongst those at this place are the finest weeping willows I have ever seen. The house steward says that his mistress. Donna Maria, has quite a passion for weeping willows. I believe I have mentioned the attention of the master of the house in sending me oysters from Aveiro. He resides there, we learn, to be ready to slip away, in case the French should come this way again. So much for the effects of fear.

Soult is believed to have quitted Spain, with 8000 cavalry. All is quiet at the outposts since the late failure of the enemy at the Puerto de Baños, which you will find between Coria and Plasencia. Joseph Bonaparte is at Toledo. The enemy has apparently relinquished his menaced invasion and plunder of the towns in the Sierra de Francia. I am going with Downman to Figueira for a few days, and shall write from thence.

Letter 32

Figueira: March 19.

According to Downman's plan, we left Coimbra yesterday to come here. Ramsay and I came from the Quinta de Gracioso on Wednesday, dined and slept at the convent of Santa Cruz, and at nine yesterday morning we left Coimbra; Ramsay to return to Anadia,—Downman, Cathcart, Harding, and myself to proceed here. Although Figueira and Coimbra are on the same (that is, the right) side of the Mondego, we yet recross at Montemor, four leagues below Coimbra. Between Coimbra and Montemor the road lies across a beautiful plain of unequal breadth, seldom exceeding a mile and a half, from the various streams of the Mondego on the right, to the foot of the hills, which occasionally recede and advance in agreeable variety, on the left.

Officer of the Royal Horse Artillery

We passed through five large and populous villages between Coimbra and Montemor; some handsome houses, and (which ought to have been first mentioned, as they were first admired) handsome girls in all of them. We saw by the way, in a dry ditch, a lizard, of a green colour, about fifteen inches long, and I fancied it was some rare animal; but was told that such lizards are at once common and harmless. I had not before seen so large a one. The little lizards, from four to six inches, are already swarming on every road, and on the steps of many houses. We reached Montemor, or rather, the ferry opposite, about two o'clock, and, as we approached the shore, saw our baggage and mules, which had left Coimbra before us, landing on the other side.

In approaching the ferry, we crossed the plain, literally through flocks of sheep, and had previously seen several mares with little colts, and cows with young calves. You may wonder at my remarking what in England are so generally to be met with; but these are rare sights here, indicating the wealth and security of property that are only to be found in those favoured parts of Portugal to which war has comparatively been a stranger. Montemor is on a rocky hill, on which the ruins of an old and extensive castle frown on the plain beneath.

The river here runs in one stream, is not fordable, and is about 200 yards in breadth. We were ferried over in a boat which held us, the orderly, and our five animals. Horses as well as mules acquire a docility in this country which is most useful; they leap in and out of boats, and up and down rocky steeps, with an ease and freedom which at first surprises one.

The houses here are generally white; the few not so are smeared with a kind of disagreeable ochre, neither brown nor yellow, but an unpleasing mixture of both. The women of Portugal walk generally very upright, from their custom of carrying vessels of water, and burdens of all kinds, on their heads. They rarely let anything fall, though they seldom apply their hands to their loads; we yesterday saw an uncommon, and I should think, an unsafe instance of this practice; in passing through the village of Majorca, a well-looking woman asked us for alms; she had a basket of some size on her head, from the rushes of which, whilst Downman was taking out his purse, a nice-looking, interesting child popped its head; yet neither mother nor child seemed to fear the fall which we could not help imagining every step might occasion in the moving load.

From Montemor to Figueira is three leagues; but after crossing a causeway of three quarters of a mile, over a low tract of country, generally, as at present, under water, the country loses its level appearance, and reverts to the common hill and dale of Portugal, interspersed with craggy rocks. Shortly after leaving Montemor we lost the Mondego, which takes a bend to the left. The day had been pleasant, though the sun was hot; but the wind, which had been light, now blew strong from the north, and the cold became quite uncomfortable before we reached Figueira at 6 p.m.

March 20.

This is a nice place. The sea runs high, and with much surf. There is a narrow passage and dangerous bar at the mouth of the Mondego. The channel does not seem to be more than fifty yards in breadth, and, we are told, frequently changes its situation, the sands shifting with the winds. We are today going five or six miles off, to the northern extremity of the bay, or rather, beyond it. Here is the Mondego Bay, where part of Sir Arthur Wellesley's army landed. There is a small point at the extreme end of the town of Figueira, another at the town of Boarcos, and a little intermediate battery (all without guns), to defend about two miles of coast. Our object today is to see some coal mines. We afterwards dine with Colonels Cathcart and Elley, who return with us tomorrow to Montemor, and proceed on Monday to Coimbra.

Letter 33

Coimbra: March 22.

I have had a good soaking this morning; the rain, which came down on my poor mule in good earnest, has been much wanted. We left Figueira about 2 p.m. yesterday, and sailed in the commissary's boat to Montemor. The distance is about four leagues by the river, and three by land. After leaving the harbour or basin of Figueira, where the river is perhaps a mile wide, or rather more, the Mondego narrows to about four hundred yards for perhaps a league. A projecting rock again narrows it to two hundred and fifty yards: at this point there is a guard of dragoons, who bring-to all vessels coming from Figueira, and make them show their passports from the *Juiz de Fora* and Commissary of Figueira. This is necessary to secure the public trade on the Mondego; the sailors would otherwise prefer following their own concerns and their private trade, to supplying the commissariat of the army.

Our party reached Montemor about five o'clock, having sailed in about three hours from Figueira. We got aground some twice or thrice, exchanged *vivas* with all the boats we met, and frightened (and were perhaps more frightened ourselves) a bull, who was feeding close by the bank in the narrowest part of the main stream of the Mondego, which for three miles was as straight and as narrow as a canal. All these perils passed, we reached Montemor just as a procession was descending from a church, amongst the ruins of the old castle, which had once, we were told, been the residence of the kings of Portugal. The procession was similar to the one at Coimbra, on the preceding Sunday; the same figure of our Saviour, the same number of little children fantastically dressed as angels; but at Montemor the flag carried after the Roman standard was green, and the followers wore white silk cloaks, with green capes reaching over their shoulders; those at Coimbra had been purple.

I find that the stomachers, bracelets, rings, and other finery with which the poor children are bedizened, belong not to the church but to the family. This opportunity is sought to display riches, as well as the beauty of the children, the most handsome being always selected. Did I mention my intention of taking a trip to the coal mines? They are at Mondego Point. Very bad sulphurous coal, but the rocky cliffs are fine, and the roaring surf dashing against them still finer. This morning at Montemor I heard the surf at Figueira very distinctly. It would be a dreadful lee-shore. I shall write again before the English mail leaves Coimbra. *Adieu.*

Letter 34

Quinta de Gracioso: March 29.

I have been delaying to write to you till nearly the last day of the mail, in the hope of having to acknowledge the receipt of another packet from you, but I cannot learn that any more letters have come from England, although the wind has been in general northerly for the last week. I returned from Coimbra on Friday evening. Our court-martial having again adjourned, I trust that duty is now over. We have no news from the army. My letter yesterday, from Colonel May, the artillery adjutant-general, mentions that we shall not move till the end of April; but no one does or can know anything of the matter.

I met a most interesting case, in Coimbra, a few days since, in a blind soldier, of the 88th Regiment, only twenty-five years old, with a decent-looking wife, carrying an infant of five weeks in her arms, and another little girl, two years and a half old, running by her side. I was struck with the children, and stopped the poor fellow to hear his story. He was going to Lisbon to be invalided, was quite cheerful, and seemed only to feel for the little girl, whom he was obliged to carry on the march, and who was both frightened and hurt when he stumbled or fell down for want of sight. They had been possessed of a donkey, he said, but it had been stolen from them. I never saw more cheerfulness, or more resignation. I could not help going to the *commandant*, and securing the poor fellow's family a passage to Lisbon by water.

The good folks here are in sad want of rain; without it the harvest will be scanty, except in wine, the flavour of which is always highest in seasons of drought. Our horses are now all on green forage, chiefly barley, some of which, after being cut, is allowed to bear a second crop, but the greater part is ploughed in. This must be bad husbandry, I should think.

I stumbled, on Sunday, on a collection of bee-hives; there were more than forty in a row, all of cork, with a little hole or two cut for the bees to go in and out, and covered with a rude piece of slate. They were a couple of feet high, circular, perhaps a foot in diameter, and surrounded by bees, "improving the shining hour."

I have had my pen in my hand to write to Gordon, at Gibraltar, but something or other always interfered. Yesterday I received a long letter from him, dated Gibraltar, the 10th inst. He had been at Cadiz, where he saw Lord Wellington at the theatre; and hearing that his lordship had been at his uncle's, at Xeres, on his way to Cadiz, and would again be there on returning towards Lisbon, managed to get first to Xeres, and to be introduced as an officer most desirous of serving with the army. Lord Wellington told Gordon's uncle:

"It is really not in my power to order your nephew to join the army; I have nothing to say to the military at Gibraltar; but let your nephew get an exchange to some place under my command, and it is likely he will be gratified."

Gordon has already ferreted out a captain at Cadiz, who will exchange with him, and I have written to another officer here to change with him again, and have also written to Lord Glenburvie (Gordon's uncle) to make interest for his succeeding to the second captaincy of Bean's troop, which will soon be vacant by the promotion of Captain Whinyates. I have no knowledge of Lord Glenburvie, but wrote on the score of his benefiting the corps by attending to the interest of a deserving officer.

Six p.m.

I am just returned from a long ride through the woods, where we saw many more cork hives, and met plenty of goats, kids, and pigs. Ten minutes ago, I was preparing for dinner, when the good steward of the house knocked at my door; on opening it I found he came to announce the arrival of a barrel of wine, as a present from the Capitan Mor, of Anos. I must tomorrow write him a civil note in return for the wine, and a very civil letter which accompanied it. You see we are on good terms with the folks here; they are very obliging. When we told the steward yesterday that we should not cut the barley of a field adjoining the Quinta, he seized Ramsay's hand and kissed it with the liveliest gratitude. We are as quiet here as if in the regions of peace. *Adieu.*

Letter 35

Quinta de Gracioso: April 13.

You will participate in the good fortune which has attended me, in having received the command of the horse artillery with Lord Wellington's army. This is the more flattering, since I have made no application for it, and since, from my present rank, I could not have expected so pleasing a distinction. It is owing to Downman's having obtained leave of absence. Fisher obtained this leave for Downman in the handsomest manner, and at the same time sent me orders to repair to headquarters, which is to be my future station, and to assume the command of the horse artillery. This I shall accordingly do the moment I may be at liberty from the general court-martial at Coimbra, which is again directed to assemble on Saturday, the 17th. However, the delay will be of no consequence; I shall go by Mangualde to see General Stewart, and take a different route to those I have yet traversed. My own employment being arranged, I naturally think of my friend Bell, for whom the situation of adjutant is now vacant.

Lieutenant Harding, who has been in that capacity with Downman, has been so obliging as to remain with me till Bell comes, which I consider very friendly. I told him candidly how Bell and I were situated.

My new appointment will have many advantages: I shall be always at headquarters, in the way of hearing and seeing all that is going on, and of making, at my own discretion, visits to all corners of the army. I shall have full employment, but in the way, I like, and trust to be of use; there is ample field for exertion. I shall, moreover, live by myself, which, strange as it may seem, I consider an advantage.

Letter 36

Quinta de Gracioso: April 20.

Nothing of a public or interesting nature has occurred since my letter to you of the 29th March. On my arrival here, I found your old friend Light. He had been on duty towards the Vouga. The first cavalry division are moving towards Oporto: chiefly on account of forage, though appearances indicate movements in the direction of Astorga. A letter received yesterday from the quartermaster general, assured General Bock that the marquis was most anxious to move the army when able. This implies that some arrangements are yet incomplete. I shall reach headquarters just in good time.

I went yesterday with Captain Marschalk, of the 2nd German Dragoons, to a convent three and a half leagues from Coimbra, in a retired dell under a rocky ridge, running from Busaco towards the Puente de Murcella. The convent (which is called that of Lordovão) is seldom visited, lying out of the common beat. A few French stragglers had been there after the Busaco affair, but had done no harm. The abbess spoke to us at the gate: she was a very cheerful old lady, but told us in reply to our inquiries for the visiting parlour, that the door was the only place where gentlemen could be permitted to be.

A nice little girl of four years was playing with her, the daughter, the abbess said, of a villager of Lordovão, but at the age of seven she must be forbidden to enter the convent, such being the rule. I think the abbess said, that after that age, children were too observant to be allowed to remain. There were one hundred and four nuns, and several (we did not learn how many) boarders in the convent. We were politely offered, but declined refreshment. We asked to see the church, which was immediately permitted. I have seen nothing finer, and in truth, nothing so fine. It has suffered no injury. Through the gratings above we saw many sparkling eyes, but could discover no person distinctly. Across nearly the middle of the church, and directly under a noble yet simple organ, an iron gate separated the space allotted to the nuns.

Their part of the church was arranged in stalls, and reminded me of the chapel at Windsor, though it was considerably larger. We saw very distinctly, in the galleries, several of the boarders, dressed very gaily, though all in white. A beautiful voluntary was played on the organ. It was simple and solemn, but was followed by the French *Marseillaise*. Never was anything more ill-timed than this sanguinary air in a church. It was probably in compliment to us as military men, and as the only march known to the invisible performers. After looking at all the shrines and paintings in the church, we returned to the entrance of the convent: thanked the lady abbess, bowed to all the ladies whom we indistinctly saw at the windows, and took our leave, pleased, yet disappointed at not having seen more. *Adieu* for the day.

Letter 37

Quinta de Gracioso: April 22.

I write a few lines to save next mail. It is now twelve, and the mules are loading. We purpose going as far as the convent of Busaco, where I will finish my letter, and return it by Captain Ramsay who accompanies us to Busaco. *Adieu* for the instant.

6 p.m.

Just arrived at the convent, after a very hot and fatiguing journey for the mules. These gardens are delightful. I have just made my bed on the bedstead on which Lord Wellington slept the night before the action of Busaco. *Adieu*, for here comes dinner.

April 23: 6 a. m.

A beautiful morning; the convent bell calling to prayers; fog clearing away. We propose today marching by Martigao and Barill St. Combadaõ, all inconsiderable places. The cavalry movement mentioned in my letter of the 20th, is not altogether on account of forage. That division will occupy the province of Entre Douro y Minho. Colonel Cathcart slept in my room at the Quinta two nights ago, and left us yesterday for Oporto. He had just heard from his father. Lord Cathcart, who, in joining the Russian Army from Petersburg, had followed the route by which Bonaparte fled. He slept at the same houses, and everywhere heard of the voracity with which Bonaparte devoured any and everything set before him.

The dead of the French Army, Lord Cathcart says, remained frozen in the attitude of despair, in which death, accompanied by the horrors of starvation, had seized them. There were 7000 bodies in one place, dead doubtless from starvation; when one reflects on these miseries, what does war appear? what it undoubtedly is, the heaviest curse on our fallen nature. God bless you and yours.

April 23.

I forgot to tell you, in speaking of the convent at Busaco, that all the doors and ceilings of the rooms are of cork, which has a pretty effect. The sun, now setting, casts a warm tint over perhaps one of the finest views in the world.

Letter 38

Mello: April 26.

We are so far on our journey; my last letter was from the convent of Busaco. In descending the mountain, we followed the road by which the enemy had ascended to the attack of the light division of our troops, and passed through Martigao and Barill, to Santa Combadaõ, where we slept at the house of the Capitan Mor, and were most comfortably lodged. In our way to Santa Combadaõ, we twice crossed, by ruined bridges, the River Criz; this you will trace on the map. At the house of the Capitan Mor, there were two full-length pictures of Catherine of Great Britain, and her spouse, as we understood it, Don Pedro the Second, of Portugal.

The fountain where the far-famed Iñez de Castro wept during her confinement, and near which she was murdered, is yet shown. It is at the Quinta de Lacrymas, and within a mile of the bridge of Coimbra. All this I learned after I had quitted Coimbra, and had lost the opportunity of visiting the interesting spot. From Santa Combadaõ, we passed by Taboa to Villa de Marto, a collection of dirty houses, where we slept.

The bridge over the Mondego, near Taboa, is most romantic: yielding to none, except that of Almeida, over the Coa. From Villa de Marto, we joined the main road I had formerly travelled.

Till yesterday, when it rained at intervals, we had fine weather; it has rained again today, and the weather is cold; the snowy mountains round us reminding me of my former trip from Guarda to Mello. We stop here today to rest our horses and mules. I find the house here, in which is the troop hospital, belonged formerly to Vasco de Gama, the celebrated Portuguese navigator. There is a beautiful passage in Thomson's Seasons about him. Tomorrow, we shall march through Celorico to Barracal, next day to Friegardas, and after that to Malhada Sorda. The army will probably move in a few days. The first cavalry division is now entering the province of Entre Douro y Minho, and will advance by way of Amarante.

Malhada Sorda: May 3.

I arrived here after a wet and cold journey. We left Mello on the 27th, and slept at Barracal, a league from Celorico: on the 28th we halted at Friexedas, and on the 29th came here by way of Freixo, crossing the Coa (swelled with rains) at the ford near Castello Mendo, one league from hence.

May 5.

I had written thus far only, when I received an unexpected. and unwelcome letter from the Judge-Advocate of the Coimbra Court-martial, directing me to attend at Oporto, where the court is to reassemble on the 7th instant. This was not to be endured, so I mounted my horse and galloped to the adjutant-general, and arranged that I was not to go. Nothing can be finer than the country when you pass the frontiers, and leave stone walls and dirty Portugal behind. It is then level turf with majestic scenery bounding the plain.

Today I shall dine and sleep at Puebla de Azava, three leagues off, returning early tomorrow morning. I hardly know what prevents our taking the field; though the rains may have some effect, I believe our deficiency of transport has more. Nine hundred mules are wanting in the Artillery Department alone, and, I believe, 3000 or 4000 in that of the Commissariat. This is provoking. We shall, as we suppose, cross the Douro in Portugal; the cavalry is already in the Entre Douro y Minho. Burgos is a thorn which must be extracted. It is considerably strengthened, but we have good information.

We are making scaling ladders here; Pasley's fellows are working hard within 100 yards of me. His school of instruction has done much, and will do more good. There is at last a regular corps of sappers and miners. Our reserve artillery, twenty-four 9-pounders, six 18-pounders, about 200 rounds per gun, a proportion of small-arm ammunition, and thirty-four large pontoons with equipages complete, is edging down towards the Douro from the neighbourhood of Covilhaõ. We wished that it should have kept the left bank of the Coa, leaving Guarda to the left, but the roads are reported impracticable, and it will cross the Coa near this, recrossing the river at Almeida. I do not know that any of the infantry divisions have moved, though I suspect they are closing up.

Our field artillery is tolerably complete, except two batteries, of which one only received its horses the day before I left Coimbra. Our horse artillery are now—one troop at Zarza Mayor, (with General Hill's corps,) one at Castello Branco, on its march to Sabugal, where I shall meet it on the 8th instant, one troop at Oporto with the cavalry of this corps, one at Mello, attached to the Light (Infantry) Division. All have 6-pounders, except the troop lately arrived from England, which have 9-pounders; that troop is yet unattached. I hope to see at least two others unattached also, and, should any opportunity offer, shall endeavour to have it so arranged.

Our arm, in high and unequivocal efficiency, should be kept like greyhounds on the slip; its value is yet but little known. Joseph is at Valladolid: of the distribution of his forces I know little. All our preparations indicate long movements. The enemy will be numerically superior in every arm; yet I think we shall see the Ebro. I imagine, but without the least authority, that we shall mask Salamanca, and advance direct upon Burgos. Toro and Zamora are said to have been strengthened, but how I know not. We remain yet in very indistinct possession of the particulars of General Murray's affair with Suchet; it appears to have been decidedly in favour of the Allies. It took place, I believe, on the 11th *ultimo*. Suchet advancing on Biar and Villena (near Alicante), took a Spanish battalion in the castle of the latter place, and pursuing his advantage, pressed the Allies, who retired before him, contesting the ground.

Night ended the action. Murray, it is said, purposely retired to a more favourable position, which, having gained, he became next morning the assailant, and, after a severe struggle, decidedly drove Suchet off the field with considerable loss. Some cavalry and ten British guns are said to have done great execution against Suchet's columns, which were thrown into confusion. The Allied loss is said to have been about 900; this is probably, as usual, exaggerated. Elio (my Buenos Ayres acquaintance) commanded the Spaniards. I have seen his despatch dated from Castalla, which you will find between Villena and Xixona: it is well written, admitting the discomfiture on the first day. If I can procure it, I will enclose it, though probably you may be already more in possession of the real facts than we are.

The priest of Puebla de Azava knew that the thing had happened some days before the despatch reached headquarters. I apprehend that before the action, some of our troops (and I know many stores) had been embarked for Tarragona:—this arrangement has been counter-ordered.

If Murray can make head against Suchet, we shall do well; his success, even partial as it may have been, is both unexpected and well-timed, and may prove of much use. We all lament the ridiculous dress of our cavalry, whom it will now be difficult to distinguish from the enemy. I observe our scaling ladders are entire; not in joints as they usually are. They are thirty feet long, two feet wide at top, and one and a half at bottom. The sappers are all busy practising both double and single sap.

No appearance of any issue of pay to the troops. Provisions here are dear; onions, sixpence each; fowls, three dollars a couple, &c. &c. The wine is excellent, light and of pleasant flavour; the bread uncommonly good, well-baked, and keeps well; the loaves are very flat.

Galloping Royal Horse Artillery

Everyone says so much of the miseries to be looked forward to, in case of want of money in Spain where ready money must be paid for everything, that I have laid in a stock of dollars; I got yesterday 400. I have met with the most friendly reception here from Colonel Fisher, whose arrangements are good. He has proved himself an excellent man of business.

LETTER 39

Malhada Sorda: May 7, 5 a.m.

We remain in repose: but the battering guns passed us yesterday, and the pontoons will today or tomorrow. On the latter especially must obviously depend our movements if we are to cross the Douro in Portugal, of which I have very little doubt. I have not yet seen the marquis; but I have seen what frightened me much more. I met a wolf yesterday, and never felt so much alarmed in my life. I had returned early from Puebla de Azava, and after breakfast walked up to the convent near this village, to receive Colonel Fisher's orders for the day, and returned alone. the road is rugged and rocky; a high wall of loose stones bounding it on the left: to the right is a ruined house, separated from the road by a broken loose wall, through a hole in which, a kind of lane leads into the country.

Just opposite this ruined house, and within ten yards of me, I saw the monster. We mutually stopped, gazing at each other; he grinned, showing teeth of which I then more feared the length, than admired the whiteness. My first impulse was to put on my gloves, which were in my hand: and my next to pick up one of the large stones at my feet. the creature seemed in the act of springing, but on seeing me stoop, stalked quietly away a couple of yards, and then, grinning more horribly than before, turned round his head, as if again about to spring; but after a moment's pause walked slowly away, stopping and turning round every few yards.

Fear, you know, is a bad portrait-painter, but so horrid a countenance I never beheld. The creature was gaunt, and looked half-starved. It is more honest than creditable to confess that my thoughts were so occupied by this gentleman, that it was not till my arrival at my own door that I discovered that I still carried the great stone. Wolves abound in this part of the country; some animals have been lately torn by them, but I cannot learn that any man has ever suffered here. They have, however, occasionally been seen prowling round the village, though seldom so very near the streets as in the instance I have mentioned. My curiosity is, however, fully satisfied.

Letter 40

Malhada Sorda: May 8.

Changes in our own corps are at hand: I yet know nothing certainly, I may rather say at all. Colonel Fisher goes home, and I confess myself sorry for this, having had great reason to admire his arrangements. Dickson will be Fisher's successor, and I can see further, that it is wished I should apply for the command of the reserve artillery. I mean to do no such thing; the command is justly thought inferior only to that of the whole artillery of the army, but I mean to apply for nothing: merely remaining ready and willing to do anything. I shall hear today how the matter is settled, and shall rest contented. Colonel Waller, being a senior officer, has been directed to remain at Lisbon; this Waller will probably not do. There is another senior Lieut.-Colonel (Tulloch) in the Portuguese service, and several senior to Dickson in the British artillery.

All these perplexities will, I fear, lead to confusion at the moment we want the cordial co-operation of all. I fear we shall have a jumble, and that the public service may suffer. This would be a real evil; all other considerations are of little importance. I shall get on very well with Dickson: he was second to me in the South American Expedition, and then obeyed my orders with the implicit readiness which I shall now transfer to his. He is a man of great abilities and quickness, and without fear of any one. I have asked Mr. Hennegan, our commissary, to dine with me today, and Mr, Butcher, who was commissary with me at Buenos Ayres. You would smile at my unconcern about the dinner; we have literally nothing but some ration beef for them.

Malhada Sorda: May 11.

I am heartily tired of riding over broken pavements and rocky roads. On the 9th, Harding and I rode over to Villa de Toro, about four leagues from hence on the other side of the Coa. It is near Sabugal. After crossing the Coa by a rude bridge of slippery stones, and the usual incidents of losing our way, we reached Villa de Tomo (for the place is spelt all manner of ways), and inspected Captain Webber Smith's troop of Horse Artillery, which had marched in the day before. It is in very fine order, and after a long and severe march looks very healthy and well. I prevailed on Smith to return with me. In an endeavour to abridge our road, we again lost our way, and rode across the country about three hours, when we reached the Coa about a league and a half above the bridge by which we had crossed in the morning.

We endeavoured to ford, but the stream was so rapid, and sands so shifting, that we were obliged to give it up, and rode along the bank through fields of standing rye, really higher than our horses, till we reached the bridge. Near it we found a poor mule, which had been drowned since we crossed in the morning. We reached home by five p.m., having set off at six a.m. On the 10th, we set off at five a.m., to Puebla de Azava, three and a half leagues off, where we breakfasted with Ross, and persuaded him and Jenkinson to accompany us to Ciudad Rodrigo, five leagues further.

The road is good, and we galloped thither, and minutely examined the works, the breaches, and the ground where our batteries and trenches were during the siege. Ross and Jenkinson knew every spot, and explained all fully. Poor Ross lost here a brother, whom I had the pleasure of knowing. He was an engineer of great professional promise, and of a suavity of manner and gentleness of disposition, superior to almost any I have ever seen. He was buried in the same grave with Captain Skelton of the Engineers, killed at the same time; Jenkinson performed the last sad offices. The grave is in a little retired valley, not far from where the two friends fell. Colonel Jones of the Engineers had placed an inscription on a small pedestal to mark the spot, and had wisely surmounted it with a cross. Many Spaniards have been seen kneeling there, and none pass by without taking off their hats.

While we purposely turned aside, poor Ross quitted us to pay a melancholy visit to the grave; he often steals over there. After four hours passed in looking about, we remounted our horses, forded the River Aguada a little below the town, and galloped back to Puebla de Azava, where we met Fisher, and dined and slept.

May 11, 5 a.m.

At five a.m. today, I mounted my horse, and returned home to breakfast, and finding the Life Guards and Blues were to be reviewed by the marquis near Alfayates, set off to see the review. The ground is about three and a half leagues from hence, and the roads to it abominable. I got there about an hour before the review commenced, and looked over the household troops, as these regiments are called. The Marquis, who is Colonel of the Blues, was in the uniform of the regiment, wore a star, and looked very well. His horse was most richly caparisoned, and had a net of embroidered gold and purple of uncommon beauty, which had been worked and presented to him by the ladies of Cadiz.

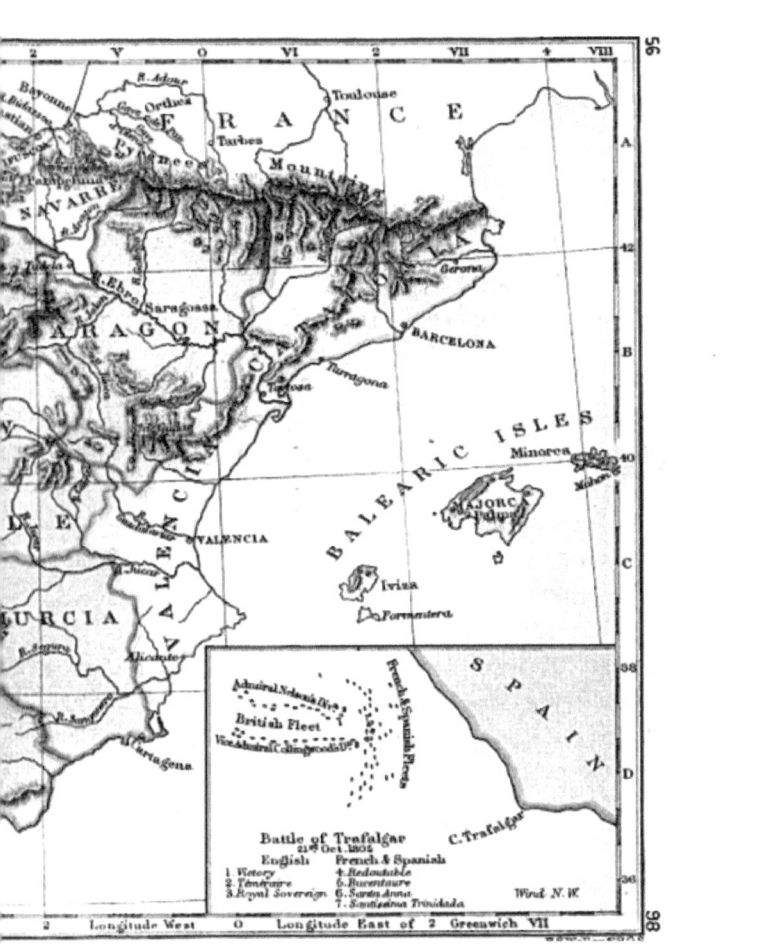

The Prince of Orange and all the great folks were there: among others, Don Julian Sanchez, the Spanish chieftain, Generals Alava and O'Lawler. Alava resides at the British headquarters, and is the organ of communication with the Spanish forces. He commanded a Spanish line of battle ship at Trafalgar. I returned home about two o'clock, tired and hot. The heat of the two last days has been very oppressive.

LETTER 41

Sabugal: May 15.

I am here with Dickson to see the pontoon establishment and reserve Artillery under Colonel Hartmann. Since my last letter most of the divisions in the rear have been moved; others have received their routes, so that we shall soon be all in motion. I left Puebla de Azava early yesterday morning, and after changing my horse joined Dickson, who was coming here. We slept last night at Villa de Toro, at Captain Webber Smith's.

Today we started at daybreak, and rode through a thick fog to Pouza Folhis de Bispo (what a name!), to inspect three hundred mules just arrived from Seville; good animals, but the muleteers the most whimsical figures imaginable. From Pouza we rode here, and have been busy with Sir Richard Fletcher, (commanding the Royal Engineers), in the pontoon park.

We have been putting our wits together to make something of the pontoons, which travel badly, break down, and in short do all that is not wished. Already have horses and bullocks been tried in the draught, but without finding that either do well. We have sent them all our spare wheels, and this moment I have been sending Ross an order to make a couple of wheels lower than any which have yet been tried.

We expected to have met Lord Wellington here, according to an appointment with Dickson, but his lordship flies. He was here yesterday afternoon, ordered one pontoon to be burnt, and vanished in the smoke. You would be dinned with the noise of the room (Colonel Hartmann's) in which I write; German, Portuguese, Spanish and English, all talking at once: a smoking and wine shop below. Today and yesterday the cold has returned: now fog with rain. *Adieu.*

LETTER 42

Malhada Sorda: May 15, 4 p.m.

Just returned with a tired horse, knocked up by eight leagues of bad roads.

May 16, 9 a.m.

I had hardly sat down yesterday before I was interrupted. I dined at the convent to meet Lord March, who is a fine youth, and one of the Marquis's *aides-de-camp*. The light division, which is commanded by General Charles Alten, will be reviewed tomorrow near Espeja. Ross's troop is attached to it, and I must of course be there. The cold weather continues. I have been sending off a man to Puebla for my appointments, but I do not think Headquarters will move before the 20th.

A number of artillery horses arrived at Sabugal yesterday evening during my visit there. There were two officers of the artillery drivers. Captain and Lieutenant Reid, and both their wives were with them. What will these ladies do? I cannot conceive a situation more uncomfortable than that of women following an army. I fear they will find neither the reality nor even the appearance of civility from any one: all are occupied with their own business and their own comforts.

Today is wet and cloudy. Colonel Fisher left us the day before yesterday, sincerely regretted by all. I hope Dickson's reign may be long, for the sake of the service, but the times are slippery. I missed seeing Don Carlos d'España on Monday last, at Ciudad Rodrigo, which I was sorry for; there is something amusing in seeing those who make what is called a figure in the world. To be a spectator of all that passes is always so, though one gets imperceptibly entangled in the puzzled skein of little politics.

May 19, 5 a.m.

My two last days have been passed in riding about. On the 17th I went to the review of the light division, commanded by General Charles Alten. This division consists of the flower of the army; the three battalions of the 95th Regiment, the 43rd and 52nd Regiments, 1st and 3rd Caçadores, (Portuguese light troops), and the 17th Portuguese Regiment of the Line, the 1st German Hussars, and Koss's Troop of Horse Artillery. Nothing can be more striking than the appearance of these troops: perhaps at this moment the finest infantry in the world. The hussars are attached but for the moment. The marquis was attended by all his staff, and many generals as spectators. The review was on the plain of Espeja, about three leagues from hence. The day was very hot, the troops went through their movements in an admirable manner, and to the perfect satisfaction of the marquis, to whom I was introduced by Colonel Gordon, one of the *aides-de-camp*.

Lord Wellington was very civil, and invited me to dine with him, which I accordingly did, and sat till half-past eleven, as etiquette forbids any one's moving from table till after his lordship, except indeed the Prince of Orange, who rose about a quarter of an hour before the rest. The party consisted of twenty-eight. The conversation at these tables is necessarily common place. Much was said of the Light Division, and more of Ross's Troop, which is certainly in very superior order. A Count de Chaves and his two sons (one a boy) sat opposite Lord Wellington, who sits in the middle of one side of his table. Nothing more amuses me than scenes of this sort; fancy is at work reading the characters of all, and smiling at the eager looks which betray the anxiety to catch a smile from the hero of the day.

The Prince of Orange always sits on his right hand. His highness seems affable and good humoured, and is a very general favourite. The boy was soon asleep, and the father followed. I talked with Colonel Arentschild till we were both ready to follow the example; and before we broke up, heat, good cheer, and champagne had made us all drowsy and stupid. All however seemed unnecessarily in fear of the great man; on his part, he talked with apparent frankness.

I returned by moonlight to Malhada Sorda, and at five rode over to Puebla to dispose of some horses lately sent from Sabugal for officers. They are sorry beasts, but I am obliged to take one, which I shall not keep if I can avoid it. On Sunday, after remaining in doors till towards evening, Harding and I walked out. We scrambled down a rocky ravine, through which a mountain torrent dashes its tributary stream into the Coa. At the point of the "meeting of the waters" is a little rude mill: it is partly hewn out of the live rock, and partly built of loose stones.

A miller was at work attending to three grinding stones; his bottle of water and a few lentils on the ground, a sorry jackass picking up some grass between the stones at the door. While we were talking to the man, his wife, ugly and brown, arrived with part of a brown loaf for him; they seemed happy to see each other. We could not help asking one another, which were the wiser and more rational beings: those who were contributing to the sustenance, or those who were about to destroy their fellow-creatures? *Adieu.*

Letter 43

Malhada Sorda: May 21.

I write a few hurried lines: where we may be next mail day I know not. Headquarters moves tomorrow to Ciudad Rodrigo; indeed, part are now moving. There is something unpleasant in leaving any place, and I confess I shall quit even this with a kind of regret, though it has as few charms as can well be imagined. Loose stones and squalid people are the dead and living objects of Malhada Sorda. Our regrets will accordingly soon vanish, and probably never amount to even a half wish to return. We have curious weather, changing *"with the varying wind,"* as the song has it. Yesterday panting with heat, today buttoned up to keep out the cold. I have just had a friendly letter from General Bock, who is coming from Oporto to join his division of cavalry at Braganza. We are sending more of our columns to the Tras os Montes, and have divided our pontoon establishment into two parts. A few days will show the meaning of all we are doing.

Enter a little singing Portuguese girl, happier, I ween, than those *"who whirl of empire the stupendous wheels."* By the way, some of our wheels here go round badly enough, and require more than ordinary pushing and oiling to get them to stir. All are packing up, and all lamenting the quantity of baggage, which yet avarice (in the disguise of provident management) prevents any from lessening. I have cut a little profile of myself for the boys. Dickson will excuse my cutting it out of his book: he is a good fellow. Between ourselves, I have had a long letter from Colonel Waller, asking advice what to do; his situation is singular. (See letter 40). I have recommended him to think of the good of the service and that only, and to do nothing of which, on calm and future reflection, he may have reason to be ashamed.

Dickson shewed me yesterday a very sensible, plain letter which he had written to him, and was just going to send off. Dickson, too, feels himself awkwardly off, but will bear his honours well. There is an open, manly simplicity about Dickson, very prepossessing. I hope and trust he will long enjoy the confidence of the Marquis: and this I should desire for the sake of the service, independently of any regard I might have (and I have a very sincere one) for Dickson. Joseph remains hitherto at Valladolid. I have a return of all his artillery now lying before me. *Adieu*:—I am called away.

Letter 44

Tamames: May 23.

Just arrived here after a pleasant ride, though a hot one, from Ciudad Rodrigo, or rather, from some ruins a mile from it. The town was full, and we bivouacked to get out of the bustle. My last letter was written from Malhada Sorda, which we left early yesterday morning. We came by Espeja, near the place of the review mentioned in one of my late letters.

On reaching Ciudad Rodrigo, we learned that besides the headquarters of Lord Wellington, including all the posse which compose it, those of Marshal Beresford and General Castaños were to be there too. My billet fell on an uninhabited, or rather, I should say, uninhabitable house. Dickson was as badly off, and no stabling at either place; so that we set off to find some snug place to pitch our tents in, and found one enclosed by a good wall. This was a great recommendation, as it is no very uncommon thing to have one's animals stolen. I was glad, too, that we quitted the town, great part of which, from its late sieges, is a heap of ruins. The streets were full of horses, mules, and baggage, and all the confusion attendant on squeezing a multitude into a small space.

After dinner we walked into the town, and were amused with the curious figures we met. On the steeple, and looking down "on the great roundabout and all its bustle," were three or four storks. They are very common in this, as in many other countries, and are protected by the people. They seem aware of this, and noways afraid of anyone. It is curious to see the little birds, such as sparrows, making themselves nests in some crevice in those of the larger birds, and living, as it were, under their auspices. I do not recollect this in Holland, or in other countries in which I have before seen storks. In the course of the morning, we had seen many of the larger vultures, as well as a bustard, the first I have seen here.

In Ciudad Rodrigo, I had an opportunity of inspecting the Spanish regiments of Hibernia and Mallorca, which marched to join the army this morning. They are fine-looking troops, dressed, the former in brown, the latter in blue. The *Caçadores* and *Tiradores* of Castile remain as the garrison.

In Ciudad Rodrigo are three Roman pillars, bearing the inscription of Augustus Caesar; they have nothing very remarkable. Two shafts of about thirty feet, of brick cemented over. They form, however, the arms of the town, and are shown as its chief curiosities. All the smart ladies of the place were walking about, some of them pretty, and many well-dressed. The marquis gave them a ball in the evening. While I was endeavouring to make out the inscription on the pillars, I observed a crowd round a kind of hurdy-gurdy, as I supposed.

On approaching nearer, I found half-a-dozen little girls dancing a *bolero* with *castanets*. I was greatly pleased; the oldest girl could not be more than ten or twelve, and, as well as one or two more, danced with uncommon elegance and animation. Their only music was a kind of little box covered with parchment, on which another girl beat with her hands, whilst some of the spectators occasionally sang. I never saw more joy sparkling in any eyes than in those of these little girls, especially when a "Bravo" burst from the spectators, who were common peasants and soldiers.

I sauntered about till nearly dark, when I left the town to avoid being shut in, and returned to my tent. This morning was very cold. After a good breakfast we set off between five and six, and got here about twelve. The marquis and marshal arrived soon after, and are lodged at the next house but one, which is occupied by General Alava. The country over which we have ridden today, eight (not six) leagues, is very fine, though there is little or no sign of cultivation. The majestic mountains, called the Sierra de Francia, and de Bejar, in the intervals between which the distant and snowy mountains near Plasencia formed a noble background, gave a grandeur to the open country over which we passed.

Columns of dust indicated the movement, on all sides, of armed men, and led the mind to contemplation on the scenes about to take place. On the highest peak of the Sierra de Francia stands the Convent of Nuestra Senora de Francia. I could not help fancying the monks occupied in gazing on the multitudes pouring out on the plain beneath them. Possibly they were all asleep, or too indolent, or too wise, to think anything of the matter. After passing the village (or what was the village) of Pedro de Toro (now a heap of ruins without a house or a single inhabitant), we reached Tembroa, and soon after crossed the River Yeltes at the village of Aldehuela de Yeltes, three leagues from hence.

Above the hill, as you cross the ford, the country is very beautiful, the road lies through fine oaks, chiefly pollard, but fantastic: to the left, a lake of water, the second we have seen. Today, among the mountains of Bejar; here is the Castle of Bejar, in an armoury of which was the sword of the Cid, a famous chieftain in days of yore against the Moors. This sword was taken from the castle, some time ago, in a curious manner. There is, in the 1st Life Guards, a Lieutenant Mayne, who came to this country with Sir Robert Wilson, and served as Colonel in the Lusitanian Legion, and carried on the war on the true guerilla system. (*The Loyal Lusitanian Legion During the Peninsular War* by John Scott Lillie and William Mayne is also published by Leonaur). Having a great desire to become possessed of the sword of the Cid, he managed to take it down, and to affix to another, which he hung up in its place, the history of the Cid's exploits. He afterwards presented another sword to Marshal Beresford, as the real sword, which he reserved to himself.

There is another story told of the same Lieutenant Mayne, who is doing duty with the Life Guards here. He was at one time in command of the post of Alcantara (on the Tagus), and accordingly considered himself Governor, and finding that all governors were Knights of Alcantara, dubbed himself a Knight. Tomorrow we shall halt there, to the great comfort of the poor mules and horses. In the morning, the Marquis will review the Portuguese Brigade, somewhere near the town. I propose looking at them, and then either riding to inspect Captain Bean's troop of horse artillery (which was here yesterday, and cannot be far off), or groins: to look at the house in which Cervantes was born; it is not far from hence.

Though the house is probably like most others, yet not to see where the author of *Don Quixote* was born would be unpardonable. The dress of the Spanish women is whimsical: hair very long, but plaited behind, and tied with a bow of ribands; petticoats very short, little tiny aprons, gowns of yellow stuff, with a broad border of blue, or the colours reversed, or at least having a border differing from the colour of the gown. Many yesterday had very wide sleeves curiously wrought. We have now bade *adieu* to Portugal; I shall not close my letter till tomorrow.

May 24. 5 p.m.

We had a very fast and hot ride to Moraleja, where we found the Portuguese Division of General Hill's corps drawn up in review order. Eight battalions of the line, one of *caçadores*, three squadrons of dragoons, and two field batteries of artillery; in all about 5000 men, exclusive of artillery. The scenery was most romantic. The line was drawn up on a rising ground, well wooded, a river rolling in front; on one side, the mountains of the Sierra de Bejar, and in the distance the snowy mountains near Plasencia. Both the marquis and Marshal Beresford were there: the marquis in his full-dress marshal's uniform. Tomorrow we go to Matilla, and on the 27th shall be at Salamanca.

There are today 3000 of the enemy there, who must retire at our approach. Our first object will be to attack Zamora and Toro. I saw at the review a person who left Salamanca last night, and says the enemy appeared ignorant of our movements. It is not probable they should be so; they are sly foxes. I regret leaving the neighbourhood without seeing the convent of the Peña de Francia. It is so cold there in winter, that the monks descend to a second convent which they have halfway down the mountain. Some of the figures today at the review were irresistibly ludicrous. One master of a band had a square-topped hat, with a feather three times as tall as any feather I ever saw in my life. The men looked healthy, cheerful, and well.

Six divisions of our infantry, and one of cavalry, are today advancing from Braganza, and Miranda de Douro. One division of infantry, two brigades of cavalry, and the whole of Hill's corps on this side of the Duero (now no longer Douro since we are in Spain). This village, or rather little town, is in ruins, at least one half of it; yet the people seem happy. *Adieu.*

Tamames: May 24.

Headquarters removed yesterday from Ciudad Rodrigo to this place; tomorrow they will be at Matilla, and on the 27th at Salamanca. This presupposes that a corps of 3000 French will, at our approach, retire quietly; if they do not, we must force them to do so. We are today as follows: the cavalry and 1st infantry division moving from Braganza, in the direction of Zamora; the 3rd, 4th, 5th, 6th, and 7th infantry divisions advancing from Miranda de Duero by the right bank of the river; the light division and Hill's corps, between the high road from Ciudad Rodrigo to Salamanca, and the Tonnes; the Portuguese division of Hill's corps, near Moraleja (three leagues from hence).

We had intelligence today at twelve, from Salamanca, which our informant left last night. The French were in apparent (it must be feigned) ignorance of our movements. Our first object is to attack Zamora; but it will be necessary to force the position of the enemy, who mean to make a stand behind the River Esla. I do not imagine they will risk a general action. For security in case of accident, we have a bridge between Miranda and the junction of the Esla with the Duero. The defences of Salamanca were destroyed beyond all capability of repair. Zamora is not strong: it is surrounded by a good common wall, and a kind of castle has been fortified, and joined by a looped wall to the cathedral, which is taken into the *enceinte.* The marquis is said to expect the enemy may leave 2000 or 3000 men in Zamora; nothing less would retard the progress of our army, and the enemy cannot afford to lose the use of so many men, who would, in all probability, fall into our hands.

Toro is still less strong. I apprehend our first general action will be before Burgos, the siege of which is resolved upon. I cannot hear that our heavy ordnance has reached Corunna; we wish it were at Santander, whence the task of removing it, and placing it in battery against Burgos, will probably devolve on me. The enemy yesterday pushed a patrol to Vitigudino, midway between Salamanca and Torre de Moncorvo. I had a hot ride to Moraleja, where I saw the Portuguese division of Hill's corps reviewed by the marquis, the whole in most creditable and efficient order, both as to equipment and appearance, and facility of movement. The division is commanded by the Condé de Amarante, a lieutenant-general. The infantry were 4480, *caçadores* 220, cavalry 230, and artillery twelve field pieces. I never saw finer troops.

I hope tomorrow or next day to see the British division of Hill's corps; it is in our front. The Spanish Regiments of Hibernia and Mallorca left Ciudad Rodrigo yesterday, to join Castaños: they are well-looking troops, but inferior to the Portuguese. Each regiment had something under 400 on parade. What think you of headquarters drawing rations at Ciudad Rodrigo for 1500 animals? it is true that the marshal's and Castaños' headquarters were there, as well as the Marquis's: it is a little army. I will write again, after our movements shall be a little more developed; all, however, looks well.

Letter 45

Salamanca: May 27, 6 a. m.

My last was written from Tamames: we left it on the 25th, and on our way to Matilla, where we halted yesterday, paid a visit to the Casa de Cervantes. 'Tis a few hundred yards to the right of the road leading from Tamames to Carrascalicho, the first village on the route to Matilla. The situation is pretty, some nice trees and a little rivulet tributary to the Henbra, give an air of romantic beauty to the spot. We peeped in at an iron-barred window, and imagined we saw Cervantes himself. One might have fancied anything, for there was not a soul in or near the house, which is a solitary one: but some peasants, whom we afterwards saw, assured us (with much eagerness, and seeming satisfaction that we should be interested about the matter) that it was the very house in which the great Cervantes was born.

It is still called the "*Casa de Cervantes:*" if your map of Spain be a good one, you will see that our road lay through Carrascalicho Sanchon, and Villa Alba. Matilla is a poor place, and, like most Spanish villages which I have yet seen, without a tree to shelter one from the sun. The house in which Harding and I were billeted, though consisting of four rooms, had literally no windows: this, I find, is no uncommon thing here. The rooms are whitewashed, and while the sun shines and the door is open, one manages to see without a candle, which in a dark day must be at all times necessary.

We (Lord Wellington's staff, including orderlies, about forty persons) left Matilla at five yesterday morning, taking the road to this place. About seven we reached the heights of Salamanca, and the baggage was ordered, when it should reach the streamlet of Valmusa, to be halted under a guard of the Blues. The road for the last two days was one of those by which our army had retreated in the preceding year; the signs of the retreat were but too evident, in the skeletons of the poor animals who had suffered.

On coming within about two miles of Salamanca, Lord Wellington inclined off to the right to gain a rocky height which commands a full view of the city, and of the adjacent country. The scene was very fine; below us our own videttes, beyond them those of the enemy: each side supported by picquets of their own. To our right, and rather behind us as we looked towards the city, were the village of Arapiles, and the two hills bearing the same name, on which was fought the Battle of Salamanca. Still more behind us we observed on two roads nearly parallel, the heads of the two columns forming Hill's division.

It began to be very hot. We looked through our glasses, and observed the enemy drawn up; a couple of battalions and a squadron to the right of the city near a ruined convent; two squadrons on one side the Tormes near the bridge, a half squadron guarding the ford about a mile above the town, near the village of Santa Marta, and a battalion in reserve behind the city. In the plain intervening between our hills and the town, the 1st German Hussars inclined by degrees towards the ford of Santa Marta, favoured by the inequalities of the ground, which concealed them from the view of the enemy.

The 14th light dragoons edged along the right bank of the Tormes, keeping beyond the reach of the enemy's fire. The enemy appeared in some confusion, though they remained stationary, as if waiting for something. Looking beyond the city in the direction of Miranda de Duero and Zamora, we could see their pickets withdrawing and their mules and baggage joining them from all sides. In this way we remained till ten o'clock, by which time the head of Hill's right column, which consisted of cavalry, and Bean's troop of horse artillery, under General Fane, were within two miles of the village of Santa Marta, and evidently marching for the ford.

Battle of Salamanca

The enemy a little before this began to move, at first in the direction of Toro, but very soon, as if wavering, bent to their right, and kept close to the Tormes in the direction of Arevalo and Madrid. Hitherto Lord Wellington, with his staff of about forty persons, had remained stationary. We now descended, and passing the head of the Portuguese column of Hill's corps, galloped to the ford of Santa Marta. We had for some time seen that the enemy would be much pressed if our cavalry, already jaded by a long march, could be thrown across the Tormes in time to hang on their rear. On reaching the ford we found that General Fane, whose movements had been concealed by the undulations of the ground, had crossed the river, and we saw his six squadrons gaining the rising ground beyond. It became now necessary to leave headquarters, and to gallop on, which Harding and I did.

On gaining the rising ground, we found the enemy retiring rapidly, but in good order. Owing to ravines and intricacies of the ground near the river, which obliged the horse artillery to make a detour, it was not possible to bring the guns into play for some time, during which the enemy had gained a league and a half from the city. At that distance, however, from Salamanca, the guns opened with effect: every shot going through the ranks of the unfortunate enemy, who retired with extreme rapidity, but in great order. In this manner, our guns pursuing them with as much quickness as very deep country, occasionally intersected with hollow roads, would allow, the enemy gained the village of Aldea Lengua.

There was at this moment an opportunity of attacking them with every probability of forcing them to lay down their arms, but strict orders having been given not to pass a ravine close by the village of Aldea Lengua, the moment (never to be regained in war) escaped. When it was just gone, we were allowed to go over, and passing the village with some difficulty, continued our pursuit for a league and a half further, pouring our fire on the enemy. By this time, we had overtaken many, unable from fatigue to march further. At Aldea Lengua the enemy abandoned the caissons of a gun and howitzer which, after firing two or three rounds, escaped: the coach of General Villatte, the French commander, had previously been taken.

About three quarters of a league beyond the village we came up with them, and after some firing, there seemed a favourable moment for a charge, which two squadrons of ours attempted, but without success; the enemy forming in squares, and repulsing them by a volley, which did, however, little execution. Some few men and horses were wounded, and three or four horses killed, but the charge was a feeble one. I was carried on with the stream, and got a blow in the leg with a spent ball which has done no harm. This affair must have cost the enemy about 300 men. I counted upwards of eighty dead on the road, besides those who must have fallen in the standing corn. Few, if any, were killed or wounded but by the fire of the horse artillery.

The poor Frenchmen threw down their knapsacks to march with greater rapidity: throwing away two sacks of excellent biscuit, and much corn. The affair ended in front of the village of Aldea Rubia, and between that village, San Morales, and the Tormes. The French general seems to have delayed his movement from Salamanca unaccountably, but his troops afterwards when in motion marched with great celerity, and bore our fire with much gallantry. I saw more than one instance of desperate refusals to surrender; one poor fellow was at length cut down by three dragoons, who in vain required him to surrender; another, severely wounded, tried to destroy himself.

The chief loss fell on the 23rd French Light Infantry: the 94th, and (I believe) 95th were their two other battalions. One of these battalions had only arrived from Ledesma (between Salamanca and Miranda) the day before yesterday. I do not know the number of the cavalry regiment: it was dressed in green, and with brass helmets. On looking with great attention at their dragoons before we marched, I could not distinguish them from our Blues: their brass helmets are the same, and the difference between dark green and blue is not distinguishable. I look forward to mistakes.

We afterwards found three more caissons; I imagine they applied the horses of the two found at Aldea Lengua to remove the guns, which were an 8-pounder, and a 6-inch howitzer. I left the field in the suite of the Marquis, and we reached Salamanca about five p.m. There were some *"vivas,"* and some ladies rushed out of the crowd and seized his lordship's hand: but altogether there was less expression of joy than I expected. In the evening there was an illumination I am told; but I was tired and went to bed, though not without some sorrowful ideas at the sight I had witnessed. There was not even the false emotion of honour where there was no danger, and to slaughter flying enemies, though duty requires it, is nevertheless shocking. I spoke to many of the wounded: none uttered a complaint.

I have yet had no time to look about, but the cathedral and square of the city are superb. I shall finish my letter after I shall have looked a little about the city. We are excellently lodged in the house of an ecclesiastic in the Calle de Milan, fifty yards from the cathedral. General Hill's corps, which we passed in bivouac last evening on our return from the field, has today moved. I have accordingly not seen General Stewart, as I had hoped to have done.

7 p.m.

We are to start tomorrow. I should have preferred staying a day or two at Salamanca, which is an interesting city, though many of its fine public buildings are in ruins. The French, however, do not appear to have committed many excesses, they had unroofed part of the Irish College, with what intention I could not exactly make out. The cathedral, one of the most beautiful buildings I have ever seen, remains entire: we went to the top of it, and were well repaid for the trouble of getting up, by the beauty of the view, which is extensive. The afternoon has been broiling: to be more hot was impossible, but we scampered away to examine the three convents of Mercedes, Gaetano, and San Vincente, which had been fortified by the French, and destroyed by us after their surrender. The inspection of this scene of utter ruin employed us till after dark, when we returned into the city and dined. *Adieu* till tomorrow.

LETTER 46

Almeida: May 28.

Though I wrote to you yesterday from Salamanca I gladly resume my pen while I have an opportunity. The marquis remains today at Salamanca: the rest of headquarters are here on their route to Miranda de Duero, for which we shall march early tomorrow morning. We shall cross the Duero in a couple of boats nearly opposite Miranda, in an order prescribed this day. The crossing will be tedious. There are but two boats, said to be small, so there will be time for rumination on the banks of the river before one's turn comes. I am glad to add to my letter of yesterday that the enemy's wounded in the affair of the preceding day were taken every care of; this is as it should be. Salamanca is a noble city, though much ruined: many of its public edifices have an air of grandeur.

The inhabitants speak of the French with a composure truly surprising when one looks round at the misery and ruin visible on all sides. Seeing *"Los Ninos Expositos"* (which means The Foundlings) written on one of the buildings, I went in, asked for the administrator, and went through all the building. Two little circular boxes in windows in the middle of the street receive the children, and a bell is pulled by the persons placing them, so that the proper nurses receive the little ones, without seeing by whom they are left. The administrator told us 317 were received in the year 1812, and about 100 since the commencement of the present year.

They are kept at the expense of the hospital until eight years old, and then sent out to service. The funds are supplied by the government, though from want of sufficient knowledge of Spanish, I did not quite make out how. The regulations as to numbering and registering the children seem pretty much the same as in our English foundling hospital. Cases had occurred, the good man said, though rarely, of parents coming to claim their children; though he added, he had never known one of a father's coming, and said with great simplicity, that the institution received all the children brought to it; "Yes," said he, "Spanish, Portuguese, French, English, and Turks, we receive them all." We were shewn into a room where the little ones lay three and four in a bed: some not above ten days old.

We are again tonight in a house without windows, but very clean; and the daughter of the host, a good-humoured girl, made us an excellent dish of eggs and bacon, and afterwards ran to the wine-house to get us a flagon of wine. The servants and mules did not arrive till towards seven, having had a fatiguing march from Salamanca of eight long leagues. We set off again at daybreak. We passed today on our left the little town and hot baths of Ledesma: the latter are well worth seeing, and are in high repute as warm sulphurous springs. The water is about 110° Fahr. No Frenchmen have ever been in this village, as the peasants tell us.

This I afterwards found to be false: indeed, a requisition for mules from the French general arrived during our stay. Some of the people seem shrewd enough, and to know what we are about. I was amused at Salamanca with observing in some streets the names of the owners cut in the freestone over the doors; one which I copied is as follows: "*Esta casa es de Antonio Obatle y de sa muger Maria de Hyerta y heredos. A. D.* 1802." *Adieu.*

May 29: 10. a.m.

Just arrived at the ferry opposite Miranda de Duero. Conceive a multitude of men, horses and mules descending by a craggy path to the bottom of a rocky chasm, in which the green Duero rolls with great rapidity, the river eighty or ninety yards wide. A single flat-bottomed boat, which with difficulty holds eight horses, is the only conveyance across. It is pulled backwards and forwards by ropes fastened from rock to rock. I have seen nothing so wild yet, even among all the rocky scenery of Portugal. In descending the path people seem going in all manner of directions. In an hour or two (as many more arrive than can be got across) the path, the only inlet, will be jammed up; there is no outlet.

I should think the rocks are four or five hundred feet high. We are going across according to a prescribed order; my turn is not likely to arrive for an hour or two. I have stolen into a retired nook of the rock, and am in quiet, though within five yards of the eager candidates for passing. It appears there is another ferry near Fermoselle and opposite Bemposta, about three leagues below Miranda. Many wish the horses had been sent round that way, and the baggage animals only had passed here. We are now between Hill's corps and the main body of the army; tomorrow we shall join the latter, which I presume we shall find approaching the River Esla. We have heard nothing of the enemy for the last two days, and indeed think little or nothing of him.

The river is sometimes so swollen that the ferry is impracticable. The only alternative for passengers then is to cross in a kind of hammock, which passes along a rope fastened to two projecting points of rock. The rope is at this moment about 30 feet above the surface of the water. No one has yet attempted it today. In truth there is no hammock, and if there were I should hesitate, unless I were assured of having assistance at hand. The life I lead is a very curious one. We live well enough and suffer no kind of hardships or privation whatever. It is more like travelling about in the gipsy style than anything else.

You would stare to see the strange figures we all are. Blue or grey slouch greatcoats are worn by all; one may almost say the shabbier the better. You would have smiled to see me last night feeling the pulse of a poor boy who is sick of a fever, with as much gravity as a professional man would have done. I will finish my letter at Miranda, when I shall have got across. There is then half a league of rocky and bad road to scramble over.

Letter 47

Carvajales: May 31.

Just returned, after almost incessant riding since 6 a.m. yesterday. It is now 10 a.m. I have lost, for the moment, part of a letter written and rolled up in my paper-case, so that you will have unconnected scraps. We have crossed the river Esla, and have taken an officer with the piquet of twenty men which he commanded. I believe we have lost a few men killed, so says report, and we have certainly had a few drowned in crossing by a very awkward ford. The 15th Hussars took the French piquet. I was not at the little affair, having been marching all night with the cavalry to another ford, at last found impracticable. On getting, here yesterday, I was told Bull's troop was but two leagues off, so I determined to inspect it. The two leagues proved six: the roads intricate, through woods and fords.

A little before midnight, I reached the village where the troop was said to be, and with some difficulty and wandering about, found the house in which Ramsay, Louis, and Blachley were seated at table, discussing the news of the day over a flagon of good English ale, brought from Oporto. After joining in the delights of the flagon, Ramsay had a comfortable bed made for me on the table, into which I had just stepped, when in came Colonel Ponsonby, of the 12th Dragoons, with an order for us all to march directly.

There is no hesitating in these cases: out we jumped, mounted our horses, and marched till seven this morning, having joined the cavalry division, and two divisions of infantry, on our way. The jumble of some thousands of men moving in different directions, in the dark, is more easily imagined than expressed. The curious figures are most laughable; it is not so, however, to see the number of little children exposed to misery and hardships. I counted more than a dozen quite little ones, besides many others too young to walk.

A pontoon bridge is now being laid over the Esla. I presume we shall reach Zamora tomorrow. The French are now destroying the bridge there over the Duero. I had already changed my horse, and set off for the ford, vexed not to have been there when the passage was forced; but, learning that all was over, and that we shall move by the same route tomorrow, I turned about. The noise at this moment in my room, defies all description; ladies and gentlemen vie with mules and asses: a greater or more discordant variety of sounds never was heard. I find that the post will be made up early tomorrow morning, so I must close this.

Letter 48

Toro: June 2.

I wrote you two hurried lines last night from Zamora, (this letter is missing), which I quitted immediately afterwards, and rode to Tusero de la Ribera, where I communicated to Webber Smith the unwelcome intelligence that his troop was removed from the hussars, and that his 9-pounders were to be divided between his own troop, Gardiner's, and Bull's. Smith is much mortified, and the events of this morning, which are just over, have not tended to lessen his chagrin. We were hardly asleep last night in Smith's tent, when Gardiner's troop arrived from Torres, bringing also an order for Smith's replacing his with the 7th Division.

At daybreak, the hussars advanced with Gardiner's troop, and, near Toro, came up with the enemy's rear-guard, consisting of the 5th, 12th, 16th, and 21st Dragoons, under the General of Division Digeon. These corps formed, as some say, twelve, and others, nine squadrons. Our hussars advanced with spirit, the enemy retiring rapidly to the village of Morales, one league from Toro, in the direction of Tordesillas. They formed behind the village, after having been cannonaded by two of our guns, which were all which the deep sandy roads would allow of being brought up at the moment.

Our hussars passed on both sides of the village, instantly charging and putting to flight the enemy, who made off at speed for a little bridge across a marshy bottom, about a mile from Morales. Finding they could not pass the bridge, they faced about, standing a charge, and by this time supported by the fire of two guns and a howitzer, belonging to the division of infantry, composed of the 100th, 5th, 103rd, and 90th Regiments of the French line, under the General of Division Daricau. The enemy were worsted in the charge, but passed the bridge, followed by part of our 10th Hussars, of which regiment Captain Lloyd, having advanced with great spirit, followed at first by a few men, was taken. Lieutenant Cotton was killed by a carbine ball about the same time.

The enemy were again pressed, and retired hastily on their infantry, who had been marching during the whole affair, but without being engaged. The result of this affair, which has been very honourable to our hussars, is a loss to the enemy of above 200 dragoons with two officers taken prisoners, about thirty desperately wounded, besides some (for I did not reckon the number) killed. Most of the killed and taken were of the 16th French Dragoons. This corps is almost annihilated. Besides the first piquet of twenty taken at the passage of the Esla, another piquet of thirty dragoons was taken the day before yesterday by Don Julian Sanchez. This regiment was the very one which charged Colonel Judson's troop of horse artillery in Holland, on which occasion I had reason to remember it. One of the officers taken today is much wounded; few of the men have escaped without some scratch. Colonel Grant, who commands our hussars, has paid the wounded every attention.

I have just been with the prisoners to the castle here, and have been urging Lord Aylmer to arrange that the officers we have taken be exchanged for Captain Lloyd. The Spanish peasants whom we met, were most loud in their "*Vivas*," and accoutred in the French brass helmets and swords, made a ridiculous appearance. It seems strange, but it is true, that within ten minutes after the affair was over, part of which was almost in the streets of Morales, the women were spinning at their doors, and the little children at play as if nothing had happened. General Hill expected an attack the day before yesterday, the enemy having shown 15,000 men near Alacjos (near Medina del Campo); there was not, however, any affair. All are much pleased with the gallantry of our hussars, whose horses, several of the prisoners told me, were better than those of their officers.

I walked back with the prisoners, who are in general very good-looking men. They talked with much coolness of what had passed, shrugging their shoulders, and merely said it was the fortune of war. I have not yet heard at what hour we shall march tomorrow; but I presume we propose to occupy Tordesillas. This is not so good a town as Zamora, nor were we received with much acclamation; yet the people seem individually very friendly. I am in an excellent house with three old ladies.

The country near Toro is fine, though, like the greater part of this province, too open. The Duero runs under the walls at some little distance. There is (or there was) a good bridge, of eleven arches, over the river; two of the arches are, however, destroyed. This was done by ourselves in the retreat from Burgos.

Letter 49

Toro: June 3.

I told you of a spirited affair which took place yesterday between the French dragoons and our hussars, who certainly show that they possess the right spirit. An order was sent to General Hill last night to move today, but on what point I do not know; unless it should be the object of the enemy to avoid an action, one may soon take place. Their force is distributed between Valladolid, Tordesillas, and Medina. If Hill should be ordered to cross the Duero, which I suspect is the case, we may avoid Valladolid, moving direct on Palencia. But near as we now are to each other, the mutual movements must necessarily much depend on the contingency of the day.

Deserters to Hill's corps all agree that we might have taken Villatte's corps near Salamanca had we but continued our pursuit for half an hour longer. We are leaving half our reserve ammunition near Zamora; this is in order to relieve the horses, which are already suffering. I can learn nothing of the heavy ordnance necessary for Burgos, though one fortunate day may put us within reach of the place. If it is much strengthened it may be necessary to break ground regularly before the horn-work. Our men look well: could they but be kept from excesses they would remain in health. The encampments will, however, do good in this respect, inasmuch as the men being out of towns, will be more out of the way of temptation.

a Mota: June 4.

Hill crossed the Duero early this morning. Tomorrow headquarters will be at Castromonte. Nothing new from the outposts. I believe the enemy has crossed the Pisuerga, between Valladolid and Dueñas; in this case we may soon make our bow to him.

LETTER 50

Amusco, four leagues North of Palencia:
June 8.

We left Ampudia yesterday morning and marched to Palencia. On approaching the town, we learned that a piquet of our own had been placed a little beyond the town on the Torquemada road. Palencia is a fine old town. Within three quarters of a mile of the place, and near a canal with two locks, there is a large paper manufactory. It is unfinished, to be sure, yet the very appearance of intended industry reminded us forcibly of home. The canal is a fine one, though I could not distinctly learn its length or direction. Our maps trace it from Reynosa (some leagues to the northward of Burgos) to Segovia, but I believe they rather trace the intention than the execution of the plan. Having outstripped the marquis, we waited for his arrival, and in due order followed his lordship towards the town. Lord Wellington rode with Marshal Beresford.

As we approached the bridges there was such a crowd, such waving of handkerchiefs, throwing up hats and shouts of "*Viva*," that the *grandees* horses took fright, and whisked about: and it was not till a guerilla chieftain (successor to the unfortunate Marquinez who was last year assassinated by a deserter then employed as his orderly) had in some measure restored order, that the cavalcade could proceed. Ten yards after passing the bridge the shouting was again clamorous, and we were stopped by the arrival of the Camera or Corporation, in their best suits and hats. Two of them spoke at once to the marquis who could not possibly have heard either, indeed the soundings of a trumpeter, who formed part of their procession, were totally drowned in the noise of the multitude. At length we moved on, preceded by a couple of mace-bearers, with wigs thrown not very straight over their heads of hair. These gentry were in purple gowns; altogether the scene was ridiculous.

The Spanish custom of showing at once respect and the counterpanes of the family, is to hang the counterpanes out of the windows; those who have no counterpanes hang out sheets. Some ladies, who possibly had neither, were good enough to show petticoats instead. Several ladies, whose patriotism was kindled by the sight of the hero, rushed forward and seized his hand. We passed on, handkerchiefs waving at all windows: till stopping opposite the Town-house a portrait of Ferdinand VII. was brought out, to which the generality pulled off their hats, and we continued our way, the people throwing flowers from the windows.

We remarked especially a shower of roses from the upper grated window of a convent of nuns. Cowper's description of the hero of the day came into my head, though the beginning only is applicable. Lord Wellington has both "purposed the salvation," and, as we trust, "has saved" Spain. I was somewhat mortified that we did not alight at the Town-house, where, I dare say, as at Zamora, a collation had been prepared for his lordship. We took the direction of the River Pisuerga near Magas, and after ascending the ridge of hills above the Pisuerga, had a good view of Valladolid and Duenas on the one hand, and Torquemada on the other.

Joseph Bonaparte had quitted Palencia the afternoon before we entered it, and the greater part of his troops left early the next morning (June 7). They passed the night, as the inhabitants assured us. in much alarm. We saw some six or seven thousand of them marching to a bivouac near Torquemada, which a letter just (4 p.m., June 8) received from Captain Bean, informs me they quitted early this morning. Part of Hill's corps now occupies their ground, and has been cooking with the wood which the enemy left on the spot. This wood is composed of the doors, window frames, tables, and drawers of the unfortunates who have houses in the neighbourhood; such is war!!

In Palencia there was not a morsel of bread nor a drop of wine, without which last, we dined for the first time since I joined the army. My room was very small, in the noisiest part of the town, crowded to excess by stragglers from the whole army, (Hill's corps excepted,) which encamped under its walls. I never heard such a confusion in my life. It lasted till we left Palencia this morning, which we did without regret; it is, however, a fine old city. The cathedral and a church or two are fine buildings, and the main street has *piazzas* throughout its length. They are high enough to be above the windows of the first floor, and the pillars supporting them, being of fine stone, give an air of something like grandeur to their appearance.

But Palencia from its situation must be unhealthy. The soil is a deep black clay, very offensive. The town is not clean. Near it are two remarkable sharp-pointed hills; on the top of one are wine caves, of which, both today and yesterday, I have seen many. They are common in this country: consisting of a cave hollowed out of any earth which will bear it, and having a common door with a padlock and key. Their appearance is strange,—a collection of doors without houses.

On our way here, we passed through the village of Fuente del Val de Perros, which means the Fountain of the Valley of Dogs. In it is an old castle now dilapidated, which we examined very attentively. The walls are twenty-eight feet thick, in solid masonry. It contains several cells, without windows or light of any kind; designed, no doubt, to immure unfortunate beings. There was also a dungeon below ground. One shudders at the scenes which may have taken place in such buildings; happy England, where such things cannot be! Coming over the road today, I saw in a string of crowded mules, an ass with the nicest pair of hampers I had seen. They were flat-sided, and comfortably roofed, and looked altogether so snug that I set down the owner as a more than usually knowing fellow.

When I had jostled through the crowd, I turned round to look again at the ass, when to my surprise I observed in one hamper that was open in front, that it was nicely lined with scarlet cloth, and that a pretty little child was fast asleep in it. I asked the boy who was leading the ass whose it was, and found the little treasure belonged to the mess sergeant's wife of the 23rd Infantry: and the mother, a respectable-looking young woman, who was riding just by, told me she had carried the little one so for more than a year very safely. This will be a comfortless night for many a poor fellow; it is just beginning to rain hard.

When we arrived here Lord Wellington had not made his appearance. His lordship had made a long ride all along the front, and, as well as several others, I was glad to spare my horse and did not follow in his suite. I had hardly shown my billet to a lame old lady, who was complaining of the miseries she had undergone, owing to the rapacity of the French,—how they had drunk her wine, eaten her eggs, and broken open all her boxes,—when I observed two of the younger women giggling in the passage, and on asking them what made them so joyful, found they were enjoying the confusion of the maid of the house, who was putting on her best stockings behind them, that she might run and see the great Lord.

We had tea in the evening: nothing is so refreshing. We asked the man of the house to join us: he did so, and liked a cup very much; and I offered one to the old lady who was much pleased, and repeated all the misconduct of the French fifty times. We suspect we shall halt tomorrow. It may be necessary to allow the commissariat supplies to come up; more than one division is without bread. *Adieu*—I am called away.

Letter 51

Amusco: June 9, 9 a. m.

It has rained all night very hard, and continues to rain at intervals. The cavalry and Portuguese troops have no tents, and our infantry not enough for all. There are more wet than dry jackets at this moment. This halt is very seasonable for our beasts, which are jaded. The marquis has just passed our window; I suppose to review some corps, as he had on his uniform and star: he usually wears a grey great-coat. Had he been in his great-coat just now, I should have followed, as he might have been going to the front. How lucky to halt today in a quiet quarter.

You would smile to see me reading the *Iliad* throuogh all our scenes of confusion. Many of the walled towns have just the turrets one fancies Troy had, and that one sees in the fanciful paintings of it. Mankind is the same in all ages, and, as somebody observes, one sees in the quarrel of two boys the germ of an Iliad; an expression which forcibly occurred to me, in a fisty-cuff battle between two boys near the spot, at Morales, where, the very day before, our squadrons had met those of the enemy.

Letter 52

Castroxeriz: June 11, 5 p.m.

Headquarters came here to day from Melgar, on the Pisuerga. This is the dirtiest town I ever saw; none in Portugal equal it. It is situated on a rising ground in a plain bounded by hills, and with mountains visible to the northward. We are yet seven leagues from Burgos, which lies eastward of us. Above Castroxeriz is a very high hill, on the top of which I passed a couple of hours this morning, observing through my glass the movements in the valley beneath, of Hill's corps, which is encamped all round us. We have many reports today both of the enemy's force and intentions, but tomorrow will let us more into the secret, and I hope to find time to add a few lines to this letter. Something decisive must take place if the enemy purposes to prevent our crossing the Ebro. I imagine we shall not attack Burgos, but leave a corps of Spaniards to guard it:

June 12.

I have been writing to twenty people, and what is worse, telling the same story, or pretty nearly, to each. The enemy was in force yesterday near Cellada, three leagues from Burgos, on the Valladolid road. He retired towards evening; 10,000 troops moved off at 4 p.m., leaving a solitary battalion at Cellada. We are trying to turn his right flank, and have sent our left column (we are in three, exclusive of Hill's corps, which is on the right of the others), under General Graham to cross the Ebro above Frias.

Graham may have done this yesterday: in this case the enemy's situation is so far critical, that he must be decided. I do not think he will risk a general action, evidently our wish and object. His armies of the centre, south, and Portugal are concentrated. That of the north, under Caffarelli, has returned to France. We shall not attempt to lay siege to Burgos at present. In truth, we have no means, nor if we had, is it an object. The reported garrison of the castle is 3000 men; a force the enemy can ill spare, nor should I be in any way surprised if the castle were blown up and abandoned. Excepting the celebrity, the place has acquired from our mishaps last year, it is of no importance in any point of view.

Prisoners and deserters, many of both are sent in daily (eighty within the last twenty-four hours), agree that Suchet's corps is expected to join; this is not likely. I believe Murray has embarked the Alicante army, and that it will menace, and possibly land on, the Catalonian coast. We are impatient to hear particulars of the reported action of the 9th May; we have confused accounts of it *via* Oporto. The enemy's prisoners and deserters are stout fellows, and well clothed. I asked a deserter the other day why he had deserted: "for want of rations," he said; yet the knave was very fat. The other French soldiers, prisoners, showed no dislike to him, as they generally do, and ought to do, to deserters.

Villadiego: June 13, 8 p.m.

Burgos Castle was blown up at 5 this morning: I have this moment returned from it. It is one heap of ruin and devastation; among the many mines exploded, some have laid open the breaches, and uncovered our poor fellows who fell in the storming. A few of us went in at a hazard with half a dozen of Don Julian's people.

The enemy withdrew his picquet, which joined its corps on the plain, a quarter of a league out of the town, where were six squadrons of cavalry, and two brigades of infantry. After looking about for some time, the enemy sent in a patrol, and we made a most precipitate retreat. Joseph Bonaparte quitted Burgos today, at 4 a.m.; eight or ten French were killed by the explosion of their mines and shells, all of which latter burst.

There was a smart cavalry affair yesterday at Cellada del Camino. We took an officer, some prisoners, and a gun.

Letter 53

Nadagiala: June 14.

I had time last night, after returning from Burgos, to write two lines to mention that the castle was blown up yesterday morning at 5. On reaching, yesterday morning, the village of Hormillas, and ascending the hill above it, Burgos rose on our view, and our cavalcade stopped, with one impulse, to contemplate a scene which recalled the miseries of the last campaign. We could plainly, though the view was distant, perceive that the castle was destroyed. We had previously had indistinct accounts that explosions were heard early in the morning; yet we were by no means sanguine in our expectation of finding that the enemy had saved us the trouble of a siege or blockade.—I am called off.

June 15, 2 p. m.

I resume my unfinished tale. I write now from Valdenvieda, a little village close to the Ebro, and in a valley laughing with every luxuriance of fruit and corn. We marched this morning soon after daybreak, and have passed over a most open and wild country. The road descends to the Ebro through a rocky chasm between two mountains; at first it looked tremendous, and I fancied it worse than any I had seen;—but I shall never get on with anything like a connected story if I do not revert to our visit to Burgos on the 13th.

After seeing Burgos at the distance of three leases, Lord Wellington desired Sir Richard Fletcher to go on, as far as he could with safety, to reconnoitre the place. Dickson, Harding, May, Woodyear, Colonel Gordon, one of the Marquis's *aides-de-camp*, and two or three others joined us, and we went on, looking about us a little, as we saw the enemy's videttes and had no troops with us. As we advanced the videttes retired, and we learnt from the country-people that they were preparing to leave Burgos.

After fording the Arlanzan, the bridge over which was blocked up, and jumping over half a dozen ditches, the little bridges of which were broken down, we reached the hills above the town, and about a mile from it we could distinctly observe the castle in ruins, and straggling people in several parts of the town; some, scrambling over the timbers and ruined remains of a church and of the castle. Still no one ventured out of the town to us, and we were apprehensive of being taken if we went in.

After hovering about for some time, we met a vidette, and, soon after, a patrol of Don Julian's people, and learned that an officer and a piquet of thirty men of Don Julian's were at hand. We had already crossed the road to Valladolid, and pursuing our route a little further, we could clearly perceive, on the plain beyond the town, the enemy in full, and apparently confused, march of cavalry and infantry, preceded by a multitude of mules and beasts of burden. Some Spaniards (peasants), also, about this time assured us that the enemy had quitted the town, leaving at the gate a piquet of fifty dragoons.

On this, Lieut. Reid, (as at 1859, Major-General Sir William Reid, K.C.B., late Governor of Malta), of the Engineers, who had joined us, and I rode forward. Reid, who had been actively employed during the siege, knowing the suburbs, was guide; we approached, and riding fast, yet cautiously, soon gained one of the bridges, and called at a house where Reid had lodged. The people were glad to see him, advised us to be cautious, but said they believed the enemy were gone. We agreed to skirt the town, and gain the horn-work from whence we could see the town, the castle, and the plain beneath.

On scrambling up the rampart we found all in utter confusion: barrels of powder lying about, splinters and shells, balls and cartridges. On looking down we had a full view of the enemy's force. Six squadrons of cavalry, within 400 yards of us, and, as it were, beneath our feet; the men dismounted and strolling. About 5000 or 6000 infantry moving across the plain, which was covered with carriages and beasts

SAVING THE GUNS

of burden. We could neither see piquets nor patrols, and fancied we had passed them. After some time, seeing no one coming towards us. we crossed the ravine which separates the horn-work and the castle, and entered it by the very breach in which so many of our brave fellows fell last year.

It had either never been repaired, or had been opened afresh by the explosion of one of the many mines tired that morning. It was so steep, that it was with some difficulty my horse, though active, scrambled up it after me, and it was easy to know from the uncertain footing, that we were treading on the remains of the brave. On entering the castle, we found it one heap of ruin and rubbish. Gates, beams, masses of stone, guns, carriages, and arms, lay in a mass of utter destruction. Several mines around us had failed; some were primed, but had not exploded, others had been ill-managed, and had blown the earth inwards. All betrayed hurry, fear, and confusion.

We were soon joined by a few peasants: one told us the enemy had burst all the shells that morning, and that in so doing many soldiers had been killed. Indeed, the rest of our party, who had soon afterwards entered the town by the upper bridge, found three dead bodies in the fields, and four in the great square, all evidently killed by splinters of shells. Our friends soon joined us, and we established a little patrol of Don Julian's, just outside of the town, some of us keeping an attentive eye on the enemy; whilst the others looked about at the scene of ruin around. The enemy had apparently done little to the castle during the winter, except, indeed, replacing the broken palisades. He had, moreover, by some strange want of foresight, attended more to building a very handsome gateway of solid masonry to the horn-work, than to repairing the horn-work itself, and putting up the palisades: of which, however, great quantities were collected. He had further built some casemates, and was preparing others in the horn-work.

We stayed in the castle about an hour, visited each of the breaches, talked over all the incidents of the siege, and returned through the breach by which we entered, uncovering by our steps the half-burned bodies which filled it. At the bottom of the hill, we stopped and sent Woodyear into the town to inquire our way to Villadiego, which we knew to be seven leagues off. Woodyear had just returned, and we were eating our loaf of bread, when we observed Colonel Gordon galloping out of the town; he called to us that the enemy had returned, finding we had no force.

Having no mind to contest the point, we mounted our horses and galloped away; but whether the alarm proceeded from Don Julian's people, or whether there really was a cause, we know not, probably the former. The townspeople were glad enough to see us, yet made no demonstration of joy; telling us the French threatened vengeance if they did not keep quiet in their houses. The town did not appear to have suffered from the explosions, but the pavement of the cathedral was strewed with broken glass ground almost into powder. The cathedral is a most beautiful building, remarkably light and airy. I speak of the outside, not having had an opportunity of going within.

Five English prisoners were found in the prison; one a quartermaster of the 10th Hussars, lately taken at the affair of Toro. Ninety-six sick Frenchmen were also found in the hospital. We left Burgos about 3, and rode as fast as we could to Villadiego, which we reached about 7, much pleased with having seen the rock on which, as Bonaparte said, the fortunes of the last campaign had struck.

I passed a very pleasant day yesterday at Marshal Beresford's. We had an excellent dinner, served up on very superb plate. The marshal's table is allowed to be the best in the army; it is furnished, as we are told, by the Regency of Portugal. Our party was of eight, and nothing could be more pleasant. I have not yet been across the Ebro, but have contented myself with looking at it. The troops are now crowding down the defile; one horse fell over the precipice and was killed. There was such a scramble of guns, dragoons, infantry, and baggage that chaos seemed to have come again. In the midst of the confusion we were amused by the men getting into cherry trees, of which we met all at once with a great number. Never was there any transition more rapid; all above rocks and barrenness, all in the valley luxuriance and plenty.

As we were coming last night from the marshal's, we met Major Buckner of the artillery, who had just reached the army. A newly arrived person is like a man dropped from the clouds, so I gave Buckner a bed, and set him off this morning for St. Martin's, at the bridge of which the third division of infantry will today cross the Ebro. We are near the Puente (or bridge) Arenas; tomorrow will see the whole army on the left bank of the Ebro.—*Adieu.*

Letter 54.

Medina de Pomar: June 16.

Never was any valley so romantic as that in which we were yesterday; our march today has just brought us out of it. After writing yesterday I took a long walk with Dickson. I can fancy nothing more lovely;

I should have called it the happy valley had my wife, my children, and other friends been there. These were denied, but roses, honeysuckles, and myrtles perfumed our steps; beans, peas, and pulse of all kinds, in profusion.

The valley is a league and a half in length, and contains fourteen hamlets. It is bounded on both sides, and nearly at both ends, by craggy mountains. We left Valdenoreda this morning a little after four. We sent the baggage off sooner, to pass by the bridge before it should be crowded by troops, and forded the river at a part where it is very rapid. For a league our road lay close by the river, which runs through a ravine formed by the boldest crags, clothed in many places with trees and shrubs so luxuriant that one could not but wonder how they could grow there. I have this moment been to see the first division file past. It is part of Graham's corps, and I had not lately seen it. The men looked well.

The curious figures of the lady and other followers, of all divisions, are beyond description. I could not help observing just now that the only smiling face which passed was that of a little girl of three or four years old; the child was tied on an ass with a string, and found amusement in playing with the end of it. For the first time in the Peninsula I have heard the French well spoken of; 4000 of them were here the week before last; a respectable-looking man told me just now that the French general in command (D'Aroux he called him) was an excellent man, and that he had placed sentries on all the wine-houses, and kept the troops in order. There were three generals and a division here. The inhabitants seem decidedly in the French interest; most of the houses were shut when we entered, and all faces looked sad. My billet is on an uninhabited house; it was locked up, but the woman of the house brought me the key, and was very civil.

We know little of the enemy at this moment, nor, strange as it may seem, are we sure who commands his army: whether Marshal Jourdan or General Cazan; Joseph Bonaparte is of course nominal, and merely nominal, commander. The enemy is irresolute, his plans seem disconcerted by our sudden advance. We know that he is distressed for provisions. All the dry corn of the little valley we left today has been carried off to Breveisca. The adjacent country has probably been equally drained. We believe that Miranda and Vitoria will both be abandoned from want of provisions, and it is possible, if we can advance rapidly, that Pampeluna may not receive a garrison from want of supplies.

We know, by an intercepted letter, that the enemy entertains great fears on account of Pampeluna, and that his difficulties in regard to supplies are very serious; our own supplies may be circumscribed, though we hope an open communication may be established with Santander, only fourteen leagues from hence. The Guerilla Longa, with 4000 men, is at hand; Mendizabel is also at hand. Espoz and the Empecinado are in Arragon; the two latter have been obliged to retire rapidly. One of O'Donnel's corps (of 15000) is said to be coming from the Madrid side; such is our present situation. Part of our army have suffered partial privation, but never have wanted bread for more than one or two days, and these instances have been rare, and possibly have occurred more from want of foresight than of means of transport. The street under my window is crowded with mules, and there is noise and bustle enough to derange the wisest head.—*Adieu.*

Letter 55

Berberana: June 18, 9 p.m.

We have been fully engaged from noon till 7 p. m., and a colder evening November seldom produces in England; wind northerly, with occasional rain. We marched this morning from San Leon, and thought of little but taking up our quarters quietly here, but the enemy must needs dispute the point, and showing about 16000 men, obliged us to take the trouble to drive him back. The French are gallant fellows and really do their part well.

The affair today was near Osma, a mile and a half from hence. There was much firing, but little loss on either side. On our first seeing the enemy today near Osma, he retreated, showing six squadrons, and as many battalions: but suddenly returned with extreme vivacity, and became the assailant in his turn. This was probably to discover our force; however, he found us in no ways disposed to turn, and again retired.

Our light division was detached early this morning to endeavour to cut off some of the enemy's battalions returning through the mountains towards Espejo. The division came up with three battalions near Villa Neuva, half a league from Espejo: charged one battalion, took about 200 prisoners, and the baggage of the other two battalions. Neither the particulars of this affair, nor that of ours of today, are distinctly known at this moment, but I write lest I should not have another opportunity. Indeed, we suspect that the marquis will send off an account of his having passed the Ebro. Orduña is ours by the operations of today; our movement for tomorrow is not yet known.

LETTER 56

Subijana de Morillas: June 19, 7 p.m.
It has rained nearly the whole day. We have had another skirmish. It began at twelve, and ended at five; much firing, but little done on either side; the enemy was forced, and gave way. Our outposts are now within three leagues of Vitoria, where we shall be tomorrow. We have just seen the whole French army; it is not easy to form a correct judgment of its numbers, partly concealed by mountains, and seen through thick occasional rain. I have but five minutes to write. The French headquarters of the army of the south were yesterday at Pancorbo, from whence they were removed late last night. It was Maucune's division which was so roughly handled yesterday by our light division.

A French brigade is dispersed in the mountains, and will be brought in by degrees by the peasants and guerillas. The divisions with which we skirmished at Osma were Foy's and Sarrut's infantry, and Courtoux's cavalry. We went this morning to Salinas, so called from its salt-works. I must describe them when more at leisure. The French were driven out of this town two or three hours ago.

Our hostess, with a nice little girl of fifteen months old, is now singing with joy at our arrival. She has been two days and nights in the mountains; the house ransacked, and all gone. The misery one sees shows war in its true light. In the field one expects to see the fate of the soldiers, but the distress of women and children sinks deeper in one's mind. We have *Moniteurs* of the beginning of June, I believe, and know of the thirty days' armistice between the French, Russians, and Prussians. The *Moniteurs* were found on the dead, and in the baggage of yesterday's affair. We must get the strong pass of Puerto d'Arlaban, between Vitoria and Mondragon.—*Adieu.*

LETTER 57

Subijana de Morillas: June 20.
We are to halt here today; whether for a longer time I know not: Lord Wellington has gone out to reconnoitre. In all probability tomorrow, we shall march again. The poor people of this house have just been to inquire how we slept. We could not but sleep well, and, idlers that we are, lay in bed this morning till past six. The poor souls had been for two days in the mountains: they returned just after we obtained possession of the village, and found their house ransacked of all but quantities of thread, of which, I imagine, there must be some manufactory at hand. When we arrived, we were drenched with rain,

had lost the orderly whose horse could not keep up with us, and were as hungry as the poor creatures themselves.

The woman brought us her little girl, hoped we were friends, and her husband offered to run to a neighbouring village to try to get us some bread. To observe the looks of these poor creatures whilst uncertain if we would permit them to take shelter in their own house, or to eat the fruit of their own labour, would move a heart of stone. In a little while the husband returned, bringing a loaf for us, and one for his wife and child, which he begged us to take care of for him: and soon after the woman came with a little jug of sop for the child, begging leave to hide it in our room. The husband has gone out again to try to get us a fowl and part of a sheep, and his wife is singing her baby to sleep in an adjoining room. When we told them that room would be left for their family, they seemed quite transported. They had anticipated another miserable night in the mountains.

I believe I have given you all the news of our affair with the enemy, of whom I rarely think, but when we see them. Yesterday we were for a couple of hours attentively examining their bivouac before our troops arrived for the attack. One has time, in looking so long at one's fellow-beings, to make many reflections, certainly not altogether in the spirit of war. Though separated by a river and ravine, we were near enough to distinguish with our glasses the countenances of the men, and to imagine what was passing in their minds. Fancy, you know, on these occasions will be busy, and will form many an airy vision. I believe I mentioned our having passed in the morning through the village (or rather town) of Salinas, so called from its salt-works. They are the simplest imaginable.

The town is on the sloping side of a mountain, two salt springs are at the tops of the two steep ravines, on the sides of which flat and shallow cisterns are supported by props. The water being evaporated by the sun, the salt remains: 30,000 *fanegas* (a *fanega* is, I think, two bushels and a half) are annually obtained here. We had the preceding day a distant view of Salinas from a rock above Espejo (near Osma), and had in vain puzzled our wits to make out what all the stages of wood could mean.—*Adieu* for today: I shall continue to write daily.

Vitoria, June 21, 9 p.m.

We have had a great day, and have been successful. The action began at eight a.m., in front of Subijana de Morillas, and lasted till dark; the enemy having been forced back at least four leagues. I write on the spot where the action ceased, *i.e.* at a village a league and a half in front of Vitoria, and hardly know what have been the casualties of the day; from my own observation, however, they are very considerable: tomorrow you shall know more.

At daybreak I shall perform the last sad offices to George Thellusson, who was killed in an unsuccessful charge of cavalry at the entrance of this village. His head was split with a sabre cut, and he received a stab just above the heart. I shall write to Lord Rendlesham on the melancholy subject.

I had an opportunity of solacing the agonies, and probably the last moments, of the French general of division Sarrut, whom I helped out of the road, and laid against a bank, under charge of Bombardier Smith. I got the poor general some brandy, and sent him a surgeon. He said he was grateful, but dying. He was sadly wounded with case shot. The action being just over I know no particulars, nor what friends may be lost. I have great reason to be thankful, having escaped unhurt. My mare was shot through the neck early in the day.

We have taken many guns. I know not how many, nor how many thousand prisoners; tomorrow at daybreak will tell us all. We are in a house gutted: furniture strewed about, the inhabitants of course fled. The enemy behaved well. His artillery was more than usually well served. I imagine he must have lost much the greater part of it. The road was in many places blocked up with the guns, and with ammunition and other carriages.—*Adieu*: tomorrow you shall have a connected account. All now is hurry, bustle, and the strange sensation which succeeds the active scenes of the day.

LETTER 58

Vitoria: June 22, 7 a. m.

I have buried poor George Thellusson close by a chapel, and have placed a crucifix over his head to protect his remains from insult. I shall preserve his watch, ring, and locket, which he had about him, and will write particulars to your brother George. The victory was complete. The Horse Artillery did its duty, and was of undoubted use; no other artillery could get up when the rout began. The roads were blocked up with the enemy's guns, caissons, and carriages. I imagine fifty or sixty guns were taken, and about three hundred ammunition carriages. King Joseph's carriages, &c. &c., are all taken. Money has been found in profusion; all is plunder and confusion.

We are advancing again. I shall try to see General Sarrut again, if yet alive. Woodyear is wounded by a spent cannon shot. Colonel May

ROYAL HORSE ARTILLERY IN ACTION

by a spent musket ball, and Swabey shot through the knee. None of the artillery casualties (all I yet know) are dangerous. My friend, Henry Cadogan (Colonel of the 71st Regiment), is said to be killed. The confusion around is indescribable. We must push on to improve the advantages of the day; if we do, the Peninsula may be our own, but the present moments are precious, and must not be lost.

Unless we lose time, we shall yet do great things. It must be our office to give the enemy no repose, though as he now flies unencumbered with baggage or equipment of any kind, he can move rapidly. He appears to have taken the Pampeluna road, but I suspect has only made a detour to gain a woody country, to prevent our destructive fire, and that he will again revert to the direct Bayonne road. I suppose the despatches may not be closed till particulars are more known. We are now collecting the scattered remains of equipments of all kinds. The wife of General Gazan is taken. The poor woman has lost her child, but search is making for the little one, and the lady will be sent after her husband today. Larpent (the Judge-Advocate-General) saved her and her equipage.

Vitoria is a fine town; houses generally of stone, a finer square with piazzas than in Salamanca, shops with French signs, and the whole assuming a French appearance. General Sarrut is dead. Poor man!! I wish now I had taken his decoration of the Legion of Honour, but though I saw it, the general thanked me so warmly, and squeezed my hand with such earnestness, that I felt it would have been ungenerous to have taken the prize.

The great pass of the Puerto d'Arlaban is yet to be forced, but all prisoners, of whom hundreds are coming in, agree that their army is in full march for France. There was a time, yesterday, when our troops were checked, and the fire of the enemy most galling. Fifteen of their guns, well served, presented a battery somewhat formidable. It was to this fire, supported by their infantry, that we had to oppose our guns, which were bravely supported by our own and the Portuguese regiments; though they could not be kept from the muzzles of the guns, which they occasionally prevented from firing.

Whilst on the hill just above Subijana de Morillas with Lord Wellington and his staff, before the action began, we had a full view of both armies. Between both, and while closing to engage, an old woman and her two boys gathered vegetables in her fields, with a philosophical composure. General Alava, with whom I was in conversation, told me the scene of action was one in which a battle had been fought in the time of our Black Prince, by the English and Spaniards, against the French who were beaten. The mountains are to this day called *"les Montagues des Anglais."*

✶✶✶✶✶✶

"The hill thus carried was called the Englishman's Hill, not as some recent writers have supposed in commemoration of a victory gained by the Black Prince, but because of a disaster which there befell a part of his army. His battle was fought between Neverette and Najera, many leagues from Vittoria, and beyond the Ebro. But on this hill the two gallant knights, Sir Thomas and Sir William Felton, took part with 200 companions; and being surrounded by Don Tello, with 6000, all died, or were taken after a long, desperate, and heroic resistance."— Napier, vol. V.

✶✶✶✶✶✶

The plan of the battle was originally that the centre, consisting of two divisions, should make a direct attack; that Hill, with the greater part of the cavalry, three divisions of infantry, and Longa's and Morillo's guerillas should attack on the right, which rested on the mountains. He was to draw the enemy's attention to that flank, whilst Graham and the remaining infantry, by a detour, should turn the enemy's right flank. A delay in Graham's movements occasioned a change in our distribution during the action.

The knowledge of Graham's expected movement made me a little anxious, but at last his guns (Bull's) appeared, at a critical moment, and in a great measure confirmed the rout of the flying enemy. Just before this we were in the waving corn fields, near Vitoria, I rode forward to ascertain who some squadrons moving rapidly, but in good order, were, and got singly amongst the enemy; no one, however, had time to bestow on an individual, and we soon gave them a salute. This was just before I met Sarrut. The colonel of the 65th French infantry lay beside him, and laying hold of the lieutenant-colonel of that corps (by name Bernard), I ordered him to attend his general.

The charge in which Thellusson fell was ill directed: the enemy having been pressed through a wood, retired in a confused mass across a plain, severely galled by Bull's troop (the rest of the horse artillery having by this time expended their ammunition); just as the French reached the defile, the cavalry charged. It was evident the charge must fail; we pushed our guns forcibly through our own squadrons, and when the enemy retired in confusion, opened a destructive fire, which soon cleared the pass. The village of Armentia, or some such name, began at the very entrance of this pass; the enemy suffered dreadfully here. On pushing through it, dusk began, and darkness immediately succeeded.

In this action, which may be decisive if we improve our advantages, there could not have been less than 100,000 men on both sides actually engaged. The ground was most difficult; rugged and rocky ravines on our left approaching the River Zadora, which runs through the plain, or rather through the very undulating and intersected ground, which may be called a plain in comparison with the mountains which bound it.

I write necessarily in a confused manner. We believe that Taragona has fallen after eight days' siege. The marquis received this report yesterday before the action, and is inclined to think it true. We are now (8 a.m.) going to Salvatierra, where headquarters will be today. Lord Wellington wisely gets his army away from this large town. I shall keep my letter folded. Our infantry on the left fired little yesterday, the 1st division, I believe, not at all. The 6th was not in the action; these divisions, consequently, are in full efficiency. General Alava has a fine house here; he is a native of Vitoria.

Letter 59

Salvatierra, five leagues from Vitoria:
June 22, 5 p.m.

Just arrived here on the route to Pampeluna. The enemy reached a position near this town at nine last night, and marched at five this morning. Their *gendarmerie* and King Joseph slept here, and plundered the town before they left it. All accounts describe them to be in utter confusion. There seems little doubt that the enemy intended to have retired by the Bayonne road. Madame Gazan (the general's lady) says, that soon after the action began, her husband wrote to her to dine early, and then to leave Vitoria and take the direct road to France. Mina's guerillas are just arrived here; you never saw such figures, dressed one day like peasants, another in captured French clothing. They have long harassed the enemy. We learn from prisoners that General Daricau is wounded, and General Gremier, I am told, is prisoner.

I was in Vitoria too short a time, and was too hurried this morning, to make much observation on the disposition of the people, but Lord Aylmer tells me that nothing could be more sad than the appearance of the town last night. There was a lanthorn at every door, but not a soul in the streets, and at the house in which his billet was, the women openly avowed their concern that their friends the French were gone. The scene this morning, in passing through the plunder of the carriages, baffles all description. I picked up a map large enough to cover the side of a small room; believing it to be of value I carried it some way. It proved to be a large map of the king's palace and gardens at Aranjuez: I gave it to Sturgeon for the quartermaster-general. I gave him also for General Murray a beautifully bound copy of the regulations of the royal household.

We have taken one hundred and fifty-one guns, and four hundred and forty-nine caissons: Jourdan's staff or baton, Joseph's jewels, plate, military chest and carriages. His portable library was in my possession, but I threw it away, having too much employment to attend to plunder, but I have a little volume which shall be sent next post. I have written a confused account, but you will make something out of it. My station at the beginning of the affair gave me a clear insight into probabilities, and acquainted me with the marquis's plans. Beresford was struck by a musket ball on the hat: we are on excellent and sociable terms. Giron is in pursuit of the great French convoy of plunder, moving direct to France by the Bayonne road. Graham's movement is not on Villa Real but Villa Franca, to head the French army should it take the route to Tolosa from Pampeluna. General Clauzel is marching from Logroño on Tolosa.

LETTER 60

Hill above Pampeluna: June 25.

We have for two days been marching through execrable roads and heavy rain which has now ceased; the rain has saved many a house from the flames. The valley through which we have been pursuing the enemy, is at once sublime and beautiful; it is clothed with the richest corn and vineyards, above which are beautifully-wooded hills: behind the hills are noble mountains, with craggy and inaccessible tops. Every village we have passed through since we left Vitoria has been on fire, houses all gutted; the inhabitants have generally fled; some of those who remained have been murdered.

Our right division, seconded by Ross's guns, has been in constant action. The enemy have lost many men and animals; of the latter, those on either side who flounder are in general lost in the deep mud. We have taken another gun; the horses being killed by one of Ross's. The column of the enemy which we now follow has, from all accounts, but one howitzer left. Our troops are investing Pampeluna at this moment. We took a picquet this morning, making seventeen prisoners, and poking the other four of the twenty-one which composed it into the river close under the walls.

The people in the town are running about, but the enemy has shut the gates and lets none of the peasantry out: yet I imagine, from the observable quietness, that they do not intend to hold the town: possibly they will leave a thousand or twelve hundred men in the citadel: half an hour ago they were destroying ammunition; they have now ceased even moving palisades, which at one time they were tearing down from the outworks. They have lost many men: they take much pains to carry off the wounded, having dismounted for that purpose a regiment of cavalry, on whose horses the wounded are carried off. Their dead they use every exertion to conceal, purposely stopping occasionally to collect the bodies and throw them into convenient ditches, where they cover them over with bushes.

We have found several such receptacles containing from ten to twenty-two bodies each. I have just seen Jourdan's baton or staff of marshal: it is covered with blue velvet, is a foot or more long, and has thirty-two embroidered eagles on it. It is enclosed in a red morocco case, with silver clasps and eagles: at each end is printed in gold characters "Le Marechal Jean-Baptiste Jourdan." There is a colour also belonging to the $100^{\text{ème}}$ Reg. de Ligne, $4^{\text{ème}}$ Bataillon: the colour is a yard and a half square; we were not aware that any battalion had colours. I spoke about the state of the enemy's army to a captain of the 55th French line, who deserted last night. Many officers have already deserted; they all say (but what will deserters not say?) that their army will disband on reaching France, for which it is in full march. *Adieu*—for a moment: we are leaving the hill to take a different view of the town.

3 p. m.

We have been riding about to find Lord Wellington, who stayed behind at Irurzun, where headquarters were last night. We have just stumbled upon his lordship eating a beef-steak by the roadside. The troops continue to invest the place. Since we entered Navarre, of the Spanish part of which Pampeluna is the capital, we are utterly unable to make ourselves understood. The inhabitants speak a dialect which (perhaps erroneously) we call Basque. It is as unintelligible to Spaniards in general as the Provençal dialect is to the people of the rest of France.

The papers will tell you that the Allied loss in killed wounded and missing in the late affair is 4910. Hundreds must be added to the enemy's loss. Prisoners and deserters are continually coming in. We have no news yet of General Giron, or of Graham. The French general Clauzel is still at Logroño (on the Ebro): he will, I suppose, endeavour to join Suchet.

4 p.m.

Strange times these. Off to Santander to bring up guns for the siege of Pampeluna *Adieu.*

5 p.m.

I have got excellent quarters on the banks of the River Arga. The village is about two miles from Pampeluna. I await my orders to start. Santander is, I believe, about forty leagues from hence; the object of my going is to meet at Santander, and tranship to smaller vessels than our ordnance transports, the heavy guns and stores required for the siege. These are, if we can manage it, to be conveyed by water to Deba, a little town somewhat to the westward of St. Sebastian. From Deba I must find means of transporting them to the trenches, which will be preparing in the meanwhile. I cannot imagine the siege of a little place like Pampeluna will arrest the progress of such an army as ours. The city (for it is one) is 1200 or 1400 yards long, by 1000 or 1200 broad, as I hear.

The chief body of those we have been pursuing have taken the direction of Roncesvalles, famous in history for the defeat of Charlemagne and the loss of the twelve paladins of France. Alava, who is a sensible man, says that Townshend's account of Spain is the best book on the subject. There are by Alava's account seven passes for carriages over the Pyrenees; twenty-eight for horses and mules; and about forty others passable by infantry. Many of the two last descriptions are not generally known. The three,—of Irun (on the north), St. Jean Pied de Port (a little beyond Roncesvalles), and of Junquera (between Bellegrade and Figueras),—are generally considered as the only passes of the Pyrenees. The mountains beyond this plain are a kind of chain connected with the Pyrenees. We have here on the plain, corn quite ripe; this is the first we have seen so forward. I shall carry this letter in my pocket to Santander, and endeavour to send it by some opportunity.

I shall send a letter to Sir George Collier (commanding the *Surveillante,* and other ships of war on that station), who will be requested to afford me every aid. I like the scheme of going hugely, shall take no baggage, and shall consequently get on very well. This village, lying out of the high road, has escaped being plundered. The good people stare at us, but seem no ways alarmed. Some well dressed women have been walking about. All since the action till this afternoon has been wretchedness, flames, and misery; the dying and the dead at every step. Here one breathes pure air and is in repose. In peaceable times this country must be delightful; it surpasses all I have yet seen for beauty combined with richness. Two shillings was the price yesterday for a sheep; none were really to be had, as they were for the moment driven into the mountains.

I have already mentioned that we have had accounts of the existing armistice between the northern belligerents. It may possibly lead to a general peace, to which our late really splendid victory may prove a step. I believe all parties are heartily tired of the war; none more so than the French armies who have served in the Peninsula. I momentarily expect my instructions, and shall set off. Fremantle left us this morning with the despatches.—*Adieu.*

June 25, 10 p. m.

I start for Vitoria on mv route for Santander at daybreak tomorrow. General Abbé is in Pampeluna with 400 or 500 men. A convoy of 600 carts reached the city yesterday. No news today of General Giron or Graham. We have taken no more guns. I enclose a volume late King Joseph's.

Letter 61

Vitoria: June 27, 4 a. m.

Whilst we are getting horses I resume my pen. We left headquarters near Pampeluna early yesterday morning, and at ten at night were here wandering in the streets and in the dark. Luckily, we stumbled on Parker, whom we found sitting down to tea and fruit and a bottle of champagne. Parker has promised to furnish us with fresh horses, which are jewels indeed, circumstanced as we are. The roads of our fifteen leagues yesterday were wretched, the whole way covered with stragglers, and in many places blocked up with carriages and mules. I thought we never should have got along.

About four or five in the afternoon we had missed our way and our horses were knocked up. One sees all the horrors of the retreat more in passing again over the ground than at the moment of their occurring. Dead horses, mules, and asses, at almost every hundred yards. The enemy in his fright having abandoned his ammunition carriages, had not the means of blowing up the bridges; if he had done so in one or two cases, our pursuit would have been greatly impeded. He endeavoured, however, to destroy them with pick-axes, and partially succeeded in several instances. Clauzel's French division is cut off; Hill and Clinton and, the Guerilla Morillo are looking out for him. I met General Hill (who is an old acquaintance of mine) on my way yesterday, and had a long confab with him. I carry in my pocket poor Thellusson's watch and trinkets; possibly I may find some opportunity of sending them to England through some naval officer.

I have an order from Alava to all authorities to be aiding and assisting. I find in Parker's room a correct plan and section of Congreve rockets, dated Punhete in 1810: the plan must have been taken from one of those fired at Santarem, where they were injudiciously thrown away, got into disrepute, and have never been used since. Whatever the value of this novel arm may be, it consists chiefly in the composition of the rockets; this is a secret, and likely to remain so—*Adieu*: I must find out someone who can tell us our route.

Posada at Berberana: half-past 1, p.m.

Thus far on our way to Santander. Our horses are knocked up, but we have got hold of Senor Alcalde and are trying to get post mules. We have still twenty-two leagues to go, but the thing presses. This house is the one I slept in after the Osma affair. Our road today has been over the fields of the affairs of Subijana de Morillas and Osma, and of the action of Vitoria. Ambition should take such rides to make it loathe itself and war. General Castaños is at Burgos, and the enemy have left Bilboa; two pieces of intelligence we have picked up on our way. Butcher and myself only are here, we have left Harding and Mr. Gilbert behind on the road; their getting on is of less consequence. My office is to report to headquarters the arrival or non-arrival of the transports off Santander, and the capabilities of the little port of Deba, where, as I have already mentioned, we hope to disembark the ordnance. It is to the eastward of Santander, and consequently nearer Pampeluna.—*Adieu*: three wretched animals have arrived; one is a mule which has never been backed.

La Serea: 10 p.m.

You never heard such a noise as there was at our setting off from Berberana; the alcalde declared he was the most unhappy man in the world; down went his hat in a rage: nobody could tell, he said, how much he suffered. "Take whose mule he would no one seemed pleased." We got here by great good luck, our animals soon knocked up, and we made fruitless efforts to replace them in two or three villages. Here we stumbled very unexpectedly on a reserve of small-arm ammunition under Captain Hutchesson of the artillery, and have borrowed horses and secured a guide to conduct us over the mountains tomorrow morning. We are in the curate's house, but neither he nor anyone in the village can tell us how many leagues it is to Santander.

La Serea: June 28, 3 a.m.

We have got a guide, and are going across the mountain road by Espinoza. It seems ridiculous, but we dispute whether we have twenty-three or eleven leagues to go. Could one draw a line across the country, I verily believe a dozen leagues would bring us to the sea. We leave here with the horses and mules we pressed at Berberana. The poor owner, who set off with us on foot, was soon knocked up, and volunteered getting behind Mr. Butcher on his mule, which was declined. I should be much mortified should any untoward circumstances prevent our reaching Santander and my getting on board some ship of war today. I hope the ordnance vessels have arrived: all this is yet unknown. If they have, I trust upon inquiry to find that the port of Deba will admit of our taking the vessels round at once, without the necessity of transhipping the stores; in this case I should go from Deba to Santander.

Laberadepsas: 12 o'clock.

Thus far (six leagues) on our way. We have had hard work of it, our horses again knocked up, and there are no animals in the village. You would laugh to see our present dilemma; we are wishing to write an order to the *alcalde* of the next village; all the villagers here, with the alcalde at their head, approve of the idea, and give us hearty *vivas*; but none can write at all, and we cannot write, that is compose, an order. A guerilla of Morillo's is here, and could write, he says, beautifully; but, having a ball in his arm, his abilities cannot be tried. In the meanwhile, the alcalde's wife is getting ready some eggs and bread: there is no doing, you see, without the ladies.

We have had the worst road today I ever saw. Espinoza is a fine old place, straggling, but with many houses wearing an appearance of decayed grandeur; the situation beautiful, and like England on a large scale: very luxuriant hayfields. No traces of war are visible. From Espinoza, the scene becomes more and more grand, till at length the

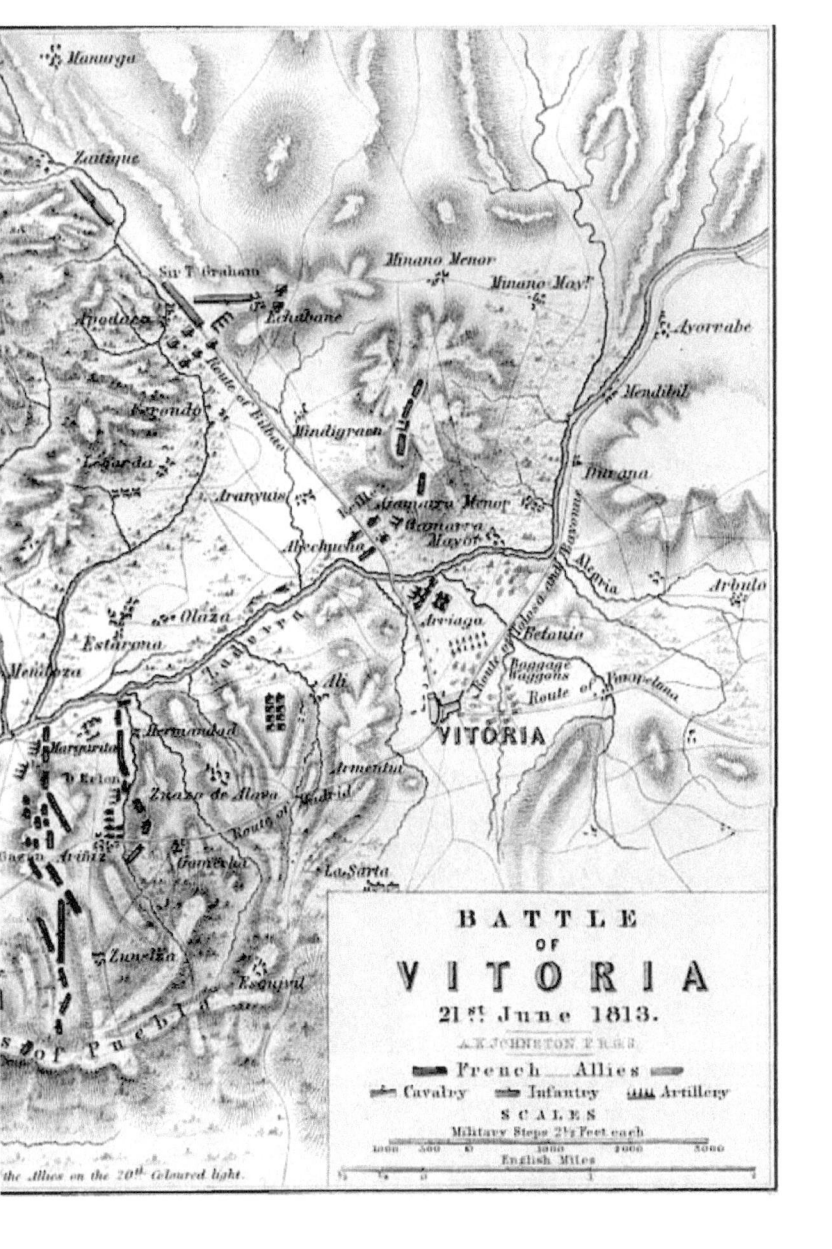

mountains are such as I have never seen; the "dread magnificence of Heaven" was indeed displayed majestically this morning. We travelled for three hours within a quarter of a league, as we were told, of this place; I verily thought we should never arrive. We pick up guides as we go along: poor souls, they are forced to go: one is obliged to be deaf to all excuses.

In one place, we had to fight all the ladies of the village; of course, we lost our guide, there was no disputing the field with the amazons. However, we soon after pressed an old man, who tried in vain to shift his office on every one he met. He had many friends, he said, but like the hare in the fable, was deserted by all when he wanted their assistance.

Letter 62

Santander: June 29, 8 a. m.

Arrived, after a most rough ride: it was not possible to get here last night. At dark, we reached a village, two leagues and a half off, where we slept. This morning, I have left poor Butcher and the orderly floundering in the mud, and have pushed on. I am in the government house, I believe; nothing can be finer. Mr. Commissary-General Ogilvie is here. After breakfast, we shall sail in search of Sir George Collier. The *Surveillante* is in the offing, we are told. The Coruna fleet is expected today; we must carry them forward at once to Deba. Mr. Ogilvie has received me very kindly. I have letters for him, and the naval commanding officer; the letters are left behind in my cloak-bag, but knowing their contents, I shall find no difficulty in introducing myself. I have a courier ready to return to Lord Wellington's headquarters with my despatch, which I shall send off the moment I can ascertain the real state of affairs.

Letter 63

Deba: June 30, 3 p. m.

Once more on dry land. I embarked yesterday at Santander, in the *Lyra*, shifted in the evening to the *Surveillante*, and again reshipped to the *Lyra* brig of war (Captain Bloye), in which I came here. The *Surveillante* had been on fire just before we got on board; the fire was in the magazine passage, but by exertion was put out. I hope tonight and tomorrow to get the ordnance and stores landed. We have no soldiers here, but sailors are famous fellows in all cases of energy and exertion. We swept the coast of launches as we came along. It is a most bold, rocky coast, open to the whole set (as the sailors call it) of the Atlantic. We ran away with ten launches from Bermeo, and as many from Lequeytio, and expect tomorrow as many more from Motrico.

The enemy, 500 strong, are at Guetaria, in some sort of stronghold. We have two companies of Don Gaspar's guerillas at Zumaya, two leagues towards Guetaria, which is three leagues off. There is a difficult bar here, and a river running up to the village of Alzola in the direction of Tolosa. I have found here Captain Webber of the artillery, who has been sent from Pampeluna to examine the road for our heavy guns from hence to Tolosa, twelve leagues, in which there are difficulties at intervals: from Tolosa to Pampeluna is ten leagues, and the road excellent. I have reported all this to headquarters since my arrival, and have sent also a despatch to Sir Thomas Graham, at Tolosa. Captain Webber is just going to repair the roads, applying for that purpose to the civil authorities for the assistance of the peasantry. I write whilst the first transport is working towards the bar.

We have had an excellent dinner; literally fish, flesh, and fowl. This is a delightful place; how shall I return to war and its miseries after these hours of quiet repose? Our hostess (I have not the least idea whether I am in an inn or private house) has been apologising for having only some French wine to offer us. It is *only* claret, and excellent. I hope in two days to finish all we have in hand here, and then to join at Pampeluna. I now wear Captain Bloye's shirt (before he offered me the means of washing, I was as dirty as a pig). I have nothing with me but a saddle and bridle, and pistol. I am literally in rags; my pantaloons not having above two days' service left.

5 p.m.

Here I am, sitting on the sand, and surrounded by a dozen little girls: one is mending my foraging cap, the rest singing "*Viva* Vellington." The first boat is arriving with ammunition, and more are on their way from the transports. Just by us, the peasants are digging up two guns of Mina's, which have been buried sometime in the sands. The secret, as three men told us, was intrusted to them only; how we all try to make ourselves of importance! It is the finest afternoon imaginable. My circle of girls increases, and is most entertaining: some laugh, others sing, and all lean over the Señor Inglese, and wonder what he is writing.

Never was a more beautiful spot than this. A rocky entrance and a difficult bar defend a nice little harbour, sheltered on all sides by mountains clothed with woods. In every little interval of valley are

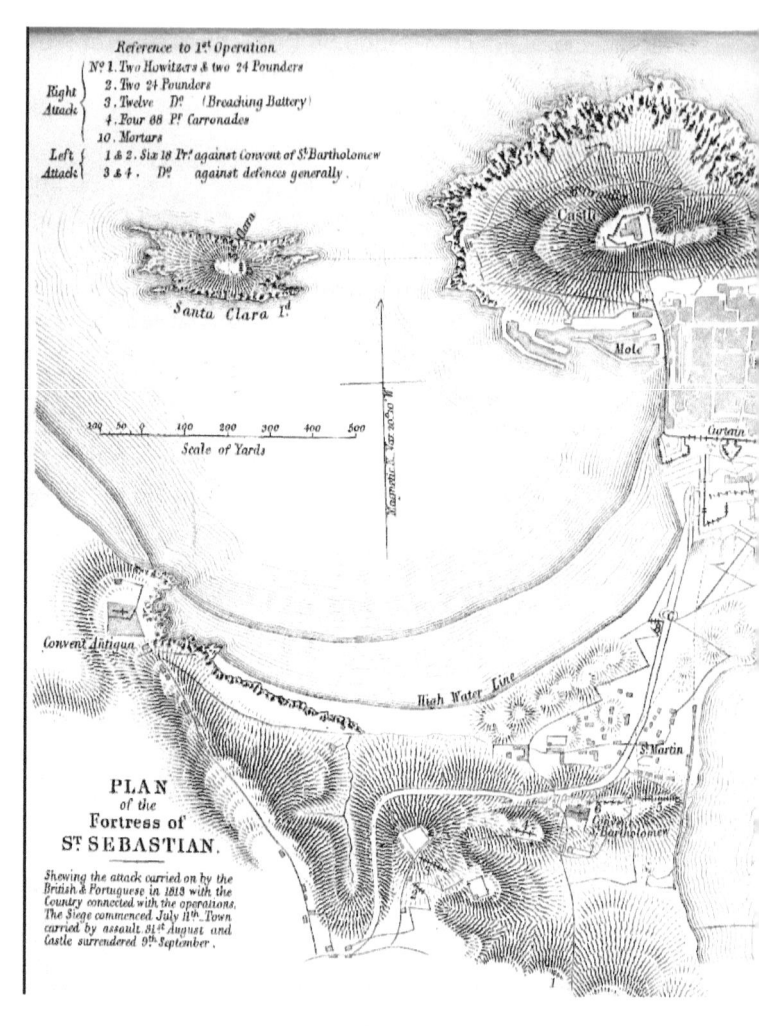

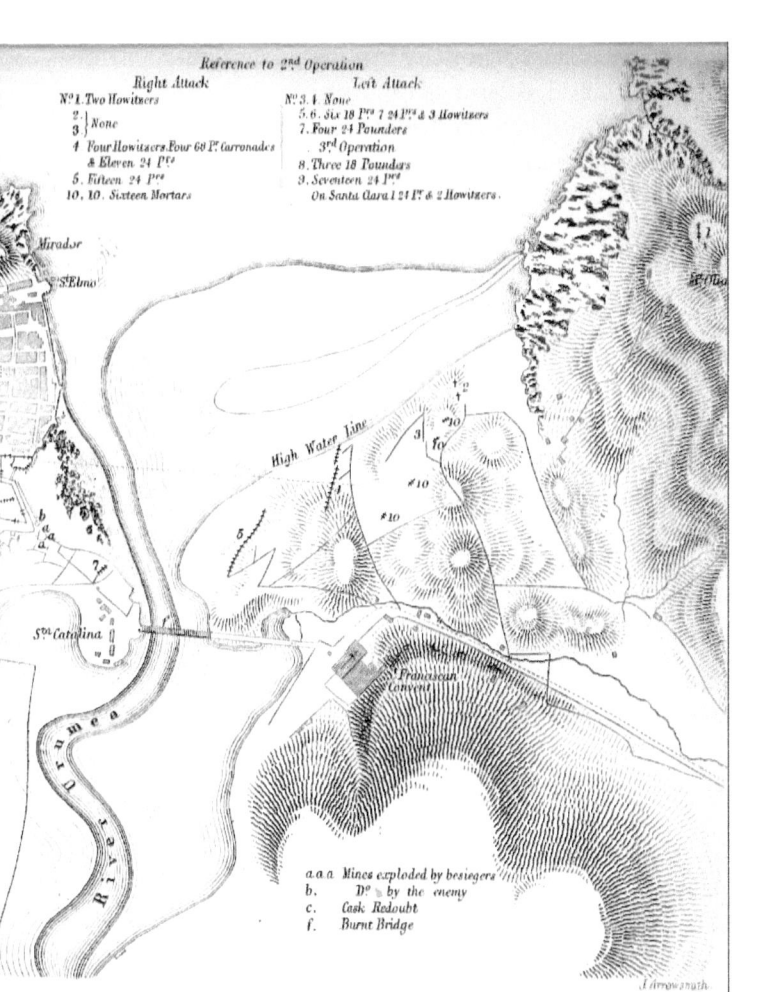

delicious vineyards. The sea washes the walls of the houses. If I am long detained here amid these scenes of repose, I shall lose all relish for more active employment; in truth, no one can return to those I am about to revisit without at least repugnance, if not disgust. I hear the most shocking accounts of the atrocities committed by the enemy in a late attack on the castle of Castro.

Castro is near Laredo, on the coast to the eastward of Santander. Enraged at finding a bridge destroyed, in consequence of which numbers of their column had been pushed down a ravine by their fellows whilst advancing to the charge, (the attack failed,) they murdered every person in the town whom they could find, and committed every indignity. They said the townspeople should have informed them of the destruction of the bridge. This story I had yesterday from Sir George Collier, who had himself destroyed the bridge in question.

LETTER 64

Deba: July 1, 2 p.m.

The *Surveillante* is just arriving from the westward; with our glasses we can see Sir George Collier coming on shore. The tide has ebbed, and we are idle. All this while the enemy is working hard at Pampeluna; but one can do no more: time and tide neither wait for, nor will be hastened for, any man.

Six p.m.

Captain Bloye dined with me; an hour before dinner the *Surveillante* arrived, and I have had a long confab with Sir George Collier, who wanted me to carry the ordnance transports to the eastward, not liking the bar here. But always disliking changes of arrangements, and in truth, not considering myself authorised, I declined the offer. The *Surveillante* has anchored, but will get under weigh, with the evening breeze, for St. Sebastian. Sir Thomas Graham is at Oyarzun (near St. Sebastian), and the enemy in force near Irun. I have had an answer from Tolosa, whither I had to send five despatches for headquarters and for Sir Thomas Graham. I have some reason to think that Lord Wellington, with three divisions of the army, may have gone in search of Suchet. Guitaria, a little fort, three leagues from hence to the eastward, was blown up and abandoned last night; this is well for us who have no troops here. All seems to be doing well, but I am for the moment out of the way of information.

July 3.

It blows very fresh. We cannot get our guns on shore, but I hope the weather will moderate. Time is most valuable now. I long to return to the army; though we have not guns, we have yet abundance of stores, and are busy loading our cars. They are the common ones of this part of the country: four barrels of powder is their load. The people here are friendly, nay, more than friendly, providing us with everything. The lady of the house waits on us at table, which she provides with a profusion of good things. I fear the transports must slip their cables if the gale increases; this would be awkward, but I shall persuade Captain Bloye to stay to the last moment.

We went after dinner yesterday in his boat up the river Deba: the scenery beautiful; the ladies accompanied us. Our object was to see if there was water enough to send our powder, shot, and shells, as far as Abzola by boats. I had hoped there would be: it proved otherwise. After rowing up about a league through the mountains covered with chesnuts we got aground, quitted our boat, and walked back. The confusion in loading the cars is most whimsical. Without forage for the bullocks, or provisions for the men, we are obliged to call on our wits for assistance at every moment; they have not yet failed us, though we seem continually within an ace of their end.

What think you of our want of gallantry, when I confess we are obliged to send *ladies* with expresses over the mountains? The *alcalde* is in despair, he says; men to carry letters can no longer be found. Captain Power, and three officers of the British and Portuguese artillery, with ninety men, arrived yesterday to assist us. I have sent Power to mend a suspension bridge, the rest are busily employed on the wharf. Not far from Deba is the little village of Anchove; can anchovies (of which there are myriads) take their name from this little sea-port? This coast now swarms with mackerel.

2 p.m.

Curious world this! All we have been doing is to be undone. Our stores to be re-embarked. Pampeluna is not to be besieged at present, but merely blockaded. I am to rejoin headquarters. Butcher to remain here. Murray has raised the siege of Taragona, as I hear, leaving his guns, &c., and all at the mere idea of the approach of Suchet, whom we must now look for and beat. All this news is brought by Pascoe, who left headquarters yesterday. I shall sleep here, I think, make my arrangements quietly, and start at daybreak. I must find from Sir Thomas Graham where headquarters are; besides, I stay to keep all quiet, and to avoid the alarm of the natives, whom our sudden change of measures may throw into a fidget.

Letter 65

Tolosa: July 5, 8 a.m.

I left Deba yesterday, pressed a horse there, and reached Tolosa at ten last night. Roads bad, weather a soaking rain, scenery magnificent. I never saw more richness combined with sublimity. This country is fertile in all its valleys, and noble in all its mountains. My leaving Deba was sudden, as the last letter will acquaint you. After collecting some hundred cars and pairs of bullocks, and landing and forwarding to the army convoys of ordnance stores for Pampeluna, the siege of that place is postponed for the present, and all is again embarking. This is owing to Murray's business, and is sufficiently embarrassing for us. Clauzel and Suchet, who may unite, may also combine a movement with the army we have lately beaten, and in this case, we should not be quite free to undertake the operations of a siege like that of Pampeluna, in addition to our other field movements.

At two leagues from Deba I met Lieut. Mainwaring of the Artillery, who had come from headquarters, with despatches for me. These only directed arrangements which I had already made, except by changing the rendezvous of the transports to Bilboa, instead of Guitaria, as had been agreed on by Captain Bloye and myself. A little further on the road we came to the baths of Cestona; the waters are like those of Cheltenham. It is a noble valley. One league beyond Cestona is Aspeytia. While the *alcalde* looked, or pretended to look, for horses, we did really look at nineteen old nuns in the convent of Escotia. All simple, all ugly, but all pleased with our visit. A double row of bars separated us from these ladies, who were pleasant enough. From the convent we ran a mile to the church (and a very nice one it is) of St. Ignatio; I believe it was founded by Ignatius Loyola. It is of marble, inside and out, and is striking. The dome within has alternately the arms of Austria and of Spain.

You know there was a time when one monarch ruled both empires. We were especially struck with some spiral columns of marble of unusual size. By the way, our host at the baths of Cestona made us remark a very fine oak plank in the floor. It was twenty-two yards long. At Cestona was a room over the door of which was painted EL JUEGODEULLAR. If at first sight you understand this to intimate that the room contained a royal billiard table, you are more penetrating than I was. I had yesterday another despatch from Sir Thomas Graham, to whom I shall go today. The general is at Ernani, three leagues from hence. Headquarters were yesterday or the day before at Ostiz, and will to day be at Lienz.—*Adieu* for the moment.

Half-past 10 a.m.

Still at Tolosa. We have had some difficulty in procuring steeds, have had sentries at the gates to press any country animals coming in, and, at last, have got two little mules. This town looks old. The women in all these towns are fair and good-looking. Since Vitoria we have seen no swarthy beauties.

July 6.

I am now at Ernani, on the high road towards Bayonne, three leagues from Tolosa, which I left yesterday, on a wretched mule, and got here about three. I waited immediately on Sir Thomas Graham, who was very friendly. The siege of St. Sebastian is resolved on. I dined at Sir Thomas's, and rode one of his horses to St. Sebastian. I am now (6 a.m.) going out again with Major Smith of the Engineers. I have seen a good plan of St. Sebastian; it must fall. A convent, detached from the place, has been occupied by the enemy, who drove the Spaniards from it, and are busily strengthening themselves in it.

Sir George Collier rode with us last night; we missed our way, and did not get back till near 10 p.m. I hope to be employed, being tired of idleness, and baulked of active employment at Pampeluna. Nothing can be pleasanter than Sir Thomas Graham's table, where I dined yesterday for the first time. I hope to make further acquaintance with the general. At this moment, I have a difficult card; I am so convinced of the necessity of an immediate attack of the convent, that I cannot with propriety conceal it, though my opinion differs from that of my seniors. However, Dickson will, I hope, be here today, and he is a sure card for decision. This country continues beautiful. Today is fine, so was yesterday; but, in this part of Spain, rain is as frequent as in our Devonshire.

The Spaniards hold Irun. The bridge over the Bidassoa (beyond Irun) is destroyed. The enemy has a strong camp near Vera. I shall stay here a day or two, instead of hunting headquarters in the mountains; they are coming, I believe, towards San Estevan. I will write again soon.

Letter 66

Zubieta: July 7.

My letter yesterday was written from Ernani, and sent, I know not how, to headquarters, which are, I know not where. I intended to have devoted this morning to writing to you, but it is otherwise ordered, and I am just setting off to be present at an attack on a convent in front of St. Sebastian, which fortress I reconnoitred yesterday. I am a little awkwardly situated; Lieutenant-Colonel Hartman, commanding the Artillery with Sir Thomas Graham's force, has different opinions as to the attack of the convent from those I entertain, and, at the request of Sir Thomas Graham, explained last night. Some 9-pounders, and a brigade of German light infantry are (possibly owing to my report) ordered to the attack. I go as a spectator, not knowing whether Lieutenant-Colonel Hartman has been acquainted with the orders of Sir Thomas for the attack in which the lieutenant-colonel's artillery form a part. The attack may or may not succeed, but I have no hesitation in saying it should be tried.—*Adieu* for the moment.

12 o'clock.

On coming towards the convent, I found Colonel Halket's German brigade, six Portuguese guns, and an English howitzer, moving forward to the attack. This is a motley force (for there are Spaniards intermixed) with which to do anything; but Smith of the Engineers is getting some garden ground cleared of the fruit trees, and an old wall will soon be pulled down. Meanwhile, some shot are heating, and, unless something untoward happens, we shall soon, or ought soon, to drive the enemy away from the building, which is only 450 yards distant. Mistakes are ridiculous things; the Portuguese shells do not fit our howitzers. In vain do we beg the Portuguese to put their shot in the fire: "*Si, si, Señor,*" all say, but not one shot arrives.

I seat myself under an apple-tree and smile, determined only to be a spectator. Zubieta, from which I began my letter, is a league from Ernani. Bull's troop is there, and I mean to stay with it till Dickson's arrival at Ernani, where he is expected. I shall learn from him where headquarters are, that I may either rejoin them, or remain for the siege of St. Sebastian, as may be directed.

Zubieta: July 8, 6 a. m.

I was obliged to leave off yesterday. We had a good deal of firing, but nothing done. Our Portuguese friends brought only three guns into play, frequently missed the whole building, and fired shot not half heated. I stayed till 4 o'clock, at which time the Portuguese had nearly expended their ammunition, and I returned here to dinner at Ramsay's quarters, from which I now write. They are in a comfortable farm-house, extremely clean, the windows obscured by delicious vines. The house is in a field, some eighty yards from a river, surrounded by orchards and cornfields; these again are bounded by some of the mountains of the Pyrenees, which surround us on all sides. It is impossible to return from ruined walls and smoking houses, on the embers of which are hundreds of human beings ready to destroy their fellows, without feeling a relief in even looking at the peaceful occupations of husbandry.

This morning I must go to Ernani to see Sir Thomas Graham, who sent me word last night, by Captain Cator, that he wished to see me. The transports I left lately at Deba were coming into Passages harbour yesterday evening. The place for landing the ordnance and stores is fixed on, and so indeed are the operations of the siege, in Smith's opinion and mine. However, Lord Wellington, Fletcher, and Dickson will determine. There are more ways than one; and provided we do but take St. Sebastian, and quickly, it matters little to our country whose plans are followed.

I have hitherto avoided mentioning one subject which has given many here great uneasiness, and, perhaps, amongst the many friends Ramsay deservedly possesses, to none more uneasiness than to myself. He is under arrest by Lord Wellington's orders, conveyed through me in the harshest terms. He remains still in this mortifying situation; having been put in arrest on the 23rd June, two days after the Battle of Vitoria, in which Bull's troop (which I have no hesitation in saying is much the best in this country) had, under Ramsay's command, been of unusual and unquestionable service. After moving forward on the 22nd June, towards the evening. Lord W. spoke to Ramsay as he passed, desired him to take his troop for the night to a village then near; adding that, if there were orders for the troop in the course of the night, he would send them.

The night passed away, no orders were received. At 6 next morning, an assistant-quarter-master general (Captain Campbell) came to Ramsay, and asked if he had any orders. Being answered in the negative, he said, "You will then immediately march and rejoin the brigade to which you belong."

Accordingly, the troop marched; and soon afterwards a written order was received by Ramsay from General Murray, the quartermaster general of the army, also ordering "Captain Ramsay's troop to rejoin General Anson's brigade." While the troop was doing this, and was halting for the moment, whilst Ramsay having the quartermaster general's order had ridden to discover the road in one direction, and Captain Cator, with a copy of the order, had gone for the same purpose in another, Lord Wellington came up, called repeatedly for Ramsay, then for Cator; neither at the moment was on the spot. His lordship then called for Dickson, whose horse being unable at the instant to clear a wide ditch over which we had just passed, I rode up to mention the circumstance to Lord Wellington, who ordered me to put Captain Ramsay in arrest, and to give the command of the troop to Captain Cator.

This I accordingly did, having soon found Cator, and soon after Ramsay, whom I sent two or three people to look after. It appears that Lord Wellington had intended that Ramsay's troop should not have moved that morning till he himself sent orders, and his lordship declared that he had told Ramsay so; this Ramsay affirms he never heard or understood, and his lordship's words, repeated by Ramsay, young Macleod, and by a sergeant and corporal, all at hand when his lordship spoke to Ramsay, are precisely the same, and do not convey such a meaning.

I spoke instantly to Lord Fitzroy Somerset on the subject, who, together with every other individual about headquarters, was and is much concerned at the circumstance. Nay, two days afterwards, when the despatches were making out, every friendly suggestion was used by several that Ramsay might be mentioned as he deserved, but I have reason to believe that he is not. There is not, among the many good and gallant officers who are here, one of superior zeal or devotion to the service to Ramsay, who has given repeated proofs of spirit and good conduct. Admitting, contrary to all evidence, that he had mistaken the verbal orders he received,—this surely is a venial offence, and one for which long-tried and faithful services should not be forgotten.

The honour of a soldier is so delicate that I should never have mentioned this circumstance to you, had it not now become my duty as commanding the Horse Artillery to report to our own headquarters at home an affair now become public. Few circumstances have engaged more general attention, or occasioned more regret. It has naturally been expected that after the first moment was over, a deserving officer would at least have been released from a situation most galling to a gallant spirit. We have accordingly, from day to day, hoped that Ramsay would have been restored to his duty. I trust this may soon be the case; but endeavouring to view the matter rather with the calmness of an indifferent spectator than with the warm feelings of a friend, I am yet at a loss to account for the delay in a point so easily settled.

In the meanwhile, Ramsay bears up with great fortitude, though he deeply feels. All I have said you had better not mention unless the matter should be spoken of by any of our people; in this case, in justice to Ramsay, it should be told in the simple manner I have related it. I have written a very long letter to General Macleod about this affair; it is a private letter, but it was necessary to write, lest the general should hear of the matter, to Ramsay's prejudice, from common report. It now rains in torrents. Heavy squalls and thunder. Thank Heaven I am not in the *Surveillante* or *Lyra*, though I have received much hospitality on board both. We shall ride to Ernani the moment it clears.

This country, we are told, is very subject to rain at all seasons, except the winter months, when there is clear frosty weather. I have been too busy to take a peep at France, but French blood has already been spilt on their own soil. Murray's abandonment of Taragona is ill-timed. If, as we hear, he has left all his battering train behind him, it will require address to explain the matter satisfactorily.

Letter 67

Passages: July 10.

I have now charge of some batteries to be erected against St. Sebastian. They will be on some sand hills to the eastward of the town. This village is close to St. Sebastian, extending to the river Urumea, over which, leading to St. Sebastian, was a wooden bridge now burnt. My present occupation is to land some guns and mortars for the siege, and I have, accordingly, taken up my abode in this village, where I am near both the landing-place and the sand hills. The village is now the scene of plenty; orchards full of fruit, and corn which grows under the fruit trees.

Some Spaniards, a battalion of Portuguese, and some companies of British and Portuguese artillery are coming. All the plenty of the village will soon vanish. I have just sent Harding with a note to the officer commanding the Portuguese for a working party, and with another to Mr. Butcher, the ordnance commissary, to hasten the landing of the guns, &c. Till Harding comes back I have finished my task. We hear nothing of Dickson, or of headquarters, though we hourly expect both. I believe Lord Wellington was yesterday at San Estevan, but we have lost sight of his lordship.

Sir Thomas Graham is not well; his wound was a little galled by exercise the day before yesterday. He is a most friendly, fine old man, and as active as any of us. It rains here always; that is, in heavy and frequent showers every day, but the vegetation is luxuriant, and the verdure most refreshing to the eye. A day or two will elapse before our guns are landed, and our batteries are ready; then we shall begin in good earnest. The place is not strong, the town is low, the castle is on a very high and abrupt rocky hill. The donjon or castle is on the top, commanding, I should think, a very fine prospect.—*Adieu*: Harding returns, and I have to make my reports to Colonel Hartman. He has command of the Artillery with Sir Thomas Graham, and I merely offered my services to be employed any way.

July 11, 6 a.m.

A good deal of running about yesterday, and a famous fatiguing work over the mountains, to discover a road (not yet found) for transporting a couple of 24-pounders, which I want to get on a height commanding, though at a distance, the castle of St. Sebastian and a battery called the Mirador which we must silence. Webber Smith, who is active, has offered his services to assist. The mule road from Passages to this place is bad, and is partly on the edge of a rocky precipice, over the rocky shore of the harbour. I had dismounted yesterday on passing a narrow place, the road being worn away and very slippery from the late rains, and was leading my horse; the flies tickled the animal, who kicked violently, and in a moment kicked its hind legs over the precipice, at least fifty feet high, and of course fell over. There were a few shrubs which broke his fall, but nothing to make it in the least probable that he should escape as he did, with merely half a dozen cuts and bruises.

No news yesterday. Lawson's and Dubordieu's companies of artillery arrived yesterday, and a Portuguese company of artillery under a Major Ariaga, whose orderly was in the act of giving me a letter when my horse fell over the precipice; the man's astonishment was quite amusing. I expect today another Portuguese company of artillery, and shall have employment for all.

July 11, 7 p.m.

We have had a very fine day, and have done a great deal, though the tide fails us; we can only work at or near high water. The harbour of Passages is very fine, a very narrow entrance, between high rocks, opens into a spacious harbour, which from neglect is filling up; within a few years ships of the line rode here with convenience, at present none but small craft, and vessels of 200 or 300 tons come in. I had a very unexpected letter today from Charles Gordon, dated Cadiz, June 29. He had obtained leave, through my letter to Adye, to visit the army, and is coming by way of Madrid. You would laugh if you were to hear our conversation here: one moment spherical case and round shot, the next tea or shoes or Russian ducks. I have sent Harding to Ernani where Lord Wellington has arrived.

July 12.

I have such a budget of letters as has quite unfitted me for business. I was busily employed calculating weights and means of transport (the latter is quite a technical term here), when I heard that the marquis and headquarters were coming to reconnoitre; all this is common enough, and in no way ruffled my tranquillity, but your letters quite overset me. I did ask Sir Thomas Graham and half a dozen of the suite into my room, and was civil enough to them; this was before I had read your letters. When I once began I went through all, and now any one may calculate what they please for me. I gave the matter up, and luckily Dickson, Major Smith of the Engineers, and the marquis are gone to the sand hills (where I have been twenty times) to look out.

The rest of the suite are dispersed, and I am as much alone in a great room as a man can be whose heart and head are filled with home and all its recollections. The people are all at work, I hope; their tasks were set them early this morning; some of them troublesome ones enough. Today details for the siege will be arranged: whatever they may be, or whatever part I may be ordered to take, I shall be equally cheerful and ready. You will long since have seen that I have no scruples in serving under Dickson. Had he been the reverse of all he really is, I should equally have served to the best of my power. It is no time to think of minor points when our country requires our exertions. It is, I think, well for the service that the command fell on Dickson, who is fully equal to it.

You will have become acquainted with the circumstances of Ramsay's arrest detailed in one of my last letters. I asked Lord Fitzroy Somerset, who came to sit with me just now, how the matter stood, and was sincerely mortified to hear that the marquis is inexorable. He was exceedingly angry when Sir Thomas Graham's letter came to him. I cannot understand all this; one is obliged, in charity, to imagine that the subject presents itself to his lordship's mind in a point of view widely different from that in which it strikes all others. I am willing to wait, and make resolutions of being calm on the subject. But it pains me greatly, and the more so since Ramsay expects with anxiety to hear from me what effect Sir Thomas Graham's letter to the Marquis had.

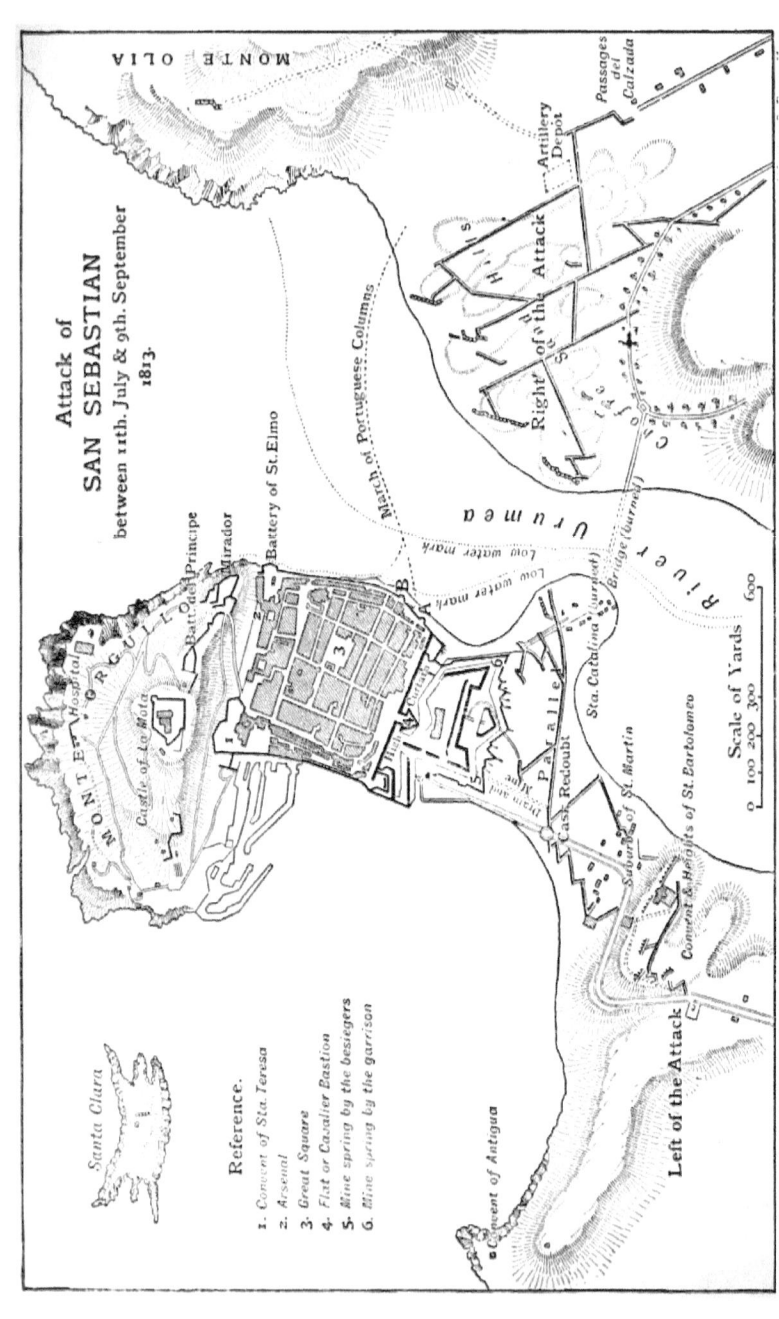

I see no reason why I may not hope to come home when the campaign is concluded. How this campaign may end, none can tell, but affairs yet look well. We shall attack St. Sebastian with spirit, and surely, as I trust, take it soon. My own path is clear: I have no favours to court, and have merely to discharge the duty which my country (certainly not any individual) may have to claim from me: and this I hope I shall have strength and health to do.

We hope soon to hear of the general joy the late Vitoria victory has no doubt occasioned in England. I am never sanguine on the greater scale of politics, and have not the confident hope which many possess that it may lead to a general peace, though I believe all sides heartily wish for peace; the country people here, the finest race I ever beheld, openly say they do. Women here do all manner of work in the fields in boots; here and everywhere, they do all that men do, and ought to do, elsewhere. They are consequently somewhat masculine, but are nevertheless most noble figures. I must now go out and see what has been doing at the landing-places, and the mountains. I shall also ride to Ernani, to see Dickson, to hear what my operations are to be; this, and taking the distances with my sextant from all the points of the fortress, will fully occupy me.

LETTER 68

Passages: July 16, 6 a.m.

You know I am now busy in making arrangements for the siege of St. Sebastian: *viz.*, the artillery part on the eastward side, where all our heavy ordnance (six field 18-pounders excepted) are to be employed. The roads are detestable. The night before last, we lost Webber Smith's howitzer in the River Uramea, and last night one of Captain Dubordieu's 9-pounders, and five horses which were drowned. The two guns have not yet been got out; we must try again.

Yesterday we had no working party of infantry, so I was obliged to run about, first here and then there, until I got a brigade of infantry placed at my disposal. General Spry's brigade has been so placed, and is amusing itself with dragging 24-pounders up a slippery mountain. We brought howitzers yesterday to take the advanced redoubt of the enemy near the convent in reverse, which they did, obliging the enemy to abandon it. An attack was accordingly made on the convent by the infantry, but somehow it failed. Today we try again, having brought more field guns rather with the view of distracting the enemy than for any other purpose. Our batteries will open against the castle and town in a couple of days, but without cars, or mules, or oxen, one looks at the carriages and piles of shot with something like wonder how they are to be moved.

I am at my wits' end, or nearly so, with the ladies here; they are everything, do everything, and are supreme; they row, unload vessels, bring shot on shore, yet I have been a week begging, praying, and urging in vain, that they should receive rations, and some remuneration. Lord Wellington has ordered it, and a commissary is said to be coming, but he does not come, and I have to make all manner of excuses to them: we exchange conversation as we pass in the harbour; they speak English, French, or Spanish, and talk all at once in all. Ten redoubts are thrown up round Pampeluna at from 2000 to 2500 yards' distance; the guns taken at Vitoria will be placed in them. No siege of that place is contemplated. The siege of St. Sebastian will well nigh exhaust our means in ammunition and stores. Sir Richard Fletcher (Engineers) arrived yesterday; we dined early and then rode round the place till 10 p.m.

Tonight, we get some 24-pounders into battery. This morning we took the convent and redoubt. There was some firing and a good resistance on the part of the enemy. I have tired my fingers in writing to borrow men for a working party for tonight. We begin the moment it gets dark enough to conceal us from the place.

July 19.

All going on well; that is, busily. I am just out of the trenches, which I leave to, look at the wharf before I return to them. We hope to open tomorrow, yet have five or six guns to land, and as many more to transport to the batteries. We begin with a deficiency, at the lowest calculation, of fifty-eight artillerymen for two reliefs. We cannot afford casualties, and the enemy uncivilly tries to break our heads with his shells, which he throws badly and hits no one. He was hard at work last night, his pickaxes made much noise. His soil is rock, ours sand, on which we tumble and cry *Viva* twenty times before we can get a 24-pounder to budge an inch. We shall have thirty-two guns in play at the east attack, and eight on the south. The Field-Marshal comes tomorrow. The 22nd is the anniversary of Salamanca, we must celebrate the day. We fired 2500 18-pounder shot (most of them red hot) and 450 shells at the convent taken the day before yesterday. We have already found a thousand of the shot, and shall look for more. The convent cost us seventy men, and the enemy 250 men; he behaved with gallantry.

The enemy has some good head in the fortress: we must feel for it. He fires and takes his measures with judgment: nevertheless, I hope a few days will give us the town and works, and some more, the rock and castle. The latter may (but I suspect will not) be defended for some time. Sir George Collier has spared us sixty seamen to help us in our batteries.

Letter 69

Passages: July 23, 2 a. m.

We began breaching the wall of St. Sebastian at daybreak, on the 20th. By mid-day yesterday the breach, of one hundred feet long, was perfectly practicable, the wall being entirely levelled. We were to have had twelve guns in the breaching battery, but mishaps of various kinds reduced us on the first day to seven, and on the second day to nine. The guns have each fired upwards of three hundred rounds, and several of them three hundred and fifty rounds, daily between daybreak and sunset; this is considered a great deal. This is a curious world; after this excellent breach they (equivocal pronoun) hesitate about using it, and accordingly I am now ordered to make another breach. It is in a part of the wall more oblique, will probably take two days to accomplish, by which time the original breach will be entrenched, and we must begin again.

I must get down before day dawns, to begin again the work of destruction. Great part of the town is ruined by our fire. The crashing of houses, and roaring of guns on all sides, make a horrible din. How dreadful must at this moment be the feelings of the poor inhabitants, and indeed, those of the garrison! Their wall ruined and an assault of course expected!! We who witness these horrid scenes do not feel them as we ought: the habit of continually seeing shocking sights takes away every finer feeling; 'tis well that it does.—*Adieu*, for the moment.

July 24, 3 a.m.

I was unable to finish my letter last night. I am now going to the battery, to see the storm of the unhappy town; it will take place in half an hour. The town was on fire when I lay down at eleven last night. We have a river between us, so, thank Heaven, we cannot, even if we wished it, go into the place till the first fury shall have passed. Poor inhabitants, how many women and children are at this moment in the agonies of despair!! I have not one moment to write. When the assault is over, as I presume the castle will of course hold out, we must begin again. We began a second breach yesterday, at daybreak, and changed it again at 8 a.m. for a third, which was in some measure practicable at dusk—*Adieu*: may you never see such horrid scenes as I must unavoidably!

Letter 70

Before St. Sebastian: July 26.

I continue well, in good health, and good spirits; the latter no ways cast down by the unexpected failure of our assault yesterday, on the breaches of St. Sebastian. The causes of all this I will detail in another letter. Delay and indecision are the principal causes of the failure which will entail more labour on our fine fellows. We have already made two breaches: we shall have to make a third, and to throw down a demi-bastion, with an explanation of which, I am sure, I will not plague you. The loss before the assault was confined to our breaching battery, in which the usual casualties occurred daily. I should not mention them, were I not sure you would be more at ease in learning the truth, than in its being concealed. In the assault, about thirty-six officers and two hundred men have been killed and wounded. The troops did not behave well, according to present appearances.

I have had a good sound sleep of several hours, and did not rise till six: quite a lazy hour. For ten or twelve days past, the exercise I have taken has been very violent; and yet, provoking to say, I get so fat that I can hardly put on an old jacket which has to relieve one which has turned black by smoke, rain, and sand. I had yesterday quite a houseful, my friends being ranged round the floor like I know not what; among others, Ramsay, and Colonel Ponsonby who is a great friend of Ramsay's. He dined with me the day before the assault, and was stretched along the floor with the rest. Today there will be little firing. The new plan of attack is digesting: I hate delay, but it will do well enough. I think none of the troops will move till success shall have attended our second assault, and a few days must elapse before our new breaches can be made.

Among the wounded yesterday was Lewis of the Engineers, whom I saw as the day broke carried off by two or three of the sapping party; he has lost a leg, but is doing well and in good spirits. Poor Taylor of the *Sparrow* (which carried to England the Vitoria despatches) is here too, wounded. Sir George Collier and he came to our battery for a moment, and an unlucky shell struck Taylor in the leg, which I fear he will lose. The weather is charming, with a delicious sea-breeze; trudging up to our ankles in sand is fatiguing, but while health and spirits are bestowed these little labours serve but to enhance the value of repose: I am very thankful that these blessings are continued to me, and I have a good and firm hope that they will still be so.

I mean to send you a drawing and plan of St. Sebastian, which I foresee will make an interesting feature in the campaign. Time alone is wanting to prevent my doing this I wish you to possess every information of what is going on, and to follow in idea all my scrambling adventures. Do not imagine that I am insensible to what you feel or fear on my account, because I seldom allude to the subject. On the contrary, I do feel more for your sake than I choose to express, or even to own to myself. But have no fears, all will be well. Things seem alarming only at a distance: danger when looked at steadily vanishes almost to nothing. I have had very great assistance in the batteries from John Parker; he is a fine fellow, zealous and determined.

July 26.

Captain Waller of the *Goldfinch* has this moment called on Captain Taylor of the *Sparrow*, (who lies wounded in my room,) and he has obligingly offered to carry to Basque Roads (for which he sails tomorrow) any letters I may have for England. I have told you I was chagrined at the failure of our assault on St. Sebastian yesterday; I am more so at the order I have just received and would willingly disobey,—to withdraw tonight the guns from the batteries, except two guns.

Our service in the breaching batteries has been laborious, but exertion is healthy, you know. I write to the last, but have to run one way for a Portuguese working party, which Bradford who has a brigade of these folks must find me, and another for bullocks.

We are to attack St. Sebastian again, when more ammunition arrives from England. I hate irresolution and doubtful counsels.

LETTER 71

Passages: July 26, 3 p. m.

I am now going to embark all the ordnance employed in the siege of St. Sebastian. The golden opportunity has been allowed to slip by, and we have lost what was within our grasp. I can safely aver, and without arrogance or ostentation, that the artillery part was performed with effect.

I have had a scratch or two in the face and head, but nothing either to spoil my good looks or spirits, and I only mention the trifle lest you should otherwise hear of it, and be alarmed. Tonight, I shall have a difficult task in withdrawing the guns from the batteries; it must be done silently, to prevent any knowledge on the part of the enemy.

July 26.

We opened our breaching battery on the 20th. It is about seven hundred and fifty yards from the walls of St. Sebastian. Twelve 24-pounders were in the battery, three of which were of the shorter kind, and borrowed from H.M. ship *Surveillante*. Six other 24-pounders at the same time opened on the breach, but at one thousand yards. Of the real breaching battery, from different circumstances, seven guns only were brought into play on the 20th, and nine on the 21st. By mid-day on the 22nd the breach was practicable; ninety feet wide, and of a good regular slope. Besides these batteries, there was one of two 24-pounders and four howitzers, and another of four 68-pound carronades, and on the 23rd a third of four 10-inch mortars, on the right of the River Urumea; on the left of which were, in two other batteries, six 18-pounders, and two 8-inch howitzers.

A sketch shall explain the otherwise unintelligible story. I fully hoped, and strongly urged, that the breach should be stormed as early on the 23rd as the light and tide would admit. From half tide to low water there is ample room for troops to move to the foot of the breach. When the tide is up the water washes the walls of St. Sebastian, and a retaining wall which extends from the right of our trenches to the ditch of the place. Instead, however, of storming, we were ordered to make another breach to our left of the first.

After battering this for some hours, information was received from a civil engineer well acquainted with the town, that the wall to the right of the breach was a *toise* thinner than elsewhere. We were accordingly directed to make a breach there, which was done, and the breach made practicable before night.

Thus, ended the 23rd, during which, while the second breach was making, our 68-pound carronades threw shells with very small charges, just to clear the breach, and prevent any defences being made behind it. This operation set fire to some of the houses beyond the breach. Before daybreak on the 24th, the trenches were filled with the necessary troops for storming and supporting.

It was agreed that our fire should continue till the moment that the assault should be made, which was to be at 4 a.m., a little after daybreak. Till then we were to increase breach No. 2, and then to turn all available guns to restrain the enemy's flanking fire from two distant guns, or otherwise assist in the operations, as the case might be. Nothing could be clearer. About an hour after daybreak we had the mortification of seeing the troops filing out of the trenches, and perceived that the assault was postponed. This, we afterwards (for the Urumea prevented any immediate communication) learned, arose from a misconception that the fire among the houses would interfere with the assault.

The 24th was passed in widening the second breach, in clearing from it the timber which fell on and into it from adjoining houses, and in viewing generally the defences of the enemy. Time was considered so valuable that we hoped to storm at 4 p.m. when the tide would have served, but the inconvenience of having only a few hours of daylight controlled this reasoning, and the assault was ordered to take place immediately after daybreak on the 25th instant.

The assault was accordingly made, but stupidly an hour before, instead of after daybreak. Lieutenant Jones of the Engineers, with an officer and nine men of the Royals, led the way, and gained with no loss the top of the breach (the large one). This party was followed by two companies of the Royals, which reached the foot of the breach, and were faced to their left, so as to front it in good order; but the enemy by this time commencing a roll of musketry, the men, panic-struck, turned, could never be rallied, and sustained loss in running back.

It was intended that, at the moment of storming the first breach, another column, passing to the rear of the first, and between it and the receding sea, should pass on to the second breach, and carry it at the same moment. The discomfiture of the first party prevented this, and no man reached even the foot of the second breach. When day broke we hardly thought anything more than a false attack had taken place. The carronade battery in which I had taken my station, is low, and within five hundred yards of the retaining wall before mentioned, and of the demi-bastion under which the storming party had advanced, and commands also a clearer view of the breach than the breaching battery itself. As the day dawned, we discovered with our glasses bodies both of officers and men in the breach, and under the demi-bastion and returning wall. We then began to suspect what we soon found to be the case, that the assault had been made, and had failed.

In a little while one or two of the enemy appeared on the breach, and one sergeant, with a gasconading humanity, ran down among the wounded, raising some, and speaking to others. We stopped our fire, which till then had been continued occasionally over the breach. More of the enemy appeared: a kind of parley took place between

THE STORMING OF ST. SEBASTIAN

them and three of our people at the head of the trenches: when a white flag was hoisted, by what authority I know not. We, of course, ceased firing. The Urumea to our left prevented communication, and during the time the truce lasted, the enemy carried away into the town such of our wounded as could be moved. I could see none of the wounded brought to our side, except Lewis of the Engineers, whom before the firing ceased I could clearly see being carried back by a sapper and two sergeants. He has lost a leg, but is doing well.

After this strange interval of inaction, which lasted about an hour, we recommenced firing, but without any definite object. We had again the mortification of seeing the troops filing out of the trenches, and the affair was over. Still we knew no particulars till first a letter from Sir Thomas Graham, and soon after the good old man himself, acquainted us with the morning's failure. The loss in this affair is thirty-six officers, and two hundred men killed and wounded.

Lord Wellington came here yesterday about 12, and remained till 4. Another attack is determined upon. We are to complete the second or half-finished breach, to throw down the demi-bastion, and to have fresh troops for another assault. In the meanwhile, our ammunition draws to an end, nor do I at this moment know whence a supply is to be procured. However, shot can be cast at foundries at hand. I lately gave an order for 6000 12-pound shot to be cast near Santander; perhaps we may pick up enough from some of the Basque Road frigates. Unluckily our 74's have only 18- and 32-pounders.

It has this moment come to my knowledge that the River Urumea is fordable at low water opposite our batteries. Alexander Macdonald of ours (a brave and daring officer) forded it last night after dark, getting under the Mirador battery of the enemy. I have sent for him, and must take steps in consequence; the enemy may otherwise pay a visit to our unprotected batteries. We have but one weak Portuguese brigade on this side the Urumea. I had often urged the necessity of solving the question of fordability, but in vain.

However, now no bad consequences shall accrue, and we must turn the matter to our own advantage. The service of the breaching batteries has been severe. Dickson having come here before the batteries opened, I selected the breaching and the carronade batteries for my own superintendence. They have been both well served, both by our own men and the seamen, of whom we borrowed a detachment from Sir George Collier. To the breaching battery the enemy has naturally directed every disposable gun; we have accordingly lost men daily.

Our chief inconveniences have arisen from two 14-inch mortars, the shells from which have repeatedly blown up every platform in the battery, and dismounted our guns. The enemy's shot have also disabled many carriages and one gun, which received in the first half-hour a shot injuring the bore, and rendering it useless. Captain Dubordieu is the only artillery officer killed. Many of our seamen have suffered: less used to the matter than ourselves, it was not till several had been killed that they would listen to my injunctions; but they did their duty nobly, as the tars always do. Three of their officers and sixteen seamen have been killed and wounded within the last three days in this battery. A few of these suffered in an explosion which took place one hardly knows how. Of two bodies which were blown to pieces, the limb of one struck me a severe blow on the thigh and head; but I escaped with a violent jar from the explosion, and two or three slight cuts in the face and ear, and am no ways hurt, merely a little deaf.

I mention these things lest you should hear them magnified, which is the more likely, since several of our own officers who were with me at the moment were also blown down. Colonel Fletcher, Lieutenant Jones, Lieutenant Reid, and Captain Lewis of the Engineers, were wounded, and Lieutenant Machel killed. Soon afterwards. Sir George Collier and Captain Taylor of the *Sparrow* came into the battery to me, and had not been there one minute before a shell struck poor Taylor, cut his head and broke his leg, which the surgeon intends to amputate tomorrow. He is now in my room, in excellent spirits, and will do well.

I have no fears for the success of our enterprise against St. Sebastian. It must be taken: the honour of our country requires it.—*Adieu*. I have just received orders to withdraw the guns from the batteries. This chagrins me; the guns are of no use in case of disaster, and in case of going on with the siege must be drawn back again. I believe the marquis has his fears of Soult.—*Adieu*, I must send this letter away without reading it over. It is probably full of inaccuracies.

Letter 72

Passages: July 27.

I wrote to you yesterday. Things crowd on us. Last night we withdrew our guns from the batteries (except two guns); today we embark them, that is, if we can; but bullocks are knocked up, and boats are not to be had. These, and many other obstacles, would prevent us if we were not determined that nothing should. This morning the enemy made a sortie on the trenches, and absolutely carried off as prisoners 300 or 400 Portuguese and a few Englishmen, and all for want of foresight on our part. Thinking the thing likely some days since, we had some of the guns of our left embrasures arranged so as to take the enemy in flank; but the guns having been withdrawn, their assistance was lost on the occasion of the sortie.

July 28.

I wrote yesterday once, and twice the day before; nothing very new. We have as yet embarked very little. Tide fails, bullocks knock up, boats cannot be found; nevertheless, we work on. Our two guns left in the batteries keep up a show of fire, which the enemy returns. Today, we get poor Taylor on board. I am much interested about him, because he was wounded in our battery, and, though merely a spectator, he seems to have suffered in our cause, as too many of our seamen had before done. I am sending my baggage to Oyarzun, where Webber Smith's troop is; this is a precautionary measure.

July 29.

We get on but slowly, yet as well as we can. Our boats sink, we have to raise them again; our bullocks knock up. Our sick and wounded, hourly arriving, take many of our smaller boats. Yet we are in no ways discouraged, and, in the consciousness that we are doing all that is possible, we are neither disconcerted nor disheartened. I am just returned from seeing the wounded on ship-board. The scene is distressing, and the more so from our utter inability to assist. What we can do, we do. The accounts from the front are perplexing. We have had no communication, nor has Sir Thomas Graham, with the marquis, for two days. We know that Longa has retired.

The enemy may, in consequence, have cut in upon our communications. I hope not, and that tonight's and tomorrow morning's tide may yet be allowed us. They may (but I suspect they will not) suffice to get off our remaining guns and stores. If not, we lose them: and what then? You'll say, and so say I. Shakespeare says, "*The uses of adversity are sweet;*" I am sure those of experience are, and that it is well worth while when mishaps occur, to reflect coolly to what they are owing.

We endeavour to do this, and I hope shall hereafter smile at our present intricacies. You see I avoid the word *difficulties*, disliking it, and banishing it from our society; were the demon admitted, he would bring with him a host of dispiriting companions. Dickson is writing

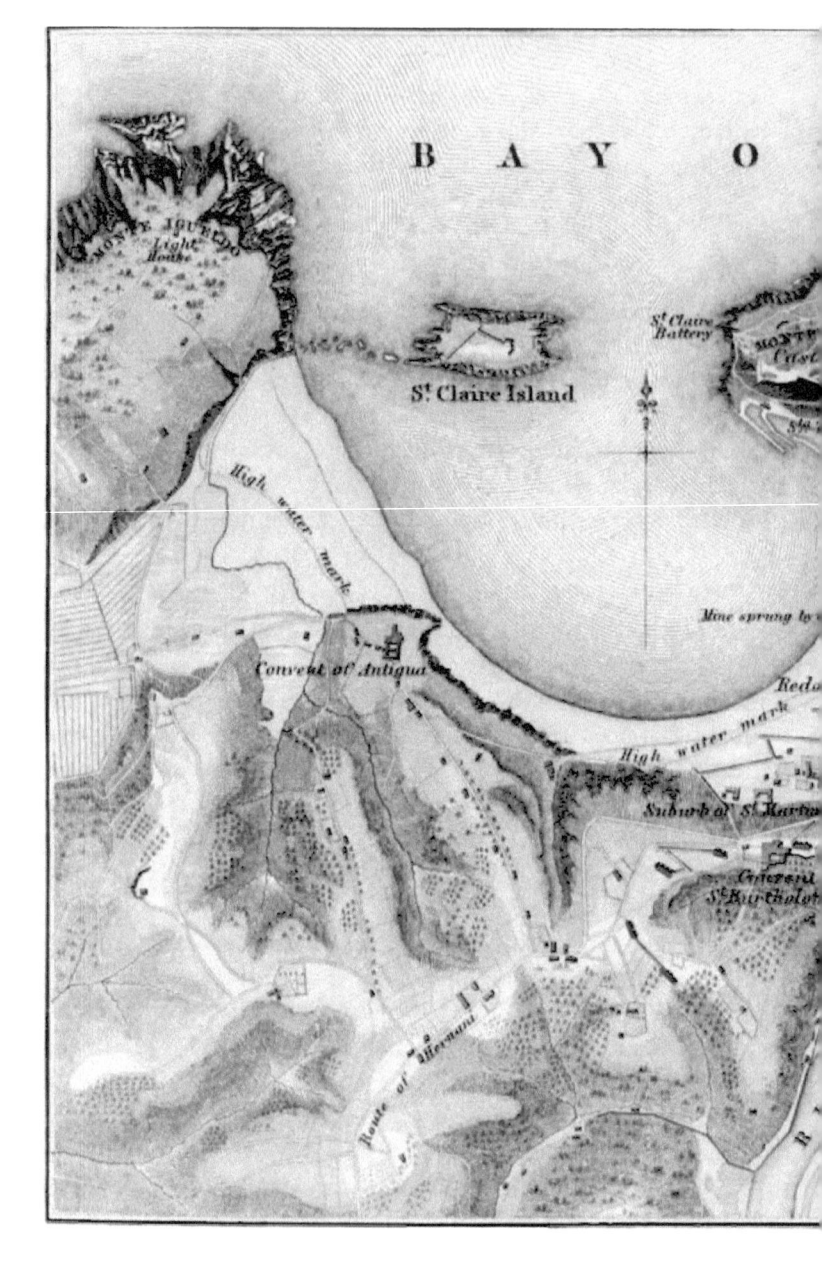

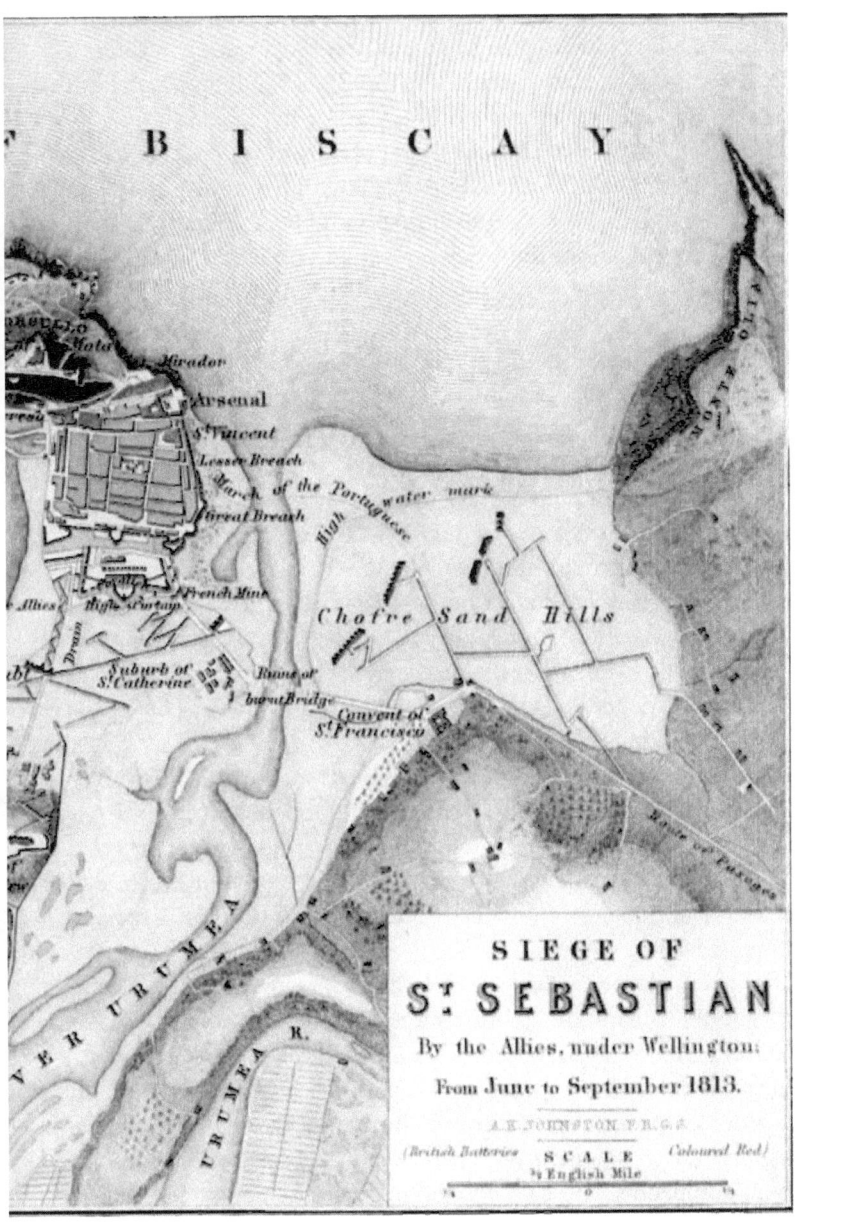

about ammunition for General Giron who suddenly sends to say he has none. We are both seated on one box, and writing on another.

Passages: July 30.

I wrote a little note yesterday, but imagine I may yet be in time to save the sailing of the despatches. On the 28th, Soult attacked Lord Wellington with 35,000 men (as some say, and others, 25,000); and, after repeated attempts, was completely repulsed with considerable loss: chiefly on the part of the enemy. Lord Wellington, by all accounts, had only the third and fourth divisions at first with him. The sixth division came up soon afterwards, and the second division joined him in the evening, when, as a letter from Sir Thomas Graham expressed it, "Lord Wellington wished he might be attacked again."

The affair happened in the neighbourhood of Pampeluna, for the relief of which, no doubt, Soult had advanced. It is said the enemy has reoccupied San Estevan, but of this I am not sure.

We embark what we have remaining on our wharfs, leaving the two guns in the breaching battery, which were to have been withdrawn last night: and we are now dragging again up the mountain two 8-inch howitzers, which were brought down yesterday. Four transports with troops from England are now in the offing. Sir George Collier writes that he hopes more are to the westward beating up. When our fresh battering-train shall arrive from England, we shall reattack St. Sebastian: that is, if things remain favourable. The attack will be on the other (or land) side.

You see the trouble occasioned by want of sufficient gallantry. We are, of course, more at our ease since the good news received last night, but shall have full employment again soon. Today will be a day of comparative ease; yesterday was the most sultry and unpleasant day I ever recollect. I was on the wharf till after dark, and had a long way to scramble home.

After being jostled by loaded mules, and somewhat out of humour, I met a poor woman; she had to conduct a stubborn ass, and to take care of two little ragged children (one at the breast), and was crawling towards the place of embarkation, whilst her husband was coming wounded, in a boat, to get on board the transport for Bilbaŏ. It was impossible not to compare our relative situations, yet the poor soul made no complaints. These accidental meetings do me good. *Adieu:*— a boat has this moment sunk in five fathoms water, with one of our mortars on board!!

Letter 73

Passages: August 1, 6 a.m.

Yesterday, Harding and I rode to Oyarzun, where I had business with Sir Thomas Graham, whom, however, I did not see. The good man had rode out to reconnoitre, so I sat down and wrote him a long letter, which I left on his table. Today I expect back from Oyarzun my mule and baggage, which some days ago, when things looked more uncertain than they have done since the marquis's late brilliant though bloody action, I had sent thither, to be more able to move in case of need. The 92nd is said to have suffered much in the late affair, but to have behaved, as it always does, nobly. Soult is now decidedly retiring, and the marquis following him; details are yet indistinctly known.

Canning, who reached Sir Thomas Graham from the marquis the night before last, told me yesterday, that our loss was 2500 killed and wounded, but that the British troops had never behaved more firmly, or more to the satisfaction of the marquis, whose presence with Hill's corps at the moment of its being overpowered by numbers, was like the prescience of a divinity. The men cheered with enthusiasm, and returned to the charge of bayonets with a resolution which nothing could withstand. We hope all this may lead to the fall of Pampeluna, which place and St. Sebastian are essential to anything like the permanent occupation of the country. We concluded our labours of reembarking ordnance the night before last; we are now ready to land them again.

Curious work, all this. Our mortar and its bed remain in three fathoms water, but I have reported to Sir Thomas Graham that it shall be got up, and accordingly it must. Something delays the arrival of the baggage and mules from Oyarzun. The road is bad, rugged, and by the cliff over the Passages water. Most of the roads hereabout, the paved high roads excepted, are very bad. In one place between this and Ernani, we are continually having accidents. Three or four nights ago, a waggon of one of our reserves fell over a precipice into the Urumea and was lost: horses saved.

The next night, another waggon shared the same fate: horses all lost. Both were overset near the same place where I may have mentioned that, just before the opening of our batteries against St. Sebastian, we lost a howitzer of Smith's troop, and a 9-pounder of poor Dubordieu's. Both were recovered: carriages of course broken, and five horses drowned. Parker's company left us yesterday: he is a fine resolute fellow, and a real good officer.

9 a.m.

The church bells of St. Sebastian remind me that today is Sunday. I hope you are quietly preparing to go to church. How much better suited to the day are your employments than mine! It has often struck me as a singular coincidence how generally our battles are on Sundays, as if war, the reverse of all that religion prescribes and enjoins, were permitted to show strikingly a breach of the Sabbath.

August 2, 7 a. m.

A letter was received yesterday from General Murray, quartermaster general, acquainting Sir Thomas Graham that on the 30th *ultimo* the marquis had taken 3000 prisoners, besides the wounded in the field. This must allude to an action on that day distinct from the one of the 28th. Yesterday morning we rode to Passages de Francia, and examined the little forts at the entrance of the harbour, which we had not before had time to do. On my return home I found an orderly from Ramsay with an account that a third corps of the enemy, of which the marquis had previously no information, were discovered in the Pass of Lanz, and that his lordship had moved to attack it. Today will probably bring us some orders for our movements. The reattack of St. Sebastian must depend on the arrival of the battering-train expected from England. Soult, we believe, has decidedly retired.

I should be glad to say that Pampeluna had fallen; it would be of great use to us,—so would St. Sebastian. The army is on the point of moving forwards. Orders are sent to the reserve artillery and the pontoons to come up. Sir Thomas Graham has also received directions to prepare to pass the River Bidassoa. I have just returned from examining St. Sebastian with Dickson; all remains in the same state. The enemy had added a retrenchment or two, but nothing of consequence. You fancied I was unwilling to serve under Dickson, quite the reverse; I like him, always did, and have no feeling of the kind.

Moreover, I should have served cheerfully under any one. I did not come into this country to make difficulties, or objections to anything or anyone; and having long since made up my mind, and taken my line of conduct, have no intention of changing the one or swerving from the other. Both seem to me to be right, and that is enough.

LETTER 74.

Passages; August 4.

I have little new to offer you. I am in expectation of receiving my orders today. They will be either to remain and land the expected battering-train intended for the reattack of St. Sebastian, or to rejoin the headquarters of the army. I should prefer the latter, but shall obey either cheerfully, and have no doubt that all will be for the best. The late successes have been very great. There have been fifty reports of their extent, as well as of the losses of provisions and baggage of Soult's army, but knowing how little reports of any kind are to be depended upon we suspend our belief. The ladies here have all been paid for their late exertions, and at every turn inquire when they are to be employed again.

A dollar a day and rations for the two ladies who manage each boat is the price fixed on, and they seem satisfied. The wounded sailed yesterday for Bilbaõ. Bloye had hard work to tow them out of the harbour. There was little or no wind; two of the ships afterwards edged nearer in shore under the castle of St. Sebastian than was desirable; all the boats of the little squadron were sent to tow them out. I sat on a rock on the mountain above my house, and enjoyed the serene beauty of the day.

The rocky coast of Spain from Cape Machichoco on the one side to the flat coast beyond Bayonne on the other appeared beneath one's feet; the ships below mere specks in the water. The road up and down the mountain is rugged and steep. Our guns fired occasionally at St. Sebastian, within the walls of which the enemy, like ants, were toiling in adding to their defences.

Both breaches remain as before, a *chevaux-de-frise* across the larger one excepted. All our batteries, lately the scenes of horror, looked so diminutive that one could not but forcibly recollect what little creatures we are, and how puny are all our efforts whether good or evil. This pause in war affords time for reflections. Those which arise are of sorrow for the surrounding miseries, and of dislike, nay abhorrence, for the cause of them. In the event of again attacking St. Sebastian, the side of the attack will be changed. It may not be easy to persuade troops to attack breaches which have once been assaulted without success; others will accordingly, I presume, be made. Our first objects will be to repair, or rather to make roads from the landing-places towards the batteries, and to establish a bridge of communication between the two sides of the Urumea River.

If nothing prevents me, I shall go tomorrow to Fuentarabia and Irun. I have not yet been at either. The bridge beyond Irun is burnt down. The advanced posts on either side are civil, and talk, as much as a space of 150 yards between them will permit. Every evening half a dozen well-dressed people pass my door; they are inhabitants of St. Sebastian, and go to take a wistful look at their houses, or rather the ruins of them. There will be more ruin yet in that town before we shall get possession of it.

Letter 75

Passages: August 6.

Yesterday passed without my writing to you, and I have little news to communicate today. I rode yesterday to Oyarzun, intending to go to Irun and Fuentarabia; but I returned without going to either. At Oyarzun I found Dickson preparing to return to Passages, and learnt that the siege of St. Sebastian was to be recommenced, and that we were all to assist. Accordingly, we began today to reland the guns just embarked, and have already sent to bring back the ordnance transport which two days since sailed for Bilbaô. I am going with Bloye to Rentoria to examine the landing-place for the ordnance for the service of the attack on the left bank of the Urumea. We shall have a pleasant row across the harbour, which, at high water, is most beautiful.—*Adieu* for the moment.

11 a.m.

Just returned from Rentoria, where we found a good place for our purpose, and set the master of a transport to work to rig out a derrick. No news from the front today. I am obliged to leave off.

Letter 76

Passages: August 11, 7 p.m.

There is little new, yet a letter and no news of the army would be shameful. What shall I say of ourselves? little that is active, but all that is the reverse. We are doing nothing, or next to nothing. We artillerymen await the arrival of guns and stores from England. The cavalry longs to eat the green Indian corn, which is prohibited; in consequence their horses are kept in good exercise in looking for straw. The infantry rests on its arms, and all expect the development of some new plan. The marquis's headquarters are at Lesaca, nor does any immediate movement seem probable. His lordship has lately received some news, which, it is supposed, has occasioned a change of plan, but of what nature the news is, if known, is not communicated, and absent as I now am for the moment from headquarters, I have no means of knowing anything beyond common report.

In St. Sebastian all remains yesterday and today the same as before;

nor is there anything materially new on our side, except the completion of a few batteries. I visited those on the left side of the Urumea two days ago. Yesterday was employed in inspecting some of the troops of horse artillery. I wished to get this over before I shall be again employed at the siege. The moon rising through a misty cloud which has all day enveloped the top of the ranges of the Pyrenees, offers at this moment one of the most beautiful sights I ever saw. It is not yet 8 p.m. and I write in the open air, and by perfect daylight. The evening is serene, the tide full in: boats crossing the harbour in all directions.

August 13.

I write now in the open air in a balcony over the water, and in the shade. The boats passing, the ships unloading, and the whole bustle of the port, as it were, beneath my feet, are most interesting. I shall never, I think, be tired of this romantic spot. I stop to listen to the singing of the boatwomen, whose boats surround a vessel not far from hence. One seems to give a verse which the rest sing after her. The harmony is simple and beautiful: the ladies sing in parts, and with some taste.

August 15.

I have been apparently busy all day, yet have done little. It is the birthday of Bonaparte, as the repeated salvos from the castle of St. Sebastian would have told us, had we doubted the fact. They fired three salvos at 8 last night, three or four this morning, and an equal number at noon today. Tonight, *VIVE NAPOLÉON LE GRAND* shines on the castle in brilliant splendour. Goodnight.

Letter 77

Passages: August 18.

I rode yesterday to Irun and Fuentarabia, and returned, after a pleasant but wet ride, to dinner. Jenkinson accompanied me. We called on Sir Thomas Graham, and sat half an hour with him as we passed through Oyarzun. Irun has nothing in it remarkable. Beyond it, at a mile distance, is the bridge over the Bidassoa (or more strictly speaking, was the bridge, for it has been burnt down). The river is about 100 yards wide. We exchanged the usual civilities with the enemy on the other side. From the bridge we returned to Irun, and from thence went to Fuentarabia, a couple of miles from Irun, but in a circling direction, so as to bring us nearly to the mouth of the Bidassoa, and three quarters of a mile from Andaye, a little French town opposite Fuentarabia, and also near the French end of the bridge beyond Irun.

All these places are filled with Spanish troops. Fuentarabia looks pretty enough as you approach a causeway bordered with trees. Its fortifications have some years since been destroyed, and we had remarked how happy for the place this was; on getting into the town, however, we found half of it in ruins, and many houses propped up with beams of wood. It bears evident marks of a siege, but my memory does not at this moment tell me when. Both here and at Passages, we saw some of the largest mackerel I recollect. Those we have lately had, though good, have been small; all are without roes.

A boat was taken the afternoon of the day before yesterday coming out of St. Sebastian. It is yet uncertain whether the officer in this boat really had been in the fortress or not; or whether (according to his own account) he had come from Guetaria. I will find out particulars this morning and let you know. Ships are said to be off the coast: if so, we may hope for our expected battering-train, which we know to have been wind-bound at Falmouth on the 2nd instant. Nothing indicates any intended movement or advance; on the contrary, the pontoons have been sent to the rear. There was a marked change immediately after the arrival, some days ago, of a messenger from home.

3 p.m.

No news. The ships (eight) in the offing are believed to be from Bilbaõ. The boat's crew remain in confinement. It will be difficult to make out anything respecting it.—*Adieu.*

Letter 78

Passages: August 22.

Knowing that you will be pleased to hear that our friend General Stewart is doing well, I enclose you a letter received this morning from him. I have little to communicate. My last letter will have acquainted you with the nothing we have been doing for some days. The *Zephyr* sloop of war arrived last night. She has convoyed some ordnance vessels, which will enter the harbour today. They contain the third proportion of our battering-train; I am glad of this. Tonight, we begin again to get our guns into battery; tomorrow night will, as I hope, complete this, so that we may open again on the 24th.

We are to lay open the two round towers at each end of the first breach; to connect this breach with the second breach (which is to the right); to add to the breach another one to the left; and to throw down, or at least utterly ruin and render untenable, the demi-bastion to the left of the whole breach, the approach to which it flanks. This done, an assault will be again tried.

Sir Thomas Graham is coming here immediately, and the mode of attack, will be again discussed. I hope two separate attacks will be made. The place is undoubtedly more strong than it was, as the enemy has employed every means in adding to its defences, and in strengthening those he originally possessed. This was the natural consequence of our former failure. It may be necessary to reduce the town to ashes. On mentioning this to Sir Thomas Graham he said he should write on the subject, and obtain a specific answer on that point from the marquis. Of course, the women and children will be permitted to leave the place. This St. Sebastian is destined to be a thorn in our sides, or a feather in our caps. "*Haeret lateri*" just now.—*Adieu*.

(Enclosure)
From Lieut.-General the Hon, William Stewart
to Lieut.-Colonel Frazer,

Villa Alba, near Pampeluna: August 20.

I did not receive your very kind letter of the 9th instant, my dear colonel, until a day or two ago, it having apparently made the tour of my division: headquarters at Roncesvalles. I feel infinitely obliged by your very friendly inquiries about my recovery, which, after two severe blows, has been uncommonly favourable, so much so that I hope to be able to resume the command of my division about the first of next month. I was so unfortunate as to be overpowered by numbers on the 25th *ultimo*, and to lose the Pass of Maya, where I received my first wound. Able, however, to remain sufficiently long in the field to recover (by arrival of reinforcements) our important position of lost ground (which was, however, abandoned in consequence of our failure at Roncesvalles on the same day).

I was obliged to go to the rear for a day or two to recover from severe loss of blood, &c.; but on the 31st, events being too serious for retrograde proceedings, as long as one could sit a horse, I returned to my gallant division, and in two hours after, at the attack of a hill, in pursuit of the enemy near San Estevan, received another severe blow; the ball entering at the wrist and having been extracted at the elbow. I am, however, doing well; and am grateful at having lost no limb.

When you hear details of proceedings at the point where I now write, and our noble commander's towering spirit and genius on the 27th, 28th, and 30th of last month, you will think the whole was a *chef d'oeuvre*. Our affairs were in a critical situation on the two first of these days, and retrieved by him and our quartermaster-general most admirably. We have rumours of peace, and its terms, from our outposts; nor shall I be surprised at their being realised, for the whole world is tired of war. Remember me kindly when you write home, and believe me, ever faithfully yours,

W. T. Stewart.

Letter 79

Passages: August 23.

Nothing very new, nor any thing decided as to a second point of attack. Much is said of attacking an island, Santa Clara, to the westward of the town. It becomes doubly valuable, now that the season approaches when ships may be obliged to leave the coast. From want of artillerymen we cannot open till the 26th, if then. It now blows hard. We had a good fag last night; I left the batteries at 2 a.m. this morning, (the 23rd,) having only got four 24-pounders, and four howitzers in battery by that time, though we began at 8 p.m. the preceding evening.

Our progress is ridiculously slow; half a dozen artillerymen were all we could get to show about 300 Portuguese infantry what was to be done. It is necessarily a work of silence, that the enemy may not hear what is going on. The bullocks are all knocked up, and the men, though willing, exhaust their strength in misapplying it. I am suddenly called away, and shall close this letter that it may be ready to go. I have not time to make the explanations to the drawing sent herewith, which would make it plainer, but I think you will make it out. Battery No. 5 is continued to its left, nearly, indeed, to the ruined bridge. Our right attack now stands thus:

	24-pounders.	8-inch Howitzers.	18-lb. Carronades.	Total.	
Battery 1	0	2	0	2	} right attacks.
,, 4	11	4	4	19	
,, 5	15	0	0	15	
				36	

August 25, 8 a.m.

We got all our guns in battery by 3 this morning. At 1 the enemy made a sortie (but not on our side, which, indeed, they can hardly do on account of the river Urumea, which they would have to cross). I have not heard the particulars of the sortie. We have fewer, though larger, batteries than before, consequently field officers are less wanted, and besides Webber Smith, Majors Dyer and Buckner are here. They are both volunteers, and most anxious to be employed. There is as much canvassing to be allowed to go into the batteries as there is elsewhere to get into St. Stephen's. Sir Thomas Graham called yesterday to show us a plan of Marshal Berwick's siege of St. Sebastian. The good man was very pressing that we should dine there today, but Dickson (for I was out and did not see him) declined on account of our occupation.

12 o'clock.

I have just been arranging all our details with Dickson. We take the general superintendence, giving Buckner, Dyer, Webber Smith, and Major Sympher (German Artillery) the more immediate regulation of the batteries. We shall begin tomorrow at 8 a.m. In the confused way in which I write you must excuse repetitions.

Letter 80

Passages: August 27, 4 a. m.

All is doing well. We opened our fire yesterday at 8 a.m. By 3 p.m. the greater part of the face of the demi-bastion came down with a crash.

Battery No. 5: 8 o'clock.

I had hardly begun this morning when I was obliged to leave off. We are continuing our fire; all well. The enemy having more points towards which to direct his fire, does less mischief at any. The island, I believe, was to have been taken last night; but all was so tranquil, that I imagine the attack did not take place. We cannot see it from our batteries on this side.

Lord Wellington was here yesterday morning; he, of course, did not come into the batteries, so that I did not see his lordship, who has wisely ordered another and more advanced battery on the left attack. Yesterday was a nice day, cool, and without sun till just before sunset, when the luminary peeped from behind a dark cloud as it was setting, showing the profile of the town and castle, on which the flashes of our guns glared with terrific grandeur.

What a goose am I to talk to you of flashes of guns! you will have fifty uneasy thoughts, and fancy me with a very grave face instead of the smiling one I wear whilst squatting under a little sandy branch of this battery, from which I direct the fire of the rest. You never heard such a row as is going on. Walls and houses falling, guns and mortars firing. When there is a moment's pause one wonders why all is so quiet. The row in general almost exceeds that of the children in your best drawing-room. Today is very hot with a broiling sun, but the evenings and nights are now cold, like the beginning of autumn in England.

We have here two English, and one Portuguese field officer on duty constantly, relieved every twenty-four hours. This morning Buckner and Dyer were relieved: how awkward my giving orders to those who, a few days since, were my superiors! Today Webber Smith and Major Sympher (German Artillery) are the field officers. We have, again, sailors from the *Surveillante*. Sir George Collier is a famous fellow; lame in both legs from wounds, he hobbles along, and is more of a boy than any of us. Bloye was yesterday introduced to the marquis, and is as pleased at the circumstance as can be imagined.

Dickson has gone to the other side of the river to arrange removing guns for the new battery. I have found my sextant of essential use; the engineer draftsmen had measured the distances wrong: tell Barker, with my regards, that I long to hear of his logarithms, and if he were here I could give him a peep through his glass (fixed in the sand to bear on a particular point, about which I am anxious), which would show him what a horrid thing war is.

******

Mr. Barker was a clergyman, resident at Woodbridge, the station in Suffolk of Sir Augustus Frazer's troop for several years, he possessed much scientific knowledge, as well as ingenuity in the adaptation of portable instruments for field purposes.

******

It is settled that we are to do the town as little damage as possible, but that little will, I dare say, extend to the destruction of half of it. I shall leave off for a little; writing in the sun is not good for gentlemen's eyes, and 1 have no shade but that of the smoke.

9 p.m.

All well, tired to death, but eating a good dinner. After all, the island was taken last night, and the few French who were in it, made prisoners. Two explosions took place today in the enemy's works from our shells. One at half-past three in the castle, and one at five in the curtain of the place. The batteries today were manned by seamen, Portuguese, Germans, and a few British artillerymen. Terrible confused work: half the number of good, well-instructed men would do twice the real service.

August 28, 4 a.m.

Nothing remarkable during the night on our side of the attack. The enemy attempted a sortie, but the fire of the batteries prevented it.

Battery No. 5: August 29, 6 p. m.

The enemy's fire is now comparatively trifling: it is hardly worth regarding.

Battery No. 5: August 30, 7 a.m.

Lord Wellington and Sir Thomas Graham came to Battery No. 5 yesterday at noon, and stayed some time. The attack was talked over. Dickson, Sir James Leith, and Fletcher, were the only persons present. After pros and cons it was settled that the assault should be tomorrow about 1 p.m. (or somewhat sooner will answer). Today we are paring down some more of the ramparts, already in utter ruin. Bravery and resolution, however, will always create defences, and will for ever do so: and time is at least as valuable to us as to the enemy.

I was glad to hear from Colonel Delancey, quarter-master general of the first division, that four hundred volunteers from each of the 3rd, 4th, and light divisions (that is, twelve hundred men), had arrived at Oyarzun, in readiness for the assault. New troops are requisite: those who failed last time will not do again. At 10 last night there was a false attack; the object was to induce the enemy to blow up the mines he is supposed to have in several places. Our batteries kept up a vigorous fire for some time. There was a volley or two of musketry from the trenches, and a considerable shouting. The enemy fired most of his guns: no mines were exploded, and there the matter ended.

The fate of tomorrow will decide much. All form their own opinions: mine is, and has ever been, adverse to delay, as breaking the spirit of the troops. We learn from a sergeant of French *chasseurs* taken prisoner in the attack of the island on the night between the 26th and 27th, that every other night five boats, laden with shot and powder, got into the place; but prisoners say anything, their accounts are always to be received with caution. The man says the original garrison was two thousand three hundred, or two thousand five hundred, and that about half are gone.

Battery No. 5: half-past 9 a. m.

All going on well. The wood and rubbish of the right breach of the former siege is in flames, and a mine near it has just blown up. We are directing part of our fire at the Mirador battery, so as to silence the guns for tomorrow. The enemy fire but little, and of that little, chiefly at the advanced battery on the other side of the river. That battery fires but slowly. I have just given a bold fellow an order on the ordnance commissary for ten dollars, for swimming over yesterday with an order in his mouth to the battery, and I believe I must find another swimmer today. I like to reward bold fellows: it animates the rest. The tide is receding. How many within the place are anxiously, and how many fearfully, awaiting its ebbing. Poor women! and poor children!—*Adieu*, I am called away.

3 p.m.

Lord Wellington and Sir Thomas Graham have been here. Tomorrow the attack will be at 11 a.m. a lodgement only is to be made in the first instance.

Three-quarters past 4 p. m.

Five little mines have this moment blown up near the hospital in the town; one of our shells found them out. A deserter came into Lesaca at five this morning. He reports that Soult, leaving a division in front of our light division, another in front of our seventh division, moved all the other divisions of his army (seven in number) towards Irun. In consequence our fourth division was marched to Oyarzun. Soult's troops reached their position opposite Irun at eight last night. Soult openly acquainted his troops that it was his intention to raise the siege of St. Sebastian. If so, he may attack tomorrow morning. Under this impression the artillery not employed in the siege are ordered, to the front.

Soult's troops are said to have expressed an unwillingness to make the attack; all this, however, can be but speculation. The last reception they met with from our fourth division may well make them shy. The "*Vive Napoléon*" on the castle before us makes now a sorry figure; it is almost entirely knocked away. Another great building under the Mirador has just burst out in flames; it was formerly an hospital: all this is very dreadful.

9 p. m., at Home.

This evening is very stormy: violent rain with thunder and lightning. Ross, Webber Smith, Ramsay, and several other horse-artillery officers, are dining with Parker. I have just been to disturb them. All the troops of horse artillery are ordered to march: an attack by Soult is expected. Much is at stake at present: more than generally occurs. The consequences of tomorrow may have a great effect on the campaign. Should Soult be successful, our siege is over: should our assault fail, we shall be awkwardly off. The stake is serious.

At the end of the Burnt Bridge: August 31, 8 a.m.

No news from Irun or of Soult. All our batteries are now beginning to play with effect. Hitherto there has been such a fog, and the smoke has hung so, that it was impossible to see anything. Bloye and Sir George Collier have just been here. There is to be a demonstration by sea, but no troops are to attempt to land; it is judged too difficult. The tide is fast receding. The enemy has fired musketry, but hitherto no cannon, this morning. The day will be a broiling one: the sun has just forced itself through the fog, and a gentle sea-breeze assists in clearing the fog away. It seems arranged that 1200 men only are to attack: this is too few—it may fail. The stake is serious, and should not be left subject to the least accident or to any chance over which we might have control.

Battery No. 5: quarter-past 10 a.m.

The assault is momentarily expected to take place. Sir Thomas Graham is here; he waits at this battery to see the event, and will give his directions from hence. It is curious at such moments to watch the countenances, and endeavour to read the minds of men. Hope, solicitude, anxiety are to be seen; frequently apathy and indifference, the effects of a continuance of scenes of danger; and now and then, though rarely, open fear. But most have the address to conceal this last acquaintance, of whom all are ashamed. None here seem more praise-worthy than the good-humoured Portuguese infantry, who serve our batteries with shot and powder. They toil all day in a slavish way, yet retain their composure and good temper through all our urgent endeavours to make them do more than human strength is equal to.

I have just had a hasty note from Sir Richard Fletcher, brought by a fine fellow who has swum over from the other side. The object is to direct seven guns, with spherical case, against a working party now toiling in the ruins of the right round tower, and not visible from hence. We are firing delicately, since we are directing our fire over points which our troops are now passing.

I have at this moment intelligence that 8000 French troops have crossed the Bidassoa. Two *aides-de-camp* have succeeded each other with the intelligence. It ought to have no other effect on us than that of invigorating our attack. This is no time for irresolution, and, after all, I hope all will be well; it must be so if we are firm. An officer of the 4th, and thirty men, are the forlorn hope, as it is awkwardly enough called; a better title should be chosen.

It begins (5 minutes before 11)! They reach the top of the breach. A mine springs, but behind them! All seems well. They reach the top and halt;—if they are supported it will do,

5 p.m.

All over. The town is ours, after a long and most awful struggle. The most determined bravery shown on both sides. It has succeeded, but there were many moments in which all seemed lost. The sight has been awful. We have had a tremendous storm of thunder, lightning, and rain; it was so dark at 3 that we could scarcely see. Our artillery has been of essential service: without the flanking of forty-seven pieces, which played the whole time from this side, the place would never have been taken. Much is yet undone. The enemy yet holds the Mirador, castle, and all the upper defences, and, I believe, a large church in the town.

I have not time nor heart to ask who has fallen, but I know my friend. Sir Richard Fletcher, is killed. Where to find his equal for kindness of heart, for urbanity and gentleness of manner, and for sterling professional worth we know not; this is a heavy blow indeed. The scenes witnessing, and to be witnessed, are deplorable indeed. I enclose my pencil notes, written from moment to moment during the assault. They will best tell, though in a confused way, the passing occurrences. There has been an action in front with Soult. I take it Lord Wellington was pushed, as we had to send away Wilson's Portuguese Brigade before our assault (in which they formed a part) was assured.

Minutes taken during the assault of St. Sebastian, August 31st.

10.55 a.m. Two mines sprung. Mirador and St. Elmo do not fire. Men run too much to old. breach—too little to junction of demi-bastion and curtain. Mirador fired one round at 11.30.

11.35: Much firing. Troops do not advance. Bugles sound advance. Head of Portuguese column cross to left in detached columns, men pass creek up to knees; advance nobly at double quick; fourteen taken back wounded with grape, about fifty more turn back; main body advance. Lieutenant Gathin, 11th Regiment, acting engineer, runs to the Portuguese to storm with them. The Portuguese get across at 11.45, but with great loss. At the breaches all is stationary. Colonel Farron, of the Portuguese service, asks me what he shall do with his 250 men. An equal number have gone under Major Snodgrass. I advise his placing his men in communication from batteries 4 to 5. Another reinforcement runs from trenches to breach.

11.50: More reinforcements. Farron did well: he was not intended to go on. More reinforcements from trenches to breach. Noon: Much grape in all directions from the enemy's batteries. Breaches are filled. A lodgement seems secure, if not mined under left round tower. Mine which burst at first in retaining wall very near where we had been.

12.10: Fire slackens on all sides. Mirador seldom fires—St. Elmo not at all (forgotten). At a quarter-past 11a letter was brought across the water by private O'Neil, of the 4th (Portuguese run from the breach), from Lord Wellington, asking Sir Thomas Graham if he can spare Bradford's brigade, as Soult comes on in force.

12.15: Advancing from breach of retired wall; smoke prevents clear view. Lodgement apparently secure. Two more mines blown up on curtain.

12.25: Ditch toward low communication filled with troops. More reinforcements from trenches to breach.

12.30: Troops again try the end of curtain; our own shots strike close over their heads. The place will be taken! Our men run from the curtain.

12.35: Cavalier gun opens. Ditch is cleared. Lull again in firing. Lieutenant Turner (sub-engineer) gone to bring off Lieutenant Gathin, assistant-engineer, who is wounded. Twenty-nine boats in offing; none nearer shore than a mile: two are gun boats.

12.40: Men going down from the old breach into the town. It will do; they wave their hats from the *terre pleine* of the curtain. Another reinforcement from trenches.

12.45: Horn-work apparently deserted. None seem to enter town from breach of retired wall. Our men fire from right of right round tower. This bounds our ground to right. Firing lulls.

12.55: Mirador again fires. We fire well at it, and at the cavalier. Enemy still holds end of curtain next cavalier.

1 p.m.: More reinforcements from trenches. This duty is well performed, whoever may direct it. Men enter the town, principally by the end of old breach next round tower. One man of 1st Guards runs alone to the part of the parapet, twenty yards

to the right of the right tower, and a sergeant and a few Portuguese by right breach of all. They gain it by getting on the old foundation of Marshal Berwick's wall. The enemy lines the stockade. The enemy runs from the rampart behind that stockade. All goes well.

1.10: Two of our shots go through the stockade; the enemy abandons it. One brave French officer and two men alone remain; they too are gone.

1.15: Enemy still holds end of the curtain next the cavalier; he should be forced at that point. The gun at St. Elmo fires.

1.20: And again,—it must be silenced. Very heavy fire of musketry in the town. Horn-work decidedly ours.

1.25: The gun at St. Elmo more and more troublesome. Firing in the town continues and increases. Few men comparatively on breaches; chiefly in hollow of retired wall between end of curtain and left tower: they are now entering the town. The flag was stuck on the castle when the assault began.

1.35: More reinforcements to breach from trenches. No fire or men to be seen on trenches. Wind very high; sand blows and destroys the view. Many prisoners brought into trenches from the town. The St. Elmo gun fires; a shot from our guns strikes the French hospital: must be prevented. Tide has begun to flow.

1.45: Heavy musketry in the town. Our bugles sound the advance in all parts of the town. General Wilson's Portuguese Brigade marches from our side of attack towards the front: this is in consequence of Lord Wellington's order before mentioned.

1.50: Our people leave the breach of retired wall, and enter by curtain. With judgment the town is securely ours, according to all appearances. Our men are pulling prisoners out by the breach. The enemy retire. Many enter the Mirador.

1.55: Fire in town slackens.

2 p.m.: Marshal Beresford and Sir Thomas Graham come to the battery. Town seems again on fire near the right breach.

2.05: News of Sir Richard Fletcher's death!

2.15: Musketry from Mirador. Firing in town continues, but is decreasing. Gabions carrying into town from trenches. Enemy from back of rock fires at gun boats, but ineffectually. Our guns in the batteries cease firing by order. Our carronades, howitzers, and mortars fire on Mirador, castle, and upper defences. The firing lulls again.

2.30: Mirador gun fires.

2.48: Great fire and smoke in centre of town near the square. Very great change of weather; really cold within the last hour, some rain falling, sky very lowering. Two mines explode in the town. The enemy still hold a church and the left part of the town.

3 p.m. Mules with ammunition going from trenches to town. Three fires in the town. Between rain, and smoke, and black sky, it is very dark.

3.30: Great fire in the town; as dark as it is generally at half-past six. Nothing of the town to be seen from excessive smoke.

8 p.m.

The town is in flames. I am just returned from the battery. Dreadful night of thunder and rain.

Letter 81

Passages: Sept. 1, 7 a.m.

I wrote to you last night and sent my letter to Collier, to whom I had to forward a packet from Ellicombe (containing, as I believe, poor Sir Richard Fletcher's will) to go to England. I learn this morning that Sir Richard was not on horseback, but talking to General Oswald, when he received the fatal ball from a musket; it struck him in the spine of the neck. Burgoyne, (present General Sir John Burgoyne, G.C.B.), has taken the command of the engineers. He is himself wounded by a musket ball, which entered his mouth, coming out at the neck. We cannot get Sir Richard's loss from our minds; our trenches, our batteries, all remind us of one of the most amiable men I ever knew, and one of the most solid worth. No loss will be more deeply felt, no place more difficult to be filled up.

We yet know no particulars of our own loss in the assault, nor of the event of Soult's attack. Sir Thomas Graham went to the front last night, and has not returned. The night has been tempestuous; thunder, lightning, wind, and rain. Our trenches are up to one's horse's knees in water in the lower parts. I have this moment returned from the batteries, where we are putting things a little to rights. The enemy has lost the entire town, but fires with angry animation from his upper defences. He also rolls shells into the unhappy town, already on fire in several places.

All that unavoidably follows an assault is going on,—the burial of the fallen, and, I fear, the pillage of the unfortunate inhabitants. I have not yet been into the town. I have no desire to witness human misery, and indeed my duty at the batteries on this side is sufficient to occupy me. The breaches have proved more difficult (as I now believe) than I had apprehended, since in many places it was necessary to apply scaling ladders in the inside to get down from the breach into the town; but I yet talk from report; I shall soon be able to judge from observation.

A new operation against the castle now becomes necessary. Rey will of course defend it with the same judgment and gallantry he has hitherto shown. The mine on the retaining wall near the entrance to our trenches was well arranged and intended by the enemy, but it burst one moment too late, providentially for our people. Tell Moor he will find the precise spot of this mine by prolonging the right face of the bastion of the horn-work as you look from the town.

The curtain was originally ten or twelve feet above the demi-bastion. The curtain was much lowered by firing. So exact was the fire of our batteries that our shot, passing over the heads of our men, then lying on the demi-bastion, carried away the heads of the enemy, who fired from the ruins of the rampart of the curtain. Had the demi-bastion been mined, the assault would have totally failed, and I looked with trembling expectation for the explosion. How this was overlooked by Rey I know not. When I get hold of any of the French engineers, I shall ask them.

Our principal object now will be to seize the Mirador, and to cut off the enemy's supply of water, which he chiefly procures from a fountain at the back of the rock; exposed, as I hear, to the fire of our battery on the island. If so, the island will be of essential use. We are making up accounts of expenditure of ammunition. Our average whilst we had only three or four mortars in play, has been more than 8000 rounds per day. We had yesterday sixteen mortars playing; our total number of pieces sixty or sixty-two. Two or three more were rendered unserviceable by one casualty or another. I trust Soult has been repulsed. The Bidassoa must have swollen much during the night; if, therefore, he has not crossed in very considerable force, he may be in much difficulty. The French flag is again hoisted on the castle. It was struck at the beginning of the assault, no doubt as a signal to the French coast.

Half-past 2 p. m.

Marshal Beresford and Sir Thomas Graham have been here, and also the marquis. I have just returned from reconnoitring the upper defences, from battery No. 1, which you know is on the height, and is the point from which the views of St. Sebastian are taken. The town continues in flames; I believe our people too are plundering it. Multitudes of all sorts of people are to be seen with towels and sheets full of all sorts of things. I shall avoid going into the town until the plundering shall have ceased: indeed, I do not see how the town can avoid being (at least half of it) burnt down. I discover from battery No. 1, that a large convent to the right of the church with the spire, and having gardens enclosed with a high wall, which reach a good way up the hill towards the upper defences, is still in the enemy's possession. I have just reported this to Sir Thomas Graham.

Unless we are expeditious, this convent may cost us dear; yet no one thinks so. It is arranged that the attack shall go on from the other side, that we shall batter down the Mirador, &c. &c.; all of which I will not detail now. Soult was repulsed yesterday, but the affair, I believe, cost us 1000 men.

LETTER 82

Passages: Sept. 3, half-past 7 a.m.

Nothing very new; but I learn that the dispatches are not made up. There are difficulties in making out the numbers of killed and wounded. Ours are 1500, of whom half are killed!!

I have been in the town, and over that part of it which the flames or the enemy will permit to be visited. The scene is dreadful: no words can convey half the horrors which strike the eye at every step. Nothing, I think, can prevent the almost total destruction of the unhappy town. Heaps of dead in every corner; English, French, and Portuguese, lying wounded on each other; with such resolution did one side attack and the other defend. The enemy holds the convent of which I spoke in my last, and from it pours certain destruction on any who approach particular spots under its fire. When a man falls, we are obliged to send the French prisoners to drag away the body, and they, poor fellows, manifest a reluctance in performing the dangerous duty. This convent must be carried, and soon; there is no alternative, it must not be suffered to remain in the enemy's hands.

The town is not plundered, it is sacked. Rapine has done her work, nothing is left. Women have been shot whilst opening their doors to admit our merciless soldiery, who were the first night so drunk, that I am assured the enemy might have retaken part, if not the whole town. The inhabitants who have come out look pale and squalid; many women, but I think few children. I had occasion, in going to General Hay, to go into several houses: some had been elegantly furnished. All was ruin; rich hangings, women's apparel, children's clothes, all scattered in utter confusion.

The very few inhabitants I saw, said nothing. They were fixed in stupid horror, and seemed to gaze with indifference at all around them, hardly moving when the crash of a falling house made our men run away. The hospitals present a shocking sight: friends and enemies lying together, all equally neglected. Many assured me they had never been seen by any medical man, and all agreed they had tasted nothing since they were brought in. This I afterwards found to be generally true, and nearly unavoidable; but on mentioning the matter to General Hay, I learned that steps had been taken for the due care of the sick.

I went on with Colonel Dickson: our first object was to reconnoitre the breaches, and to discover, and concert with the engineers, the proper spot for the erection of batteries against the Mirador and upper defences. We agreed with Burgoyne that the batteries should be made in the ditch of the curtain; the curtain itself we found too narrow for our purpose. In examining the works from within, the effects of our own guns were most striking, not above one or two of the enemy's guns remaining mounted, and all repeatedly struck and ruined by our shot; most had their muzzles carried away.

In the demi-bastion lay dismounted an English 5½-inch howitzer (No. 388). One was taken, I have heard, at Albuera. In ascending the breach, the descent into the town looked tremendous: three joints of scaling ladders (the joints are of six feet each) were then fixed against the descent, and did not reach the top. Many of our poor fellows lay dead on the roofs of the adjoining houses; the roofs seemed almost to have fallen in with the number of the dead. Below the descent of the centre of the breach was an excavation, and at some feet further back, a barricade, so that men descending found themselves, as it were, in a kind of pound.

It would have been unavailing to have descended till the flanking fire from the crest of the right round tower took the enemy on the curtain in reverse. In standing on the ruins of this tower, and looking about attentively at all around, and the flames of the burning houses at ten yards' distance, we discovered at our feet the *saucisson* (as it is called), or train of powder to fire a mine. Henry Blachley, who was with us (for he and Charles Gordon had followed us,) cut the train with his knife, and we scrambled on to the right breach of all. In a barricade between this breach and the right tower, the unfortunate enemy seems to have had no retreat. His men lay there heaped on each other. In the horn-work and low communication across the ditch, the defences of which and those of the cavalier we had not attacked till the morning of the assault, we could not but remark that the French artillerymen lay dead by their guns.

The square of the town is small, but very handsome: there is a fine *piazza*. The houses are of four stories, with handsome balconies: at the west end stands (or at least stood last night) the town house. The north side was in flames when I left it; and before Gordon left the town, and returned to dinner, had fallen down. I spoke to several prisoners, generally good-looking and good-humoured fellows; they had always, they said, been well fed with salt meat, had plenty of water, and soft bread, by which they meant to explain they had never been reduced to eating biscuit. One who was in the hospital slightly wounded, and attending the rest, seemed more than usually intelligent. He said that the garrison originally was of 3800 men.

On my expressing surprise, and seeming to doubt, he replied, "You may rest assured that I speak the truth, and that I know the number and strength of the regiments."

"How many are now in the castle?" said I.

"There are," he answered, "nearly as follows:—

" 22nd Regiment of the Line	350
72nd ,,	200
1st ,,	400
Chasseurs des Montagnes [1]	200
34th Regiment of the Line	300
Artillery	200
Sappers	50
Miners	20
Pioneers	40
	1760 "

[1] Raised in Gascony about four years ago.

Nevertheless, I doubt the fact. We know from General Key's secretary, who has been taken prisoner, that on a muster on the morning of the assault, there were, exclusive of servants and sick, 2004 effective bayonets. This secretary confirms the report that we have repeatedly heard, that General Key is by no means disinclined to surrender: all the prisoners concur in this, and that another officer,—some say the chief of the staff, and others, the chief of the artillery,—alone prevents it. Our prisoners all say they have been treated remarkably well; the wounded, too, have been taken good care of. Jones, (present General Sir Harry Jones, K.C.B.), of the engineers, after all, is still in the castle. We now hear, and it is believed, that all the officers who were taken in the former unsuccessful assault, were to have been sent to France on the night of the day on which the island was taken. At this moment, a false report that the castle had hoisted the white flag, sent us to the top of the house. The fact is, the French flag still flies on the castle, but a flag of truce has just been sent into the Mirador. We yesterday visited the arsenal of the artillery: very few guns, fewer carriages; quantities of small arms in utter confusion, and an old red coach!

As you leave the arsenal gate, where there is a sentinel, you find yourself suddenly under the Mirador battery. I had stopped a moment in the surprise of suddenly looking two or three of the enemy in the face, when one of them laughed and pulled off his hat, which salute I returned, and not trusting too much to the continued attention of the gentry against whom I had not more than an hour before been sending directions to fire, walked back again. We paid a second visit to the corner of the town, under the fire from the convent of St. Therese, where a mine is preparing, about the immediate success of which we are anxious, and then came home. General Hay's *aide-de-camp*, with whom I spoke, in a little while afterwards incautiously exposing himself, was killed. He had peeped round the corner, and stood on some steps to no manner of purpose, and fell the certain victim. In the midst of all these scenes of horror, are the most striking and whimsical contrasts.

The people of St. Sebastian are robbed and plundered; those of Ernani and Passages come with smiling faces, and purchase their neighbours' goods. Soldiers, sailors, and muleteers are to be seen dressed in women's clothes, and with every remnant of tawdry finery. How all these things are brought out is surprising. Sentries are placed at all outlets, and the plunderers forced to lay down their ill-gotten spoils; but all that can be carried about the person undiscovered, of course escapes.

In the avenue leading to the batteries, two nights ago, a regular plundering party stopped, after dark, all who passed. Gordon, who had sent his servant for his dinner, wisely sent two soldiers to guard the man on his return. The master of a transport, who had taken a walk, "good, easy man," to look about him, complained to Parker that he had been robbed of his coat, his shoes and stockings, and his money.

"What shall I do?" said the disconsolate man.

"Why," said Parker, "if you wish to keep your shirt, you had better return to your ship."

Tonight, we are to begin to draw our guns through the river Urumea. It must be done after dark, to avoid the enemy's fire, and is only practicable at low water (if then).

Imagining that the enemy, in the confusion of a general fire, might not know how many mortars we had, we fired several salvos of shells after dark last night: this was a prelude to the flag of truce to be sent in the morning, but I do not imagine he will surrender a post yet capable of a strong and protracted defence. His bravery hitherto authorises the opinion that he will defend it to the last.

One hears with regret that the enemy received almost regularly supplies of powder and stores by sea. I fear this has been the case, but shall be particular in my inquiries by and by on the subject. All is quiet in front, where we have had no loss for a day or two, except that of Mr. Larpent, the judge-advocate-general, who having (as I hope) a clearer knowledge of law than of military positions, wandered into the enemy's lines on the 31st, having mistaken them for ours. He timed his mistake well: law is silent here.

P.S.—I find I have made two mistakes in my letter relative to the assault:—

First.—The advanced battery of the left attack really did fire during the assault, and was of essential use; being on the opposite side of the Urumea, and not under my immediate direction, its fire had escaped me. It consisted of three guns, the fourth having been disabled by the enemy's fire. Captain Power, (present Lieut.-General George Power, C. B.), commanded in it.

Second.—The enemy's mine, which threw down the retaining wall of the glacis, did more mischief than I had supposed. In passing yesterday, I reckoned seventeen bodies, of which parts were visible; these were of men, whom the falling of the wall had crushed.

Sept. 3, quarter-past 11 a.m.

All firing has ceased by order. Sir Thomas Graham sends word that another message is expected to be sent into the town in the course of the day. Dickson has gone into the town to meet Sir Thomas.

Letter 83

Sept. 4, 5 a.m.

I sit down more dirty, and as wet as ever I was in my life, having for the last two hours been wading through the Urumea. What with lazy folks and sleepy ones, tired working parties, and worn-out bullocks, we have got over only two carriages and one gun. We were obliged to discontinue our fun when the day broke, the battery of the King of Rome staring us in the face. The unhappy town continues in flames, which no one could extinguish, even if the experiment were made; which it neither is, nor will be.

The continuance of the siege of the castle was communicated to Dickson last night, in the following letter from Sir Thomas Graham;—

My dear Dickson,
I have received Rey's answer, and have written to say hostilities will recommence at nine this evening. Do not, however, do more than fire a few howitzers till the hours we agreed upon for our salvos, which you may direct to be continued at least three times on each occasion, making about nine in all during the night. I send to tell Hartman and the engineers.
       Ever yours,
                  Thomas Graham.

A subsequent note, received during the night, mentioned Rey's expression, that his men "have sworn to defend their post to the last extremity." This is always said, and really means nothing.

                            Sept. 4.

Hundreds passed and repassed the Urumea yesterday: avarice swallowed all other considerations. Had even the enemy's fire continued, it had been disregarded. He made overtures relative to prisoners, but in reality, to sound our terms; but I suppose they were a little less easy than he expected, for he rejected them; and, in the true Gasconade style, has sworn "to defend his post to the last." All this is mere expression, and we are going to work again.

The town continues in flames. Nothing can be more magnificently awful than the conflagration after dark; our salvos of shells adding to the horrors of the scene.

All the wounded and dying are removing from the church, hitherto our hospital, which the flames are beginning to reach. I should have been well pleased to have been spared this third siege, for so the operations against the castle of St. Sebastian may be called; not but that I applaud Rey, and also shall do our own fellows if they beat him out quickly; there is room for genius on both sides.

I have the pleasure to say we have got the convent of Santa Theresa;

this was a thorn in our side. The whole town is now ours, and will very soon be nobody's: it is utterly sacked, and wholly on fire; I do not believe one single building will be saved. The troops are retiring to the ramparts, the flames driving them from their more advanced stations. The harbour of St. Sebastian affords little shelter except for small craft, which can run alongside the mole. I do not imagine that vessels of above six or eight feet water can run in; but the mole is hitherto forbidden ground, or at least neutral: both sides command it.

I *did* mean "want of gallantry" at the *first* assault of St. Sebastian. Some deny this now, since the defences have been really made formidable; but they were much less so at that time.

Moreover, our fellows took it for granted they were all to be killed, and turned tail without looking at the reality of the danger, which, as usual, the cowardly magnified. But all this should be forgotten, since the tarnished laurels have had all stains wiped away in the late really bold assault.

Twelve hundred volunteers were ordered (as I have already mentioned) for the assault. The terms used in communicating the orders on this subject were singular and animating:

> Men were wanted to volunteer, such as knew how to show other troops the way to mount a breach.

On communicating this order to the fourth division, which had to furnish 400 men, the whole division moved forward. While this spirit shall remain, what may not troops perform? Yet as the really brave always fall in a day of open assault, our late loss is in truth a severe one. It was impossible to look at the dead in the breach without admiration of the brave men who had fallen. Their wounds all in the front; and filling, when dead, the places they filled whilst living. Purcell will recollect a better version of the idea in *Catiline's Conspiracy*.

★★★★★★

> John Purcell Fitz Gerald, Esq., of Bredfield House, at whose hospitable mansion the officers of the Artillery at Woodbridge were always welcome guests.

★★★★★★

But I must not wander into Sallust, but come back to plain matter of fact.

We have sent home again for another proportion of battering ordnance, and three more proportions of ammunition. Our proportions are:—

                14 guns, 24-pounders.
                4 68 lb. carronades.
                6 8-inch howitzers.
                4 10-inch mortars.
                ─
                28
                ─

                1500 rounds for guns.
                1000 rounds for howitzers.
                800 rounds for mortars.

Soult is manoeuvring in our front. Letters received last night mention that Lord William Bentinck has fallen back, and is awaiting Suchet in position. This may be true.

Our ordnance requires reform. I send you a drawing of the vents (by no means the worst cases) of some of our guns. In the desire to avoid bursting, I fear we have made our iron too soft. They sent us, too, wretched shells. Nearly half burst (I speak of the eight-inch) in leaving the howitzers. I believe the last proportion were picked off the ramparts of Portsmouth.

I was called up last night by Sir George Collier, with the news that Austria had declared against France, and that an action had been fought, and twelve pieces of artillery taken. *Apropos: the British Artillery have never lost a single piece of artillery in the Peninsular War.* The Portuguese have occasionally.

                    Sept. 5, quarter-past 5 a.m.

Just returned from the river. Our guns are all over: that is, fifteen. We do not intend taking more. Our men have worked famously. Blachley has literally been in the water all night, where, to be sure, neither he, nor those with him, were a whit wetter than those who were on shore, for it has rained incessantly. Messieurs the enemy are very civil; though in broad daylight, and in the clear view of their batteries, they did not fire a single shot. This was generous enough; had they fired, a confused multitude of six or seven hundred men, and seventy or eighty pairs of bullocks, pulling heavy loads, might have suffered severely.

The morning's occupation will be to determine upon a convenient road to our new batteries from the spot under some ruined houses where we have left the guns. I must revisit the town today, otherwise I should have willingly avoided it. How different from what I first saw it! rich, beautiful, and flourishing; now a scene of ruin and desolation. The remnant still burns in despite of the rain: and the flames, I imagine, will only cease with the houses which feed them.

Half-past 8, a.m.

My constant wish to return home has not suffered any diminution. Be assured that when honour and the trust committed to my charge will permit me, I shall do so. But many things remain yet to be done; nor does the war seem to be drawing to a conclusion. The late marks of honour and of favour I have met with, doubly tie me to the service of my country. I see, however, no reason to distrust my being enabled to return after the campaign, at least for a while. Be not alarmed; I have no idea that anything can or will detain me. I hope never to come but with honour. I mean not the romantic sense of a shadowy thing, but the solid principle of a conscientious discharge of the duties I owe to the country to which we have the happiness to belong.

If the same Providence which equally and in all places can protect, and has protected me, shall permit it, you will, as I hope, soon see me. From the mercies of the past I augur well of the future. I have, as you know, no favours to court, no complicated part to play; and am unconnected with any party, or any other feelings than those of earnest desire to serve my country. I have no tie beyond that country which can keep me here: but I trust never to desert her cause, nor to leave my station but with honour.

12 o'clock.

I have just been with Dickson across the Urumea again to look at the new batteries, and to arrange about getting guns into them to-night. We called upon General Hay, and found him in the house over the gateway as you enter at the guard house: he had been burnt out of his former one. The one in which we were two days ago, was also burnt. All is misery and ruin. We found in the streets a few peasants; they had white tape round their right arms, as a sign that they had leave to go in. They were prowling about to see what they could find. We entered a house close under the ramparts near the Plaza Vieja, (or old place,) where there is a little space across which the flames had not reached, but the rapacity of man had reached it, and we found nothing but a wretched starved cat, and the remnants of furniture.

Fires are kindling on the breaches to consume those of the dead who yet remain unburied. The smell from the mines and other pits into which the heaps have been thrown, and but slightly covered over, is most offensive, tainting the air around. We saw one respectable man and his daughter, a fine-looking girl of twenty; they were looking at the remains of what had been a good house; they made no complaints, and we pulled off our hats as we passed them. We were glad to leave this wretched place; the occasional crash of falling houses alone disturbs the silence which now reigns, where but a few days ago all was noise and confusion.

A very small part of the town yet remains unhurt, but that part is under the enemy's fire, and of course we kept from it. The King of Rome's Battery fired a shot or two, but ill-directed. We are firing occasional shells, but shall not open in earnest until the 8th. Tonight, after dark, we shall begin to place our guns in battery, but the batteries are yet unfinished, and we have our magazines, &c. to remove.

The terms which Rey wanted for the garrison of the castle were fifteen days' suspension of hostilities, to see if Soult would relieve the castle, and then a free passage into France for the garrison. Quite inadmissible. Soult had communicated to the garrison that he would deblockade St. Sebastian on the 1st of August. This hope probably increased the vigour of the defence. I hear unexpectedly of the sailing of a frigate with Sir Thomas Picton, who is ill. *Adieu.*—We begin again on the 8th. All is well. No news of or from Pampeluna. All quiet in front.

I have to lament another old acquaintance in a cousin of Sir Howard Douglas's—Captain Douglas of the 51st. He fell the victim of his humanity in endeavouring to save a wounded soldier of his company. Poor Fletcher! what will now his sister say? What will his children feel? Here, too, Fletcher has many, very many, to regret his loss; it is indeed one which we cannot forget. His funeral was over before I was aware of it or could attend, as all the engineer officers did who were on the spot. No man has fallen in the Peninsular War more regretted, and more justly regretted, than Fletcher: none whom the country has more cause to lament.

I saw this morning Reid of the Engineers, (present Sir William Reid, K.C.B., late Governor of Malta); he has recovered from his wound surprisingly soon. He joined previous to the late assault, but Fletcher, knowing Reid's gallantry, and doubting his strength, took that care of him which zeal made him forget for himself, and would not permit him to accompany the storming party.

Letter 84

Passages: Sept. 7.

We made a very good evening's work yesterday, and were home and in bed by 11, after placing seventeen guns in battery on the hornwork. Sir Thomas Graham, whom I saw in the morning, wanted me to dine with him, but I excused myself, expecting we should have found our evening's task less easy than it has proved. I must find out today about a poor little child, who, Sir Thomas Graham mentioned yesterday, had been seen in a house not safe to approach, in the town, where the poor little thing (of 3 or 4 years) was supposed to have been without food for two or three days. General Oswald, who was sitting by, said he had heard of it, and had offered any man five guineas who would rescue the child. This, during the flag of truce then flying, would be easy, and one of the general's staffs-officers, with whose name I am unacquainted, left the room to see what could be done.

The loss of poor Woodyear, (Captain Lumley Woodyear, of the Royal Artillery, killed on the 31st), has affected us all, though, in these turbulent times, the finer feelings, if not quite lost, are so blunted that they are seldom called forth. The horrid sights always before our eyes make almost all callous; this, after all, is perhaps a greater evil than any other produced by war. We are going to make the necessary details for the batteries, after which we shall visit them all.—*Adieu*.

Sept. 7, 1 p.m.

All arrangements are made. The men on the left bank of the river take the batteries one day; those on the right, the other. In consequence, Colonel Hartman commences tomorrow.

5 p.m.

I have been applied to to be second in a duel, and have peremptorily refused; nay, more, shall prevent the meeting at all hazards. Fine time this for fighting amongst ourselves, when we are all wanted to fight against the enemy! I hate duelling, nay, hold it in utter abhorrence, as a highly sinful, unjustifiable, and, to talk more lightly, foolish and ridiculous mode of ascertaining the justice of any cause, or making reparation for any offence. I am at this moment a little perplexed: a blow has been given, and that publicly; but I trust some mode may be found of arranging this most unpleasant affair. We have been laying four or five heads together in the hope of settling it, and shall meet here at breakfast tomorrow morning early for the purpose.

Sept. 8, 5 a.m.

I was called up about two hours ago by a note from one of the parties in the unfortunate occurrence I alluded to last night. What a time for squabbling! yet what is war but quarrelling on a larger and more murderous scale? But a truce to all this: in a little we shall open on the castle. This occupation will employ all squabblers, and many others whom I trust are not so.

I believe changes are at hand; but we are to be silent. Even the almost nothing which has been hinted to me, has been imparted under the expectation, if not injunction, of secrecy. I despise all their secrecies: yet they make half the importance, and sometimes more than half the employment, of folks in office.

8 p.m.

St. Sebastian has surrendered: that is, the castle. We opened our fire at 10 a.m., at 12 the white flag was shown at the Mirador. The articles are signed. The garrison, about 1750 strong, of whom 1250 are effective, will lay down its arms at the great gate at 12 tomorrow. They will be embarked at Passages, and be conveyed to England as prisoners of war. We had about 60 pieces in play today. Except a few rounds of grape, the enemy did not fire a shot.

Delancey, Bouverie, and Dickson, were the officers on our side; they met Songeon, chief of the staff, and Brion, commandant of artillery. Rey, on displaying the white flag, said he would send officers to confer on terms: Sir Thomas Graham replied that he had no others to offer than those he had already named; that of the garrison laying down its arms, and being prisoners of war. The garrison has lost 2400 men during the siege.

Sept. 9, 7 a. m.

It rains in torrents. The garrison have little cover but holes dug in the rock. I long to see the place. I shall look out for Rey and the staff, and introduce myself. We shall have a famous fag in undoing all we have been doing; embarking our guns, &c. I have written long letters home relative to our guns, &c.; there are some points requiring reform. The marquis arrived here just after the white flag was shown at the Mirador.

This was fortunate, as it prevented delay in referring to him.

10 a.m.

I have just had a friendly invitation from Sir Thomas Graham to dine with him. I hope to meet Rey there.—*Adieu.*

LETTER 85

Passages: Sept. 9.

We commenced firing at the Mirador, and upper defences of the castle of St. Sebastian at 10 a.m. yesterday: at 12, the white flag was suspended from the Mirador; firing ceased, and in the course of the day, articles of capitulation were signed. The garrison will lay down its arms at the great gate at 12 today, be embarked at Passages, and be conveyed to England as prisoners of war. We had almost 60 pieces in play, and found at first the Mirador so hard that our balls split on striking it. Nevertheless, we had peeled the wall, which was beginning to come down; we were breaching three points at once. I yet hope to send you a plan, having enticed my friend Theodore (Dickson's Portuguese adjutant) to copy one for you.

Rey's garrison is, as I hear, of 1750 men. This seems to tally with what I had before heard. The garrison was chiefly burrowed in holes in the rock, and suffered of course many privations. Our prisoners were sent from the castle last night. We are glad this siege is over. I think Rey should have held out longer in the castle, though he probably reflected that when taken, as it must have been by assault, few would be spared. I have written long letters home on the subject of the vents of our guns, and recommended their being bushed with fine copper as was done at Elvas, after the first unsuccessful siege of Badajos, when the Portuguese iron ordnance was ruined in a similar way.

There is much security against bursting in keeping the iron as soft as it now is. Possibly guns, when bushed, will be more valuable than before. We have nothing new from Pampeluna: its fall would be very opportune. I suspect Abbe means to blow down the works and attempt to escape. It rains in torrents: the summer seems to have passed, and we have now autumnal weather.

I am going, an hour hence, into the castle, having already, by Dickson's directions, sent thither competent officers to take account of the ordnance, &c., and to place the necessary sentries. The marquis was here yesterday, and is expected again today. Rey and his garrison are particularly anxious to be embarked at Passages, and to be under British protection; they fear the Spaniards, and with reason. We hear nothing of the Alicante Army.

Letter 86

Passages: Sept. 10, 7 a.m.

Soon after I left off writing to you yesterday, I set off with Dickson and Sir George Collier to see the garrison of St. Sebastian lay down its arms. We forded the Urumea on horseback, and found the British and Portuguese troops filing towards the town. The Portuguese were formed in the streets, the British on the ramparts. The day was fine, after a night of heavy rain. A little after 12, the French garrison marched out at the Mirador gate: General Rey at the head of his men, followed by Songeon (chief of the staff), and Colonel St. Ouary (commandant of the place); the remains of the French regiments following. The officers saluted General Oswald as they passed him; this was at the Plaza Vieja, near the great gate of the town. Many of the French soldiers wept bitterly: all looked sorrowful. The bands of two or three Portuguese regiments played occasionally; but altogether the scene was dismal. A few inhabitants were present, and only a few.

After some little delay, for the ruins of the place prevented the garrison from keeping any precise order, the French laid down their arms in silence. During this interval, after bowing to General Rey and Colonel Songeon, I went up to Colonel St. Ouary, of whom I had heard many good accounts from our officers who had been prisoners, and to all of whom he had been uniformly attentive. The colonel spoke good English, said he had been twice prisoner in England, that he had been 52 years in the service of France, and that on the 15th of this month he should have received his dismission (that is, his retirement from future service). He was 66 years of age, he said, and should never serve again: and that if he could be permitted to retire into France, instead of being sent to England, he should be the happiest man imaginable. I recommended his writing to Sir Thomas Graham on the subject.

At this moment, for the troops were still filing past, I recognised the face of the officer who had so gallantly come down the breach after the first assault to assist our wounded. I ran up to him, and offered him my services. I found his name was Loysel de Hametière, captain of the grenadiers of the 22nd regiment. He said:

There are the remains of the brave 22nd. We were, the other day, 250: not more than fifty now remain.

He was soon surrounded by many other officers, who came to express their admiration of his gallantry. While we were talking, Dickson came up, and I went with him to introduce myself to Colonel Brion, chief of artillery. We found him a plain, sensible man, and of very pleasing manners. Rey is a great fat man, not pleasing, at least in appearance; Songeon decidedly not. St. Ouary very gentlemanly. Colonel Brion wished to see our battery in the horn-work. I was at that moment firing a salute of twenty-one guns, in honour of the Spanish flag then hoisting at the castle. He expressed surprise at the facility with which we had thrown up the battery, and repeatedly said that the fire of the artillery during the siege had been admirable. In the interval, we had left Pascoe to assist in getting quarters for the artillery officers, and had left one or two of our gunners to guard their baggage.

On returning into the town, we took leave of Colonel Brion, and went to look at the castle and upper defences. We ascended by the Batterie du Gouverneur, which was that we had called the Battery of Theresa, and proceeded by the castle, descending by the Mirador. The batteries (those in the sea-line excepted) were utterly ruined; guns dismounted, and carriages broken; the castle utterly in ruins. In all nooks and corners, little wretched holes made as splinter proofs for the garrison to retire to. There were no barracks or any covering for the troops except these holes, many of which were full of water from the rain of the preceding night.

On viewing the batteries, our surprise that they had not fired ceased: the guns were generally unserviceable, and of those able to fire, the carriages were knocked to pieces. The French officers agreed that all the horses of the garrison had been eaten, and some of them spoke of this circumstance with much more disgust than seemed reasonable. By the time we returned into the town the prisoners were placed in a convent yet remaining, and the officers were lodged in the few houses, close under the castle, which had escaped the flames. It was now about 4, and we were leaving the town, when Colonel Delancey, from whom we had separated, returned, bringing an answer from Lord Wellington to Sir Thomas Graham, to Sir Thomas's letter relative to the articles of capitulation, of which his lordship approved; and Dickson and I returned to communicate to General Rey the approval of his lordship.

Among the articles was one, that an officer should be sent to the headquarters of Soult, to acquaint him with what had happened. In a prior conference, Songeon had adroitly wished his own name to be inserted as the officer to be sent to Soult. This, it was easy to observe, had given offence to Rey, to whose choice Lord Wellington referred the name of the officer to be sent.

In another point, too, Rey seemed quite chagrined; one of the articles expressed that a commissary, who had under his charge the widow and two daughters of his brother who had been killed (as lieutenant-colonel) at Pampeluna, should, if possible, not be sent to England, but be exchanged for some British officer of equal rank. To this the marquis acceded, giving the officer permission to remain at Passages till the one sent in exchange for him should arrive. Rey was angry that such an article should appear. Using an opprobrious and vulgar term he said:

What! such an article about women in the capitulation of such a garrison, and after such a defence.

We had previously called on Colonel St. Ouary, who accompanied us to Rey. We found the colonel sitting with the very ladies in question, and immediately told them of the permission their relative had received. They were most grateful, as they had a great horror of being sent to England. I spoke chiefly to the mother, who seemed young to have such daughters; the youngest was apparently fifteen. After leaving Rey, we galloped to Ernani, and dined with Sir Thomas Graham, who had not been well, and had been indoors all day. Marshal Beresford was to have dined there, but sent an excuse, being ill; he is going to Lisbon for change of air. If I can manage it, I will go today and pay my respects to him; but I have full employment, having the arrangements to make for the re-embarkation of the ordnance and stores, and the return to their stations of the several companies withdrawn from their brigades for the duties of the siege.

Jones of the Engineers is well; that is, recovering from his wound, which is through the right arm near the shoulder. Colonel St. Ouary had been most attentive to him. He says many of our own prisoners were killed by our fire, there being no shelter for them. All here seem to agree that, previous to the surrender of the castle, the siege had cost the enemy in killed and wounded (including some few deserters) 2400 men.

One thousand two hundred and thirty-four effectives laid down their arms yesterday. There were no eagles of course, nor any colours but the little flag of the castle, much such a one as you made me for the Sutton Batteries. Besides the effectives, there were about 600 non-combatants, of whom 272 were severely wounded. The rest were disabled from former wounds not healed, or were old and worn-out men.

Soult is now moving. Dickson has gone to headquarters to see the marquis. I have a host of folk below stairs, waiting for orders about bullocks, cars. &c.; besides, the *Freya* has arrived, as I hear, and our horse artillerymen of course: they will be very acceptable. Tell Moor the *Beagle* sloop of war is ordered into the harbour of St. Sebastian. This is an experiment to see how the harbour will suit for small vessels of war. They must, I believe, be moored stem and stern, but I will learn all this and let Moor know. We are going to work on the breaches directly,—destroying one day, building up the next!!

By-the-by, I asked Colonel Brion after some old acquaintances in the French artillery. Navalet, whom I knew as colonel of horse artillery at Strasburg, is dead. He died as general in Poland. He died suddenly, Brion says, after passing the day with him. Moray, who gave me the picture of the lady which used to be in our rooms, is colonel, and is at Bayonne, where he is commandant of artillery; if so, we may renew acquaintance.—*Adieu*.

Ninety-three pieces of artillery taken in St. Sebastian, of which:
    56 in Town.
    37 in Castle and upper defences.

Total   93

Letter 87

Passages: Sept. 12, 6 a.m.

We are going to place thirty-five of our English guns in St. Sebastian, and to repair the breaches. I have not yet seen Burgoyne, to learn whether any alteration will take place in the form of the works. Major Dyer, of our corps, will be placed there to manage our department. The garrison of St. Sebastian marched by my window yesterday afternoon to embark at Passages. Rey and Songeon are at variance. Without knowing the merits of the case, I should be inclined to suppose Rey in the right. Songeon said openly yesterday that he should be disposed to shoot Rey on their passage to England. However, they go in different ships, so that their shooting will be distant.

I am glad to learn that Sir Thomas Graham has written to the marquis in favour of St. Ouary; I hope the old man may be permitted to retire unmolested to France. Dickson mentioned at Lord Wellington's table what I had told him of the gallantry of Loysel of the 22nd French infantry, and of his attention to our wounded at the first assault. Lord Wellington said he was a fine fellow, and that he would send him to France. Unluckily, Dickson did not recollect his name, which no one knew: but I hope the thing will not be forgotten. I shall try today to see St. Ouary, if not embarked and in the offing, which I fear he is. Marshal Beresford has embarked in the *Challenger* sloop of war for Lisbon. I am vexed I did not see him before he embarked.— *Adieu* for the moment.

Sept. 12, 10 p.m.

I ranged again today over the ruins of St. Sebastian, to determine what guns we should leave there. Miserable and shocking remnants of human bodies yet remain; those of women as well as men. In spite of all the burials and burnings, the air is tainted. The rain now falls in torrents, and the season is evidently changed. In a few days I shall return to headquarters. Our batteries have already vanished, the natives pulled them down for the sake of the fascines for fuel, and we are filling up the trenches. There are twelve or fourteen feet water, at high water, along the mole of St. Sebastian.

The *Beagle* is in the harbour, where at low water there are twenty-five feet water. Captain Smith, of the *Beagle*, says there is room for three or four similar vessels, but they must be moored stem and stern. There is a regular land and sea breeze on this coast except in stormy weather, so that vessels may leave the harbour almost optionally. Goldfinch of the Engineers writes that Pampeluna will hold out till the middle of October. I know not on what his calculations are founded.

Letter 88

Passages: Sept. 15.

No news. The enemy is understood to be cooking ten days' provisions, and we are about to do the same, or nearly so. All this looks like movements, but what the marquis's plans are we do not know. Much will obviously depend on the fall of Pampeluna; of the probable time of this we are yet ignorant, or, at least, know nothing new. Dickson is going to headquarters. I remain to rummage together and embark odds and ends. All this goes on a little slowly since we have lost our men on the one hand, and our bullocks on the other. I shall ride to Oyarzun to call on Sir Thomas Graham, who is most attentive, most friendly, and entitled to all the respect I can show him.

Letter 89

Passages: Sept. 19, 7 a.m.

I write for a quarter of an hour before I sally forth to superintend the work at the wharfs. We get on but slowly from the want of bullocks and boats; besides we have now neap tides, which are little favourable. I hope a couple of days more will suffice: I shall be glad to rejoin headquarters in case of a move. Today, I suppose I shall pass as yesterday, riding from one wharf to another, then on board ship, then to St. Sebastian, where Dyer is busy in getting things in something like order. He has succeeded in some measure, and the wretched place is less offensive, but yet bad enough.

After rummaging yesterday over one of the magazines, we went under that of the Cavalier (the name of a work about the middle of the town front, and higher than the rest), where we visited, by the light of a candle, the theatre of the place, a little dark misery of a place without any possibility of a window, and hardly possessing airholes enough to make it wholesome. The theatre was painted prettily enough. On the hill yesterday I visited the bakery, which is a kind of natural cavern in the back of the rock. There are three large ovens. One of our shells had found its way down the flue of the chimney, which it destroyed on bursting, but without doing further damage.

6 p.m.

I have spent this morning like other ones. Tonight, we begin again to work at 9, when the tide will be up, and allow of our boats coming to both wharfs. I hope much will be done to night. With some difficulty I have secured twenty large boats, which will carry off a good deal.

I had two days since a most flattering reception from the officers of the three troops of horse artillery, who invited me to a very elegant dinner given at La Sarte, where Webber Smith's troop is. We sat down seventeen, and had a very pleasant day. I was obliged to leave them rather early, having two leagues to ride home in the dark, and to ford the Urumea. Nothing can be more flattering than the honour paid me by my brother officers, whose conduct was very marked towards me. I was almost sick today going to the island, there was so much surf. I assure you I was still nearer being kissed by some boat-ladies on the quay at St. Sebastian, for interesting myself about their getting their boats back to Passages, where I had first the honour to form their acquaintance.

Our men are becoming sickly, especially those who have been employed during the siege, when their labours were occasionally both laborious and incessant. I felt a little jaded myself, but am quite well again.

LETTER 90

Passages: Sept. 25.

I must say three words of the passing news before I close my letter. The allied (more properly Portuguese) garrison has quitted St. Sebastian, and a Spanish one has arrived, or rather is arriving: for their troops straggle in, as it were, by a kind of accident. We leave there a company of British artillery and another of Portuguese, or rather a confused jumble of remnants, amounting to about two companies. All the ordnance and stores intended to be re-embarked have been put on board, and all arrangements are made. Headquarters remain at Lesaca, where, on the 27th instant (the anniversary of Busaco), Lord Dalhousie, with Generals Packenham, Murray, and, I hope, Stewart, will be installed as extra Knights of the Bath. I shall accordingly go to headquarters on that day or the 28th.

The roads have been reconnoitred, and the points determined on for our pontoon bridge over the Bidassoa; all, however, remains quiet in front. Near Irun, the enemy has two brigades covered by two divisions.

Soult, as I have already mentioned, is understood to have quitted his army, now under the command of Count Gazan. Gazan is esteemed by his own people, and commanded the three last divisions with whom we had to contest the valley of Bastan after the Vitoria affair. How Soult has gone, whether in disgust, or that he has been recalled, we do not hear.

Of Lord William Bentinck we hear nothing; that is, being absent from headquarters, I do not hear the common news of the day. We are forming depots, or something like them, of prisoners near Pampeluna, ready to pop them into the place when it shall have surrendered. I can hardly yet think a very general movement can take place till this event. I hope soon to have good news for you. We are yet without any very distinct account of what is going on in the north of Europe, though we hope for the best. What torrents of blood are now flowing all over the world!—*Adieu.*

Letter 91

Passages: Sept. 26.

We are quiet here, but it is the prelude to the reverse. We are about to advance; I hardly know the precise direction. I have before me a sketch of our positions from Roncesvalles on the right, to St. Sebastian on the left. I shall try and copy it for you before next mail.

Sept. 29.

I go tomorrow, *via* La Sarte, Zubieta, and Adoin, towards headquarters. This is a sad round, but I wish to inspect Ross's, Ramsay's, and Smith's troops again. The movement of the army will take place on Saturday, so that I dare say the mail which carries this will also carry intelligence of the result of the movement. Sir Thomas Graham is, I believe, going home, and Sir John Hope coming out to relieve him.

All this, though little known here, is probably no secret at home. I shall quit Passages, and the house in which I write, with regret. There is a good-humoured sentence about this kind of feeling in Pope's Letters, in which he says:

> One would hardly wish to have the old posts pulled up which one recollects as a child.

Adieu. I fear I shall not be able to write more to you today.

Letter 92

Village near Oyarzun: Sept. 30, 8 p. m.

I left Passages this morning with regret. Tomorrow I shall continue my route for Lesaca, paying a visit to, and taking my leave of. Sir Thomas Graham, by the way. I have ever received the most friendly and most flattering attentions from him. We sent the servants straight here, and found all ready for our reception. On our arrival tomorrow, we shall separate from Charles Gordon, to the regret of all. He is a fine fellow, and has done me a hundred good turns. The house in which I now write will be his quarter. I shall send you a sketch of this part of the country which he has copied for me. I will continue my letter tomorrow.

Oct. 1, 7 a.m.

The servants are now packing up, and I wish to have my letters ready, as we were told the army would move on Saturday, which is tomorrow, but I doubt the fact. Something detains us, though we know not what it is. Our news from England is favourable as to the state of affairs in the north, though nothing very certain seems to be mentioned in any papers which I have seen. Private letters received here from Bayonne and other places in France all agree that the French Army has been worsted, and all mention a report that Bonaparte has been wounded. It is certain that though despatches are received at the French headquarters every day, a silence has lately been observed as to their contents. This, at least, seems to admit that the enemy has no news favourable to himself to communicate.

Lesaca: Oct. 2, 8 a m.

I am in the same house in which I wrote yesterday. The marquis is gone to Roncesvalles, but is expected tonight or tomorrow. I sometimes suspect that orders from home control our entering France; but this is mere unauthorised speculation. The fall of Pampeluna is no doubt anxiously looked for, though little is yet known, and deserters,

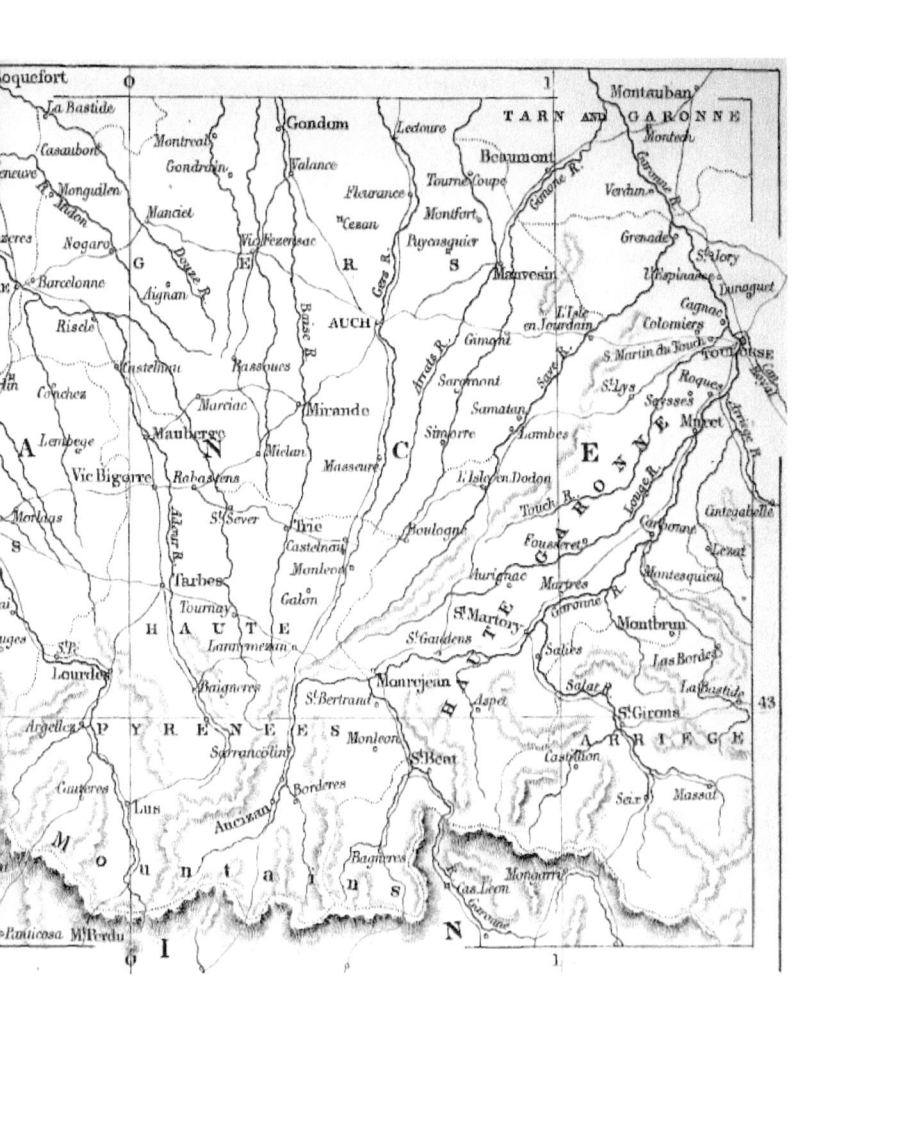

a few days since, from that garrison, do not describe the troops as in any degree suffering from want.

Oct. 3, half-past 8 a. m.

It is a close, rainy day. Lesaca stands in a little valley of 200 or 300 yards wide, with a little stream running through it into the Bidassoa, distant about a mile. The Bidassoa is thirty or forty yards wide, running rapidly through a rocky channel, and very subject to sudden rises from rain. We rode yesterday over the bridge near Lesaca, to Vera or Bera, near which the line of our position crosses the Bidassoa. At the bridge of Vera, the enemy lost 1000 men on the day of the assault of St. Sebastian. The river having risen after they had crossed by a ford, and had been repulsed, they were obliged to retire by this bridge, not wide enough for more than three or four to pass abreast, while some of our troops poured a continual fire on the bridge from the walls of a neighbouring convent.

Had we been able to have spared a sufficient force to this point, a very considerable part of Soult's army might have been taken. It is curious to see two opposing armies quietly looking at each other from the mountains; each butted in a rude manner on the projecting points. Nothing more convinces me how little we really are than the contrast between the magnificent mountain scenery, and the diminutive appearance which we and our field-works make. With difficulty one discovers the little huts, and the less beings who inhabit them.—*Adieu* for the present.

Oct. 3, 3 p. m.

I called in my way on Sir Thomas Graham at Oyarzun, and heard the good news of Blücher's victory, as mentioned in the *Courier* of the 21st September. I trust it will prove true. It is not doubted, save by some few, who having been often deceived have become suspicious. Poor Moreau! I believe him to have been an excellent man. When I was in Germany, the picture of Moreau was to be found in all the peasants' houses where his army had been. He was then the only French general abstaining from plunder himself, not admitting it in others, and carrying on war without forgetting humanity. Perhaps I am wrong in saying *the only*, but he certainly was one; and his conduct was a marked exception to the general system of rapine, then, as now, usual in the armies of France.

The marquis is gone towards the right, and will not return until tomorrow night. All idea of immediate movement seems to be given up. I believe I told you Soult had quitted his army. We now find he only left it to visit Bordeaux. He still commands in the front, and today is at St. Jean de Luz. There is hardly a breath of air stirring, of which all, who have been any time in this town, complain. There is a convent, or rather nunnery here, which has escaped the general fate of such institutions in this country. I have not yet seen it, but hear there are seventeen old ladies there. The valleys in these regions have iron foundries in them; they are frequent in all this part of Spain. Near Tolosa, the best gun-barrels in the Peninsula are said to be made. They are now scarce, though I saw lately at Oyarzun several very handsome ones, which had been presented to Sir Thomas Graham.

I rode yesterday to Vera, at which point our position crosses the Bidassoa. We found yesterday, what I have before seen though it still seems strange, a considerable part of a Spanish corps in French clothing; one cannot divest oneself for the moment of an idea that one has changed sides.

These Spaniards were generally good-looking fellows. They certainly behaved well in the late affair, and we are willing to hope it may prove the Busaco of Spain: that it may confirm the Spaniards, and teach them to stand boldly and bravely against the French. Not that the Spaniards have been wanting in bravery, but without officers, without a government, without an object, as it were, to fight for, can we wonder that they have frequently betrayed a want of confidence in themselves? When I say without an object, I am wrong: for they have the noblest which man can fight for,—Freedom;—yet the freedom they have is but a whimsical one.—*Adieu.* I am called away.

Letter 93

Lesaca: Oct. 4.

I wandered this morning into the mountains. The mountain I selected is abrupt and crowned with rocks. The view from it is noble:—Fuenterabia, the sea, the mouth of the Bidassoa, the river itself occasionally seen for a moment as it rambles through the rocky channel, Lesaca, Vera, and Echallar under one's feet, with the tents and huts of the contending armies, diminished to little specks, hardly visible. The quiet solitude of the place left room for reflections favourable to anything rather than war.

Oct. 6, 9 a.m.

I hardly know where my letter last night left off, but I believe I have not told you that the day before yesterday we revisited Vera, and turning to the right ascended the mountains, and reached the craggy top of a summit overlooking the Pass of Vera, and that of Echallar. From this point we looked down upon St. Jean de Luz, Bayonne, and all the little towns and villages of France, as far as the eye could reach. Beneath our feet were the French piquets. Many battalions under arms: some at drill, others in little squads: some adding to fieldworks, others throwing up entrenchments. Some of the enemy on an opposite rock contemplating, like ourselves, the noble scene around. The country below us had ranges of mountains, as at any other time we should have called them; comparatively to our Pyrenees they could but be called hills. The country, however, looked, and I dare say we shall find it, hilly as far as the River Adour, on which Bayonne stands. We lingered on this enchanting spot till the day began to close, and then rode home fast to dine with. Colonel May. It was quite dark before we arrived there.

At dinner, amongst others, was Mr. Larpent, the Judge-Advocate-General, who had so lately been exchanged. He had been, he told us, at Mont de Marsan, which I think is the principal town of the department of Landes. He had in the first instance passed through St. Jean de Luz to Bayonne, where he had been ten days. He described the country all the way to Mont de Marsan (which is half-way to Bordeaux) as sandy and barren. The people with whom he conversed spoke generally of peace,—of the desire, the great desire, they had for it,—but that they did not expect it. Many officers observed their emperor's ambition would ever prevent it.

Of course, none expressed any opinion of Bonaparte. He saw Soult, but in a room with many other generals, and did not know well which he was: but had much conversation with Count Gazan, who spoke much of the state of affairs in the north, and said he considered that the losses of the two sides there were pretty equal: that they were just where they were, with the exception that the French armies were now concentrated, which, in the event of another attack of the Allies and its failure, would give Bonaparte an opportunity of directing to any one point his whole force.

Mr. Larpent further learnt from Count Gazan, that Soult would readily enter into an exchange of prisoners, nay, that he would regularly and always exchange them, provided his officers were always restored to him direct. The count said:

When they are sent to England, and then to France, they get

into the hands of government, and *we* have no more to do with them.

This is worth observation, as implying a separate interest between the general government of France, and the particular army of which Soult is chief. The count continued:

As far as the Loire, we can command, beyond it we have no control.

At Mont de Marsan they are building a *prefect's* palace, and courts of justice, and a house for the commissary of war; all handsome buildings, to make way for which an old bridge and some houses have been pulled down. Generally, Mr. Larpent said, this and other towns through which he had passed looked thriving. Those with whom he had conversed said, the expected coming of the English was well enough, but all spoke with horror of the atrocities they expected to be committed by the Spaniards and Portuguese.

All said the peasantry would rise, and cut off all that they could. This is probable enough, since two days ago when the Portuguese surprised and took a French piquet, they were fired at by some peasantry, of whom fourteen were taken, and have already been marched to Passages to be embarked for England as prisoners of war. This may stop the ardour of the peasants, who seemed surprised when they understood they were considered as prisoners of war.

At Bayonne, Mr. Larpent says, there are 6000 troops at work. He was for a moment on the works, but not knowing anything of fortification, can give us no account of them; he was not afterwards permitted to look at them. Bayonne has been for some time declared to be in a state of siege; in consequence, all there is under martial law, and all houses within 1000 yards of the place have been pulled down. The enemy in general seemed ignorant of our position, and all believed that we had detached divisions to act against Suchet. In answer to my question whether the country through which he had passed seemed generally thriving, Mr. Larpent said, certainly: yet it might be accounted for by the great traffic it has had with Spain, being the direct route of all the forces which for some years had gone thither.

I took a long ride yesterday with Dickson and May. We set off at 7, and ascended the mountains called the Peña de Haya or Les Quatre Couronnes, of which I spoke in one of my last letters. We went by the village, or rather the chapel, of San Antonio, which is in a deep valley on the road leading from hence towards Oyarzun. We here turned to our right, passing an iron foundry, and gained by a rugged path, and with many stops to breathe our horses, part of the position on which the attack of the 31st of August had been made. Here we quitted our horses, and left our coats and hats, and set off in good earnest to clamber up the mountain, making many pauses by the way to take breath, and to gaze at the world beneath.

When we had reached halfway, a flock of wild geese passed over us, and at some distance some vultures, as if longing, yet afraid, to attack the geese. Above all, and soaring majestically, were three eagles. The day was yet undecided, and volumes of fog rolled amongst the valleys between the mountains, which looked like the monstrous billows of a raging sea suddenly arrested.

At length we reached the top, from which we had the double view of the valley of Oyarzun, the well-known St. Sebastian, the little sea of Passages, Fuenterabia, Irun, Andaya, Urogne, St. Jean de Luz, Socoa, Bayonne, and the numberless villages of the plain. A convoy of our own off St. Sebastian, with the commodore firing signals, added to the scene. Ships were also visible in the Nivelle and the Adour. The first is the river at whose mouth is St. Jean de Luz, the last, the Bayonne River.

We could not but observe, although at the direct distance of four or five leagues and in the midst of noble features, that St. Sebastian made a prominent figure; from the pinnacle on which we stood, a good glass might have made out the attack. While we were gazing in almost breathless admiration of the scene around us, we were enveloped by flies or ants. They literally swarmed so that we could see nothing, and were glad to remove to another point to get rid of them.

On looking towards Bayonne, we saw a considerable explosion, probably that of blowing up some buildings near the works.

In looking towards St. Jean de Luz, we could plainly observe a strong working party throwing up an intrenchment from the fort of Socoa towards the town, and could almost make out the form of the works of Socoa. This Socoa is a fort on the tongue of land forming the western part of the harbour of St. Jean de Luz. It was intended that there should have been an anchorage made here for twelve sail of the line, but the plan, whatever it was, had not been completed.

There are, I believe, bomb-proofs in the fort, capable of containing 1000 men. This place, on our advancing, must be taken; but in my next letter I will describe it more minutely, as I shall then have seen a plan. It is said to be too small a place to be capable of making much resistance: still. I suppose, we shall have another little siege.

On descending from Les Quatre Couronnes (so called because, in some points of view, the rocky pinnacles of the mountain are said to resemble four crowns), we rejoined our horses and continued our route to examine the positions intended to be taken by our batteries, which are to cover the establishment of the bridge over the Bidassoa. This is near the little village of Biriatu, and on the points which I had previously sent Gordon to reconnoitre. Near this spot is the Convent of St. Marcial, near which the Spaniards behaved so well in the late action. Their corps remains halted all about, and they are very fine-looking young fellows. These heights are near (though of course in front of) Irun. From them, as from others near the enemy, were to be seen his battalions on parade, some at drill, &c. &c.

As we returned, the day was getting to an end. We repassed Lord Aylmer's brigade, composed of regiments lately from England. The officers of one corps were all out of their tents, observing, as they said, a very heavy firing of shells towards our right, that is, towards Maya. They saw, as they said, several distinct shells in the air at once: in vain we observed that we had no guns, nor had the enemy, in that direction; they could not be mistaken, they said, they had seen too many shells fired at St. Sebastian while their ships lay off it, not to know well how to distinguish their smoke from any other.

In short, we were glad to see that which we really did not, and to take our leave: but in reality, these good people, who being young in the country, are a little more alive to the possibilities of war than their neighbours, had seen nothing but the clouds converging as they do in mountain scenery. We had an adventure coming home; the road down the mountain leading to the iron foundry before mentioned is narrow and steep, cut in the little zig-zags usual on the slopes of steep mountains.

We had suddenly turned the corner of one of these, and were near a kind of hole which I had slightly noticed on coming up, when we observed several Spaniards about it, and some coming out of it. In the path lay a poor bullock, bleeding at the mouth, and trembling violently. We learnt on inquiry that a pair of bullocks had tumbled into the hole, which was of considerable depth, but slanting down; that they had pulled out one, but that the other, which had been killed by the fall, was still in the subterraneous passage. I looked down the place, which was not so steep but that a man might crawl down. It was too dark to see the bottom: a man or two were then in, tying a rope to the horns of the bullock, which, being very large, repeatedly stuck in the sides of the cave, and prevented their pulling the beast out.

Nothing could more forcibly remind one of *Gil Blas'* cave of robbers, which had just such an entrance. We waited a long time to see whether the men would get the poor beast out, but all in vain; the rope slipped,—then it broke,—then slipped again. They were tired,—they laughed,—they gave the cavern and the bullock to all the *demonios* they could think of. At last we went on leaving the bullock to its fate.

While I write, Dickson calls to give me two very interesting pieces of intelligence. The one, that an English mail has arrived, the other, that we shall attack the enemy tomorrow morning at 7 o'clock. The attack will be at three points, opposite Fuenterabia, above Irun, and near the point which we visited yesterday. We are now packing up, and I shall go to Oyarzun or Irun, so as to be on the main road by which the troops will advance. My point tomorrow will be that of the batteries near the pontoon bridge by Biriatu.—*Adieu* for the moment.

Letter 94

Near Oyarzun: Oct. 6, 10. p.m.

We attack tomorrow at daybreak. Hill commences rather sooner, and makes a false attack near Roncesvalles. We cross the Bidassoa, on three points, at Fuenterabia, above Irun, and again a little higher up near the village of Biriatu. Near this last, and to cover the establishment of a pontoon bridge, the batteries of artillery, of which I shall have charge, will be posted. This point is of sufficient importance: the others are not less so, and, in truth, the enemy's position is every way formidable. But success is necessary to us, and we must exert ourselves like men determined not to be foiled.

There is every reason to expect a sanguinary struggle. Much hinges on tomorrow. We cannot long maintain our present position, and must absolutely advance or retreat. If successful, our situation will be much improved. If all goes well, you shall hear again. I have every confidence; our leader is excellent, and his followers of tried valour. The issue of tomorrow decides the campaign; as it may turn out, France or Spain receives us for the winter.—*Adieu.*

Sir John Hope is here, and well; he arrived today. We have difficulties more than usual to overcome tomorrow, and must accordingly exert ourselves to overcome them. I trust the storm will soon be over: rain would add much to the difficulties, already sufficient, of an attack.

Letter 95

Lesaca: Oct. 8, 5 a. m.

I wrote you a few hasty lines from Oyarzun on the evening of the 6th. I now write in a hurry; we have been called up; the marquis's horses are ordered, and his lordship is at breakfast; when he moves, so shall we. We left Oyarzun at midnight of the 6th. The columns which moved by the direct road to Irun (and it was not possible to advance by another) completely filled it. The night was at first stormy; thunder and lightning, and some rain. It afterwards was so sultry as to be the subject of every one's remark; the little wind there was was like the breath of an oven.

The road was so blocked up, that though the distance is but two leagues from Oyarzun to Irun, it was daylight before we reached the latter. All seemed quiet in the enemy's position. On reaching Irun, Ramsay's troop inclined to the right, leaving the high road. I here learned that Michell's battery (late Parker's) was to join me when it came up, which it soon did: and we found 400 infantry waiting to pull the guns over the mountain to the places previously intended. Bull's horses never want assistance; they were soon posted on a height with some Spanish horse artillery.

The affair began at 8; a column of our infantry having crossed previously at Fuenterabia, opposite to which place they forded the Bidassoa. Another column crossed by fording just below the burnt bridge at Irun, followed close by Webber Smith's troop. Another column, at the same time, about a mile higher up; and the Spaniards, as if impatient, rushed down the mountains, a little to the right of the enemy's village of Biriatu, and in spite of every opposition forded the river, and carried the mountain called (even in orders) the *Montague de Louis XIV.* During this time, our guns and those of the Spanish horse artillery played on the enemy; but he made a very feeble resistance, and, at 9 o'clock, the burning of the huts of the mountain posts showed that he had abandoned them.

Finding that the affair was losing all appearance of becoming serious on our right, I quitted Ramsay's and Michell's batteries, sending them orders to cross at the burnt bridge at Irun, and crossed myself the river at this point, which is close to the high Bayonne road, and leaves to its left the Isle de la Conférence, where Louis XIV. and Charles IV. of Spain had the conference from which the little isle takes its name. The moment after I had crossed, I saw the marquis approaching the ford, and rode up to report to Dickson what I had done. I had also previously ordered Ross to leave the mountains and to cross.

This last was left to my discretion, but I had no instructions relative to the other two batteries, and though clear in my mind that they should advance, I was not so that it would be approved, since at times his lordship allows no troops to be moved, but in obedience to his own orders. Dickson thought my having moved them hazardous, and I sent Bell off again to stop them where he might find them, but with orders that they should be ready to move rapidly forward when ordered, which they afterwards were. Indeed, Ramsay having found out a new ford, had already crossed the Bidassoa, and had gained the road communicating with the main one to Bayonne.

At this time, the enemy had retired from the river at all points, and had fallen back on what I presumed to be his second line, from a redoubt in which he opened a fire of a few guns, having previously fired three or four 24-pounders only from a battery a little below Andaya, which battery had been immediately taken by our troops, who crossed near Fuenterabia. The redoubt was also immediately taken, and on our ascending the height we found the troops formed somewhat in advance of it. An instantaneous hurrah burst from the line on seeing Lord Wellington, who rode on a little towards the left, where the enemy yet showed a feeble line but disputed some woody ground. In the front was the village of Urogne, which our advanced troops were then entering. On a height, not above 1400 yards beyond it, were two French divisions, drawn out before their encampment, which was partly intrenched and had an apparently strong redoubt which they strengthened with fresh troops.

About a mile to their left, before the encampment, were two field-pieces, the first they had shown. From these, they cannonaded the village and our troops then entering, which were the German and other light troops of the first division. On looking attentively at the village, the inhabitants appeared in a body in a field adjoining the road. There were women and children among them. This was before the field-pieces played much on the village. The inhabitants disappeared, I know not how but suddenly, for on turning round, after looking for a little at what was doing on the left, they were gone.

The enemy's fire from the two guns became more rapid, and the village was obviously on fire. Whether this may have been from the enemy's shells (if they fired any), or from our troops setting fire to the houses, I do not at this moment know, but I know that the troops who first entered got drunk, and that many were laden with plunder. I shall make more particular inquiry, since it was distressing to see the first French village (or little town, for it is of some size) on fire. I imagine, too, that had the enemy shown more enterprise he might have easily taken the troops who entered the village.

It soon became necessary to withdraw them, and the affair ended about half-past 12 (one hour after Urogne was on fire) by our assuming a position a little retired, and nearly the same one on which the second line of the enemy had rested in the morning. On questioning the prisoners, they agree that some battalions and many guns had marched that morning for Bayonne, that Soult was at last really gone, and they believed to Germany: and that Suchet had slept the night before at Bayonne, and was come to take the command. It is certain that they made a very feeble resistance, being as it were taken by surprise, or at least, without preparation.

The guns taken in the redoubt are old iron ship guns, on sea carriages. They showed no field guns but the two near Urogne, during the firing of which their tents were struck and sent off. Their redoubt beyond their encampment and to the left of it apparently commanded the approaches from the Pass of Vera. No attack seemed to have been made through this Pass, but more to our right there was much smoke. I am not yet aware of what has been done on our right.

Little can be seen in these mountainous regions beyond the next mountain, and the fatigue and difficulty of communication are beyond what could be imagined. Few lives were lost yesterday, I know not how many, but as the action was fought over much ground, many fell in detail. I saw several Spanish bodies in the nooks of the river. The Spaniards behaved nobly.—*Adieu*; I must quit my pen for the saddle. I will send you a sketch if I can.

9 p.m.

I returned about an hour ago, after a long ride, and a good scramble on foot in the mountains. The enemy still holds one of the highest, called *La Montague de la Rhune*. I have been under it with the Spaniards all the afternoon. Tomorrow it must be carried. Soult is certainly gone. He has been appointed to succeed Berthier, who has retired. In consequence, Soult goes to Germany. Is this appointment designed to draw him from his army? Soult is keen, thoughtful, and quite a man of business. He allows himself but one hour for dinner, and five only of the twenty-four for sleep. He is said to be ambitious. Does our modern Caesar fear another Cassius? Soult is thin as well as thoughtful.

Suchet is, or was at Bayonne on the night of the 6th. All prisoners agree in this, and that he was to have reviewed his troops on the day of our attack, which they all say was altogether unexpected. Seventeen officers and 350 men were marched from hence, this morning, to Passages, to be embarked for England as prisoners of war. This is exclusive of officers and men who are wounded, and exclusive too of those taken on the left. The affair has been more warm than I had supposed. Our loss in killed and wounded, I believe, is about 1500. We rode early today after Lord Wellington, but missed him, and taking the mountain road on the left instead of the right of the Bidassoa (by which we had returned last night), suddenly came to an utter end of the road, which terminated in a great rock. This was below the village of Salinas, and is the point to which boats can navigate the river.

After this adventure Dickson and Bell turned homewards. May, Pascoe, Ord, and I, whisked about, passed through Vera, and ascended the craggy mountain, learning that the Spaniards, who had already a strong corps posted there, were about to attack the Montague de la Rhune by both flanks. We left our horses half-way up, and scrambled up the remainder on foot. We found the Spaniards and the enemy firing a good deal, but to no purpose; and seated ourselves quietly among the rocks and looked very attentively at Socoa, Urogne, and St. Jean de Luz: all of which we took in reverse, as it is called, that is, we saw them as it were from behind, and had a more distinct view than before of Bayonne, where we could see the walls, as well as the houses, very plainly.

At Socoa and St. Jean de Luz, the enemy was busily employed in throwing up works. Socoa seems to differ a little in shape from what I had supposed; but distant views are deceitful, and I hope to have a nearer inspection. After sitting till we began to fear that day would decline, we returned to our horses, and turned over the mountains to look at the batteries and intrenchments carried the day before by our light division. It is not easy to imagine a stronger natural position, strengthened, as it also was, by redoubts, by abattis, by intrenchments at every knoll, and with paths, where there were any at all, hardly practicable. It is highly honourable to our troops, as it is little so to the enemy, that this strong position was forced.

You will judge of the steep ascent when I tell you that we were glad to lead our horses down, though tired enough with walking. We met a large Spanish body ascending towards the Montague de la Rhune, which I trust will be carried tomorrow, when the attack will commence at daybreak in front of Maya, but will no doubt be general.

I hope to finish my letter by saying that we have been successful. We found three mountain guns (4-pounders) in Vera; they were taken yesterday, and are like the little guns the boys of our Woodbridge artillery school used to drill with.

In Vera we found also an hospital with about 400 of our wounded in it. In descending the mountain, we stumbled on the paved road leading through one (for there are two) of the Puertos de Vera, into France. By the way, the little town of Urogne seems to have suffered very little from the fire of yesterday. In looking from the mountain this morning, we could hardly observe any difference. In the mountains today, we saw more than one entrance into the iron mines with which this province abounds. We suspect the hole under La Montague des Quatre Couronnes, into which the poor bullocks had fallen, to be the shaft of one of these. On the mountains, one meets occasionally with great boundary stones; these are believed to mark the limits of France and Spain, though I doubt the fact. On one, a little way from the Bidassoa (which near this point is the undoubted boundary), was carved an inscription, implying that desertion beyond this limit will be punished with death. The stone and characters are very old.

I took my leave this morning of Sir Thomas Graham, and shook him most cordially by the hand, wishing him every happiness, and assuring the good man how happy I should be to serve under his auspices hereafter.

Letter 96

Headquarters, Vera: Oct. 10.

The Spaniards go by troops to plunder the little that can be found in the French houses. The part of France we have entered is, perhaps, a league and a half wide, by three or four long. It is hilly, or rather less mountainous than the Pyrenees; but, except towards the Nivelle, is anything but flat. There are hedge-rows, like those of England, and lanes: in short, already do we see a different country. "*Bon jour, mesdames,*" said we yesterday to a couple of brown beauties; "*Demonio!*" said they in return, "*Somos Portugueses.*" You see in all this how strongly the love of country enters into all bosoms, since these ladies, who were shoeless and without handkerchiefs, indignantly repelled the idea that they were French.

I have not yet learnt the particulars of the fire in the village of Urogne. I only know that the misconduct and plundering of the troops there have occasioned very severe animadversions from the marquis; and that his lordship has, in consequence, ordered three officers home. It has occurred to me that the enemy himself may have set fire to the village, in part of a fixed plan of driving the country before us; and that on reoccupying the village he may have put out the flames.

How far he may act on this principle of destruction I know not, but it may soon be proved, since I apprehend a day or two will see us successful or foiled in an attack on St. Jean de Luz, which is a considerable town, having a capacious harbour, and a mole, which, with corresponding moles on the side of Socoa (as I have already mentioned in a former letter), were intended to form a secure anchorage for a dozen sail of the line. I meant to have given you a good account of what we have been doing, but shall not have time, as I hear the mail is making up.

I have already detailed the part I saw of the affair of the 7th instant. On our right the affair was more contested. The light division and the Spaniards have suffered considerably. The light division drove the enemy, by dint of bravery, from redoubts, intrenchments, and abattis, such as men *ought to have defended forever*. The Spaniards too, behaved well, but were foiled a little; nothing, however, can have exceeded their gallantry of late.

I passed the 8th instant in reconnoitring La Montagne de la Rhune, and yesterday our present and the enemy's late position. I believe he retired in the course of yesterday from the mountain of La Rhune, which towards us towers to a craggy cliff, surmounted by the ruins of a hermitage, whence it is usually called La Montague de l'Hermitage, but recedes by gentle slopes towards the enemy. It would accordingly have required a considerable detour to have turned the mountain, which the marquis intended to have done yesterday, and to commence his attack at the village of Sarre? I meant to have gone thither, but had orders to accompany Dickson towards our own left, which we examined from Andaya (opposite Fuenterabia) to the same side of La Rhune that I had previously examined.

This Montague de la Rhune is the prominent one hereabouts; and frowns over the lesser ones. The enemy was jealous of it, and we were the same. He fired quite uncomfortably at two or three of us the day before yesterday, whilst reconnoitring his position in the mountains. In short, he was quite rude. The mountain formed an excellent *appui* to his left, but cut us, as it were, in two. The present positions are rather detached.

In this singular country one leaves an enemy's division a league in one's rear without fear, as in truth without danger. Andaya has been in ruins since the Duke of Berwick's time; that is, something less than a century ago; a little fort was then blown down; but on the frontier of France, properly so called, on which our left now rests, there is not a soul; all have retired, and all are to retire before us, as the prisoners agree. This is politic on the part of the enemy, who has not, however, destroyed the houses, nor had he time to remove the Indian corn still growing, though over ripe.

The country changes the moment one has passed the Bidassoa near Irun. Hedges appear, and the face of the heathy country, interspersed with fields, reminds one of England. In the sea battery near Andaya (a place in which much brandy is still made amongst the old ruins), are four iron guns: one an East India Company's gun, taken, I suppose, in some Indiaman. We sent three of the guns to St. Sebastian, and the fourth over the cliff. In a redoubt are four other good, but ship guns, on ship carriages, which come into use in our position, in which we yesterday placed forty-six guns, including six field 18-pounders.

Today headquarters move to Vera, a league from hence. We should have gone sooner, but one of our hospitals had to be moved. I saw there, about two days since, 400 wounded English from the affair of the 7th, which I dare say has cost at least 2000 killed and wounded. I include Spaniards, and then am sure I underrate the numbers. We have now two pontoon bridges and one boat-bridge over the Bidassoa, to which our position on the left is too close; one likes to have elbow room. I imagine the marquis will throw bridges over the Nivelle and boldly cross that river, so as to take in flank St. Jean de Luz, now apparently well-fortified in the field way. I mean the position in front of St. Jean de Luz; which town is on both sides of the Nivelle connected by bridges of wood (as they appear), on stone piers.

In St, Jean de Luz there seems to be a castle, watched by one of our men-of-war brigs. As no attack took place yesterday, I have no doubt the Montague de la Rhune is ours. This assures the Passes of Vera and, as I believe, of Maya: but all this is my own idea. It is difficult, without personal observation, to comprehend much in this mountainous country, of which the maps I have yet seen give little idea.

Three hundred and fifty prisoners, and seventeen officers, marched from hence on the 8th, to embark at Passages. This was from this point only, and of course exclusive of prisoners wounded or overlooked in the mountains, of whom numbers are found from time to time, and generally stripped by the Spaniards, who, I believe, think they have great charity if they refrain from murdering the oppressors of their country. On our way home yesterday from Irun, we were necessarily forced to follow the little rocky path by the channel of the Bidassoa, where we met a string of wounded getting along miserably enough.

The last man was a Frenchman, who limped in great pain after the rest, who were chiefly Portuguese, and on mules. A Spaniard was immediately before the file; he was in high glee, and had been singing all sorts of airs. He was well dressed, but not a soldier. The moment he saw the Frenchman, all his singing was at an end; he spurred and beat his own beast, swore by every god and demon at the wounded man:—he ought to be murdered, he ought to be flayed; he ought, in short, to have suffered any, and everything: and I have no doubt that had this man met with the wounded man alone, he would not have confined his anger to mere expressions.

I hope in a few days to announce more news. By-the-by, on the 2nd General Cassan (or some such name), who is now said to be Governor of Pampeluna, sent to Don Carlos d'España, commanding the blockading army, desiring that he would furnish rations (7000 daily) for the inhabitants of Pampeluna, whom he could no longer afford to feed. Don Carlos replied, that he held him responsible that the inhabitants were equally fed with the garrison, and that he should strictly inquire into this on the surrender of the place; and that, of course, he should not give a single pound of food. One thousand two hundred infantry are just arrived from England; we have full employment for them. *Adieu.*—The mail is, I hear, closing.

P. S.—I hear with pleasure that the marquis has marked, by a strong order, the displeasure his lordship feels at the improper conduct of the troops in Urogne during our temporary possession of it. I enclose you a copy of a general order issued the day before yesterday; and of an extract from one given out on the 9th July on the first probability of the allied troops entering France.

Adjutant-General's Office,
Lesaca: Oct. 8.

1. The commander of the forces is concerned to be under the necessity of publishing over again his orders of the 9th July, 1813, as they have been unattended to by the officers and troops which entered France yesterday.

2. According to all the information which the commander of

the forces has received, outrages of all descriptions were committed by the troops, in presence even of their officers, who took no pains whatever to prevent them.

3. The commander of the forces has already determined that some officers, so grossly negligent of their duty, shall be sent to England, that their names may be brought under the attention of His Royal Highness the Prince Regent, that His Royal Highness may give such directions respecting them as he may think proper, as the commander of the forces is determined not to command officers who will not obey his orders.

Adjutant-General's Office:
July 9.

1. The commander of the forces is anxious to draw the attention of the officers of the army to the difference of the situation in which they have been hitherto among the peoples of Portugal and Spain, and that in which they may hereafter find themselves among those of the frontiers of France.

2. Every military precaution must henceforward be used to obtain intelligence and to prevent surprise. General and superior officers, at the head of detached corps, will take care to keep up a constant and regular communication on their right and left, and with their rear; and the soldiers and their followers must be prevented from wandering to a distance from their camps and cantonments, on any account whatever.

3. Notwithstanding that these precautions are absolutely necessary, as the country in front of the army is the enemy's, the commander of the forces is particularly desirous that the inhabitants should be well treated, and private property must be respected as it has been hitherto.

4. The officers and soldiers of the army must recollect that their nations are at war with France solely because the ruler of the French nation will not allow them to be at peace, and is desirous of forcing them to submit to his yoke; and they must not forget that the worst of the evils suffered by the enemy in his profligate invasion of Spain and Portugal, have been occasioned by the irregularities of the soldiers, and their cruelties, authorised and encouraged by their chiefs, towards the unfortunate and peaceable inhabitants of the country.

5. To revenge this conduct on the peaceable inhabitants of France would be unmanly, and unworthy of the nations to whom the commander of the forces now addresses himself, and, at all events, would be the occasion of similar and more evils to the army at large, than those which the enemy's army have suffered in the Peninsula, and would eventually prove highly injurious to the public interest.

Letter 97

Vera: Oct. 11, 7 a.m.

I hope for a quiet day; there never was a finer: the mists are cleared away from the mountains, there is hardly a breath of air, or any sounds to disturb the tranquillity of the scene before me but those of a little saw-mill, and the tinkling of the mules' bells. I have a little room to myself; the window looks to the rising sun, and over a little plain of some 200 yards wide terminated by an abrupt mountain. Such is Puerto de Vera before me. Can you fancy the place? Can you fancy old stone houses with rude balconies and overhanging vines? Houses with eaves projecting so as equally to fence off sun or rain, and a nice little clear rivulet rolling over a pebbly bed?

On the left are the mountains which, after a ravine or two, lead to the point from whence, three days ago, we eyed the greater mountain the Rhune, then in the enemy's possession but now in ours, and thither I shall make my way when I shall have finished my morning occupation. So much for the day and the scene before me.

The little child at St. Sebastian, about whose fate you are anxious, was saved, as I hope I have already told you. I have now forgotten particulars, except that an honest infantry soldier (of the 38th I think) carried it away, declaring it should never want while he or his comrades had a morsel of bread. When I see the 38th regiment, I will ask Colonel Deane, whom I know, about the child.

I hope I have mentioned that Gordon and Blachley were of use at St. Sebastian beyond what I can express. They really understand what they have to do; and half-a-dozen such are worth more than a multitude of stupid, ignorant people. I confess I tasked them to their full strength, but they well repaid all the confidence reposed in them. Should another siege be intended, I shall strive to have them again; no one can tell the value of well-instructed people on these occasions. I wrote to Colonel Chapman yesterday, to inquire what was doing or was done for Fletcher's children. Poor Fletcher! we cease not to regret him. I see with pleasure all I had recommended, regarding Webber Smith, Parker, Morrison, and Power, is realised.

Letter 98

Vera: Oct. 13.

I sit down to write in preference to going to Sarre, where there is at this moment heavy firing, and where two hours ago the enemy poked the Spaniards out of a redoubt which is, I dare say, by this time retaken. I have my horse ready in case caprice should lead me where I have, in reality, no business. Since the affair of the 7th, all has been quiet till this morning, nor do I now think that anything serious is intended: nor should I be surprised if even this attack by the enemy were meant as a prelude to his retiring tonight.

We are cautious in our movements,—this mountain warfare requires us to be so. Beyond the very next range of mountains one literally knows nothing; but that we are about to move, I have no doubt. Our battering-train ships are ordered out of Passages harbour, already much too full. We have about 100 heavy pieces embarked, exclusive of the injured ones sent home. They will be sent to Santander, where they will be equally ready for any future service. The enemy still works hard at his intrenchments in front of St. Jean de Luz: of this, all his prisoners complain as a useless labour, since he will never remain there, in their opinion.

Of Catalonia we know nothing. Having again and again examined the positions from which the enemy was driven on the 7th, I am the more surprised that they should have been forced. It is a toil to get up to most of their intrenchments, even without arms, or anybody to meet when at the top; but bravery will, generally speaking, do any and every thing. The firing at Sarre gets more heavy, but more distant. I imagine a reserve brigade or division to have got up to assist the Spaniards, and that the enemy is, at least, checked; but one may imagine anything, as well in England as here, for we are a league from the scene.

The scenery here is indeed noble; words cannot express the variety of woods, rocks, rivers, ravines, and mountains, by which we are surrounded. One may travel up to what the poet calls the "sublimest peak," and wonder why we diminutive creatures can be quarrelling, instead of enjoying all that nature has spread before us.

I think I sent you a plan of the operations against St. Sebastian. There was one sailor's gun on the mountain below the lighthouse.

No other guns were drawn over mountains except those in battery No. 1, where in the first siege there were six, and in the second two. I could get no one to undertake to get the guns there but Webber Smith. I begged hard that they might remain, and not be withdrawn after the first failure, but was overruled, and could never get any more guns up. Two of the howitzers remained. But the enemy confessed that this battery, though distant, plagued them out of their lives. We re-embark our guns as a matter of necessity. Our means of transport are limited, and our heavy guns can readily be carried coastways and landed where we want them hereafter. This will probably never be far from the sea.

We have had a little rain, but the season must be an uncommon one, for on our first coming to this province (by-the-by, I should say kingdom, for a stone, a mile and a half from hence on a bridge, divides Guipuscoa and Navarre), we were taught to expect a good deal. Your accounts of good harvests are most pleasing. Here, did we not eat up everything, there would be abundance; as it is we have to send four, five, and even six leagues for straw. Yesterday our mules foraged in front, but at the expense of being fired at; some animals were lost, and it brings a fire on the covering party, to say no worse.

I have shown to several of Fletcher's friends the little memento of him which you sent me. He deserves, and more than deserves, every syllable said of him. We shall scarcely find Fletcher's equal, take him for all in all; his loss will be long and sensibly felt. Of the praises of the dead I confess I am jealous. I know (as my namesake the emperor once said) that all this praise (like the sorrow of which he spoke) is unavailing; and that is the very reason why I desire to see it paid. It is the only tribute we can pay to departed merit, and is consolatory to one of the strongest principles of our hearts,—that of wishing to live in the memory of our friends.

Many beside myself will lament the loss of Sir Thomas Graham, but he has judged right. Sir Thomas is no longer young, and the fatigues of the late siege pressed somewhat upon him. I have a high regard for him; there was a *bonhomie* about him that led to the most pleasing and kind attentions. Sir John Hope's coming is most creditable to him, he has filled many military stations, and has seen many a hard-fought day. No man is more looked up to, and with just reason. All does indeed seem to be going on well in the north. These are eventful times, such as the world has rarely seen.

I find hostilities have begun before Dantzic, where our rocketeers are gone to spread the flames of war more widely. The Prussians seem indeed the Prussians of older wars. Blücher's conduct after Jena showed what he was and would be. The death of Moreau is a remarkable event, the "finger of Providence" is there; but where is it not? *Adieu*: I shall mount my horse and ride to Sarre. Even Falstaff would now go thither, for the firing is over.—*Adieu*.

Oct. 14.

On riding towards Sarre we found the dying and the dead being brought back. It was a "pretty affair" everyone said, and had not cost above a couple of hundred lives to the Spaniards. I thought of Lord Byron, and his *"tools, his broken tools."* I saw a wounded Spanish general and colonel, but knew not their names. The Spanish surgeons use steel splints in binding up broken limbs. The enemy we found had surprised in part the Spanish advance: had taken one redoubt, but had been repulsed in the attack of another. The Spaniards only were engaged. One division, the 4th, had moved up as a support, but had not been in action.

The firing continued *"en tirailleur"* when we reached the front, where we continued until sunset; the enemy showing, besides his light troops, something more than a brigade, and having a division posted in reserve. While we remained, the regiments of the 4th division were ordered to retire by companies to their encampments. In following the companies (which marched separately), one could not but observe that there were from twenty to thirty men only in each; all, however, were complete in officers and non-commissioned officers, and had their colour-sergeants. This new rank (that of colour-sergeants), I think, will be of use; the badge is as good to the sergeant, as the star is to the officer.

At Sarre we saw Sir John Downie, who is a curious figure. He is Lieut.-General in the Spanish service, and has troops dressed in the old Spanish costume with slashed sleeves, &c. &c. Sir John has a great black patch on his face to cover the wound of a grape shot. Of two orderlies who followed him, one I observed carry a good-sized flat cask, well filled, I dare say. "Lieut.-General Sir J. Downie" was marked on it; this looks jolly.

Oct. 16.

The corvette which had taken shelter in St. Jean de Luz, and put to sea the other night, was afterwards driven on shore somewhere towards Bayonne, and lost. More rain: roads getting worse. No ap-

Reitendes Raketeur-Corps
(Royal Artillery. Mounted Rockett Corps.)

Reitende Artillerie
(Royal Horse Artillery.)

1813.

ROCKET TROOPS

pearance of a movement, yet one must be near; we cannot, I should think, remain here much longer. Even before the affair of the 7th, the supplies for many of the Spanish corps were carried to the mountain positions on the heads of men and women, of whom strings were to be seen toiling up the steep and slippery ascents.

All is quiet in front. I suspect a movement of some of our troops to our right, that is, towards the army which was Sir John Murray's. Pontoons have certainly moved that way *via* Tolosa. When Sir John Murray's name is casually mentioned here, I observe that no one speaks with asperity. Not a word of Pampeluna, yet all daily expect its fall. We hear that Bonaparte is known to have been at Dresden so late as the 28th *ultimo*. We are naturally anxious to hear again from home; never was there a more interesting period; a few more weeks must decide much.

Oct. 17.

I believe we meditate an attack on Laredo near Santoña, which posts the enemy still holds. They are both near Santander.

I passed a most pleasant day yesterday at headquarters. Speaking of Pampeluna, the marquis said that the governor had really applied for 7000 daily rations for the inhabitants of Pampeluna, his lordship continued:

> While the impudent fellow knows perfectly, that I am aware that there are but 3000 inhabitants in the town, and that in the 7000 he includes his garrison. Pretty blockade we should make of it on such terms.

Speaking of the facility of vessels making the coast:

> It's very hard if our sailors can't make one of the four harbours we have.

"Four," said the Marshal Beresford, "why, we have but three!"

"Ay, but please God," returned his lordship, "we'll soon have St. Jean de Luz."

I had a great deal of conversation with both the *grandees*, and the day went off uncommonly well.

Letter 99

Vera: Oct. 18.

I have just returned off "La Rhune" mountain; on the summit is the ruin of an hermitage. The top of this mountain is craggy, composed of rocks in layers. The neighbouring mountains, on the contrary, though rocky, have their masses of rock composed of small stones joined together. There was a keen cutting wind, and it was cold and comfortless on the top of this wild mountain, where the troops were sheltering themselves in little hovels formed of flat stones, piled together as well as they could. We are making some works there under the direction of Captain Reid, with whom I ascended La Rhune after breakfast.

This day is keen, but clear, and we had a better view than ever of Bayonne. We are sending to Lisbon about forty of the guns captured at Vitoria: they are generally French guns. Many, however, are Spanish. On one, a 12-pounder cast at Seville, 15th January, 1790, and named "Dragon" (all Spanish and French guns have names, or rather had, for the practice is somewhat discontinued), is an inscription between the muzzle and the dolphin, signifying that "the king having laid the gun it hit the mark."

Baring, General Charles Alten's *aide-de-camp*, went two days ago into the enemy's lines, with a flag of truce, on some business connected with supplying money for prisoners. He met an officer commanding the Nassau brigade in the enemy's army whom he personally knew, and with whom he had been on terms of familiar acquaintance formerly. This officer, on Baring's mentioning his name, recognised him, inquired after Alten and many officers of the legion; and said he had letters from Dresden of the 8th instant, when Bonaparte was still there. This conversation was in German, and seemed to excite jealousy in other French officers, who approached to hear what passed.

A letter just received from Ramsay mentions that Captain Shandy, in whose company Gordon is, has died at Cadiz, after thirteen hours' illness. I believe a fever now prevails in Cadiz. Gordon's going vexes me, but it cannot be avoided. He will do well anywhere, and already in a note to Bell says he is ready to set off. We shall keep him for a day; perhaps we may have news by the expected mail, which may change our plans.

Marshal Beresford will leave headquarters tomorrow I believe, and take the command of a corps of the army: when we advance, the army will be in four columns, of which the marshal will have the right centre, the marquis the left centre. Sir Rowland Hill and Sir John Hope, the right and left corps.

Our 8-pounders taken in the affair of the 7th instant have been lost; the boat in which they were embarked, to be conveyed from the Bidassoa to St. Sebastian, having been overset. I never heard a harder gale than blew at times last night. I am going to find out the 51st regiment, to get from the officer commanding all the particulars relative to the death of poor Charles Douglas, who was killed in the attack which Soult made on the day of the assault of St. Sebastian. Douglas had a company in the 51st, and was, I believe, a half-brother of Sir Howard Douglas, who, in a letter to Ramsay, which I saw this morning, bitterly laments his loss.

No mail, nor appearance of any. There are reports that the wreck of a vessel has been seen near Passages, supposed to be that of the packet; but these reports have probably no foundation. The late gales, however, have been most violent; such has been the ground swell in Passages harbour, as to occasion even fears there for the loss of the transports moored stem and stern. The vessels there are moored in rows. Though strongly confined by moorings, yet in the swell some have been driven forward by the rising of the swell: whilst others, close alongside, have been driven backwards by the fall of it, so that the bowsprits of some have been entangled in the mizen chains of others.

This, though scarcely conceivable, Mr. Butcher, who has just been here, assures me is true: and that, in consequence, they will be moored in future with their sides to the tide. Our battering-train ships have not yet sailed, weather alone detaining them. There are twenty of them, and nine with the field train on board, going to Santander. Twelve more, with field train also on board, will remain in Passages. The expedition against Laredo is yet secret and stationary, but is ready; the ordnance required will be taken from some of the ships going to Santander. Gordon will stay here for a few days, to see what may be seen, and then start across the Peninsula for Cadiz, a distance of upwards of 800 miles.

This is a bold undertaking for a man who travels alone,—that is, without society, for he takes his servant, horses, and baggage; we are managing to get him a passport from General O'Lawler, so as to secure him a good reception by the way. He will go *via* Vitoria, Burgos, Segovia, Madrid, Toledo, Andajar, Luciana, Antequera, and Malaga; from thence, by way of Gibraltar, or Ronda, as may seem best. Gordon is a fine fellow, and is quite cheerful about the journey and the voyage at the end of it. Nevertheless, 'tis a cheerless prospect: The West Indies offer but a beaten track.

After I left off writing yesterday, we set off for the encampment of the 51st Regiment. It is on a high mountain, about a league from Echallar. The road to Echallar lies by the rocky banks of the Bidassoa, which you keep to your right. Whilst joking or talking with Gordon we met Sir John Downie, with whose figure and face I have made you acquainted. He is a Scotchman, and one of those extraordinary characters who really seem to like fighting. Among a variety of odd adventures, he fell into the hands of the enemy at Seville, where, after his horse had leaped a broken part of a wooden bridge, in which none of Sir John's men followed him, he received a grape shot in the face, which brought him to the ground. His horse releaped the bridge, to which Sir John was near enough to stagger, and to throw over amongst his companions his sword, which was, I think, that of the Cid, formerly mentioned in some of my letters.

This was at the moment when he saw that his being taken was inevitable. On being taken to the French general Villatte, he loaded Sir John with every opprobrious abuse, and ordered him to be tied to a gun, which was literally done, and Sir John remained on it for some distance, till he fainted with fatigue, anger, and vexation. Ever since his exchange, he has never ceased to upbraid Villatte with his ungenerous conduct; writing to him to demand either an apology, or a duel, all of which, he told us yesterday (for Gordon knows him, and introduced me to him), he was about to repeat, as he commanded at one of our outposts, and Villatte at the posts opposite. Altogether he conveys more the idea of a Quixote to one's mind than any man I ever saw. The study of character is ever interesting. If we remain quiet I shall go to see him in a day or two: his post is near the redoubt of the village of Sarre; I anticipate information and amusement.

On pursuing our journey, we overtook a young and weakly boy, who told me he belonged to the 83rd Regiment, and that he had obtained leave to go home. He was going two or three leagues further, and should return to Passages in a day or two.

I told him he would find the journey long for one day, and offered him bed and board as he passed, which he thankfully accepted, and he will be here tomorrow. Gordon afterwards found out for me that his name was Jones, that he came from Gloucester, that he knew the family of our friend Jones by report, but not otherwise.

Near Echallar, which is a little town on a tiny plain surrounded by mountains, the road leaves the Bidassoa, turning suddenly to the left, and, after a rocky ravine or two with an occasional iron foundry (common hereabouts), passes through a solid portion of rock, which is cut through some twenty-five or thirty feet in depth. On reaching the camp of the 51st Regiment, we found that Colonel Mitchell, who commands it, was sick, and not in camp; but Major Rice, the next in command, received us very civilly. I could gain little about poor Charles Douglas's death. Major Rice had not been with the regiment at the moment. All he knew was that Douglas had been killed in a skirmish; that he had fallen universally regretted, and, he added, and was joined by another officer who was present, that there was never any man more amiable. "He was the only man," said both in a breath, "whom we may fairly say to have had nothing in the least approaching to any vice."

His few things have been sold, and Colonel Mitchell has written on the subject to Sir Howard Douglas. I could only learn, in addition to the above, that the men of his company had carried him off the field, and, as a mark of respect, had taken great pains in making his grave. Every little detail is of value to relatives on this occasion, and "*affection*" (as I think the "Man of Feeling" expresses it) "*will sometimes build on the paring of a nail.*" Business calls me away: so, *adieu*.

Oct. 21.

I have just been out. Whilst writing, observing a funeral party passing with most of the officers of a regiment following, I went out to accompany it. During breakfast, we had observed a grave digging under a sloping hedge at a little distance. On coming to the grave, the Rev. Mr. Jenkins, chaplain to the fourth division, was reading the service. Many officers seemed affected, they were of the 52nd Regiment (Sir John Moore's). When the service was concluded, Mr. Jenkins told me that the officer's name was Frazer, that he had lately been wounded and had died at Vera; and that a brother of his, in the Fusileers, had been killed some time ago.

"This is the first regular funeral I have seen since I left Lisbon," said I, "and you are the first clergyman whom I have had the good fortune to meet."

Mr. Jenkins replied that he had been long attached to the fourth division; and in answer to my asking who was the chaplain at headquarters, replied the Rev. Mr. Driscol, who was daily expected to join from England, whither he had gone two years ago on account of sickness. These scenes feelingly remind us what we are. There was a more than usual decency in this funeral; the officers yet remain lingering about the grave, as if unwilling to leave the spot. On my mentioning to Mr. Larpent my having attended a funeral, he said that while prisoner he had witnessed the funerals of two French colonels at St. Jean de Luz, and of General Martinière at Bayonne; all conducted with great solemnity and even splendour. These French officers had all fallen in late affairs with us.

The Laredo expedition waits the arrival from Santander of ships to convey the troops. One thousand British will be employed, and 3000 Spaniards; these are already in the neighbourhood. Four months' hay has been demanded from England. Forage now is exceedingly scarce, our troops and brigades near Urogne are reduced to grazing their horses, which must soon lose their condition.

Oct. 22.

The wind continues high. We have had heavy gales during the night. Marshal Beresford left headquarters yesterday morning to join his corps. We learn that placards are stuck up at all corners of Bayonne, strictly prohibiting any political conversations on pain of severe penalties; and announcing that all persons not having a year's supply of provisions must be ready to quit the place. A flag of truce is going in this morning with some money lately transmitted for a French officer at Vitoria, but the poor man having died the money is going back again. This is one of several similar little arrangements which are pleasing enough.

I have been reading a Cadiz paper of the 27th September, in which is a most severe article relative to the misconduct of our troops at St. Sebastian, violently written, and ascribing the burning of the town to a premeditated intention of destroying a maritime town, carrying on, in time of peace, a commerce with France most prejudicial to Great Britain. I shall try to send the paper. Lieut.-Colonel Smith of the Engineers, I hear, has answered the article. The young officer of the 83rd Regiment, whom I mentioned, is here. He arrived an hour ago, drenched through; however, we shall give him some good soup, and make him comfortable for his journey to Passages tomorrow.—*Adieu.*

Letter 100

Vera: Oct. 25.

I was out yesterday examining roads on the mountains till almost dark. We met Ramsay and Macdonald, who were coming to see me. Ramsay and I soon got into earnest confab, and were wandering very peaceably towards the enemy's lines, when Gordon and Bell hailed us. It would have been ridiculous enough to have been taken in this way. I have been looking over old orders in search of a point I wished to ascertain, and find that in the present month 70 officers have obtained leave to go to England, and 102 to go to stations in the rear, on account of ill-health; and that in last month 75 obtained leave to go home, and 177 to the rear, for the same cause.

This is the day on which we have expected Pampeluna to surrender; but I learn that De Grammont of the 10th Hussars, who was sent into the place on the 21st to caution the governor against blowing up or injuring the works, which it was suspected he intended doing, was politely received, offered wine and a fresh loaf; and declares that the men whom he saw looked plump and jolly. This, however, may be, and probably is, mere deception. The garrison can hardly fail of being ill off. It has for some time been believed that the enemy had mined the works, and Don Carlos, having lately received accounts that the mines were charged, applied to Lord Wellington for instructions how to act in the event of the garrison attempting to escape after blowing up the works. It is understood (though with what truth I really do not know) that the marquis has ordered Don Carlos, in this case, after making the garrison prisoners, to put the governor and all the officers to death, and to decimate the men.

Making this known will probably prevent the necessity of recurring to so severe a measure, which the breach of the usual rules of war might, perhaps, justify; but which one cannot contemplate without horror. If De Grammont has communicated to the governor of Pampeluna Lord Wellington's resolutions, and indeed orders, I dare say it will have the desired effect. I believe I mentioned to you that Gordon was called upon to give evidence against some Spaniards, whom he found robbing a Portuguese muleteer on the road a few days since. Dyer is also here on the same errand.

Oct. 27.

Nothing very new. Colonel Elphinstone dined with me yesterday, and showed me a letter from Colonel Goldfinch, the engineer employed against Pampeluna. On the 24th, Baron Maucune, chief of the staff of the garrison, came out to see Don Carlos. He would tell his business to no one, and Don Carlos being out of the way, the baron, after waiting some hours, returned to the garrison, evidently chagrined. Of course, he and his attendants were well feasted. Gordon and Dyer attended yesterday to give evidence in the affair of the robbery before mentioned.

Among other curious questions they were asked whether, after committing the robbery, and before the men were secured, they had, or could have had, time to have gone into a church, as in that case, whatever crime they might have committed, they could not be punished with death. I was not aware that this old custom still existed.

The morning is exceedingly cold and raw, with a heavy fog. Ross's troops and two batteries are coming over the mountains, by the road we reconnoitred on the 24th instant. Eoss has just been here.

11 a.m.

Adieu: I have just received an order to go to the left, to assist in getting the batteries over the mountains.

Oct. 28, 8 a.m.

I have been wandering since 10 last night in intricate roads. On leaving off writing yesterday, I rode to the left of the line, where Ross's troop with Major Sympher's and Captain Douglas's batteries were to meet me, and received orders to pass after dark the advanced posts, so as to reach the piquet at the foot of the mountain before daybreak. However, after losing as I thought much time in examining roads, and arranging with General Wilson (who has a Portuguese brigade) how some *caçadores* should be posted to protect the movement, it was 10 at night before Ross's troop could reach the point of departure, and such was the intricacy of the road that it was 4 this morning before it gained the advanced piquet, where we found Colonel Colborne with 300 of the light division waiting to protect us. You never saw such roads: nothing but tumbling down every step, carriages oversetting, &c.

Sympher's and Douglas's batteries are yet on the road. I have been sent forward with Ross. We took all manner of strange doublings to avoid the enemy's posts, between which and the piquets placed by General Wilson's desire, there was some trifling skirmishing. The wind this morning has been most violent, in squalls. We had an hour's good sleep, from 4 to 6, in a wood, round a jolly fire made by our 95th Regiment, but the envious rain poured down. No certain accounts yet of Pampeluna, but we believe it has surrendered, and fully expect to hear so in the course of the day.

LETTER 101

Vera: Oct. 29, 10 a.m.

The moment I left off writing yesterday I was idle enough to go to bed, ostensibly to read and to shelter myself from the cold, which was intense; but study ended in sleep or slumbering, in which every one of us in the house lay till dinner-time; when Ross, Day, and Mr. Halaghan, Ross's surgeon, dined with me, and we had a very jolly day, enlivened by Gordon's arrival a couple of hours after dark from the mountains, where Douglas's and Sympher's brigades are yet toiling; and Gordon has returned to assist them. The snow lies on all the higher tops of the mountains, and it yet rains heavily in the valleys. Unless the weather shall clear we cannot advance, which we all desire to do, and are clearly intended to do the moment Pampeluna shall fall. Of this we have even yet no intelligence.

Our movement last night alarmed the enemy, who was for some hours under arms yesterday morning. All is again quiet. The Bidassoa is very considerably swollen, and fords are no longer passable. Gordon has just come down from the mountains (3 p.m.) with an account that the two batteries of artillery are safely arrived at Salinas, the village adjoining Vera. The use Gordon was of the other night when there were difficulties is not to be told; he did more than any twenty others, and I verily believe, without his exertions, one of the batteries would have stuck by the way till daylight had invited the enemy to make a push for the guns. In a day or two Gordon will have to set out for Cadiz, which is but a dreary ride to take alone at this season, and with the prospect of a West India voyage at the end of it!

However, no man takes all this in a more manly way than he does, and in the interim he works as hard as if the guns were his own, and is as good humoured, and as full of fun, as if he had not a care in the world. The Cortes have removed from Cadiz to the Isle, on account of the epidemic now raging at Cadiz.

Oct. 30, 10 a.m.

After a very rainy night the weather is clearing. Our mules still remain on the other side of the Bidassoa. We have been sending some food for our men. The Governor of Pampeluna has broken off the capitulation which had been entered into. He wished to be allowed to march into France, and to carry six pieces of artillery with his garrison; this was of course refused. All this will end, we believe, in the surrender of the fortress in a few days; during which our troops are suffering. But, under any circumstances, we could hardly advance for forty-eight hours, owing to the state of the roads from rain.

We strolled out yesterday before dinner, although it rained; at last it pelted so hard, that hearing the castanets, Gordon and I popped into the old house, where on a dirty earthen floor, in a kind of ruined place, filled with guerillas, mules, and horses, and with a smoky fire made of wet wood, two girls were dancing *boleros*. There was hardly a roof, the windows were blocked up with loose stones. You never saw a scene which more reminded you of a group of *banditti*. At first our appearance seemed to stop the singing and dancing, but on retiring to the door, and seeming to take no notice, the ladies continued. It was much too dark to see their faces, but they really danced well, both with execution and grace.

I am glad that Captain Loysel has been. sent to France; poor St. Ouary ought to have gone too. By the way, Soult said some little time since, in the hearing of Mr. Larpent (then prisoner), that were he Lord Wellington, after having acquired such a name in Europe, he would go home.

"Your English generals," added he, "may retire when they please; we cannot."

No news today from Pampeluna. Gordon stays for our approaching advance. *Adieu*.—We have just heard that a telegraphic intimation has been received by the enemy of some successes of Bonaparte in the north; they are said to be over the troops of the crown prince, but Lord Wellington disbelieves them, and imagines that, if they have taken 3000 prisoners, the affair in which they have been taken has not on the whole been disastrous to the Allies. A *gendarme*, who deserted yesterday, says that 10,000 conscripts had just joined Soult, but that they were such mere boys, that the older soldiers laughed at them.

Letter 102

Vera: Nov. 1.

The Governor of Pampeluna has again made overtures, and a renewal of conferences has taken place. The officers appointed on either side, met at 10 on the 30th *ultimo*, and were in close divan at 2 p.m. on that day. This is our latest intelligence from that quarter. The surrender of the place is no doubt at hand. Four ounces of bread, and four ounces of meat, has been of late the daily ration. The rain returned last night, and now pours in torrents; this may prove a serious obstacle. The horses of our three batteries of artillery are now without corn; if the rain should continue a supply may not be procured, and leaves alone are but slender fare.

The enemy has for the last two days distributed a paper (of which, if I can, I will send you a copy) inviting deserters, and vowing vengeance against the English Army if it shall enter the territory of France. This paper is in all languages. That extraordinary character, Sir John Downie, has been to the outposts with his letter of challenge to General Villatte, whom he has invited to meet him between the advanced sentries of the two armies, to settle their quarrel by single combat.

I can form no opinion as to the probability of our besieging Bayonne; I presume much must depend on the weather. The marquis has certainly not yet consulted either Dickson or Colonel Elphinstone on the subject. We shall have guns enough, I imagine, but I would rather have more. I would have thirty or forty more, and embark for this special service all the Woolwich, Portsmouth, and Plymouth artillerymen, and carry the place by an unremitting fire from the moment the batteries opened. I find our rockets have been adding to the flames in the north; some are coming out here.

I saw De Grammont yesterday; he was lately in Pampeluna. All the officers declared they were heartily tired of the war, and wished for nothing so much as to get into France, and to quit the service.

"But your tyrant will not let you," said De Grammont.

"*Ah pour cela*," said they, "many of us have served forty years, and, after that, he can hardly call on us for more."

None made any exception to the appellation applied to Bonaparte, which seems odd.

Rain (1 p.m.) increasing; I never saw a completer shower-bath.—*Adieu*.

Paper printed in all languages, and thrown into the allied advanced posts, from the enemy.

The soldiers of all nations, French, Italians, Germans, Polanders, English, Portuguese, and Spaniards, are advised that the deserters coming to the French Imperial Army, are perfectly well received; they are paid for the arms, and for the horses they bring with them; none of them are obliged to serve. Passports are delivered to them to return to their native country if they choose, or to go to the inner parts of France, where they may freely exercise their professions. They are, moreover, treated with all sort of regard.

They are also warned, that the whole French nation is armed, and that in case the English, Spanish, and Portuguese armies should tread this territory, they would find nothing but death and destruction.

Thrown in at the outposts, on the nights of the 30th and 31st October.

Letter 103

Vera: Nov. 2,

Pampeluna has at last surrendered. An *aide-de-camp* of Don Carlos arrived just after my letter of yesterday was sent off. We are yet ignorant of particulars, and have many reports of the state of the place, among others, that there are but fifty guns in it. All yesterday, and for the greater part of last night, the rain continued. It is now (9 a.m.) fine, the sun shining, and we are glad to bask in his rays. Some signals were observed along the enemy's line two days ago, supposed to indicate their knowledge of the surrender of Pampeluna. They fully expect our attack, are always under arms at daybreak, and remain in their redoubts till past 8 o'clock. A day or two of fine weather will make much alteration in the roads, and enable us to move forward. There is, in truth, such necessity for advancing, in order to obtain a more convenient line and to shelter the troops, that we shall certainly not lose one moment after the roads shall be somewhat more passable. I take for granted that the garrison of Pampeluna will be embarked for England.—*Adieu* for the moment.

5 p.m.

I am just returned from Sarre, and from examining the roads by which our guns will have to move. The day has been beautiful: every one out of the huts and encampments which we passed, and seeming to enjoy the sunshine. The enemy has built a smart red house in the redoubt near Sarre. The advanced sentries are very near each other; near enough for one to observe the rings in the ears of the French ones. A couple of officers came to look at us, but our gazings were not accompanied by civilities on either side. We hear that some vessels have reached Passages, after a short voyage from England, that Bonaparte has quitted Dresden, and that the French headquarters are at Leipsic. All this we hope to be true. No further particulars from Pampeluna.—*Adieu* until tomorrow.

Letter 104

Vera: Nov. 3, 10 a.m.

A most dismal day: the rain returned. This is much against our advancing. Some vessels have certainly arrived at Passages from England. If the news they bring be correct, the Allies are between Bonaparte and France. His situation seems critical, yet he has extricated himself from others equally so. We know little yet about the surrender of Pampeluna; but are told that one article stipulates that the garrison, which is in a weak, reduced state, shall not march further than three leagues a day, and that the men look very wretched.

A Portuguese battalion is filing past my window; the poor fellows look jolly enough, though drenched with rain. They are slipping and tumbling towards the front. The Portuguese troops are remarkably well clothed: in truth, their whole appointments do Marshal Beresford great credit, but their men have neither great-coats nor tents. They had their choice of a greatcoat or a blanket per man on taking the field this year, and preferred the latter. The British soldiers have great-coats, and blankets; as well as tents, in the proportion of three per company. I now learn there was in Pampeluna a complete park of fifty-six guns. I am called away, and have, in truth, nothing more in the way of news to communicate. Very cold and foggy day.

Letter 105

Vera: Nov. 4, 8 a. m.

Another cold and foggy morning; the cold has been very intense in the mountains, and several men have perished by it near Roncesvalles, in the neighbourhood of which our advanced piquet was really snowed up. Parties were sent to remove the snow, and to get the poor fellows back. Bullocks were driven before the parties as a kind of precaution against falling into chasms, or concealed pits. Three guns of Captain Maxwell's battery (which is attached to General Stewart's division) were obliged to be left, on the 1st instant, in an advanced redoubt near Roncesvalles, all attempts to withdraw them were fruitless. They were accordingly buried under the snow in the ditch of the redoubt.

It is reported that the enemy has withdrawn a considerable force from his left, and is concentrating towards his right, that is, towards St. Jean de Luz. On our side, it is said that Sir Rowland Hill's corps is coming this way. (*General Rowland Hill* by Edwin Sidney & Alexander Innes Shand is also published by Leonaur).

The approaching severity of the season renders our movement more and more necessary. The 77th Regiment has arrived from Lisbon, about 800 strong, and about 2200 recruits, partly from Lisbon, and partly from England; these are seasonable supplies. A Captain Pomade (seriously this is said to be the man's name) arrived here yesterday, and was to dine at headquarters. He is *aide-de-camp* to Count Cassan, the late Governor of Pampeluna, and is today going to Soult with an account of the surrender of the place. Talking yesterday about the daily consumption of meat by the army, we were told by Mr. Commissary Dalrymple, that 300 bullocks were killed daily, and that the commissariat department had at present about six weeks' consumption in reserve at this rate. He added, that government intended in future to send out 100 oxen monthly from Ireland: this is but a small proportion of supply required; nevertheless, it is something.

Half-past 11.

Colonel Jenkinson brings me word that we shall not advance till the 8th. This looks as if Hill's corps were really moving nearer us. The horses of Ross's troop have been two days without corn, nor is there any immediate prospect of any. Talking yesterday with Sir Lowry Cole, who commands the fourth division, he told me that for the last two months the Portuguese brigade of his division (which averages from 1900 to 2000 men) had not sent a single man to the rear from sickness, till within the last two or three days. Yet these troops, as I have before mentioned, have neither tents nor great-coats.

The mail going from hence to our first division, was taken two days ago; this is awkward enough, but these accidents will happen now and then. Captain Pomade says, that on our first approaching Pampeluna, there were 3000 men in garrison, and provisions for 100 days. That 1000 effectives, and 500 sick, were afterwards thrown into the place, but they had had no supply of provisions, nor had the garrison any intelligence from Soult during the whole blockade. He admits that the works were mined, but says the mines were not charged. He remains here till after our approaching movement. Twenty thousand stand of arms were found in the citadel of Pampeluna. I find I am to be attached to Sir Lowry Cole on the 8th. 'Tis useless, or nearly so, to speculate on military movements, but as Soult has the radical defect of a river in the rear of part of his position, I doubt his fighting very obstinately.—*Adieu.*

Nov. 9.

We are still here, but tomorrow our long intended, and often deferred attack on Soult's position will take place. We are in all respects ready. Tomorrow may see us near Bayonne, though how near, or where the tide of war may carry us, none can tell. I write in the greatest haste, and by starts, having occasional orders to send relative to making fires to dry the roads, to cutting steps to obtain footing for the horses, to close up to let Spanish columns pass, and twenty other matters. Whilst I write I find that three men have attempted to desert from the enemy near Sarre, two were taken in the attempt, and instantly executed, the third made good his escape to our piquet.

But I must conclude, I must turn to a few other matters which require adjusting. Only that our enemy is no ways enterprising, we should be a little awkwardly off tonight, for the Spaniards will be withdrawn before the British advance, and our guns will be what is termed *en l'air*, that is, unsupported.—*Adieu.* I hope to send you good news, and soon.

LETTER 106

Hill half a league from St. Pé:
Nov. 11, 11 a.m.

Success has again attended us. We attacked at daybreak yesterday, opening with eighteen guns on the advanced redoubt, near Sarre. The enemy hastily withdrew his piquets, affording an opportunity for the horse artillery to gain the ridge on which the redoubt was, and to open within 400 yards of it. It was not, however, till after an hour's firing, that the enemy, seeing that our columns of infantry approached on all sides, abandoned a redoubt, made with every care, having a deep ditch, an abattis in front and *trous de loup*. Flattering compliments were paid by all on the undoubted service of the three batteries of artillery on this occasion. The next redoubt on the enemy's left, against which we rapidly advanced our guns, cost only a quarter of an hour, the enemy abandoning it with discreditable precipitation.

But by this time, though the ground was most difficult, the infantry were advancing with great celerity. One of those bursts of cheering, which electrify one, now indicated the presence of Lord Wellington. We advanced through rugged roads, and up and down heights more than difficult, to the village of Sarre. By this time the action became general, from La Rhune on our left, to near Roncesvalles on our right, advancing columns forcing their way on all sides through difficult passes. In front of Sarre, the affair was checked for some time; the enemy, as if ashamed of having too hastily given up his first line, rushed from his second; but on seeing our troops advancing retired, after some skirmishing, to the redoubts and heights of his second line, from which he cannonaded us with great spirit.

It was some time before we could get our guns up, and we had obviously not the best of it. But the infantry, at length moving up, forced a kind of lower ridge in the centre of the position, opposed to our two central columns (I can speak but of these), which we immediately occupied. Here, however, it became necessary to shelter the troops under the steep edge of this ridge, the enemy still playing with vivacity from four fieldpieces, and as many more heavier guns in his redoubts. At last the hill on his left, which was surmounted by a redoubt, was forced by the infantry; the redoubt on his right, in which was a battalion of infantry, remained firm.

The allied troops gained the upper ridge by all passes, and the artillery attempted to follow. Ross's troop alone succeeded and that at the expense of two hours, and the utmost exertion, and by partially making a road. On pushing forward with Sir Lowry Cole, I found the third, fourth, and seventh divisions had gained the ridges, and that the enemy, still fighting *en tirailleur*, were disputing the ground. The redoubt, last mentioned, still cannonaded us, and though, as we advanced, it became isolated, we nevertheless had to expect a rush of the enemy from it. Surrounded, however, by the light division (which had advanced over La Rhune, and after severe loss had forced the enemy in its immediate front, and had moved against the redoubt in question in its gallant progress), our fourth, and a Spanish division, the colonel commanding the 88th French battalion surrendered with his men prisoners of war; and after considerable hesitation, and requesting to hold council with his officers, and subsequently with his non-commissioned officers, laid down his arms on the glacis.

Myari, a little village below St. Pé: 4 p. m.

When I had written thus far, a violent shower of rain obliged me to leave off. I must indeed have done so in all events, as the marquis rode to the front to reconnoitre. I followed of course in the suite, and Ave passed on through the Bois de St. Pé, a wood of considerable extent, and in about a league reached the very advanced sentries. The roads are very bad, the rain continued, and we got along with difficulty. Had the weather been as bad yesterday, the troops could not have marched even without their arms over the country from which they drove the enemy.

From the advanced sentries, the line of the enemy's fires was very visible, but we could discern no vidette or piquet, except one of about thirty men on the top of the singular conical hill called La Barbe. The exact position of the enemy I cannot at this moment learn, but I understand he has abandoned St. Jean de Luz. At this instant there is a heavy cannonading to our left, whilst at the very advanced sentries two or three peasants were brought in.—(*Adieu*; interrupted again. I thought our billets were here. I find we are to go elsewhere. I now write on a log of wood in a kind of open space in the village, which is on the left bank of the Nivelle.)

Nov. 11, night.

I have had two houses since I last wrote, but am now, as I hope, fixed for the night. The house I am now in is a large, and I dare say was, an opulent town-house. It is now plundered of all furniture, in confusion, and remnants of chairs and tables scattered about. Most of the houses are filled with wounded. The last I was in had five wounded in it who had seen no one, and had neither eaten nor drunk since they were wounded. In this house I found a wounded man of the 14th Light Dragoons shot through the head, the ball passing through one eye; but he seems to be doing well.

The troops are licentious; a Brunswicker killed a peasant in Sarre without provocation, and was hanged for it in that village. Another Brunswicker I just now saw hanging, and a piquet placed round the tree to keep the body there. A paper, on which was written, "For plundering and outrage," showed the passing troops for what he had suffered, yet within five yards of the spot I met Colonel Elley, who had just, he said, been thrashing a Spaniard for driving off a sow and her whole litter of pigs.

Now to resume my story. On the surrender of the French 88th Regiment in the redoubt, I received orders to move all the guns of which I had charge to St. Pé, a village on the river Nivelle, and about a league from where we then were. I could only then take Ross's troop, the other guns not having gained the height. On reaching the heights about St. Pé, we found our troops in possession of the village, but the enemy endeavouring to retake it; and the stone bridge over the Nivelle was an object of eager contest. Half a mile lower down the Nivelle there is a wooden bridge, and a little lower, at the village of Agare about a mile from St. Pé, a stone one. The river is twenty or thirty yards wide, rapid, and not fordable.

After severe skirmishing, the troops crossed the bridges in three columns. The enemy had shown considerable bodies of troops on the heights on his side, which were of difficult access through vineyards, and were surmounted by woods. Ross's guns played on the enemy with visible effect, and just before dark the heights were carried. During the whole day we could distinctly hear, and generally see, the heavy firing on our right, which proceeded from Sir Rowland Hill's corps, and the enemy opposed to him; but the projecting base of La Rhune entirely prevented our seeing, and the wind, which was a steady fresh breeze towards the sea, (that is, towards our left), hindered our hearing what was going on with Sir John Hope's corps.

I cannot form even a tolerable idea of the loss on either side, but as the various grounds over which I had to pass in the course of the day had dead bodies scattered in all directions, I should suppose the loss to have been considerable. A French general was killed, but I have not heard his name. When we reached Sarre the inhabitants were generally in their houses, and many women saluted us from the windows: calling out, in French, "Welcome, welcome the English." This, however, is unnatural, and was probably the effect of fear. Three houses were afterwards, I learn, burnt in the village, but during the time I was there, and under a severe cannonade from the enemy, our mounted staff-corps, under Lieutenant During, was most active in preventing disorder amongst the Spanish troops, some of whom, nevertheless, forced their way into some of the houses.

A proclamation has been issued both in French and Basque, assuring the inhabitants that their property and their persons shall be respected; and General Pakenham (Adjutant-General), told me that one of the peasants, who had been taken to Lord Wellington near our outposts this morning, having been asked where he was going, and having answered that he was going to drive his sheep to Bayonne, was told he might go where he pleased, and take his sheep where he pleased. This ought to produce confidence on the part of the inhabitants.

Early today I pushed to the front, and on reporting where the guns were (for Sympher's battery had joined Ross during the night, and Douglas's had reached St. Pé) I was sent back to detach Sympher to the fourth division, and to bring up Ross and Douglas. On passing St. Pé, I found a French prisoner plundering a house; he had stolen a shirt; no one was there. On my return, seeing the owner, I told him what I had seen; but the man, like the generality of the peasants, understanding nothing but Basque, could not comprehend my meaning, but he called the curate of the village to me.

The curate who was in his best sacerdotal robes, seemed a middle-aged, respectable man; and on my saying how desirous we were to restrain pillaging, said he was fully aware of it; but in time of war, added he, "men rob and plunder when they can, of which no people are more convinced than we." I suspect he alluded to their own soldiery, who by all accounts have plundered their own peasantry a great deal.

About 3 p.m. yesterday, the enemy blew up some magazine or work, at Mondarain, a rocky ridge to our right. He also blew up a couple of tumbrils of ammunition just in our front, and abandoned one gun, which is the only field-piece I have yet heard of as having been taken. The other three which he showed escaped. On the whole, the French did not show a determined spirit of resistance. In more than one instance, I could observe their officers making every endeavour to bring them on, without success; yet they fought like brave troops, but like dispirited ones. There was no flight, nothing like a rout.

The marquis's object was, as we believe, to force Soult to fight a pitched battle: this, the action of yesterday, though a general one, was not,—the enemy retiring before it came to the push, but retiring skirmishing. The ground over which the affair was fought was so rugged that it would be difficult to attempt a sketch of it. You must fancy rocks, and hills, and woods, and mountains, interspersed with rough heaths, and rivers, and everything but plain ground.

In St. Pé the names of the proprietors of the houses are carved in stone over the doors. It is a nice little town enough. The houses are full of good forage: the hay is excellent, made, of course, from the meadows in the little valley of the Nivelle. As we returned through the town, on our way here, we found the head of a Spanish column just entering, drums and fifes playing. How different must the feelings of the people be! how changed are times! There are in this house two little girls of ten or twelve years of age; one of them could not restrain her anger at seeing the Spanish column filing towards the town, and hearing a band playing. This was more natural than the contrary conduct of the women at Sarre.

Nov. 12.

We now know of fifty-one guns which have been taken, of which five only are brass. Sir Lowry Cole told me just now that his division (the fourth) had only lost 400 men in the late affair. The fog clears, and we shall ride on; but nothing of consequence can be done today. Soult is still retiring, we believe, though to where exactly I know not; tomorrow, probably, we shall push on and feel his pulse. Twenty-eight guns are taken on the left. We were with Hope's corps this morning: their task seems to have been easy, the enemy never fairly standing to meet our troops *Adieu* for the present.

7 p.m.

The events of the day were confined to pushing forward our advanced posts about three quarters of a league beyond Bidart (which is a little bathing town in front of St. Jean de Luz); and occupying with our third division the conical hill of St. Barbe. There was some heavy firing and musketry to our right. We believe General Campbell's brigade (which is the left of Hill's corps) to have been engaged, but have, as yet, heard no particulars. On gaining the left, near the village of Guetary, we turned to our left, towards St. Jean de Luz, but did not go there. The town is entire. The mayor retired with the French troops; the other public functionaries remained, and a deputation from the town was sent to Sir John Hope before his column advanced.

In consequence, the necessary safeguards were furnished. The column filed through without doing the least mischief. I believe I have mentioned that two men were hanged for plundering. Talking on the subject as we returned home tonight with Sir Edward Pakenham (the Adjutant-General) he told me a singular anecdote. Soult shot, three days ago, a French captain of infantry and member of the Legion of Honour, who had been sentenced to that punishment by the summary verdict of a court-martial at St. Jean de Luz, under the following circumstances. Just before the French quitted St. Jean de Luz, the officer in question had his company quartered in a certain part of the town. A woman came to complain to him that his men, expecting to leave the town, were beginning to plunder her house. The officer paying little attention to her entreaties to befriend her, and to restrain the excesses of his men, she observed, "that if they, who were the natural defenders of the country, would not protect them, the English might as well be there at once."

"Oh," said the officer, "if you are a friend to the English, you shall see how I will defend you;" and thus saying, he himself set fire to her house.

A *gendarme* being present, exclaimed that though he could not take the officer into custody, nor prevent him by force, he would immediately report the circumstance to the marshal (Soult), which he did; and the officer, who was before that time esteemed as a brave and good man, was tried, condemned, and executed.

Baring, *aide-de-camp* to General Sir Charles Alten, and another German officer whose name I have not heard, are denounced as spies in the general orders of the French army, their persons exactly described, and rewards offered for their apprehension. I now suspect that Baring had himself obtained the information, which he lately gave me, of the defeats of the French in the North. I asked General Pakenham whether he had heard of this, he replied he had, and that he had seen the orders in a French orderly book, and that he should feel it his duty to acquaint Baring of the circumstance.

Altogether the late affair has ended well. The enemy abandoned St. Jean de Luz with hardly a struggle. Socoa, a little fort opposite St. Jean de Luz, is also given up; the gun-carriages burnt. Tomorrow we shall decidedly push on, but I do not expect anything like a general action. We are here two leagues from Bayonne, which a woman in this house told me is full as an egg. The inhabitants, having sent most of their effects there, are woefully afraid of our taking it by storm. I do not just yet see where our present movements will end. Bayonne will probably bring us up; it will, of course, stand a siege.—*Adieu.*

******

Note.—From the 11th to the 25th no letters were received, the *Little Catherine* packet, with the intermediate mail, having been taken.

******

Letter 107

St. Jean de Luz: Nov. 25.

There has been little new, except a severe skirmish two days ago. In making a fresh disposition of the line, the light division, which was somewhat retired, was advanced in order to connect itself by a shorter line with the 3rd and 5th divisions on its right and left flanks. In doing this there was necessarily some skirmishing, and the 43rd Regiment is said to have lost about seventy killed and wounded. A Captain Hopkirk, of that regiment, is taken prisoner. On the 22nd we lost some men and horses in foraging. A company of *caçadores*, and a squadron of the 12th Dragoons were sent out to protect the foragers, which duty they performed with great gallantry. The 12th lost eight men and horses, but the batmen, straggling, and getting into houses, many of them were taken. Bull's troop had two gunners, two horses, and a mule taken.

Among other officers who lost animals on the occasion, I hear of Colonel Barnes of the Royals who lost four mules, and Lieutenant Sinclair of the Artillery, who lost a horse and a mule. The general orders of yesterday give strict directions for future foraging, curtailing also the number of horses and animals kept by officers; this is by way of precaution against the probable want of forage during the winter. The enemy continues to strengthen his entrenchments in front of Bayonne; on our side we are forming lines, and throwing up redoubts on the favourable points of our lines. Future movements remain secret. I suspect the marquis waits for further accounts from the North. Our next movement would entail the necessity of besieging or blockading Bayonne; and there are considerable difficulties in doing either, unless we could insure fine weather.

This morning arrived a gentleman announcing himself as belonging to the house: he is come from Bayonne. He says he is not the proprietor, but his foreman; that the proprietor is a tailor, and has gone to Bordeaux; that Bayonne is exceedingly full of people, and in great confusion; that understanding the English committed no excesses, but protected the inhabitants who had remained in St. Jean de Luz, and respected their property, he determined to return and continue his trade; and that accordingly permission having been obtained from the authorities at Bayonne, about 1000 people returned yesterday from Bayonne to St. Jean de Luz. He adds that the roll of the men of the party was thrice called over at different stations before they quitted the French lines, and that they were passed over under the protection of a flag of truce. I asked the name of the Governor of Bayonne, of which he professed ignorance. I am glad the people are coming back; it looks well.

Major Cator tells me he has just seen a well-informed man from Bayonne, who says that Bonaparte has been at Paris and has ordered a conscription of 300,000 men *Adieu.*

Letter 108

St. Jean de Luz: Nov. 27.

We continue quietly cantoned here. Some of our troops are near Bayonne: it is not more than a mile and a half from the point of our line to which it is opposite. This point is occupied by the light division. We have no real information, but in revenge millions of reports. Many think we are on the eve of moving; it is certain we are getting to the front all our pontoons and means of crossing rivers, but a siege being an important step, and one involving grave consequences, I doubt our undertaking one at this season. Soult, who is between the Nive and Adour, is said to be ready to cut and run behind the latter on our approach.

Altogether, I suspect we await news from the North. The times are so big with events, and a little while may produce so much, that in looking forward one hardly knows where to stop. Among other reports, Bourdeaux and Bayonne are said to have manifested great unwillingness to furnish their contributions of men and money, and that the senate is said to have demurred about the conscription.

The marquis has had late *Moniteurs,* some of which are said to have been sent direct from Soult; but I believe we ought rather to believe none of these reports, which are probably invented by way of hoax.

I yesterday walked to the end of the street to look at the sea. Though the day was quite calm, there was a great surf. There is an ingenious, and very strong wall of masonry to keep off the incursions of the sea, which is said to be gaining on this coast. The upper part of the wall is eight feet above the wash of the beach, and the front towards the sea is a very gradual slope. This reminds me of Holland, where all the banks, which were made by great industry and ingenuity, have the same imperceptible slope, that the waves may exhaust themselves by meeting with no direct opposition. This wall is about 300 yards long, ending a little short of the mouth of the Nivelle; but as I hope to send you a sketch of St. Jean de Luz, from our own observation, I shall stop here.

The Marquis has issued another proclamation, continuing the laws and constituted authorities, but requiring quietness, and a total cessation of all intercourse with France. I have not yet seen this proclamation, but will send you a copy. This is a pretty place, as I hear, and hope to see. All speak of the lines in front (which were turned by the attack of our centre at Sarre on the 10th) as exceedingly formidable, and most people believe we should have failed in endeavouring to assault them. Our force is now nearly as follows:—

BERESFORD — *Centre Column.*

3rd Division,	British	-	-	-	4000
„	Portuguese		-	-	2500
6th „	British	-	-	-	5000
„	Portuguese	-	-	-	2000
7th „	British	-	-	-	5000
„	Portuguese	-	-	-	2500
			Total	-	21000

HOPE — *Left Column.*

1st Division,	British	-	-	-	6000
„	Portuguese	-	-	-	2000
5th „	British	-	-	-	4500
„	Portuguese	-	-	-	2000
			Total	-	16500

COLE — *Reserve.*

4th Division,	British	-	-	-	4000
„	Portuguese	-	-	-	2000
			Total	-	6000

ALTEN — *Separate.*

Light Division, British		4000
" Portuguese		1500
Total		5500

HILL — *Right Column.*

2nd Division, British		6000
" Portuguese		6200
Total		12200
General Total		61200

COTTON — *Cavalry.*

British and German about		6000
Portuguese		1200
Total		7200

Artillery, 102 pieces; and a dozen mountain guns.

LETTER 109

St. Jean de Luz: Nov. 28.

Nothing new today. The belief of an approaching movement gains ground, yet it is difficult to see through intended operations.

Bayonne being divided into three distinct parts, it follows that the force in it is applicable against the assailants at any of the three; yet there is no leaving it in the rear.

Not being able to undertake offensive operations, I have been thinking of defensive ones, and have been reading Carnot's work on the *Defence of Fortified Places*, from which I enclose you some extracts, as you may never have heard of the work, which, however, is the standard one in France, and contains much useful information. Should the Allies not continue to be as successful as we hope, France will owe her safety once more to her triple line of fortresses.

Carnot cites, in his book, instances of good ancient and modern defences, preceded by instances of culpable and base conduct of some governors. In a subsequent memoir, he recommends some changes in the works of places, and in another, a novel mode of defence by vertical fire, both too long for me to enter into the discussion of their merits. But, throughout the book, the inculcated principle is, that much longer defences ought to be made than are usual; that in a good fortress the garrison should never yield; and that while ammunition, provisions, and wood remain, they never can be driven to the necessity of so doing.—*Adieu.*

Letter 110

St. Jean de Luz: Dec. 2.

We have little news. All is still quiet, and the intended movement of our right wing, delayed, as we suppose, on account of the weather. We have had some very heavy rains, and last night hail accompanied a thunder storm; but no snow, or severity of weather. Intelligence from the side of Bayonne leads us to believe that the lately ordered conscription is felt somewhat severely; the people say no former conscription has so oppressed them. It is supposed that, although 300,000 be the avowed number of conscripts to be raised, that many more will really be taken; but that the number is diminished to keep the minds of the people quiet.

Major Dashwood, Assistant Adjutant-General, who went into the enemy's lines yesterday with a flag of truce, says they admitted that there were commotions in Switzerland, and in Holland; and that the Scheldt fleet were ill-disposed. They were very anxious to know the cause of our having fired from the *Challenger,* supposing it to be owing to some great news, and asked if it had been in honour of Marshal Wellington's having been created duke of some town in France. The firing was merely a salute to the Prince of Orange as his highness went on board.

A letter from Major Dyer, yesterday, mentions that there has been a fire in St. Sebastian, at the house next the church containing the powder, which had occasioned much alarm; and had been put out with difficulty, the Spaniards fearing to work lest they should be blown up. However, by dint of exertion, the fire was put out; and their fears were subsiding when Dyer wrote. The fire was an accidental one in a house occupied by Spanish troops.

Dec. 4, 4 p.m.

A vile rainy day after a stormy night of thunder. The surf yesterday was very high. To the left (as you face the sea) of the wall, which is, I find, 460 yards long, the Nivelle runs between two stone quays into the bay: it is, perhaps, forty yards wide. Such a quantity of sand was driven into the mouth of the river by the surf that the river was quite choked up; one might literally have walked across between the billows. In consequence, there was for the whole day a high tide at the wharves and quays, and part of the town was overflowed. This shutting up of the river occasionally happens, I understand; and when accompanied with rain does considerable damage.

We have no particular news today. Colonel Ellicombe tells me that his landlady arrived last night from Bayonne, and says that Soult has lately been sending regiments from his army into the interior: chiefly foreign ones. It is probable enough that he should fear their being ill-affected.

Dec. 5.

Nothing new; we remain quiet on both sides. I hope next week to have something to announce. No mail, as we hoped there would have been. We are anxious to hear what is doing in the north; and where our militia heroes are to be sent.

The troops continue very healthy: they have not yet been long enough in cantonments to feel the inconveniences of being comfortable. How strange this sounds! yet the thing is very true. There is still a good deal of surf, too much for any boat to venture out.—*Adieu.*

LETTER 111

St. Jean de Luz: Dec. 7.

All at headquarters is quiet; but not a word is said whether we are fixed for the winter or not. The truth is, so much depends on passing events that all is uncertainty. The movement of General Hill's corps, which I have so frequently mentioned, has not yet taken place; but I have no doubt that it will, whenever the weather shall permit. We have daily arrivals from Bayonne, chiefly women; indeed, all women and children, except such men as escape in women's clothes, which some do. They are not allowed to bring anything with them; and all agree that the conscription becomes oppressive, that the *gendarmerie* are distributed all over the country to enforce it, and that insurrections are expected.

Dec. 8, 9 a.m.

When I had written thus far yesterday, I heard of the arrival of an English mail. Three or four hours, however, generally elapse before letters are delivered, so to while away the time I ordered my horse and rode to Socoa, which I had not before visited. Except a loop-holed tower with one gun in the upper storey, the works are merely temporary field ones, not well designed, and unfinished. At the wharves there were two brigs, and twenty-three *feluccas* or *galliots*, all landing supplies, which a host of mules were carrying away. I should mention, that we expect hay from England and straw from Portugal, and corn from both.

Ross's troop will march to Cambo from St. Pé today. Captain Michell's battery moved last night from Urogne towards Ustaritz: another battery from Fuenterabia will move there today; and the long intended movement of our right will forthwith take place. I am not yet sure whether I shall be employed or not; but am of course ready.

5 p. m.

All is arranged for our moving in the morning. The marquis, we hear, has just gone on to sleep at the marshal's, near Ustaritz. We have reports of all kinds: some state that almost all the troops have left Bayonne on account of insurrections in the interior, others that there has been a commotion in Bordeaux, and that the white flag is hoisted there. The mayor here certainly encourages these reports. This morning the woman of the house came into my room, and asked me whether it were true that the Emperor really was dead, and if it was true that he had shot himself. The minds of all are certainly prepared for any event which may take place.

We have received our letters, &c., and are yet in a ferment about the good news from Holland and elsewhere, brought by the mail; nothing else has been talked of since. As usual, what we have already heard only makes us more impatient for that which one hopes to hear. The Prince of Orange left us in good time. I have no post assigned in the affair of tomorrow, but shall ride with Dickson, and follow in the usual suite of the marquis. We shall set out at 2 or 3 in the morning, so as to reach Ustaritz before daybreak. It would be curious to get hold of Bayonne without the trouble of a siege; but we have no reason to suppose so improbable an event.

8 p.m.

The rain has returned, and may spoil, that is prevent, our moving. I hope not; the thing must be done, and therefore the sooner the better. We have just had a message that the marquis is to be called at 2 o'clock, and that his horses are ordered at half-past. We have given similar orders for ourselves. Our former intelligence that his lordship was gone to Ustaritz, was unfounded. Bell, who dined out, has just returned, and brings a bad account of the weather; this rain is *mal-à-propos*.—*Adieu*.

Letter 112

St. Jean de Luz: Dec. 10.

We had yesterday a long and cold day. We got up from hence a couple of hours after dark. Not much was done, though I hardly know what I write whilst waiting for my horse to go to the front. We were up yesterday at 1 o'clock, but it was near 4 before we set out. We rode a couple of leagues on the main road before we turned to our right. The day had broken before we reached Ustaritz, which we passed through going to Cambo. The troops had just crossed the Nive at both places, and with hardly any opposition.

Opposite Ustaritz is an island, (the Nive being there in two branches): this island is of considerable extent, and our piquets having previously occupied it, a pontoon bridge had been thrown from the left bank of the island during the night. This was of course of advantage on the first movement. The permanent bridges both at Ustaritz and Cambo had been destroyed. At Cambo, the troops crossed by fording below and above the bridge, but chiefly just above it: ten men of the 6th Portuguese Caçadores (the first regiment which crossed) having been drowned in attempting the lower ford.

When we reached that point, the infantry were filing over the bridge, scrambling down the broken slope of one part, which had been hastily and insufficiently repaired. Very few men succeeded in getting over. A Portuguese regiment of cavalry was passing just above; there was no time to be lost, as the river was swelling a little from the rain then continuing. We crossed at the lower ford, which was good enough for cavalry, but could not be generally used on account of the steepness of the left bank. On advancing through some swampy meadow land, and very deep roads, we soon found ourselves in the main road leading from St. Jean de Luz to Bayonne.

The enemy retired skirmishing, our troops following and pressing them. The country in this part is hilly, and certainly very strong in a military sense. The troops with which we now were, were those of Sir Rowland Hill. There was a good deal of skirmishing, and some partial contests for particular points, but nothing serious. About noon, the enemy's left seemed to be strengthened, both behind the main Bayonne road, and to our right of it. He made a show of advancing, and brought forward three field-pieces, which played with vivacity, though with little effect on our troops, which were then resting till the centre columns should have moved on a little.

Our own guns had been left at Ustaritz and Cambo and an intermediate village, from which points they had played when our troops first advanced. However, three Portuguese guns coming up answered those of the enemy. Ross's troop came up, but was not sent on. It seemed that we were not to push on our right, already somewhat in the air, as it is called. We waited on a little hill on the right, from which we could see the movements of both sides, till about 3 o'clock. We were cold as ice. We then moved to our left, to another hill, which had been just taken by the sixth division. To our right and front, the enemy remained steady, showing, perhaps, three divisions, and making fires beyond the slope of the hill, as if intending to remain.

To the left of the hill on which we found our sixth division, was another, a mile or more from it. A French corps, which occupied it, suddenly quitted it, and, soon after, as suddenly returned, as if ashamed of retreating so hastily. Below this hill, on the top of which was a large cross, is a village, (Villefranque,) from the detached houses of which there was a galling fire. Our sixth division receiving orders to advance, carried these houses, village, and hill. It was then almost too dark to distinguish objects, but after the loud cheering which precedes a rush forward, we could observe the enemy giving a hasty volley or two and retiring. The marquis now announced his intention of sleeping at Marshal Beresford's, at Ustaritz.

We, who had no time to lose, having a much longer journey, made the best of our way, and crossing the Nive at Ustaritz, reached the main road from hence to Bayonne, through intricate, perplexing by-roads, which we never should have found but for the guidance of Colonel Ellicombe. We learnt that on our left. Sir John Hope's corps had pushed on towards the outer works of Bayonne, as there was a good deal of firing in that direction during the whole day. I dare say there has been some loss in detail, but I am yet ignorant of particulars, even of the loss where headquarters were. Ramsay was twice struck yesterday by musket-shot, but with trifling injury. He has come off with a graze in the chin, and a contusion in the breast, a ball having struck the button of his waistcoat. We saw few killed or prisoners. Some of the latter were mere boys of conscripts, who laughed and seemed quite pleased to be safe in our hands. They were excellently clothed.

Whilst we were at the first hill, I learned that a large good-looking house just before us, in a wood, was the Château de Garat, belonging to Garat the advocate, who, I think, conducted the proceedings against Louis XVI.; further, but not in sight, is the Château de l'Empereur, a royal residence.—*Adieu*: the horse is at the door.

9 p.m.

We have just dined, and I am in a bad cue for writing, but I write knowing that tomorrow will be a busy day. Such, indeed, has been today. We have had a sharp affair on our left. Having seen what was doing on our right yesterday, I determined this morning not to return there unless there should be firing in that direction, which on going towards the front there did not appear to be. Not expecting anything, I had left Bell at home, and rode with Gordon beyond Bidart, to where our piquets were on the main road. On reaching the piquets we found them warmly engaged, and the enemy advancing in force, and attacking with great spirit. There was only the second brigade of the fifth division on the spot, the first division having returned to St. Jean de Luz about 11 o'clock at night from the movement of the day before. Ramsay's troop, and the 16th Dragoons were also up.

The enemy, however, pushed our troops a good deal, and we began to give way rather in disorder. To add to the perplexity of the moment, the fifth division, having been separated during the night, and the ammunition mules not being forthcoming, had hardly a round left. I spoke to Sir John Hope on the subject, and sent Gordon back part of the way with an order to Bell to send for 150,000 ball cartridges from the reserve near the Bidassoa. There was nothing to be done but to hold our ground as well as we could, till more troops and ammunition should arrive. The ground was little favourable for bringing many guns into action at a time. To our right, and close to the road, was a low thick wood; to the left a rugged heath, intersected with gulleys and ravines.

At one time the enemy had gained the wood. A little before this, Sir John Hope was struck in the shoulder, and had a ball through his hat; General Robinson, commanding the second brigade of the fifth division, was severely wounded, and carried off the field. In this situation, ebbing and flowing, repulsing the enemy, and being ourselves forced back, we continued till about 2 o'clock, by which time a considerable body of troops had arrived in detail, and we learned that the first division was at hand. Captain Moss's battery of guns (late Lawson's) had also joined.

The marquis now arrived from the right, where all was quiet, the enemy having withdrawn his left during the night, and Hill's corps having this morning moved on till it touched the Adour. Early in the morning, the enemy had also attacked the post and village of Arcangues, (near the centre of our position), and at first made an impression on our light division which was there, but which repulsed the attack. On Sir John Hope's mentioning to the marquis the want of ammunition, I received orders (Dickson not being on the spot) to send for the reserve depot to move up. The attack still continued, and the fire of both cannon and musketry was severe. It was clear that the enemy, imagining we had weakened our left by throwing forward our right yesterday, had with his whole force made a vigorous attack on our left, in the hope of pushing on to St. Jean de Luz.

The enemy showed much spirit: a little more and our column would have been in great confusion. Several moments were awkward enough. The affair continued till dark, when we remained on the ground we had occupied in the morning. The only fruits therefore of this affair are the losses on both sides, which I imagine have been very severe, I only yet know of Colonel Lloyd of the 84th who was killed, Baron Decken of the 1st German Hussars, and Cairnes of ours, wounded: both too, being merely spectators, Cairnes' battery being at Fuenterabia, and Decken being *aide-de-camp* to Sir Stapleton Cotton, who was not in the field. Cairnes is wounded in the head, but I hope and believe not dangerously. Decken has a ball in the thigh.

You will see other names in the *Gazette*, but no one has fallen whom I believe you know. I never could get more than ten or twelve of our guns into action at a time from the nature of the ground. The enemy showed more, and played with more than usual vivacity. The day was cold and raw, and after 2 o'clock very rainy. We stand tonight thus: Hill's corps on the right of the Nive, and with his right resting on the Adour: the sixth division recrossed the Nive after yesterday's affair at and near Ustaritz: the third division at Arbonne: the light division at Arcangues: the first and fifth divisions at Guetary and Bidart. I do not know where the fourth and seventh divisions are. In this position the Nive cuts our line in two, but a third bridge over this river will be established tonight near Villefranque.

Tomorrow we shall be ready for another attack, if Soult should offer one; or we may, perhaps, ourselves move forward. I saved a long ride to no purpose by not going to the right this morning. In the present deep state of the country one grudges every step one's horse takes; I have ordered mine again at 3 o'clock tomorrow morning, at which hour we learn the marquis's horses are ordered. Ramsay is well, his face merely grazed; his side sore from the contusion. He had one man killed, a corporal and five men wounded yesterday: I have not yet received his report of today, but believe there are not more than three or four wounded, and a few horses killed. His troop fired today with great precision, and of course did considerable execution.

Tomorrow we may find Soult has retired, or he may risk a general action; though I doubt the latter. The marquis was a good deal exposed today, and unavoidably so. It was necessary for his lordship to ride from point to point, as there was no hill or rising ground from which the whole field of action could be seen. The wood too, which I mentioned, prevented our seeing, and was in every way an annoyance; it will be cut down during the night.—*Adieu*. I shall lie down, and take rest for tomorrow, which may be a decisive day. I have today seen few prisoners: not more than 100. In returning home we overtook a party of sixty-nine prisoners, and six officers. I hope tomorrow to add to my letter, and to give you good news. I do not exactly see to what our present movements are to lead; a little more rain and the country will hardly be passable.

Dec. 11, 4 a.m.

Today will enable me, as I hope, to add good news, yet I hardly expect much to be done. Troops rarely fight on three following days, but the positions of both armies are critical: they cannot long remain as they are at present.—*Adieu*: it is yet dark, but I imagine we must set off in a few moments.

9 p.m.

I write after a good dinner. We got home just before dark. On setting out, when we had got a mile from hence, the marquis received a letter from Sir John Hope. A light was procured from a neighbouring cottage: the letter was, we understood, a report that all was quiet at the outposts. On passing Sir John Hope's house he joined us, but limping. Besides the contusion in his shoulder, he had suffered from a wound in the ankle. On reaching the front we passed through the wood (not cut down), or rather on one side of it where the chief loss on both sides had been on the preceding day. Many a fine fellow lay on the ground.

The fifth division was brought a little forward beyond the wood, and the advanced skirmishers on both sides were soon within forty yards of each other; neither side, however, fired for some little time; and during the time of advancing the division, we learnt that three German battalions had come over to us from Soult's army during the night. When we were talking about this unexpected circumstance, the officer commanding them arrived to pay his respects to Lord Wellington, who received him with great affability and politeness.

It appears that there were with Soult two regiments of German troops: that of Nassau, and that of Francfort; each having two battalions. These regiments have long wished for an opportunity of leaving the French service, but having been suspected, have, under various pretences, been kept in the rear. In the affair of yesterday, Soult, having brought forward his whole force to attack our left, these regiments were in advance. They were in General Villatte's division, and the general being severely wounded, the division was for a time without any special commander.

The officer commanding the Nassau regiment proposed to a colonel commanding a French regiment, that his corps, the two battalions of the Nassau regiment and one of the Francfort battalions, should occupy a height a little in advance of where they then were. This was proposed with the view of coming over, and agreed to by the French colonel without suspicion. The officer commanding the second Francfort battalion having been wounded, no communication of the intended movement was made to that battalion. As it got dark, the roads being intricate, it was further proposed that the battalions should file to their ground by different routes. In the interim a Francfort officer had made his way to our fourth division, announcing the intended defection of the three battalions on condition that they should have the word of honour of a general officer that the troops should be well received, and should be sent to Germany.

No general being on the spot, and time being precious, Colonel Bradford, I believe, Assistant Adjutant-General to the division, gave his word; and means were immediately taken to apprise the three battalions, who came over in a body, and as it is said, unperceived at the moment by the enemy. These battalions are said to be very fine troops, and in the highest equipment. There are 1300 men, who are now here; of course, left armed, and perfectly free. The individuals whom I have seen are fine men; they will move tomorrow to Passages, and be embarked for England as soon as ships can be got ready. The commanding officer dines today at headquarters; he seems a gentlemanly man, and I dare say will give the marquis some useful information. He had hardly quitted us when the firing began: it was rather sharp, but the enemy giving way, the marquis rode off to Arcangues, where the fourth and light divisions were, who were also skirmishing with the enemy, and rather pressing him.

We remained here till 2 o'clock, the skirmishing continuing, but without any particular advantage on either side; our object being probably to prevent Soult from detaching to his left to attack Sir Rowland Hill. The day was exceedingly raw and cold. Finding that nothing was doing, I returned to the left with Colonel Cathcart. On rejoining the fifth division we found a strong column of the enemy forming as if to attack it; after waiting some time we continued to the left, and found the troops as we had left them in the morning. After talking half an hour with Ramsay, who had orders to return to his cantonments at Bidart, and finding that the marquis had also come to the left, we walked homewards.

Soon after we had passed Bidart, a roll of musketry and a brisk cannonade announced that the enemy had attacked the fifth division, which had been ordered by Lord Wellington to withdraw to the ground which it occupied in the morning. This day has, therefore, been passed in skirmishing, each side maintaining its own ground. Of course, there has been some loss in detail, but to what extent I know not. Tomorrow we shall not attack, but be ready to repulse the enemy; so, at least, we hear, but I rather think the day will be quiet. The last three days have been harassing to the troops on both sides.

Our present position is one liable to attack on both flanks, and will therefore be an uneasy one during the winter. I imagine we shall soon change it, either by advancing or retiring; in either case Bayonne is of great value to the enemy.—*Adieu.* I should mention that the German battalions, which came over last night, have left their baggage and money behind; the step was a decided one with them, and it seems to have been well managed.

Dec. 12, Half-past 10 p.m.

We have again had severe skirmishing (in the same wood), which began at 10 and lasted till 3. Soult showed three or four divisions. The affair, however, was confined to the wood. The loss fell chiefly on the Guards, who had three officers killed and three wounded; these losses, in detail, are vexatious. The troops, too, are necessarily harassed, remaining continually under arms. We have brought up our reserve troops, and tomorrow I imagine will produce something decisive.

To the right of the wood, already mentioned, I had sent a couple of guns of Moss's battery by Sir John Hope's orders; they were not, however, intended to play, unless the enemy's columns, forming immediately in their front, should attack; and were even to suffer some cannonade without returning it, our object being not to provoke an affair. Unluckily the orders, which I had sent by Captain Moss, did not reach the spot before the guns had fired, and the skirmishing soon became general and not to be controlled; on such trifles do actions and the lives of men depend.

Sir John Hope has been hit three times, and his horse twice, within the last two days. All his staff, too, have had themselves or their horses wounded. We believe even Lord Wellington has requested Sir John to recollect of what consequence he is to the army, and not to expose himself so much. But nothing but Sir John's extreme gallantry saved an utter confusion at one of our awkward moments on the 10th. The enemy today is throwing up a battery opposite Arcangues. We shall do the same, but we must manage to push Soult over the Adour, where, uncivil that he is, he is very unwilling to go! The colonel of the Nassau troops (whose name is Krüse) and his field officers, dined yesterday at Lord Wellington's, and were highly pleased with their reception.

Colonel Krüse is a Bavarian, but was brought up in Hanover, and was for some years in the Hanoverian Guards. His troops formed part of those of the Confederation of the Rhine. He complains bitterly of the treatment they met with from the French, till very lately, when (probably with the view of inducing them to remain) great attention has been shown them. They have been entirely new clothed, and have received pay to within six months, though the generality of the troops of the French Army is eighteen months in arrear.

Colonel Krüse has written to General Villatte, thanking him for attentions whilst under his orders, but explaining that having received the orders of his sovereign (which is the case,—Nassau is a small principality on the Rhine, near Mayence), his troops have quitted the service of France to return to that of their own country. The colonel recommends the women and sick left behind to the humanity of the general, observing that his brother officers and himself freely give up their personal baggage, in performing an act prescribed by their duty.

In conversation. Colonel Krüse, who seems a good man, rejoices that he was enabled to effect the escape of his battalions without firing on the French. A courier has been sent to our troops in Catalonia, with the news of this event. There are yet with Suchet two battalions, and a squadron of these Germans, who, it is hoped, will also come over, if they can receive the intelligence from us before Soult shall send orders, as he probably will, to disarm them. As our line of communication is shorter than Soult's, we hope this may be the case.—*Adieu.*

Letter 113

St. Jean de Luz: Dec. 14, 4 a.m.

I despatched a long letter for you to Passages yesterday, not knowing whether the mail was made up or not; though I hardly think the packet will be permitted to sail till something decisive shall be done. Yesterday was a murderous day; more so than any of the four preceding ones. The attack was confined to Hill's corps, which completely repulsed Soult's attacks. I left St. Jean de Luz about 6 yesterday morning: never was there a finer frosty morning. Dickson remained to make arrangements about some guns to be placed in battery at Arcangues. On leaving St. Jean de Luz, the marquis suddenly struck off by a byroad to the right; and after what was more like fox-hunting than anything else, for a couple of hours, we found ourselves near Arbonne.

By this time we heard very heavy firing in the direction of Hill's corps; and soon after, on reaching Arcangues, learnt that Soult had just vigorously attacked Sir Rowland. I received Lord Wellington's orders to send for the reserves of musket ammunition from San Pé and Arbonne, and to forward it to Ustaritz; to deposit at Guetary all the great reserve of small arm ammunition, which had reached Guetary during the night; to send back the carts to the rear for a fresh supply; and to send gun ammunition, for the batteries of artillery with Hill's corps, by every means in my power. It was necessary to write orders for these purposes, which were sent off by Gordon, who was with me. This cost me a quarter of an hour, and I did not overtake the marquis till he had gained the front.

I crossed the Nive by a new bridge of seventeen country boats, near Villefranque, and gained the hill above that village, on which hill the affair of the 9th ended. On pushing on, I found Sir Rowland's corps warmly engaged, having already thrice repulsed very determined attacks of the enemy, who, then foiled, was again returning. The loss on both sides at that point was severe. Ross's troop and Tulloh's Portuguese battery were then firing very steadily but cautiously, from the value of ammunition. The roads were heavy in the extreme, literally above one's horse's knees in stiff mud and clay.

You will see from the map, that our front was necessarily very confined, extending (at about a league from Bayonne, which was full in view) from Petit Mouguerre, on our right, to a swamp near the Nive, on our left. Soult's front was still narrower. Bayonne in his immediate rear, with his entrenched camp at a little distance from the town, to which camp, or rather under the cover of his guns placed in position, his troops retired when beaten back by our people. Soult showed about four divisions, that is, about 20,000 men, which, drawn up in two lines with supporting columns, looked more numerous than they really were, from the confined ground on which they acted. Our troops were very favourably posted, the ground admitting only of one or two points of attack, of which one was by the main road, leading to St. Jean Pied du Port.

The country here is beautiful, and studded with country houses, meadow fields, vineyards, woody hills, and large sheets of water in the valleys; these, with the Adour, Bayonne, and the shipping in the river, made altogether a view of great beauty.

After a great deal of firing, and many movements of troops, the affair was confined to a general skirmish along the front of both lines. We posted Ross's troop (of which four guns only were in the field, two having been detached with the 14th Dragoons towards Hasparren) and a battery of Portuguese guns as much in advance as was advisable, and kept the enemy in check on the main road. One of Ross's guns was dismounted by a shot which broke the axletree, but a spare carriage being at hand, the gun was soon replaced in action. I was glad to shake hands with Sir William Stewart, who was all animation and life, said the affair was a second Albuera, and added many obliging things about the service of the guns.

Sir Rowland Hill and the marshal, to both of whom I communicated the dispositions made of the ammunition in reserve, were very friendly. Determined not to give way on our right, the marquis had ordered up the third and sixth divisions forming the marshal's corps, and the fourth division was also sent for and placed in reserve. While I was talking with Sir Henry Clinton, a few prisoners were brought in; amongst them a most gentlemanly man, the Lieut.-Colonel of the 16th French Infantry. I never saw a man of more pleasing manners: I observed his decoration of honour, which was very handsome; it had Napoleon's head in the centre, in gold, on blue enamel, encircled with laurels.

On speaking to the lieut.-colonel, he answered in English, said he had been brought up in England, and had been at school at Richmond. He said they had news from Paris in seven or eight days, and that Marshal Soult, receiving his letters by *estafettes*, generally got them in six days. Before I had the opportunity of asking him any interesting questions, he was given to an officer of the mounted staff corps to be taken to the rear. For some time, previous to this, the sun, which had shone bright in the morning, had been obscured, and the smoke hung so that we could scarcely perceive what was going on.

Lord Wellington now moved to the right, and, passing a very deep ravine, rode through Petit Mouguerre to the end of the tongue of land extending from that village towards Bayonne. We were here out of the smoke, and saw Bayonne as it were in reverse. Cavalry and baggage were filing over a bridge of fourteen arches, wooden, but on strong piers; the fourth arch had a drawbridge. Boats, too, were continually crossing, apparently filled with baggage. The view here was of singular beauty, to which no doubt the haze of the day added. After looking about here for some time, the marquis returned again to the left, where we remained till about 4 o'clock, when the affair terminated in a continued skirmish.

Finding that Lord Wellington intended sleeping at Ustaritz, I accompanied Colonels Elphinstone and Ellicombe to the left. The road is most intricate: we crossed the Nive by a ford half a mile below the bridge near Villefranque, the water being low, (the tide affects the river higher up than this point,) and riding along the piquets of the line and looking out very sharp (as not knowing whether our left or any intermediate point might not have given way a little,) reached the main road just at dark. We were somewhat perplexed, the wood near the main road having been cut down, as well as two or three other groves which used to be landmarks. A house or two which had been of annoyance were burning. We found that the enemy had retired on the left. I know no particulars of loss yesterday, though I have heard several names. If we hold our right, we hope that Soult, finding he can make no impression on either flank, and that we can prevent his receiving supplies by the Adour, will cross the river, leaving a strong corps in Bayonne, and the entrenched camp.

Dec. 14, 2 p.m.

Just returned from the front; all quiet. Sir John Hope is confined today to his house: Ramsay the same. Now that the necessity for exertion has ceased for a moment, their wounds, though not severe, are troublesome. We hear no news of Soult or his movements, but are sending more batteries of artillery to our right. I send a common brass ornament of an eagle; I picked it up yesterday in the field. Never did more dreadful sights present themselves than I saw yesterday; the main road in several places literally running with blood. But enough of these horrid subjects.

Letter 114

St. Jean de Luz: Dec. 15.

All is quiet today, and all are so busy writing that I have heard no new details, nor am I acquainted with our losses: but these the *Gazette* will inform you of. Our position remains a singular one, and but that we are accustomed to victory, would be an awkward one. We have a river which cuts us in two, and have two others of difficult and uncertain passage in our rear. Soult's position, too, is critical, but Bayonne and his entrenched camp in front of it form a den into which he can retire out of our reach. On the evening of the 13th, when Hill's corps had squeezed his crowded masses into the angle formed by the Nive and Adour, I would have staked my life in doing great things with a good Rocket corps, which would have scattered dismay in a situation not likely to occur again in many years. 'Tis well to notice these things, and to be ready to apply one's observations, as opportunities occur: 100 mortars would have played the deuce with an army so placed; but mortars are not portable: indeed, how our guns got along is wonderful, even to ourselves; but our equipments are good.

We have been existing the last five days on a pound of corn per horse and the little grazing which can be managed after the business of the day is over. On our left, and during the fire, our fellows, not actually engaged, grubbed up what fodder they could among the furze bushes or fern: but corn is now arriving; hay or straw we have none. Soult's troops which have fallen are his best, and better no marshal need have. Ours were so shaken at one time on the left, that to Sir John Hope's extraordinary coolness and gallantry we owe our maintaining, or rather regaining, the ground we had lost on the 10th, which, although little in extent, formed the strong point of our position. It is said that Lord Wellington has requested Sir John in future not to expose himself so much.

I have had the good fortune to have been at all points at the most decisive, or at least at the most interesting, moments, and have been the bearer at the moment of handsome acknowledgments of the services of our guns. This is infinitely more flattering than anything said afterwards, and so our fellows felt it. The horse artillery has escaped with hardly any loss, and has behaved very well. Ross and Ramsay only were engaged. I think we meditate to cross the Adour above our present right, yet the roads are execrable; one swims as it were in mud.

I have no misgivings, but Soult works on our inner circle, and can apply his whole force to either flank. His troops, too, are comfortably housed, ours are in the field. I should be pleased, therefore, that we were over the Adour. Both sides at this moment are taking breath; it is a kind of trial of obstinacy. All prisoners (although they are but few) agree that the enemy's loss has been very great. The mayor of this town, who has daily news from Bayonne, says 7000. Soult is said to be in want of provisions. Dickson is made colonel in the Portuguese service: I wish he were a general; he fully deserves all that can be given him, either as honour or reward *Adieu.*

Letter 115

St. Jean de Luz: Dec. 20.

All has been quiet since the 13th. Soult having detached three divisions to his left (on the right bank of the Adour) to disquiet our right, has since returned them to their former position near Bayonne.

We are sending two brigades of cavalry, a division of infantry, and some horse artillery towards Hasparren, to clear the country of the enemy's cavalry under General Paris. Hasparren is to the rear of our right. Soult has nine divisions, exclusive of his lately-joined conscripts. The rains have returned, the country is almost impassable; the weather for the last two days has been uncomfortably warm, and we have had a good deal of lightning. Some deserters have just come in, but they bring no intelligence of any interest. Our horses have been starving; we got a little hay for the staff horses yesterday, but we had been for many days without hay or straw, or any substitute. There is no grazing, though the exercise of moving does the creatures good.

Dec. 23, 2 p.m.

A stormy, rainy day. Not a syllable of news here, except that the floods have carried away all our bridges over the Nive; but they will soon be repaired: a dozen pontoons moved towards the front this morning. An English mail has arrived. In a letter from Colonel Robe to Dickson, he mentions, what you will be very glad to hear, the provision made for Colonel Fletcher's family. The young baronet has his father's pension of 500*l.* a year continued to him, and each of the other children have 120*l.* allowed them, the boys being, moreover, considered wards of government: all this is very liberal, and gives Fletcher's friends real pleasure.

Have I told you that Downman expects to have charge of the eastern district during Sir George Wood's absence?—so Downman assures me. I imagine he has by this time sent you an engraving of St. Sebastian. By the way, there has been another fire in that devoted town, the house occupied by the English and Portuguese artillery having been burnt by some accident, not well explained, on the night of the 20th instant. Notwithstanding the rain, the weather is very mild. I now sit, without a coat, in a room without a fireplace. Deserters come in daily from Soult's army, which they describe to be in want, though they probably say this, knowing how much we wish that it should be so.

Dec. 24.

Captain Lane, of the Artillery, has arrived at Passages, with a rocket detachment of fifty men, but no horses. Lord Wellington has permitted a division of the rockets to be tried. The division means two carriages of rockets, of which each carriage conveys about fifty rockets, and there will be a couple of carriages in reserve.

There has been today some skirmish on our right, or rather in rear of it. Some Spanish cavalry, having been pressed by the enemy's cavalry, was supported by two squadrons of the 18th Hussars, which have suffered, as we are told, having advanced till they were entangled with some concealed infantry. Major Hughes, of the 18th, is said to be wounded, and Captain Bolton killed: all this, however, is mere report. I rode this morning to Socoa, where all was bustle; the wharfs were crowded with little vessels. A ship, with artillery horses on board, lately put in there, partly from mismanagement, partly from stress of weather. The horses, of which there are twenty-five, are all safe: they stood in the hold, up to their knees in water. Of the last hundred horses sent from Portsmouth to Santander, twenty-two died on the passage, which appears to have been uncommonly rough. This has been a bright and fine day.—*Adieu.*

Dec. 25.

We have been to Divine Service. I never heard a better or more appropriate discourse than the one we have had from Mr. Driscol; yet there is much distraction in attending service, however well performed, in the open air.

Today the weather is beautiful, clear and frosty, not a breath of wind, yet much more surf than usual. The surf broke at least half a mile from the shore of our little bay, the sun shining beautifully on the spray, which I never observed so far from land before. It is now 2 p.m.: at 3 we shall set off for Bidart, to dine with Ramsay.

There is today but little new. An emigrant is now here, who comes from the interior of France, that is, from the country near us. I know not his precise errand, but he has for the last four days dined at headquarters, and has certainly received 300 or 400 *doubloons*, which no doubt are to be well applied. He brings an overture from the servants of De Grammont (of the 10th Hussars), to pay him their rents, and an assurance how much they wish for old habits and masters. De Grammont's estates are in the neighbourhood of Pau. Soult's headquarters, by all accounts, are at Dax, which is the second day's common march from Bayonne towards Mont de Marsan.—*Adieu* till tomorrow.

Dec. 26.

The day is again beautiful, frosty and clear. Gordon and I returned from Bidart this morning. You would have laughed to have seen us last night at Ramsay's: there being no fireplace in his room, we adjourned after dinner to the kitchen, where we invited his host and hostess to partake of our wine, which they did. The lady, a fine, handsome woman, sang two or three little songs very well. Her husband, who is many years older than the lady, told us he had been for nine years prisoner in England; that he had been at Leek in Staffordshire. He had been master of a merchantman, and had lost his vessel. He has only returned home since we have been here, little expecting, I dare say, to find his house full of Englishmen. They both seemed very well contented with the guests.

One of the *stanzas* the lady sang was a little in praise of the emperor, who, as the words said, "conducted them to honour." "Pretty honour!" said the lady, half to herself, after finishing the song.

Gordon heard yesterday from his brother at Xeres, near Cadiz. The letter was dated the 10th instant, and mentioned that the communication with Cadiz was again open, that the Cortes were about to proceed to Madrid, and that they were daily expected to pass through Xeres.

I was amused by an anecdote Mr. Larpent, the judge-advocate, told me of the Lieut.-Colonel of the French 16th Regiment, mentioned in one of my late letters as having been taken prisoner. Larpent had known him as *aide-de-camp* to Count Gazan, when he had himself been prisoner, and being willing to return the civilities he had received, offered the lieut.-colonel any money he might require, which the other declined. Larpent asked whether he had been at all ill-treated when taken, to which the lieut.-colonel said, no, not at all; that nothing had been touched or taken from him; that a Captain Cameron, (I do not know the regiment, although I saw the officer at the moment,) to whom he was immediately taken, asked him instantly if the man had taken anything from him; "and I assure you," said he, with frankness, "I felt quite vexed that I had been so well treated, since I am sure your officers would not have been so well used by our men." There was an honesty of national feeling in this.

More inhabitants are returning almost daily, A banker came in from Bayonne yesterday: he is a corn-factor, as well as banker, and is said to have wished to have a contract for supplying the troops. It is observable that both this man and all others who come in begin with eager inquiries whether any of the Bourbon family are with the army.

Bonaparte's speech to the Conservative Senate has been received, but I have not seen it: report says it is a moderate one; but it is easy to make speeches. Suchet is said to have joined Soult with two divisions: so report says, how truly I do not know.—*Adieu.*

1814

Letter 116

St. Jean de Luz: Jan. 1, 1814.

Little has been done here since my last. I dined at headquarters the day before yesterday. The day went off unusually well: the party was twenty-four. The French emigrant, whom I have lately mentioned, was also there. I find his Spanish name is Don Juan de la Rosa, his French one O'Reille; that he was an inspector of troops in the French service, long resident at Xeres, near Cadiz, and that he has been in correspondence with Lord Wellington for nearly two years, having made himself personally known to his lordship immediately after the Battle of Vitoria.

After dinner, French papers were brought to the marquis: they were the *Journal de l'Empire*, and contained Soult's accounts of the late affairs to the 12th instant. The marquis read them, and there was much laughing at the false statements they contained. Among other lies was an account that the Basques and Bearnois were waging a terrible war against the English, and that they even penetrated to St. Jean de Luz. These people, you know, are the natives of this country, who, poor souls! care but little for either side, only ardently desiring peace.

I should have mentioned that in the morning we had an alert, owing to a false alarm that the enemy was moving a body of troops to attack Arcangues. The report was sent in by General Charles Alten. The marquis was out hunting, and soon rode to the front; but before he reached it, the alarm was over. I had a long visit that morning from General Victor Alten, who gave me an account of the late skirmishing with the 18th Dragoons. It appears that the Spanish general, Morillo, wishing to make a reconnoissance, applied to General Alten to lend him a couple of squadrons, which was reluctantly complied with; General Alten not knowing whether the other was not the senior, and as such able to command compliance with his request.

The country is very much intersected with small woody ravines, and the 18th Dragoons, having unluckily quitted the main road, and inclined to their left, had to pass some intricate ground by files. This being seen by the enemy, some infantry were sent against them, and before the cavalry could retire from a situation in which their horses were only of disservice, they lost several men and horses, killed and wounded. Captain Bolton, of the 18th, was taken prisoner, after being mortally wounded. General Alten sent in an officer with a flag of truce, to see Captain Bolton, and soon after, the surgeon of the regiment, whom Captain Bolton wished to attend him in preference to the French medical officers. The enemy paid great attention to the captain, and to the other wounded who fell into their hands. General Alten mentioned that the trumpeter who went in with the flag of truce saw many German soldiers, who all said they wished to desert, but were afraid of being taken, and were uncertain how they would be received in our army.

At our headquarters table, the marshal spoke a good deal of our advanced posts, mentioning a point or two which Colonel Sturgeon and I, on comparing notes, found we did not quite know, and accordingly agreed to ride and see. We set off yesterday morning at 9 o'clock, and returned home about 6. The day was beautiful, but the roads were execrable. I thought we should have stuck fast twenty times: as it was, we were occasionally obliged to whip and spur, and were sometimes for a hundred yards together up to the horses' bellies in thick mud stiffened by the frost. We were, however, well repaid by the view of Bayonne, seen very distinctly from a near point between the Nive and Adour. From this point we took part of the entrenched position in reverse: that is, we saw behind it. It was the part which approached the left bank of the Nive.

A working party of perhaps 1500 men were busily employed in strengthening the entrenchment, and another, but smaller, party were throwing up a work in our front. We had a good view of the little stockaded bridge (over the Nive) connecting little and great Bayonne. The Château de Marrac was directly before us. It is the royal residence which I have before mentioned as having; once belonged to the royal family of Spain, that is, to one of the families of the Bourbons, and afterwards, (though I forget at this moment how,) having become the property of a Bayonne merchant, it was purchased by Bonaparte. By-and-by, perhaps, we may be better acquainted with this *château*, which is, however, merely a good country-house, with no particular beauty or grandeur about it.

On our side, we are busy throwing up works near the main road in front of our left, at Bidart, at Arcangues, and on almost every knoll. Some of these redoubts will be strong. One cannot help feeling for the inhabitants. It happens frequently, as at Arcangues, that a *château* is fortified; that is, every part is pulled down which does not suit the purposes of defence, and all the noble trees round the house are felled: the owner himself looking wistfully at all the mischief doing to his property, and wishing, no doubt, the whole art of war at the deuce.

On our regaining the main road, we found a confused multitude coming in from Bayonne, and soon learned that about 400 ladies and a very few old men had been allowed to pass the French outposts. Many of the girls were really beautiful: on my observing this to the Mayor of Bidart, who is a gentlemanly man, and the owner of the house and woods mentioned in a late letter, as the scene of the attacks on the 10th, 11th, and 12th December, he told me that the natives of this part of the country were always admired, and especially the women, for the beauty of their complexions, he added:

> Ay, and the girls are good as well as pretty. It was a rare thing to hear of a false step till this country became the theatre of war and was filled with both armies. The instances were so rare that they used to be cited.

From the excellence of the ladies we turned to that of the soil, which he said never required to be idle. In truth it appears even now to be in high cultivation, and I dare say deserves all the praises bestowed upon it. He spoke much of Bayonne, and deplored the probable fate of the town, saying that the houses being very high, and having much wood about them, and the streets being very narrow, there appeared an almost certain prospect of its being burnt in the event of a siege. So much for the mayor, who ran over the usual miseries of war, which, he said, had cost him one house burnt to the ground in the war of 1793, and two others utterly pillaged in the present war, together with all his stock and grain.—*Adieu*.

Today has produced no news, except, indeed, a report that Soult has gone to Paris. I should have told you, that after we rode yesterday we had an excellent dinner at Sturgeon's house. We invited his hostess and her two daughters, Eugenie and Antoinette, to favour us with their company. Eugenie had been to see her father (who is a civil engineer at Bayonne) at the outposts that morning, having had only one tumble from a mule of Sturgeon's by the way. The girls laughed as girls usually do: the old lady would have been equally funny, but had her apprehensions,—not of the French, whom she had no doubt we should always beat,—but of the Turks.

"Oh, those terrible Turks!" she repeated a hundred times with the most whimsical gravity. "What sort of creatures are these Turks? how I dread their coming."

"Indeed, mamma," said the girls, "we dare say they are very good people."

Once more, *adieu*.

Letter 117

St. Jean de Luz: Jan. 3.

There is little news, and not the least appearance of any movement of consequence on either side. Switzerland has made common cause with the rest of Europe: 18,000 newly-raised conscripts are said to have joined Soult's army, and General Harispe to have reached Bayonne from Catalonia. Harispe is a native of Beam and is understood to have offered the French Government to raise a corps of Basques and Bearnois. General Thevenot, formerly governor of these provinces, has the command in Bayonne. The day before yesterday we took from the enemy, without opposition, a small island in the Adour, near Mouguerre. It may be useful to us, but I do not imagine we shall soon attempt to cross that river. The roads are so execrable, that our communications and supplies form the chief obstacle to advancing. Our horses are eating chopped furze, of which, in the absence of hay or straw, they seem vastly fond. There are rumours of insurrections at Pau, and of almost general desertion of conscripts from Dax: and fifty other reports, with little, or, more probably, no truth in them.

Some time ago, you asked about the number of men who had suffered death in this army; I mean by summary justice. I learn on inquiry from the judge-advocate, that thirty-seven men have been executed during the last twelve months. This number includes all who have suffered by sentences of courts-martial or otherwise. Those who have suffered without regular trials, are not more than four or five. There is no doubt that great judgment is shown in the exercise of the powers of life and death vested in Lord Wellington, nevertheless, the number of executions startles one when thus shown in its aggregate.

The average number of executions in England is fifty-five a year, and these out of about 500 persons who are sentenced to death, and out of about 5000 who are confined in gaols for offences of all kinds. This is on Mr. Larpent's authority, who told me that he was frequently applied to, and by well-informed men of his own profession at home, to know how many men suffered; whether seventy were not executed at once; and twenty other questions, arising from reports at home.

Nothing can be more creditable than the extreme pains taken to preserve discipline, nor more pleasing than the general acknowledgment of the good conduct of the army by all the inhabitants, who talk to us on the subject without reserve, and with apparent sincerity. I believe no army ever behaved better, even in its own country, than the British Army is now doing here; this is owing to Lord Wellington's wholesome regulations. Another fire in St. Sebastian has occasioned another remonstrance from the Spanish Government, which either is or affects to be persuaded that we are at least not unwilling to add to the miseries of that devoted town. In consequence of the remonstrance, our artillerymen (the only British in the place) will be withdrawn.—*Adieu.*

Letter 118

St. Jean de Luz: Jan. 22.

Except one trifling alert, nothing of interest has occurred since the date of my last letter; but we have fifty, I may say five hundred, reports daily; and almost hourly some amuse themselves by inventing, and others by believing, these tales of an hour. The prevailing report of the day is, that preliminaries of peace have been signed; this story was coined at 4 p.m.; at 2, it was said that the enemy had retired from his advanced posts, and had taken shelter (from the weather, I suppose, as we have had a little snow) in his entrenched camp in front of Bayonne; this is probable enough, though not the more so from being current here.

Three divisions of the enemy's army are believed to have been removed into the interior; this, if true, will probably oblige him to withdraw his whole force to the right bank of the Adour. Soult has but nine divisions in his army, of which three or four have lately been manoeuvring in rear of our right, but to little purpose, except that of harassing both sides. He has some armed boats on the Adour, and we are going to have some too; I do not, however, look forward to our attempting anything just yet, the roads get daily worse.

Cameron, of the 92nd, arrived with his regiment today; it is come for clothing, of which it has great need. Cameron had a narrow escape on the 13th December, having his horse shot under him. Some of our corps are very sickly. There are brigades which do not amount to more than five or six hundred men effective for duty; but the new clothing will much assist in restoring our poor fellows. Those regiments which have not yet received their clothing make but a sorry figure. The horses keep their condition surprisingly, the chopped and bruised furze has proved invaluable; hay and straw they have none. We, at headquarters, get hay in the proportion of about one-third of the regular allowance. We have been giving about 5000 barrels of powder to the Spaniards, for Pampeluna and St. Sebastian; they declare there were only 800 barrels in Pampeluna when it surrendered!! You will see a spirited letter to Sir Henry Wellesley from the marquis, relative to the withdrawal of the British troops from Cadiz and Carthagena; I hear of no news from Catalonia, nor from the interior of Spain, nor do I know what the Cortes are doing.

We have had some very severe gales: a few nights ago, a brig was blown out of the harbour of Socoa, carrying away a great post to which she was moored; and was driven on shore on the opposite side of the bay. She was forced nearly a couple of hundred yards over rocks having not above a fathom of water on them, and lies high and dry on the sand: her crew of five men took to the jolly-boat, and were lost; a woman alone remained on board and was saved. The master was on shore; her cargo was hay and biscuit, both necessary articles and in great request.

Jan, 26.

We have been expecting a mail from England for some days, one, if not more, being due. But Colonel Banbury, who arrived from London on Sunday (the 23rd), says that when he sailed from England, the Falmouth road had been blocked up for four days; in this case we must have recourse to patience. We are in the depth of winter, and a very keen biting frost. On Sunday the marquis suddenly rode out, and, as we afterwards learned had been to the mouth of the Adour. He picked up a small escort of cavalry by the way, but met with none of the enemy's parties. Burgoyne tells me that about three-quarters of a mile above the mouth of the river (at which there is a shifting bar) the Adour is confined, for nearly a mile, between stone quays. It is at this place above 500 yards wide, and flows with considerable rapidity; I wish I had been of the party. The marquis and suite only looked about for a few minutes, and returned.

I rode yesterday to the advanced posts, which I had not visited since the enemy had withdrawn to his entrenched position. On approaching the village of Anglet we turned suddenly to our right; and at the distance of a mile, reached a *château* called *Belle Vue*. We had a good view of Bayonne from the ruins of a mill close by.—*Adieu* for the moment; I am called away.

4 p.m.

The frost has disappeared, and we have returned from Urogne in the midst of heavy rain. We went to Urogne to look at the rockets, of which one of each kind had been sawn up, that the inside might be visible. Like true boys, we could not resist the temptation of burning the pieces, after which, and taking away the shell from one of the smaller rockets, we set it off without a stick, expecting it would have no range at all; but after running irregularly along the ground, it suddenly mounted into the air, whisked over the end of the village, and fell three or four fields off. We were pleased when we found no mischief was done. I much doubt these rockets being ever tried in this country, there is a prejudice generally against them; but we shall have another trial for our own satisfaction.

I have seen Alava today, and have received a passport and a letter for the Governor of Pampeluna, which I wish to see; I shall go with Webber Smith. The expedition will take me half a dozen days; I shall set off from hence on the 80th. Alava showed me a very handsome sword which the town of Vitoria had presented to him; the hilt surmounted with a casque; his arms on one side of the grasp, his cipher on the other; both encircled with diamonds. Beneath, on the ear of the sword, were the arms of the town. I have not seen a handsomer thing of the kind for a long time.—*Adieu.* I have some little arrangements to make, and some orders to give to the man whom I send forward with the horses, on the road towards Tolosa.

Letter 119

St. Jean de Luz: Feb. 4, 8 a.m.

My last letter announced to you my intention of setting off for Pampeluna, from whence I returned yesterday much pleased with my excursion, though made in five days of more than common rain and snow. I rode to Usnibil on the 30th, where Smith's troop is quartered, arrived there about 4 o'clock, saw his troop out, and then dined at the house of the curate, at which the officers mess. The curate is a respectable old man, of about seventy, very active, formerly the best shot, as he assured me, in the province, and still, occasionally, partaking of the sport. He had that morning (Sunday) been up at 5 o'clock to meet a corpse on the mountains, and, besides the usual service of the day, had walked a considerable distance to visit a sick person.

These fatigues did not prevent his enjoying several boyish sports over the kitchen fire in the evening; among others, chalking the floor, and getting up again without tumbling; and another game which consisted in placing the feet in the nooses of ropes suspended from the ceiling, while the person so placed walked backwards on his hands, to chalk at as great a distance as possible from where he set out: here, as before, the difficulty was to avoid being tumbled over. You will think these games singular ones for such a day and such an age, but the good old man seemed to enjoy himself as much as the youngest of the party: he supped soon after, being waited upon by a *duenna* who reminded us forcibly of Dame Jacinta in *Gil Blas*. The supper consisted of a kind of bread-soup, an egg, and a roasted apple: so much for the cheerful curate, whose income I learned was 240 dollars a year.

He spoke with great animation of his little town, in which he had been for forty years. It is prettily situated on the River Orio, and has several good houses belonging to late inhabitants of St. Sebastian, the fate of which town is spoken of with great warmth. A very severe memorial is about to be presented to the Cortès by the inhabitants of St. Sebastian: I did not see it, but suppose we shall hear of it by-and-by.

We rose next morning so as to start at daybreak; our road lay over the mountains. We joined the high-road at Andria, about a league from Tolosa, whither we had sent horses the day before (Webber Smith, Lieut. Saunders and I, formed the party). At Tolosa we turned to the left, leaving the Vitoria Road, and keeping the Camino Real, (or Royal high-road,) to Pampeluna, which lies in a narrow valley with precipices on each side, and the River Orio, swelled with rain, rushing with great rapidity. This road is the finest imaginable. It is well made, but not paved, and having been less used than the Vitoria Road, is in high repair.

For about five leagues from Tolosa it rises by an almost imperceptible slope, but near the village of Betelu it ascends a mountain by turning and winding, and parts from the River Orio, which has its source in one of the adjacent mountains. Here the weather changed; and from torrents of rain we had got into the regions of snow and hail. A little beyond Betelu we reached Lecumberri, a very wretched-looking village, about half way between Tolosa and Pampeluna; here we changed horses again, and, continuing our journey, began immediately to descend, having thus crossed a branch of the Pyrenees.

The River Arga was now on our left hand, and, leaving the open country, we again entered for a couple of leagues the narrow and romantic pass through which the Arga runs. About three leagues from Pampeluna the country becomes again, in some measure, open, and a few vineyards are to be seen; the snow, too, disappeared, and the rain returned in torrents. We reached Pampeluna about 5 in the afternoon, half drowned, and eagerly inquired for the best *posada* or inn. All agreed that the best was in the Plaza de Castilo on the square of the citadel: thither we went, but were told that one was full, that another had no stables, and that the host of a third had gone out.

In short, we began to think we should sleep in the streets, when we obtained permission to sit by the kitchen fire of a *posada*, of which the mistress was out, till the lady should return and signify whether we might be permitted to remain and spend our money, which, we took occasion to observe, we were very ready to do. Insensibly we got into conversation round the fire, and began to be amused by the curious figures who came in, when the mistress arrived. She seemed glad to see us, and showed us into a room up four pairs of stairs, where there were two beds, and a third was promised to be made on chairs; this, with a hot supper, and a pan of wood-ashes laid on the floor, made us quite comfortable, and we supped in high glee, having a couple of mountain beauties to wait on us, who vied with each other in telling us all the scandal and news of the place: as these ladies were at once cooks and waiting maids, we had already scraped acquaintance with them over the kitchen fire.

We retired to bed early, resolving to rise betimes next morning, and to wait on the governor with our letter of introduction; however, it was 10 o'clock before we could prevail upon ourselves to put on our wet clothes again, and after a good breakfast we sallied forth in a snow-storm, and were graciously received by Don Rosiella. We had our fears that we should have been asked to dine, but the alarm was needless; he was very polite, sent an officer round the works with us, and we took our leave.

We walked very attentively over the citadel and works, which were extensive and strong, in perfect repair, and well supplied with artillery. The officer who accompanied us was communicative and intelligent; and, in despite of the snow, we were much interested. The citadel especially is very strongly occupied. Walking round the works and over the city, looking at the cathedral and one or two other churches, and poking into several shops in search of we knew not what, occupied the whole day, and we returned to our *posada* about dark, and had a most excellent dinner of soup, stewed partridges, woodcocks, and roast meat,—and all, at our earnest entreaty, dressed without oil or garlic, two essentials in all Spanish cookery. You would have smiled to see our dinners roasted on both days; the spit is turned by hand, and is committed to anyone sitting by the fireside, so that the meat may be said to be roasted by a kind of accident.

We procured one bottle of champagne by sending out for it, had a libation to the health of absent friends, and went to bed determined to start at daybreak; however, it was 10 o'clock before we could get our breakfast, and we set off in a very sharp frost which soon changed to heavy snow, so that before we reached Lecumberri, the snow was sufficiently deep on the road to make us satisfied that we had done wisely not to defer our return. From all this you will have seen that we cannot boast of our society at Pampeluna, which nevertheless I am very well pleased to have visited. The works are a great deal stronger than I had supposed, and I have no doubt it is well we did not attack them, since I think we should have failed.

The town, or rather city, for so it is, (and is moreover a bishopric,) has few fine buildings though many fine houses, generally four or five and occasionally more storeys in height; the streets are rather narrow, and altogether it is a sombre-looking place. On two sides the River Arga runs under the walls, which are very high, and on these sides not accessible. The players, for whom we had inquired, had gone to Tafalla, which is on the Zaragoza road; the shops contained nothing very tempting, and I purchased only one or two trifling articles. So much for Pampeluna, where besides the numerous guns on the ramparts, there is on the esplanade a very complete park of about sixty pieces of artillery.

On retracing our steps, we reached Tolosa at 5 o'clock, changing our horses at Lecumberri by the way: we had taken the precaution, as we passed through Tolosa, of bespeaking dinner and beds at a *posada*, and were agreeably surprised to find that the people recognised us and were preparing our dinner. Here, too, as before, we were glad to sit by the kitchen fire, and heard all the news of the place from a very interesting girl, the daughter of the house. It seems some English commissaries had given a ball a few nights before, but had not invited the Spanish officers of the garrison; in revenge, these officers gave another ball, and, to outdo the commissaries in civility, purposely omitted to invite any of the ladies who had been at the first ball. These interesting jealousies had put the whole place in confusion. Had we had our clothes, we should have been glad to have gone to the ball; as it was, we were too dirty to go anywhere, and could only join in the conversation with the ladies round the kitchen fire, who were making all manner of remarks.

After our supper we were glad to go to bed, and had left the supper room (which was our bedroom) to have a warm by the fire, when it was announced that the grandfather of the girl I have mentioned, who had long been ill, was dying. Upstairs bolted the whole family; but immediately returned, saying, but without any visible emotion, that he could not live many hours: however, on inquiring the next morning, we learnt that the sick man was no worse, and after breakfast we set off. I parted from Smith and Saunders at Andria, and continued my route hither, changing my horse at Astigarraga, between Ernani and Oyarzun, and reached home by 5 o'clock. So much for a dull story of a very wet trip, though an interesting one.

The Duke d'Angoulême and some other person of the Bourbon family are here. I had met Lord Wellington's carriage at Oyarzun; it had been sent there, it seems, for the illustrious personages, but they had found another before its arrival. The marquis had gone to St. Sebastian the day before, to receive them; but they had not then arrived.

Two divisions and 200 artillerymen have quitted Soult's army for the interior. The Bayonese report that the Allies have been worsted in a sharp affair at St. Dizier, near Châlons, and beaten in a still sharper one at Breda. I disbelieve both. It has been said that the Alicante Army was marching hither, but I doubt the fact altogether. We shall move when we can, our pontoons are at Bidart; but their bullocks are again sent back to procure some kind of sustenance near Irun, where the pontoons have hitherto been. The enemy has many gunboats, or rather armed boats, on the Adour, with which some of our mountain guns (the only ones we can move) exchange shots; and now and then convoys of provision boats get down the Adour into Bayonne.

All otherwise is quiet; but we expect to move, though individuals can hardly budge a step when they leave the high road: never was any country so deep. The rains, too, have returned, and every little streamlet is swollen. General Buchan's brigade (which is a Portuguese one in Hill's corps) was lately four days without bread or meat, owing to the swelling of a little rivulet, which prevented their receiving their supplies. Money is very scarce here; dollars are selling as high as eight shillings: we hear that 300,000*l*. is coming out.

Sir John Murray will, I think, never be tried: government wishes his trial to take place here. Sir John is at Valencia, and the evidences, among whom are three or four Spanish generals, an admiral, and two or three naval captains of ours, all on the other side of the Peninsula. After Admiral Hallowell, his most violent accuser, is a General Copons, a Spaniard: the charges are three, and the principal one is for not having sooner re-embarked his army, so that any imputation for not fighting is out of the question; a fourth charge founded on Copons' letters to Lord Wellington, was disapproved by our government and withdrawn.—*Adieu*.

Letter 120

St. Jean de Luz: Feb. 8.

I have but little news for you; there has been some trifling affair in Catalonia, but this Lord Wellington's last week's despatches will probably have mentioned. I have as yet no correspondent in what we call the Alicante army; but I wrote yesterday to Major Williamson, commanding our corps there, in the hope of enticing him to send me from time to time a notion of what is going on.

It appears that about the 24th January, part of our army, with some Spaniards, advanced from Villafranca to surprise some post of the enemy, near the River Llobregat (near Barcelona); that after some fighting, in which our troops behaved well, and the Spaniards under General Sarsfield equally so, the enemy retired; but that a corps under the Spanish General Copons, which was to have intercepted the enemy's retreat, having been delayed from the badness of cross roads, the enemy was not cut off as had been intended. The Spanish loss is stated to be two colonels, and about twenty men; the British do not appear to have suffered. Suchet is said to have retired towards Gerona, leaving 5000 men in Barcelona.

The letter from which I take the above story, (the correctness of which I have no immediate means of ascertaining), is written from near Taragona, by an officer of our corps, and dated 24th January; it was received here this morning. The General Copons mentioned, is the Spanish general who preferred charges against Sir John Murray, as I mentioned in my last letter. It appears that the enemy has still posts in Valencia, of which Saguntum and Peniscola are two; the name of the third I have forgotten. I believe I have also mentioned that we have transferred the horses of a battery of artillery, and of one of our gun reserves (that is, of the convoy of artillery waggons with reserve gun ammunition) to the pontoon establishment, which consists of thirty-six pontoons in marching condition; these with their attendant carriages require about 600 horses.

Feb. 9.

Last night we had a bulletin from Bayonne, announcing an alleged victory over the Allies near St. Dizier, on the 27th and 29th January. Bonaparte is said to have moved after it to Brienne; we have, indeed, all manner of reports, among others, one that the senate was requesting Bonaparte to make peace; but these reports are not worth mentioning till one can ascertain their truth a little, which I have not now the means of doing. I am called away.—*Adieu.*

Feb. 11.

I could not find time to take up my pen yesterday; we were all at Fuenterabia with the rockets, of which we fired a good many, and in various ways; some of them answered well enough; I have no doubt we shall find them useful on the Adour. We shall soon move; all is getting ready. Hill, with his own corps, and another division, will move to the right; this, however, will be only a feint, we shall really pass the Adour near its mouth, but more of this hereafter. A brig arrived here the night before last; she is said to bring papers to the 31st January, announcing a report, which we had before heard, that the Paris Bank had stopped payment.

We hear, too, of insurrections in Brittany. We learn that in all parts of France there is an unwillingness to furnish the quota of men for the army, which has at last amounted to a refusal to send men for general service, though the authorities declare the people are willing and ready to defend their homes. I believe this much to be well authenticated. I went to a ball last night at the *Salle de la Mairie.* The room was very full; about thirty women, some fine women, none remarkably handsome, nor of high rank, but rather the contrary; *cotillions*, English country-dances, and waltzes, took their turns. The room was of a good size, with the Gallic eagle in *bas-relief* opposite the door as you enter, and a pedestal remaining at the upper end of the room, on which had stood a bust of Bonaparte, now broken to pieces. The marquis and marshal, and all the smarts were there, including Count Dumas, and some other French noblemen in the suite of the Duc d'Angoulême, who, however, was not present: so much for the ball.—*Adieu.*

Letter 121

St. Jean de Luz: Feb. 13.

We begin to be in a bustle: Hill's corps and the third division moved to the right yesterday; Hill moves on the Gave. This, it is conjectured, will produce a corresponding movement of Soult to our right, in which case we shall suddenly throw a small corps over the Adour, near its mouth, secure some batteries there, so as to afford safe entrance into the Adour for vessels, and protect the passage of more troops, and the formation of a bridge of boats about a mile above the mouth of the river; this operation will be ticklish, nevertheless I hope and believe it will succeed. We shall employ our rockets with the first body of troops sent across; here is one instance in which they may be usefully employed, as guns cannot be got over at first.

If Hill succeeds in drawing Soult after him, he will suddenly counter-march, and cross the Adour at some intermediate point, probably in the neighbourhood of Peyrehorade. From our having sawn up into planks for the pontoon brigades all our platform sleepers, I conclude that there is no intention of besieging Bayonne; our game must, in truth, be a bold one, and I take it that, investing Bayonne, or rather blockading it, we shall rapidly advance.

A proclamation, in the name of the Bourbons, is hourly expected, and that it will accompany our advance; dies are making to cut out *fleurs-de-lys* for scarfs to be worn on the arms of those who may wish well to the old cause. A village or little town in the direction of St. Jean Pied du Port, has shown much disaffection to our cause, the inhabitants having armed themselves against our foragers; you will see the little place in the map, where it is called Bidarry. I believe that orders have been given to burn it; notice had been sent to this village that some severe measures would be resorted to, and that the inhabitants must be unequivocally enemies or friends. I yet hope their houses may be spared. All looks well, but as the wind and weather are necessary to our operations, I wish we were well on the right bank of the Adour.

Feb. 15, 10 a.m.

The marquis and staff have followed Hill's corps; Dickson remains here to forward the operations of the corps on this flank. At this moment the Guards are moving out to occupy the ground in front of the mayor's house, in the neighbourhood of the scene of the affairs in December. There is nothing new, nor is the effect of Hill's movements yet known. If Soult should not have followed Hill, he will probably try to make our left uneasy. I am going to the front, after giving Gordon and Blachley their directions. I have just seen Lieutenant-Colonel Arentschild, of the German Artillery, who has ridden post from Lisbon in eight days; it is about 200 leagues.

There has been a violent riot at Vitoria; a cart belonging to a French merchant's house, and which really contained contraband goods, was stopped by the police, and sentries placed round it in the marketplace, while the matter was to be investigated by the magistrates. During their deliberations the mob assembled, and under pretence that there was some correspondence carrying on with the enemy, destroyed the cart, carried off the goods, and proceeded to seize and throw into prison all French inhabitants, of whom many had been for years resident in Vitoria; the mob also seized and destroyed or carried off all property which they supposed to be French, and it was not till after two days of riot that the tumult was ended by the interference of the military, who attended, it is said, not to prevent, but to regulate, the seizure of whatever was supposed to be French.

Three lives are said to have been lost in the scuffle; this may be called an ebullition of the deadly hatred between Spaniards and French. Yesterday our host came to me deploring our approaching departure, and dreading, as he said, (and I dare say honestly enough), the arrival of the Spaniards; he hoped he said, some English authorities would remain. There is no doubt that if the Spaniards were not restrained, they would severely retaliate for all the insults and injuries they have suffered from the French.

Letter 122

St. Jean de Luz: Feb. 17.

We know nothing more of what has been doing on the right, than that there has been an affair, and that our people have driven the enemy back on the river Gave, and that we have taken about 200 prisoners, having lost ourselves about the same number in killed and wounded. Captain Clitherow of the 3rd Guards is amongst the former; he was *aide-de-camp* to General Byng: General Pringle has been wounded. If you consult the map, you will find the position of our people near Navarreins, in the direction of Pau; all on the left has been quiet, but we are ready for a start. The passage of the Adour will be exceedingly interesting. The river is 400 yards wide, rapid, and occasionally agitated; there is a difficult and shifting bar at the mouth of the river: our place of crossing will be about a mile above.

I am now going out to reconnoitre the road by which our guns will have to advance. The French ship of war *Sappho* (I believe of forty-four guns) is anchored in the river, and one of our objects is to destroy her. In her present anchorage she is protected by the enemy's entrenched camp. We meant to have gone down to the mouth of the Adour, but met a piquet of the enemy just beyond the village of Anglet, and learned from some women that a patrol of *Chasseurs à Cheval* had just past. We took one straggler from the infantry piquet; the poor fellow was without arms, and exceedingly frightened; he said he was a Genoese, and told us where his piquet was, so we let him off. A sailor deserted this morning from Bayonne; he says there are twenty-five gun boats there.

No further news from the right; our bridge, from the non-arrival of some vessels with planks, cannot now be ready till Monday night. I begin to suspect it will not be ready so soon. Lord Wellington has two reports daily of its progress, and will not, as we are told, return here till it is quite ready. Instead of the proposed beams and a quantity of earth to be laid upon them to hold the cables on the right bank of the river, it is now proposed to hang an 18-pounder over the stone quay at the end of each cable. In all the bustle of the preparation, I have hitherto had little or nothing to do.

In the expectation of the arrival of horses from England and Ireland, the artillery part of headquarters has been directed to remain here during the movements on the right; but unless our reinforcements should come within a day or two we must move without them. We have had another instance of what I mentioned in a letter two months ago; the Nivelle has been again shut up by a bank of sand formed at its mouth. Fifty men were employed for some hours the day before yesterday in clearing away a channel; they had to cut down at least six feet before a drop of water could escape; but the river once disengaged, soon forced a passage, and most of the vessels in the harbour had got out yesterday. Ten Spanish regiments, under the marquis de Chastellan, were to reach Oyarzun yesterday; I imagine they will be here tomorrow. The Spaniards confidently expect peace; they are always in extremes.

Feb. 20.

I have sent Gordon and Blachley off to the front with rockets, but have not myself been out: I have no arrangements to make in case of moving, but to mount my horse; but I now (12 o'clock) find that there is a delay in our movements; the wind blows from the very point on which our vessels have to steer, and we must either wait or alter our plans; and as the Marquis and Admiral Penrose are at this moment closeted, this point is probably determining. It is curious to consider how little one feels affected by what is to take place; such is the effect of habit, that we are going to undertake an operation of considerable difficulty, with all imaginable composure, and with a confidence that it will succeed, which even those feel who know nothing of the matter. I hope we shall have comfortable weather, for the sake of our men, and indeed for our own; wet and cold are but bad companions.—*Adieu.*

Letter 123

St. Jean de Luz; Feb. 21.

All arrangements are suddenly changed. The marquis, with seven divisions (including Hill's corps,) has moved to the right, and between manoeuvring and force will cross the river higher up than we had expected yesterday; we had repaired for artillery the bridge over the Gave d'Oléron, near Bidache. There will be some interesting movements which I shall not see, having, together with Dickson and the other artillerists of headquarters, been directed to remain here and "see Hope's column over the river." This, including the attack on the *Sappho* frigate, and the throwing over our bridge, will also be interesting. Our force with which we watch Bayonne, is now reduced to two divisions, the first and fifth: Sir John Hope is rallying, but is not yet able to mount his horse; this is *mal à propos*. You shall hear all when anything shall have happened.

Feb. 22.

We should have moved yesterday, had the wind permitted our vessels in the harbour of Socoa to get out. In approaching movements, rockets are assigned to me. You never saw such a jumble: people scraped together who know nothing. There is nothing for it but to laugh and go on. I have sent Bell off to Bidart, where the rockets are, to bring particulars of what they have and what they have not; in an hour it will be determined whether we move today, but from the appearance of the wind, I do not think we can.—*Adieu.* I must go for orders.

Half-past 1 p.m.

We are just going to try the crossing without naval co-operation. I have no doubt all will do very well. The troops will be crossed over in rafts formed of pontoons, carrying 100 men each; these will be towed each by one boat. If the wind will allow, the gun boats and other vessels will get into the Adour tomorrow about 2 p.m.

A vessel consigned to the Mayor of St. Jean de Luz has arrived from Bordeaux. She brings intelligence that the congress at Basle is broken off, and adds that Bonaparte has been defeated in a battle with the Allies. I write while waiting for my orders; unless our movement shall be again postponed, it will be over before I shall have the pleasure of receiving your letters *Adieu.*

Feb. 25, 10 p.m.

Again, returned here, and going to bed; tomorrow morning I will resume my pen.

Feb. 26, 7 a.m.

Our plans for the day are not settled. I hope to find that I can devote an hour to you before we go out, as I suppose all is quiet on the right. The marquis is at Garris: Sir John Hope had had no communication from him when we left the front yesterday.

I take up my pen after breakfast to begin my story. Bell has gone out to learn what is to be done. I hope to remain quiet for an hour or two, for we have arrangements to make, so that I shall write by fits and starts.

We left St. Jean de Luz, about 3 p.m. on the 22nd. I had to manage the medley called the Rocket Corps, composed of men hastily scraped together, utterly ignorant of the arm they were to use, the rockets equipped in five varieties of manner and liable to as many mistakes; the corps was further divided in three parts, of which one followed the route to the mouth of the Adour, the two others followed the main road, accompanying the 18-pounders destined to attack the *Sappho* French corvette and to play on the gun-boats which might come to her assistance. The *Sappho* was anchored in the Adour, so as to flank an inundation protecting the right of the enemy's entrenched camp.

It had been supposed (for the ground could not be reconnoitred till the enemy's piquets were driven in, and this was avoided till the last moment, that no alarm might be given) that the 18-pounders might be brought within 700 or 800 yards of the *Sappho*, and that she would be sunk; but as it was necessary to place these guns so as to be sheltered from the guns of the entrenched camp, they could not be brought nearer the *Sappho* than 1500 yards; at this distance about 400 rounds were fired at her, of which twenty or thirty at the conclusion were hot shot: the *Sappho* returned the fire with one or two guns only, was repeatedly hulled, and after some hours retired from the contest, under the protection of the citadel. We learn that of a crew of forty men, she had thirty-four killed and wounded, including the captain, who died after having an arm amputated. Twelve gun-boats assisted the *Sappho*, of which five played on our 18-pounders from behind. These fled after a few discharges of rockets—of which one hulled a gun-boat,—and the whole ran with precipitation up the river. Thus, ended the affair on the right, during which the Spanish corps under Don Carlos d'Espana made a demonstration on the enemy's entrenched camp, so as to prevent any troops being detached. All this was over by 3 or 4 p.m.; the object of destroying the *Sappho* was to prevent her being sent down against the bridge at the mouth of the Adour.

To return to the column which marched to attempt the passage near the river's mouth. It consisted of the first division, (except the second brigade of Guards, which accompanied the guns playing on the *Sappho*,) to which were added eighteen pontoons and six boats, forty rocketers, and an officer with a few artillerymen destined to spike the guns of a battery on the enemy's side of the river. From difficulties in getting the pontoons forward, it was found, about an hour before daybreak, that three pontoons only could be got to the water's edge before daylight, and it was judged advisable to withdraw the troops and postpone the enterprise.

The original plan had been to make six rafts of three pontoons each, each raft containing 100 men; to pass over in two turns 1200 men before the day should dawn; and to have 1200 more ready to follow them, while they held their ground supported by the fire of twelve field pieces from the left bank of the river. Sturgeon directed the column, and we walked together at its head. I had previously passed a night of curious adventures, as I will by and by relate. Sturgeon, Burgoyne, and I, examined the most favourable point for putting the rafts into the water. The sentry on the opposite bank challenged, to which, of course, no answer was returned.

On Sturgeon's learning that only three pontoons could be got up before daylight, the troops were ordered to withdraw out of sight; they were thrown behind some sandhills, and the pontoons drawn back on the sands. At the moment of Sturgeon determining to withdraw the troops, I had laid down on the sand, and had fallen asleep. He came to me to say what he had done, and to inquire whether he had not, in my opinion, acted according to the spirit of his orders; which, on his repeating them to me, I thought he had. Whilst we were talking, the troops moved off. The orderly, with Bell's horse and my own, followed the infantry into the sandhills, and in the dark, we missed them entirely, and had a fatiguing walk of three hours on the sand, till meeting Bull's troop, I got a troop horse, and succeeded in an hour more in finding my own.

The troops, consisting of Bull's troop. Captain Carmichael's battery (that is, half of it), three squadrons of the 12th Dragoons, two squadrons of the 16th Dragoons, first brigade of Guards, and a couple of German battalions, were formed in a valley between sand-hills, and the pontoons were drawn there with great exertion to join them; this occupied us till near 12 o'clock, when the river became passable, the tide (still running out) being nearly slack: for this we had waited. Sir John Hope having previously sent orders to attempt the passage at all hazards when the tide would permit, and having himself been down at daylight. Our fleet was visible, but at a considerable distance, and was rather losing than gaining ground; the wind being unfavourable, but not violent.

While this was doing we made no show of men, and could only see a trifling piquet of the enemy on the opposite side of the river, which appeared at low water to be about 200 yards wide. The piquet seemed at a loss what to do, and the moment our first boats were carried to the water's edge on men's shoulders, fairly ran off without firing a single shot, the advanced sentry's piece having missed fire. The six boats were soon in the water, each carrying six soldiers only, and the tide coming in, soon increased the labour of passing. After some time, a raft was made, and soon after two others, each carrying from fifty to sixty men. After two or three had passed, the tide came in with such extraordinary force, that it was found impracticable to get our raft either backwards or forwards from the middle of the current, where she remained tide-bound; the united strength of all on board who could pull being unequal to haul with any effect on the line which was passed from one side of the river to the other. By 5 p.m. about 500 men had been passed, when we ceased working.

The enemy had retired, and the few seamen (Portuguese), whom we had, were exhausted with fatigue. All was now quiet and apparently over; towards dusk, however, the enemy pushed down his 27th and 87th Regiments from the citadel; they came on with apparent spirit, but after having a few rockets fired at them (the rocketers under Captain Lane having been the last troops passed over) hastily retired, not having more than twenty men killed and wounded, of whom several fell by the rockets; one rocket having killed one man and wounded four others seemed the signal for retiring, which they did precipitately.

On the 24th I reached the mouth of the Adour before daylight, crossed and went to the outposts, looking attentively over the ground of the affair of the preceding night, so as to ascertain fairly the effects of the rockets. Our little fleet was in sight, some vessels pretty close to the bar standing off and on; the fleet, including *trincadors*, and boats of all kinds, might amount to sixty vessels. The admiral was in the *Porcupine*, a small frigate. We continued our crossing as we could, and passed a division of Bull's troop on rafts, some few cavalry by swimming, and infantry in the course of the day, so that 4000 were over by 4 p.m.; before this, the admiral had learnt how anxiously the entrance of the vessels with the bridge was desired; Elphinstone had apprised him of it through the naval agent at Socoa, who, immediately after we returned on the night of the 23rd, set off in his boat to get to the mouth of the Adour. He had no pilot, and mistaking the bar for the proper entrance into the river, beached himself on a spit of sand.

The boat, however, eventually cleared the spit by the help of her crew, and after being pulled, sails standing, over the spit, got into deep water. O'Reilly's boat, which led the way into the river, was dashed over by the surf, having all her crew bruised dreadfully, and four of them drowned. O'Reilly, and Captain Faddy, of the Artillery (who had charge of fifty artillerymen sent in our five gun-boats), escaped with great difficulty. Soon after, some other boats (small boats, for the tide being out the water was too low to allow vessels to attempt coming in) were swamped, and their crews lost, except here and there a man.

We sent what boats we had to assist in picking up the unfortunate men whom we saw occasionally struggling for life, but I saw but one man saved; some, after regaining their boats and clinging to them, being again washed into the sea. As the tide rose, the vessels attempted the bar. I have never seen any scene so awful; in crossing the bar they were agitated in a most extraordinary manner, sails flapping, and all steerageway lost; as each passed it seemed inevitably lost, as indeed several were. Though I was on the spot I hardly knew what happened, but I believe two vessels went down entirely; a gun-boat and two other vessels and a boat were driven on shore.

We had several poor fellows struggling for life in the surf literally within ten yards of us, without being able to save one of them, though we had men on the beach tied with ropes, and apparently, as the waves receded, close to them. Captain Elliot of the *Martial* gun-brig, a lieutenant, a surgeon, and, as we are told, about fifty men, are lost in all. The surgeon's fate was hard: after being swamped in the *Martial's* boat he was picked up by the gun-boat, and on her striking the ground was killed by a 24-pounder oversetting upon him from the shock the vessel received. About thirty vessels, however, got in, including three gun-boats. Yesterday night, I hope, would see our bridge in good forwardness.—*Adieu*: I am called away.

9 p.m.

We returned from the front to a late dinner. Bayonne is invested; Lord Wellington has crossed the Gaves d'Oléron and de Pau. In a note to Sir John Hope, dated yesterday and received this morning, his lordship desired Bayonne might be reconnoitred "with the view to a siege." We shall therefore have full employment: I hope we shall get our heavy ordnance over the bar into the Adour; this, though difficult, would much abridge labour. The bridge over the Adour is not finished, but promises well; and I have no doubt will be finished tonight. Our naval loss, on entering the river, is yet imperfectly known. Captain Bloye's nephew, a fine young man, midshipman in the *Lyra*, is amongst the sufferers. We shall move, as I believe, to Boucaut tomorrow. There have been no late communications from Paris at Bayonne; this seems strange. The Duc d'Angoulême is out with us every morning; he is affable, but apparently very anxious. A considerable corps of Spaniards crossed the Adour this morning.

The boom will be finished tonight, and I dare say the enemy will send down upon it either the *Sappho*, or any other vessel which may be disposable. We have placed our 18-pounders in battery to protect the boom, and play on any vessels which may come down to annoy our bridge. Our advanced posts are beyond Bayonne, towards Peyrehorade; I hope tomorrow the marquis's corps will form a junction with Sir John Hope's. I like the idea of a siege, as offering employment. We shall have full occupation, since all our platforms have been cut up for the bridge, and new ones must be made. 'Till we shall have seen Lord Wellington, we shall not know what is really intended. The citadel fired today a few shots at our people, merely as a hint to keep their distance.

By the way I was to tell you our adventures on the night of the 22nd: though I left home by 3 p.m., it was dusk before I could get Lane's rocketers to move; when they did, the party (with which I was to go) was to follow the pontoons; the roads were detestable; one pontoon overset after another; it became quite dark; the roads were over rough heaths with undulating hills separated by swamps. Having nothing to do with the pontoons, I gained their front, for they stopped every moment. The night was piercing cold, and I determined to push on to Anglet, then in the possession of neither party, and to take up my abode for an hour or two. I knew the village well, having prowled into it in daylight; however, the darkness of the night deceived me, and after passing several houses without seeing a light, I struck out of the road towards a light and knocked at the door, demanding entrance.

Bell and an orderly were with me, and I told them to look about whilst I was talking to a man who answered from within: he put out the light, and a female voice called out that they were in bed, and could not open the door. Whilst I was imagining something might be wrong from the man ceasing to speak, I heard two voices behind me, and turning round, rode up to two soldiers, challenging them in French, and demanding who they were and what they wanted: speaking sharply and seizing one by the collar. I observed they were French soldiers with their side arms, but without firelocks; they said they belonged to the 64th Regiment, were on piquet just by, and had come into the village to buy brandy; showing me their empty kegs as a proof of the truth of their story.

Observing from their mode of speaking that they took me for one of their own patrols, I desired them in a sharp tone to rejoin their piquet and not leave it again; in this probably I used some phrase different from what they expected, for they suddenly said, "You are of our side are you not?"

"Certainly, but return to your piquet;" which they immediately did, wishing us goodnight; and we separated, probably mutually pleased.

Whilst this conversation was going on, I anticipated the arrival of the piquet, which no doubt was within call; and therefore, felt it necessary to betray no haste or desire to leave them. We returned the way we had come, and with difficulty got within our advanced sentries; and after wandering for a couple of hours more found ourselves just where we had left the pontoons in the evening; nor was it till we borrowed the assistance of a corporal and a file of men from a neighbouring piquet, that we were able to get into another road, leading down to the beach, and to overtake a German battalion composing part of the column with which we intended to move.

I never was better pleased than in meeting with these Germans, for we began to be again puzzled; and, besides the chance of wandering into the enemy's lines, we had already gone over I know not how many ditches and fences. I have been over the same ground both today and yesterday, and find that we wandered round and round in a circle; and had got into the swamp at least a dozen times. The night was bitterly cold, a keen frost and piercing wind.

On the night of the 25th, I slept in this same village of Anglet at Webber Smith's, who had moved into it with his troop in the course of that day. Smith's wine was soon out, so we sat round the fire and had punch with the old man of the house, his wife, and four daughters; and had a very merry evening. The girls said they had a brother in the French Army, but had not heard of him for eight months; they seemed solicitous to go to Boucaut, where they said they had a house, and it was arranged that one of the girls should come next morning to the river side, and we would manage to pass her over, which we did accordingly, O'Reilly giving us a boat. They said they were much surprised at the good treatment they met with from the English; that all their neighbours felt quite at ease with our troops, and that they now only feared having the Spaniards amongst them.

Letter 124

St. Jean de Luz: Feb. 27.

I write in haste: the last few days have been passed in such hurried scenes, that I have hardly had time to tell you in a confused way what has happened. We shall, as I hope, remove from this today. Our bridge, which I left last evening, I hope to find completed this morning, and that the boom, too, will have been completely laid. You shall hear of both. The bridge, as I have already mentioned, is near the little village of Boucaut, the inhabitants of which, and the adjacent villages, were ordered to take up arms, and refused; in consequence, the French troops committed some excesses on leaving them. At this moment, our patrols are pushed towards Peyrehorade. Our battering train is in Passages harbour. Our guns are as follow:—

24-pounders	52
68 lb. carronades	22
8-inch howitzers	23
10-inch mortars	28
$4^{2/5}$-inch mortars	20
	145

For our guns, we have 1500 rounds each; and for mortars, about 1000.—*Adieu*, I am just going to the front.

Feb. 28, 9 a.m.

I have just returned from the front, and intend remaining here quietly for a day or two. Yesterday, the bridge being completed, Sir John Hope deemed it expedient to invest the city of Bayonne more closely than he had done before, and attacked the village of St. Etienne, which he carried, having taken a gun and some prisoners from the enemy; arid his posts are now within 900 yards of the outworks of the place. We had some sharp skirmishing near the citadel; amongst others, I received a musket wound, the ball passing through the shoulder, without injuring the bone, and I hope to return to my employments in a few days.

March 1.

I can give you no account of anything, but report says that an affair took place in the centre yesterday; that Don Carlos d'España was killed, and Lord March dangerously wounded; I sincerely hope all this is without foundation. Don Carlos is one of our most efficient and stanchest friends, and Lord March is a very promising young man, and an honour to the illustrious family to which he belongs. 'Till lately, his lordship has been on the marquis's staff, but had rejoined his regiment, (the 52nd,) to do the regimental duty requisite to entitle him to promotion. Headquarters were yesterday at Orthes; the peasants on the other side of the Adour, volunteered to repair the roads for us. I shall continue to write and give you all the information I can collect.

March 3.

We have had a dreadful gale (scarcely yet subsided) for the last thirty-six hours. Of fourteen vessels at anchor in the bay, thirteen are totally wrecked: amongst them, the *Gleaner*, man-of-war schooner; her crew are, however, saved; the beach is covered with wrecks, and with corn and brandy. Some soldiers are said to have died from excessive drinking, though every care has been taken to stave the casks as they floated on shore. About twenty lives are said to have been lost; this number is comparatively small. The *Jupiter*, man-of-war schooner, after parting her cables, ran to the mouth of the Nivelle, struck on the bar, and after receiving several violent shocks, and losing a mast, was forced over the bar into the harbour. The rain and hail have been nearly incessant for two days.

Yesterday evening, I had a letter from Bell: Dickson and May have gone to find Lord Wellington, believed to be at St. Sever and Mont de Marsan. Our cavalry had also moved upon Dax, which the enemy was believed to have evacuated. I hear nothing of the siege of Bayonne, and rather fancy it may not take place. The enemy had for the last two days continued a sharp fire, which our people do not return: a day or two will decide the question of siege.

March 4, 11 a. m.

Last night was a violent one; most dreadful thunder and lightning, with rain and a storm of wind. I have been out for an hour on the sea wall, the wind is still high, though the sun has been shining. The whole bay is covered with wrecks. I find seventeen vessels have been lost; several remain in some degree entire on the sand, others are utterly gone to pieces. Casks, chests, logs of wood, and bodies, floating in all directions.

I never saw a grander or more terrific scene: the clouds of sea fowl hovering over their prey, seemed almost to dispute the bodies with those who were rescuing them from the waves; the beach itself is more altered than I should have imagined possible in so short a time: beyond the sea wall stood the remains of an old quay of very solid masonry; thirty yards of this have been beaten down by the waves; and an old wall, which, a few days since, was some yards within high-water mark, now stands like an isolated pillar, the surrounding earth having been totally washed away. A *galliot* had the singular fortune to run at midnight into the Nivelle, and has held her anchors, it seems, after all other vessels had gone ashore. In my walk, I joined an old captain of the French navy, who said that from the appearance of the sky, more bad weather must be expected, and that there would be many wrecks between Bayonne and Bordeaux.

March 7,

I have just had a visitor from St. Sebastian, where I learn that four vessels have been wrecked yesterday. Mr. Williams, an Ordnance Commissary, is my informant; he says the minds of the people near St. Sebastian are much inflamed by the late manifesto on the subject of our burning the town. Mr. Williams adds, that his own servant was murdered a few days ago, and that Lieutenant Grimes, of the artillery drivers, was robbed and stripped in his own quarters, where he was left tied to a bed-post: all this sounds strangely, there must surely be some exaggeration.

Talking yesterday with Mr. Robb, one of the Hospital Inspectors, he told me that about three weeks ago the aggregate of the British sick in general and regimental hospitals was about 7000. This is no great number, all things considered; there are now 2000 wounded at Orthes, of which number 1400 are British. At Orthes, the inhabitants are chiefly Protestants; there is a Protestant church there, and, within the memory of many living, the Catholics could not pass to and from mass without being insulted. It is said to be one of the prettiest towns in the department.

March 11.

I have had several interruptions this morning, and several little arrangements to make for supplies of ammunition. Forty vessels of forty tons each are required for our ammunition for the siege of Bayonne, and Colonel Buckner has just come to me with an order for him to superintend the removal from Passages to the Adour of a couple of millions of musket-ball cartridges, of which half will be sent by boats, if we can manage it, to St. Sever.

General Walker, who did command the seventh division, told me just now, that when he left St. Sever on the 9th, Lord Wellington intended moving the marshal (Beresford) with the light and seventh divisions upon Bordeaux, and that the Marquis himself would move on Toulouse with four divisions, in which direction Soult had retired. About 1300 men are said to have quitted Soult, and to have returned to their homes.

Now then seems to be the decisive moment; it is believed here that after several severe actions, the headquarters of the French are, or rather were, at Troyes; but that Bonaparte himself has been severely wounded, and carried back to Paris. Lord Wellington is understood to have acted with great caution, and to have repressed the ardour of the people to rise in favour of the Bourbons, until it shall be clearly understood how politics are settled, or whether it is intended that peace should be made with Bonaparte. We hear the Austrians have declined further contests; in short, we hear fifty things. But a very little time must show the issue. I enclose a letter from Jenkinson, giving some account of what was going on in front on the 26th and 27th ultimo.—*Adieu.*

(Enclosure.)
Extract from a Letter from Major Jenkinson, R. H. A.

Grenade: March 4.

In a former letter to you I endeavoured to bring down our

operations to the 25th February inclusive; since which their interest has been increased tenfold, and we have fought a general action, the result of which has been as glorious as important. I will begin with the first movement of the army, and endeavour to follow its operations in such a manner as will enable you, by a reference to the map, to partake in the interests of our movements.

They commenced by Sir R. Hill's corps turning the Aran and marching upon St. Palais, whilst the third, and fourth, and seventh divisions, threatened the positions the enemy had taken up successively upon the banks of that river and the Bidouze.

At St. Palais there are two bridges over two branches of the Bidouze, both of which the enemy was preparing to destroy when Sir R. Hill's corps arrived, and found about two divisions of the enemy in position; but Lord Wellington's movements were too rapid for them, and he attacked and drove them through the town at the point of the bayonet, and preserved almost entire those most important passages over the Bidouze, the result of which was of course the immediate abandonment of its banks. Soult then concentrated his army, and took up a position upon the right bank of the Gave d'Oléron, covering his front with that formidable river, having his right upon the Adour, and his left upon a strong height near Sauveterre.

Lord Wellington consequently collected his force and threatened the enemy's position in front with the third, fourth, sixth, and seventh divisions, whilst the light division and Hill's corps passed it by turning the Gave de Mauléon by a ford at Navas, and the Gave d'Oléron in the same way at Villenave; and towards the evening we were in full march for Orthes.

On the morning of the 25th the enemy were seen retiring in all directions, and we pushed on to the commanding heights beyond Orthes, whilst the remaining divisions of the army crossed the river and closed up.

It had been determined that the passage of the Pau should be effected by Marshal Beresford on the morning of the 26th at Peyrehorade with the third, fourth, and seventh divisions, and at Depart and Biron above Orthes by the right division and Sir R. Hill's corps; and that the sixth division should push through the town, if possible, and establish the communication between the right and left columns.

Sir Thomas Picton having observed a ford at Berenx, he was desired to cross there; and a flank movement was made by the light and sixth divisions to support him, Sir R. Hill also moving to his left to take our place.

Early on the morning of the 27th, therefore, the third, fourth, sixth, seventh, and light divisions of infantry, Colonel Vivian's and Lord Edward Somerset's brigades of cavalry, Ross's and Gardiner's troops of horse artillery, and Maxwell's, Sympher's, Turner's, and Michell's batteries had crossed the river, over which a pontoon bridge had been established during the night. The enemy was soon discovered to be in a position with his right upon a strong height near the villages of St. Marie and St. Boés, and his left covering Orthes and the fords between Depart and Biron.

The fourth division, supported by the seventh, commenced the attack on the enemy's right; the light division was on their right, the third and sixth to the right of them, and Sir R. Hill was directed to force the passage of the river, and establish a communication with us.

It was evident that the enemy's whole army was there; and he boldly and confidently offered us battle. We accepted the offer, and moved rapidly on: and about midday both armies were closely engaged along their whole line. The contest was severe, but never doubtful; and at the date of this letter, the passages of the Adour and Midou in tranquillity, the capture of six pieces of artillery and 2000 prisoners, and the seizure of the enemy's immense magazines at Mont de Marsan and Dax, sufficiently attest the glorious and important victory we have gained, and which I conceive to be second to no one which has hitherto crowned the persevering efforts of the British Army.

We have of course been daily engaged in pursuit, and now occupy Aire, Cazeres, Barcelone, Grenade, and Mont de Marsan; and though we are not in possession of Bordeaux, yet as the enemy have uncovered it, we may consider it as in our power.

The enormities and depredations committed by the French Army are equal to any they were ever guilty of in Spain and Portugal, and they retire with the just curses and execrations of their countrymen, who hail us in every town and village as their deliverers. You will, I am sure, be glad to hear that all the General officers speak in high terms of the services of Ross's and Gardiner's troops, as also of poor Sympher's brigade: twice had we the eighteen guns in line, and never did I see better practice; nor will you be sorry to learn that we had not a man or horse touched; and I believe that Gardiner was as fortunate. Poor Sympher's brigade, which we were close to nearly the whole day, suffered severely; and long shall I regret the loss of its commander, who was so justly esteemed in private and valued in public life.—*Adieu.*

Letter 125

St. Jean de Luz: March 17.

I am still at this place but hope to set off tomorrow for headquarters, which are still at Aire. It is said that Marshal Beresford entered Bordeaux on Saturday the 12th instant, that the mayor and principal inhabitants came a considerable way out of the city to meet the Marshal, and that they had previously proclaimed Louis XVIII. This is a decided step; there is now no retreating; should Bonaparte ever again have the city in his power, what miseries would it not undergo! It is said that Bordeaux, previous to the arrival of our troops, had been six days without intelligence from Paris: this seems singular.

I have been interrupted by the commandant (Colonel Benton) and a young officer of the staff corps, who is sent here to repair the bridge for the passage of the heavy ordnance for Bayonne. We have been together to the bridge, have arranged what is necessary to be done, and went to the mayor to get carpenters; the mayor, however, was not at the town-hall, where, while we waited a little for his worship, I observed the paper of the room, which I had not noticed before. It consists of alternate N's and crowns interspersed with imperial eagles and bees: quite a Bonaparte paper.—*Adieu,* for I am again interrupted.

Letter 126

Between Bayonne and Dax: March 19.

I left St. Jean de Luz yesterday and rode to Boucaut, where I waited on Sir John Hope, who wanted me to dine and sleep at his house; but having previously promised Webber Smith to pass the day with him, I pushed on here today. I have been to Biaudos, about three leagues from hence and on the road from Bayonne to Peyrehorade. I went thither to see Bull's troop, which is excellently well off there. Tomorrow I march to Dax, next day to Tartas, then to St. Sever, and after that to Aire. We have no news today; a few shots have been fired from

Bayonne in the course of the morning, but nothing of consequence. We have no arrivals from Bordeaux, nor any news from headquarters.

LETTER 127

Dax: March 21.

Behold me in a comfortable inn in the suburbs of one of the prettiest towns I have seen, and which, notwithstanding a very heavy rain, I have run over with great pleasure; I must describe the town first, and then tell you how I got hither. Dax is a nice, though small square town, on the left bank of the Adour, navigable here for large barges which are towed against the stream by bullocks. The town is surrounded by an old wall, with round towers at the usual intervals; on the west side, there is something like the faces of bastions. The Adour runs under the north wall; a wooden bridge crosses the river, which is, perhaps, 120 yards wide, with a very rapid stream. I got here about 11 a.m. The road is over a barren and sandy heath, is but half made, and is consequently very deep; stones are, however, collected in great quantities, to make the road, and the patches which are finished are excellent.

"What is there to be seen in your town?" said I, on entering the inn, to a good-humoured landlady.

"There are, sir, many things; there is the boiling fountain, the cathedral, an excellent hospital, and the mud baths;" so away I trudged.

The *Fontaine bouillante*, I found to be a warm mineral spring; a handsome public bath is building, something in the style of our English one at Bath, and there are already several little private baths built by an individual on speculation, with the usual comforts of warm baths. From the baths, we (Mr. Bradley and I) visited the cathedral, old and solemn, but of no remarkable size or beauty; from thence, going out of the town to the south, we visited an hospital, so nice, that one might wish to be sick to enjoy its comforts.

On speaking to the porter, he called one of the sisters of the house, (a nun,) who received us very politely, and introduced us to the administrator, a young man of thirty, who obligingly walked round with us, and showed us everything. We began with a well-arranged surgery and store of medicines; from this we passed to the lingerie, where the napkins, the white bed-curtains, and other linen, were arranged with much taste; the beds have green curtains in the winter, and white ones in summer. We next visited the sick wards, which were cleanliness itself; there were wards for men, others in a distinct part of the building for women and children, and in a third and separate part, a dozen little foundlings.

The foundlings, as is common, are received in a little round box, the person placing the child in the box rings a bell, and the servants of the house attend to receive it. In the room with the foundlings was an interesting-looking woman. She was there, the administrator said, in much distress; "perhaps you could tell us," added he, "what to do."

She was married to a French officer, when in Spain, by a Spanish priest, and they were to have been married again on the arrival of the officer in France; but he was taken prisoner in the affair near Sarre, in November last, and thus she was left destitute with their child. The object of the poor mother was to know whether her husband could be exchanged, or, should that be impossible, whether she might not be permitted to go to England, to join him. I am to hear her story detailed, and shall consider what can be done.

In the hospital, we were shown an Englishman, a private of the 84th Regiment, who was wounded and taken near Bayonne, in December, and afterwards recovering from his wound was sent to prison; he was there taken ill, and was sent to the hospital, in which, he says, every possible care had been taken of him. In the chapel of the hospital was a very beautiful painting of the founder ascending to heaven in the midst of the prayers of the sick, I could not learn the name of the painter, and am sorry to say I have at this moment forgotten that of the founder.

One story has been repeated to me by every person to whom, in the course of the morning, I have mentioned the hospital. It is, that the superior of the nuns, a woman of the most amiable manners, and whose life was devoted to charitable offices to the sick, was guillotined here during the revolution; all talk of this with the utmost detestation. So much for the hospital, which is the very best I ever saw. It is said to be the admiration of all who visit it.

Having seen all the sights the mud baths excepted, I set off for them; they are by the water's edge, where there is a house with beds, &c., for people who use them; the mud and warm water (a warm spring, and the warmest I think, I ever met with) are mixed in a trough, and the limb to be cured is placed in the trough, until it becomes quite black. There are other and larger baths, in which the patient may wash himself clean afterwards. So much for my morning's excursion.

This town has not suffered in the least; there is said to be very good society amongst the inhabitants, who, having refused to arm themselves against the English, have remained quietly in their habitations.

Yesterday, Louis XVIII. was proclaimed here, and at the neighbouring towns, but little enthusiasm or rejoicing was manifested. The people looked I know not how; glad, yet frightened, and more than one have said to me, that should affairs take a different turn, and should Bonaparte return, they would be irretrievably ruined; "but," said a lady, "were one person, (whom I dare not name) but dead, or taken prisoner, all would be well. We should have peace and happy times."

I should tell you that on my way here I called on General Vandeleur, and accepted his invitation to dine. The general is lodged at the house of Monsieur de Martin, the *Seigneur* of the village, who, like the Vicar of Bray, has joined every prevailing party for the last twenty years. He is said to have 8000*l*. a year, but to be miserly and much disliked by the inhabitants. He told us that before the revolution he had been the Baron of Breton, where his estates chiefly were. I was lodged at the inn: a large comfortable house, very full both of passengers and people, attracted by the circumstance of proclaiming the king; this was done in the church, and in obedience to a circular letter written by the Prefect of the Department to the Sub-prefects and the Curates.—*Adieu.*

Letter 128

Tartas: March 22.

Today our journey has been from Dax, of which pretty town I have already given an account. Between Dax and Tartas the road is over a barren, sandy plain, and is yet in an unfinished state. The only village we passed through was Pontons; this offered nothing remarkable, nor indeed does Tartas, as far as I can learn.

The bridge over the River De Midouze has been burnt, and a ferry now supplies its place and but badly. Tartas is twenty leagues (of the country) from Bordeaux, from whence the diligence, loaded and lumbering, has just arrived. The town offers nothing curious: a building formerly a convent is now a cavalry stable for 500 horses. We are lodged at the Hôtel de l'Empereur. The landlady is what the French call "*un peu fière*:" but landladies sometimes are so, and after dinner I shall be a better judge of her good qualities. Ham, she told me, is 4 *francs* a pound, and at that price she had rather not sell it, expecting it would be dearer still. There was a considerable depot of forage here, the enemy having had 10,000 cavalry cantoned in this neighbourhood; the depot is however nearly exhausted.

Of headquarters I know nothing, but that they are not at Aire:

tomorrow I shall learn something from the resident commissary at St. Sever. I had a visit last night from the secretary of the hospital at Dax, with the written petition of the wife of Captain Girard of the French 88th Regiment, who with her child of eight months old is in the hospital. The poor woman is young, pretty, a Spaniard, and not legally married. The 88th Regiment was taken in a redoubt near Sarre on the 10th of November; Captain Girard is consequently a prisoner, and probably in England. The poor woman wishes to be allowed to join him: but suppose Monsieur Girard should not be so ready to receive the lady! in this case to obtain leave for the poor girl's being sent to England would be the worst thing one could do for her.

I should like to be of use if I knew how, feeling interested for the poor girl and her child, which is one of the finest I ever saw. I think it would be well to write to Captain Girard, telling him the case and asking him whether he would receive his wife and child. I recollect as we were standing round the redoubt in which the 88th Regiment was, and before it had surrendered, that an officer came out to speak to us; this I suppose was considered a little premature, for someone within called out, "*Monsieur Girard, on vous demande*;" and this may be the very man.

Letter 129

St. Sever: March 23, 10 p.m.

I write by a comfortable fire in a most luxurious room elegantly furnished; the proprietor of the house is one of the principal men of the town; he is not here at this moment, but I waited upon his lady and had a very pleasant hour's conversation with the first well-bred lady I have seen for a long time. As Louis XVIII. has not been proclaimed here, the Prefect of Mont de Marsan (appointed in the name of Louis XVIII. by the Duc d'Angoulême) sent orders that the king should be proclaimed here. The mayor, having been appointed by Lord Wellington, replied that having submitted to his lordship who had conquered the province, he should apply for instructions how to act. He did so, and his lordship in reply observed that it might be premature to take any step during the present state of affairs; that he considered what had occurred at Bordeaux as premature, but that he would not interfere. The proclamation was accordingly deferred.

Sensible people here are afraid of showing their sentiments, and well they may; but go into the cottages or talk apart with any man who thinks he may safely speak his mind, and it is evident that Bonaparte is detested. Our march today has been a short one of four leagues; the road and country improving, the latter much reminding me of Essex,—a little heath and a good deal of cultivation. The country people wear coarse shirts over their clothes like our English ostlers, but with a hood superadded which gives the men a singular appearance.

From a delay in passing the ferry at Tartas it was nearly 2 o'clock before we reached St. Sever, which is singularly and beautifully situated on the left (or south) bank of the Adour, which river we again crossed in order to enter the town. The country we had previously travelled over was uniformly flat. St. Sever stands on the brow of a hill perhaps 150 feet above the level of the country we have quitted, yet is itself on a plain to which the eye traces no boundary.

The town offers little remarkable; the "college" or seminary has now ninety-five students educated in the classics; the building is capacious and commodious, and the superior showed us much attention in going round the apartments. I learn that headquarters have left Aire, and were on the 20th at Tarbes, where I hope to find them. There has been no general affair; but I fear my friend Colonel Sturgeon has fallen in a skirmish. I yet know the circumstances very imperfectly, but I fear the fact is certain.

LETTER 130

Barcelone: March 25.

Yesterday we left St. Sever early, and intended to have halted at Aire, but there being no bridge we determined not to cross the ferry, but to push on here, which is a couple of miles on our road, and a tolerable village. We afterwards walked to Aire, which is a small, dark-looking town with nothing remarkable in it; at the top of the hill beyond the town is a college which we went to see; there are two colleges or schools in adjoining buildings, one for boys and the other for young men destined for the church.

The person who showed us round the buildings said that there are one hundred of these young men at present, paying each 300 *francs* a-year for board and instruction: for simplicity's sake one may call a *franc* a shilling, so that 15*l*. supplies a good education (at least I hope so), and four meals a-day. To judge by the quantity of fish and the number of hams which we saw in the kitchen, these young men have excellent cheer. Aire looks deserted; I have not seen since we entered France so sombre a place: it is on the left bank of the Adour, but the stone bridge of seven arches over the Adour having been carried away twenty-five years ago has never been replaced; the materials have been collected for some years, but money has been wanting. In this village there are some good houses, but all showing decay and want of common repairs; all say there are no men.

We dined yesterday at a bad inn, and were charged extravagantly, thirty *francs* for four of us; however, the dinner was a good one, but four or five *francs* ought to procure an excellent dinner in this cheap country. On this side of the Adour (the right bank) the country continues flat and low, so that Indian corn is still common. Flax is also very common. Spinning is the occupation of all the elder women. The people with whom I have conversed all join in expressing detestation of Bonaparte, but frankly avow the fear of speaking their real sentiments.

We have lost the bullock cars now, and see nothing but small four-wheeled carriages drawn by little horses yoked like bullocks; they draw indeed from their shoulders, but the pole serves instead of traces, of which there are none. Today we shall reach Trie, six leagues from hence. I have sent the baggage forwards, and shall overtake it on the road; there is no depending upon the news one hears, but it is reported that Marshal Beresford has quitted Bordeaux, and is marching on Toulouse by way of Auch.

Trie: 4 p.m.

Just arrived, after a longer ride than I had expected, through a country generally flat, though the last two of the seven leagues were a little hilly. Today, as yesterday, we have seen a good deal of flax intermingled in small patches in the cornfields; today we have passed many vineyards, and it is impossible to help remarking that there are no young men to be seen; the only middle-aged man I have seen today had but one eye, which possibly saved him from the conscription. I am well lodged, and wait the arrival of the mules. On going to the mayor's I found him at table, to which he invited me. At his house I saw the Duc d'Angoulême's proclamation, together with that of the mayor of Bordeaux, whose name I observe is Lynch, probably of Irish extraction; so indeed, said the mayor.

I have had half an hour's conversation with a most gentlemanly man; his object in waiting upon me was to engage me to take a letter for him to General Murray, who was quartered in his house. The letter contains some complaints of the general's muleteers. The gentleman says he was formerly in Louis's Guards; that he has a wife and six young children dependent upon him for support. He tells me that it is reported that peace is to be made with the existing government; he added:

In which case Bordeaux will be razed to the ground; but in this part of the country, we all wish you well; there is not a man who dares to speak his sentiments, but hates the tyranny which oppresses us. If we had but your English Government, &c. &c.

That the people do wish us well I fully believe, and they hope that nothing may oblige Lord Wellington to retire: they justly fear the return of their own army. I shall reach Castelnau tomorrow.—*Adieu.*

Castelnau: March 26.

I find on arriving here that it is too true that poor Sturgeon is killed; he received a fatal ball at the village of Vic Bigorre. This seems a fine town, but it rains so that hitherto I have not seen more than the cathedral, which is large, but without any thing remarkable. From all I can learn, headquarters were yesterday at L'Isle en Dodon, a dozen or fourteen leagues from this, on the route towards Lombez. We are puzzled here for forage; no corn is to be had; there is, however, some bran and hay. We are evidently moving on Toulouse; the road is said to be not altogether safe, but this one always hears. We are again in a new department, that of the High Pyrenees, of which this is the chief town.

On leaving Maubourget, the Pyrenees, covered with snow, were full in sight, and we have been approaching them all day. This place is in a fine plain; you approach it, having meadows carefully irrigated on each side of the road; little sluices at 100 yards asunder, afford facilities for laying the adjacent meadows under water. The style of the houses has altered, the roofs being generally slated. Cocked hats for all ranks of men have taken the place of the Basque bonnet; but the women are less pretty than they were. I begin to get impatient to rejoin headquarters.—*Adieu.*

Letter 131

Boulogne: March 29, 7 a.m.

We arrived here yesterday. Near Tarbes we lose the straight roads so general in France, and are pleased to find the winding ones we are used to in England; at Trie, I was lodged at the mayor's, who overwhelmed me with civilities. We are on the point of setting off for Lombez, through roads so bad, that we expect all manner of difficulties.

Headquarters are at St. Lys, as we believe, that is, six or seven leagues beyond Lombez: for two days we have had beautiful weather; it now rains heavily. This is a curious little old-fashioned town: both here and at Trie there are *piazzas*, rude and simple, round the market-places, and in some of the streets; probably intended as a protection from heat and rain, and certainly very convenient when either is violent. The Pyrenees, to our right yesterday, were noble and majestic; they are covered with eternal snow: we could distinctly discover between these regions of solitude, the pass of Jaca; it is not believed to be yet traversable.

I am interrupted by a man who has just come from headquarters, which are at St. Lys. I have sent him to engage a guide for us; he describes the road as very bad. Yesterday afternoon a deputation waited upon me from a neighbouring village; the object was to induce me to depose the existing mayor in favour of one of the embassy: of course, I told them that we did not interfere in matters of civil judicature, and so the conversation ended, but not for an hour; their people and several others yesterday reminding us that they had formerly been under the English Government: "Would to Heaven we were so again!" said several. The country we passed over yesterday was beautiful; we met several runaway conscripts; I taxed them with being so, they laughed and said, "To be sure we are!"—*Adieu.* I must set off.

Lombez: March 30, 7 a. m.

I take up my pen again, whilst the baggage is getting packed; we reached Lombez yesterday about 4 o'clock in the afternoon, after a fatiguing day through roads deserving all the bad accounts we had heard of them: however, we met with no accident, except that one of my mules fell into a hole in the road, and was with difficulty got out again. We passed perhaps twenty horses and mules, which, in different parts of the road, had been suffocated in the mud.

A league from hence, we found a better road, and, by way of giving the servants time to get in before us, went into a cottage, in which were three nice children, besides the father and mother, grandfather and grandmother, and a good-looking, laughing fellow, who said he had just run away from the army. In a room below, they showed us a sick soldier, one of our 18th Hussars, whom they had taken in; we have met before with several similar instances, and in all, the natives have behaved with the greatest tenderness and kindness towards our men. I am here lodged in a beautiful house, elegantly furnished; in the drawing-room is a collection of beautiful engravings by the best masters; the family consists of a gentleman, his wife, and a boy of eight or ten years old.

It seems we have made a strange round in coming from St. Sever, pursuing headquarters rather than moving on any fixed point; this could not be avoided, and we have seen the noble Pyrenees, worth going a hundred leagues out of one's way to look at.

Headquarters are said to have been moved from St. Lys to Seysses, a league nearer Toulouse, and perhaps we may after all find them in that city, which a lady, who arrived from thence last night, says is open to us; she also says, but on what authority I know not, that Soult and Lord Wellington understand each other; I do not believe this.—*Adieu*, I must look about and get the servants ready; we shall have more bad roads, and apparently more bad weather today.

St. Lys: 12 o'clock.

Headquarters are still two leagues further at Seysses. I am merely halting to bait the horses, and shall push on to headquarters; if the baggage gets here tonight, it will certainly not get further. I never saw a worse bit of road than about a mile of what we have passed, stiff deep clay up to the horses' shoulders. All is quiet in front, and I am glad that it is so.

Seysses: 5 p. m.

Safe arrived, but without baggage; we hope to cross the Garonne tomorrow; a want of boats in sufficient number to form a bridge has prevented our getting over sooner.—*Adieu.* I hear a mail is making up.

Letter 132

Seysses: April 1.

I fully expected this morning that we should have had something to do, but we have returned from the outposts nearest Toulouse where all is quiet; it is now 10 o'clock. We were of course out before daybreak, Soult's troops remained in position on the rising ground beyond Toulouse; as the day dawned we saw them distinctly enough; there might be some 18,000 or 20,000 men, all infantry. He has probably a division in the town, and is throwing up intrenchments (which will come to nothing), in front of the suburb, called St. Cyprien, which is on his side of the Garonne. We had anticipated either an attack or movement on the part of Soult; neither has taken place; Hill's corps crossed the Garonne yesterday by a pontoon bridge thrown over the river near Roques, a league from hence.

They marched on the bridge over the Arriège at Cintegabelle, five leagues from Roques, of which bridge they took possession without opposition. It had been intended to have taken up the bridge by which Hill crossed, and to have laid it lower down, just below where the Garonne is joined by the Arriège. I think this will be still done tonight, and that we shall push forward tomorrow. We must beat Soult soon, I hope and think; and after that which way shall we turn? The seventh division remains at Bordeaux, and Bayonne is to be besieged; orders for that purpose have been sent. Besides the siege of Bayonne (by the way a vigorous sortie was expected on the 22nd *ultimo*, when my last letters were written), another siege is to take place of the fortified castle of Lourdes; our field battery of six 18-pounders is destined for this service. Lourdes is to the southward of Tarbes, and 400 men under an enterprising officer there alarm that neighbourhood. A few *banditti* in the neighbourhood of Mont de Marsan frighten the multitude on that side, and lately made a successful attack on some baggage belonging to the seventh division.

An *aide-de-camp* of the crown prince has been here lately; he is now I know not where. It is said here, that he went to Pau to pay his respects to the relatives there of his patron, and that after dressing himself at the entrance of the town in his fringed ———, as Sterne would say, he waited on the mayor and demanded to be shown the house of the prince's father.

"Oh, that old rascal," replied the mayor, "thank Heaven he has been dead some time."

"Is the brother of the prince alive?"

"No, thank God, he is dead too. He was, if possible, a greater rascal than the father."

"Are there none of the prince's relatives left?"

"Yes; let me see. Ay, there is one over the way, that dirty fellow selling onions."

You will anticipate that the ambassador of vice-royalty stayed to hear no more. I send you a letter which I have just received from Major Jenkinson, giving some account of the entrance of the British troops into Bordeaux, and of their reception there.—*Adieu*.

(Enclosure.)
From Major Jenkinson, Royal Artillery,
Bordeaux: March 20.

My dear Colonel,

It is almost impossible to describe the joy and enthusiasm of the people at our entrance into this celebrated city. I will, however, endeavour to do it, for memorable indeed will the day be, should it be that of the restoration of the Bourbons.

On the 12th March, 1449, the British troops evacuated Bordeaux; on the same day, three hundred and sixty-five years after, they again entered it, and were hailed as its deliverers from tyranny and oppression.

When we were within two miles of the town we halted, to close up and refresh the troops; Marshal Beresford then put himself at the head of the column, to make his public entry into the town; about one mile from which the mayor met us with a numerous retinue, all in full dress, forming a *coup d'oeil* truly superb.

As soon as the usual salutations and compliments had passed, the mayor drew from his pocket a paper, which he read in a most audible, dignified, and manly voice. 'He came,' he said, 'to express the joy and gratification of the inhabitants of Bordeaux at the approach of those who might be justly termed the saviours and deliverers of Europe; and to request the marshal's permission to hoist the white flag, and to declare for their legitimate sovereign, Louis XVIII.,' at the very mention of which name the air was almost rent with cries of '*Vive le Roi!*' '*Vivent les braves et les généreux Anglais!*'

When silence could be obtained, he continued: 'For twenty-five years the Bordelais have been suffering under the most galling oppression, which has reduced their once flourishing and opulent city to a most degraded and impoverished state; and long have they wished for that moment which now offers itself, when the people could spontaneously declare their unbiassed sentiments and wishes, which are for the restoration of the Bourbons, and their legitimate sovereign Louis XVIII.' After this the municipality and national guards formally tore from their hats and waists their tricoloured sashes and cockades, and substituted white ones, and '*Vive le Roi!*' '*Vivent les Anglais!*' were again loudly vociferated from all parts of the crowd; and it is computed that there were at least 50,000 spectators of this most interesting scene.

Marshal Beresford then spoke, thanking the mayor and inhabitants of Bordeaux for the kind reception the troops had met with, and assuring them that no opposition would be offered on his part to the spontaneous declaration of the people; but he trusted that no false hopes had been held out to them to induce them to take the decided step they had. Principals, under existing circumstances, we could not be, though we should of course always wish well to such a cause, which must however hope for, and derive its best support from, their own exertions. This was answered by '*Vive le Roi!*' '*A bas le tyran!*' '*Vivent les Anglais!*'

The mayor then joined the marshal, and we moved to the commune, where the municipality and principal inhabitants were assembled to receive and be presented to him, and they there renewed their assurances of attachment to their legitimate sovereign. The marshal again cautioned them not to commit themselves without being determined to support their declaration. The reply to this was a deputation bearing the white flag, and requesting permission to hoist it; and hoisted immediately it was.

To describe the reception of the Duc d'Angoulême two hours afterwards, or his reception at the theatre the night following, would be impossible; never did I see more enthusiastic loyalty, and so crowded was the house, that one could barely move in the lobby.

This city exceeds in size and magnificence anything I had ever heard of it, and is in truth much, very much, finer than Paris.— *Adieu.*

Letter 133

Colomiers: April 3.

A sudden order to march readied us this morning at Seysses, just as I was sitting down to write to you; I had no idea that we should have moved, but in a moment, we were on horseback, and are here for the afternoon, in a small village on the road from Auch to Toulouse. We shall cross the Garonne tonight; a feint will be made above Toulouse, but our real point of crossing will be below. I have not seen the point at which our bridge will be thrown across; the ground is said to be favourable at a bend of the river which is 130 yards wide; the bank a little high on our side, but low on the other.

So far, so well: we shall move in the course of the night, so as to reconnoitre the point, and get our guns well placed. *Adieu*—I must now run to Dickson, somewhere at the other end of this straggling village. Being on a rising spot on the plain, Toulouse is in full view:

tomorrow may see us in it. I shall not be able to resume my pen today.

Grenade, on the Garonne, four leagues below Toulouse: April 5, 6 a. m.

We left Colomiers at midnight on the 3rd instant: it then rained in torrents. Before daybreak we reached the point, about three-quarters of a league higher up the Garonne than Grenade, where the bridge was purposed to be thrown over the river. On reconnoitring the banks, to ascertain the most favourable point for our batteries, we could see a few of the enemy's cavalry patrolling on the opposite bank; from some little delay in getting the pontoons to the spot, it was 5 o'clock before the first was brought to the water's edge; by 9 the bridge was completed; the bank on one side is high, perhaps fifty feet; just before the bridge was finished, the day became beautifully fine; a few men had been sent across in small boats, before the bridge was laid, and were posted in a wood on the other side. The enemy's cavalry retired, and we expected every moment that their troops would appear to oppose the passage. But not a man showed himself.

At length the troops filed near the bridge, the bands playing "British grenadiers," and the "Downfall of Paris." It is impossible to conceive a more interesting spectacle. By this time all the neighbouring villagers were collected on the spot, and when Major Gardiner's troop of horse artillery (which followed the 4th infantry division and Colonel Vivian's cavalry brigade) crossed, the peasants pulled the guns up the opposite bank with all possible alacrity. By way of precaution the horses were taken out, and the guns unlimbered; the cavalry passed in single files; the infantry by threes.

The river is exceedingly rapid, and we had our fears for the bridge, which, in despite of four stays made fast to trees on the sides of the river, soon assumed a circular shape. When three infantry divisions, two brigades of cavalry, and twelve field-pieces had passed, his lordship, who had sat the whole time looking earnestly at what was doing, crossed over attended by the usual suite; after reaching the village of St. Jory, and gaining the road from Toulouse to Montauban (or, as others call it, to Paris), we turned towards Toulouse, passed through the village of Espinasse, and about half a league from it came up to our advanced posts of hussars, which were on the main road; two of the enemy's cavalry had been seen, but had retired. The bad weather returned, and so did his lordship, and we reached Grenade, a smart, pretty town, about 6 o'clock. *Adieu*—off again.

11 a.m.

Just returned from riding halfway to Hill's corps, having been sent back with orders. All is quiet today. From the rain in the night, the Garonne has risen two feet, and by way of precaution the platform of the bridge has been taken up. Marshal Beresford, who had been separated from his corps, has just crossed in a boat. His staff are left behind; a good house on this side tempted the marshal to fix his headquarters here last night; but I dare say he is well pleased now to find himself on the other. I am glad to have been sent back, and shall remain here quiet, unless there should be anything to do. The roads are in a sad state; near the bridge one is up to the horses' knees.

Our position at this moment is as follows:—On the right bank of the Garonne (over which we have no actual bridge at this moment) about 15,000 infantry, three brigades of cavalry, and eighteen field-pieces; with General Hill, his own brigades and some few Spaniards. This corps is immediately in front of Toulouse. One division (the Light) remains in position, between the pontoon bridge and Hill, ready to support either flank. It is wished to find a convenient point, a league or two above the present bridge, whither the bridge might be taken. Hitherto no favourable point has been found.

Eighteen pontoons with all the requisites for another bridge ought today to reach Muret or Roques, (above Toulouse) from the rear. The remainder of the army is at present—one division at Bordeaux, and the rest besieging Bayonne. From all this you will see that we are for the moment cut in two. Soult may attack either flank, though under circumstances the movement might be an awkward one for himself. He yet remains near Toulouse, as far as we know. A decisive step must shortly be taken on one side or the other.

April 6, 6 a.m.

Waiting for orders; the morning fine, after very heavy rain during the night; today will, I should think, surely produce something decisive.

April 7, 5 a.m.

Still at Grenade; yesterday passed quietly; the Garonne fell three feet six inches in the night between the fifth and sixth, but rose again yesterday. I hope the bridge was laid again in the course of last night: this is a fine morning, and the night has passed without rain. Yesterday, arrived here an officer and thirty men of the Blues, escorting the mayor of some village near Tarbes; this mayor has been made prisoner for some refractory conduct. The Prefect of Montauban is also said to be actively employed in endeavouring, but ineffectually, to raise the country against us. From the Paris papers, we learn that Bonaparte, after being in the rear of the Allies, has suddenly returned to Paris, in consequence of "an unexpected and most unforeseen event;" what this alludes to, we do not precisely know. Deserters to our troops on the right bank of the Garonne, say that Soult fully expected an attack yesterday and the day before: desertions from his army are very numerous. Our guns (18-pounders), which are to be employed at Lourdes, reached Tarbes on the 4th instant. We do not know that the siege of Bayonne has commenced; on the contrary, we believe that the wind has prevented the vessels with ammunition from Passages, from entering the Adour.

I went yesterday to the church here which, tradition says, was built by the English (as well as many others in this country). It is a large and fine church, adorned with several paintings—scripture pieces of an unusual size. Preparations are making for the celebration of Good Friday, which will be tomorrow. One hears every day of the miseries of the conscription. The lady of the house where Dickson is lodged told us she had paid 20,000 *francs* to save her son; paid probably in bribes, and she seems to be in middling circumstances only.

A note this moment received from English, of the Engineers, who has charge of the bridge, says, the river is falling; that he is getting a sheer-line across, and that he hopes to have the bridge ready by the middle of the day. I have been to Dickson's with the news. Dickson dined yesterday, (the anniversary of the taking of Badajos,) at headquarters. As they were sitting down to dinner, Major MacMahon suddenly broke in, with letters from Paris, announcing, that after a desperate action, in which Bonaparte had lost 100 pieces of cannon, the Allies entered Paris on the 1st instant.

This may be true. Major MacMahon is the senior captain of the 53rd Regiment. He has been twenty years in France, I believe as a prisoner originally, and subsequently by permission of both governments; he married a lady of Toulouse, and has a daughter married there. On the approach of our army he was ordered to Montpellier, and received his passports to go thither, but making a detour joined our headquarters some days ago. Should the news he brings prove true, it must have a decided effect on the peace, so ardently desired by millions. I have little doubt that we shall move in a few hours.—*Adieu.*

Letter 134

St. Jory: April 9, p. m.

Headquarters were suddenly moved here today from Grenade. I was just going to write to you the common news of the day, when I found an order to pack up. I have made acquaintance with a lady and her son whom I accidentally saw some days ago; the lady is sister to a Monsieur Cazalès, well known in England as a literary character, and as a friend of Burke's. Soon after the French revolution, Monsieur Cazalès died at Toulouse, of which city he was a native. I have promised to find out and procure a safeguard for his sister and niece still resident in Toulouse. I shall introduce myself to them when we get into that city, which is, at this moment, in a dreadful state of uncertainty.

The shops are shut, the women are forbidden to appear at the windows, or the men to be seen in the streets, unless armed as National Guards; such are Soult's orders, but the inhabitants are believed, and I may say are known, to be friendly to our cause.

The sister of Monsieur Cazalès, who resides at Grenade, is Madame de Castelbajet; her husband, to whom she introduced me, was extremely polite, and all urged me to dine with them today, but that was impossible. Madame de Castelbajet's house was, as chance would have it, directly opposite my billet, though, as the courtyard opens into another street, I had not observed the family before. Beside the sister and niece at Toulouse, I have promised protection to a Monsieur Cabanis, who is ill there, and nursed by his young wife. If all goes well, I may pass some pleasant hours in their society.

Major Grant, who has succeeded poor Sturgeon as chief of the military communications, tells me that the English mail will be made up tomorrow. I shall therefore finish my letter while I may; tomorrow perhaps may not afford me leisure to continue it. I took leave with regret of the good people at whose house I was lodged at Grenade. After I was on horseback, the women brought me a little girl to kiss, and shook hands with me with great earnestness, wishing us every success. Soult remains in his position; his estates are near Toulouse. It seems we have pushed our troops over the River Dordogne, which joins the Garonne at Bourg, a few leagues below Bordeaux.

The united stream then receives the name of the Gironde. Two of our seventy-fours, a couple of frigates, and some smaller vessels of war had entered the Gironde. Our advanced posts on the right of the Dordogne were, on the 3rd instant, near St. André de Cubsac. The siege of the castle of Lourdes is countermanded; the 18-pounders are

Battle of Toulouse

ordered up. It is thought that the garrison of the castle is disposed to surrender. Our second pontoon train, which should yesterday have reached Muret on the main road from Tarbes to Toulouse, has by some mistake wandered from the high road, and has got-into the difficulties of the bad roads by Boulogne.

I write from a *château* near St. Jory, in which all the artillery staff of headquarters are placed for the night: a finer afternoon cannot be imagined; the windows are open, the Spanish troops are filing over the plain, and a brigade of heavy cavalry is formed under the window. In the distance one can just, and but just, see the lofty Pyrenees, which might almost be mistaken for clouds. I have just seen English; the bridge will be taken up tonight, and laid down again at Blagnac, a league above its present spot.—*Adieu.*

Letter 135

St. Jory: April 10, 3 a.m.

You will have learnt from my last letter our proceedings as far as yesterday, which was spent in reconnoitring. We should, I believe, have attacked Soult, but some unexpected difficulties in laying the bridge delayed us. It was more than mid-day when the bridge was completed, and it was then too late to make our movement. As we were returning to the front, Lord Wellington received a proclamation, which had just been published in Toulouse by the prefect of the department (Haute Garonne), announcing the fall of Paris; the intelligence restored the good humour which the delay of the bridge had interrupted, and we got home about 7 in great glee.

All was quiet yesterday, except that, towards our left, the enemy reoccupied a little bridge from which our people were obliged to retire; the bridge was afterwards blown up. The country in our front is studded with country-houses and gardens, the latter already full of flowers; indeed, the weather is more than warm. I hope today will give us possession of Toulouse, and that whatever fighting there may be will not take place in or near the city.

A decisive victory here would be a noble thing for the common cause, but we must not be too sanguine: the horses are saddled, and we are only waiting for the signal to mount. I believe I told you of the spirited cavalry affair of the 18th hussars the evening before last, and that Colonel Vivian had been wounded in the right arm: there are hopes he will not lose it. I should go on, but learn that his lordship's horse is bridled.—*Adieu.*

St. Jory: 10 p.m.

I am too tired to say more than that we have had a remarkable day, but have carried our point, though with severe loss.

April 11: 4 a. m.

We are up again, and setting off. I write while the horses are bringing to the door.

LETTER 136

In front of Toulouse: April 11, 10 a.m.

I have stolen into a corner to write a few lines whilst we are waiting to get the troops formed. Yesterday we had a busy and an obstinate day. At one time, the Spanish corps on our right gave way totally; nothing for a while could be more inauspicious. However, the day was retrieved, and Marshal Soult was driven from his position, naturally strong, and protected by redoubts and entrenchments.

There was much cannonading on both sides, especially on that of the enemy, whose artillery was served with unusual steadiness and correctness; but as I purpose sending you a sort of account of the day, I will not anticipate the story here. The troops remained last night in the position they occupied at dusk. Headquarters, after all was over, galloped back to St. Jory, which we again left before daybreak this morning.

At this moment we stand as follows:—Sir Rowland Hill's corps on the left bank of the Garonne, having in the course of yesterday possessed itself of the enemy's *tête de pont*, or work thrown up, as I hear, 1000 paces from the bridge. One pontoon bridge remains at Blagnac, a couple of leagues below Toulouse. On the right bank of the Garonne, and close to the river, is our third division, advanced in the suburbs of the town to where the land meets the river; to the left of the third division, is the Light division, extending with its left resting on the road from Toulouse to Alby (the direction towards Lyons). The right of the Spaniards here takes up the right redoubts occupied yesterday by the enemy: to their left is the sixth division, on whom the brunt of yesterday's action fell; to the left of the sixth division is the fourth; to their left the hussars and other cavalry, stretching a league below Toulouse, and upon the canal.

A considerable body of the enemy's army has certainly quitted Toulouse, and taken the Carcassonne Road, which is that of Montpellier. But a considerable body, though an uncertain one, still remains in the city which, though not fortified, has yet an old wall capable of defence. There is no doubt of the wishes of the inhabitants, and we learn from an officer who deserted last night, that during the action of yesterday, the national guards (I mean the citizens forced by Soult to take up arms) threw away their arms. But if there should be means of subsistence in the city, and a good gallant corps be left there, it may puzzle us how to get in.

I cannot at this moment estimate our loss yesterday. That of the fourth and sixth divisions, (chiefly the latter,) the marshal just now told me he believed to be 1500 men. The third division has also suffered, and the Spaniards have sustained considerable loss. The failure of the Spaniards yesterday must, however, be admitted to have afforded another instance that these troops are not to be depended upon; it has shown the enemy too that the Spanish troops are not really improved.

I get on badly with my story. I am writing with people sitting all around, and the sun shines on my paper, and the wind blows, and we are sitting for shade and shelter under the lee of a redoubt, which affords neither today, and, heaven knows, afforded none yesterday. It is the centre one, and the key of the enemy's position; it is round a house built like a church, (though not one,) and called St. Andry: to approach the redoubt yesterday was awkward, as we repeatedly found.

The marquis has left us to ride round to Sir Rowland Hill; in the meanwhile, the troops are getting ready and forming for an attack on some entrenchments yet between us and the town towards our left. Luckily, our weather continues fine and dry: were it otherwise, to move would be next to impossible. I never saw a stiffer or more heavy clay. Soult, aware of this, had roads of planks made from redoubt to redoubt, for the passage of his artillery, which, with the exception of one 4-pounder, he managed to withdraw.

In looking at Toulouse, we have already ascertained several buildings: that of the School of Artillery, formerly a convent of Chartreux. It has a handsome dome with a statue on the top. The cathedral is a solid, but not a handsome building; near it is the foundry. By the way, this may account for the superior practice of yesterday.

We have ascertained that about 100 guns and 200 tumbrils were lately sent from Toulouse to Montauban, and as many to Castres. Mentioning Castres, reminds me that Soult's estates are there. How one's ideas scramble on; mine are at this moment running to Aire and Orthes, whither we have sent Lieut. Newland to ride post, that the reserves of gun ammunition may be ordered to Auch, whither we are sending our empty waggons. To procure shot we are paying 6*d.* a

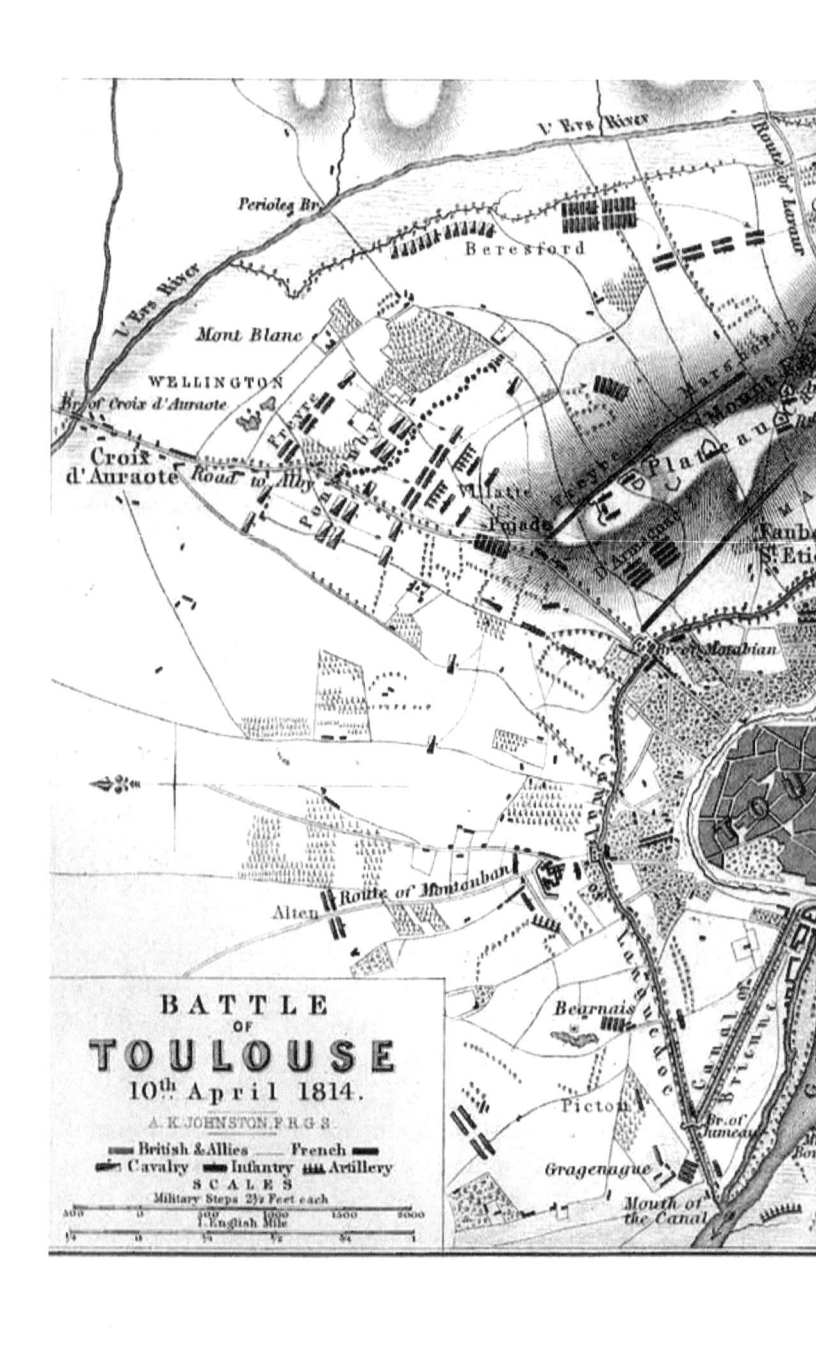

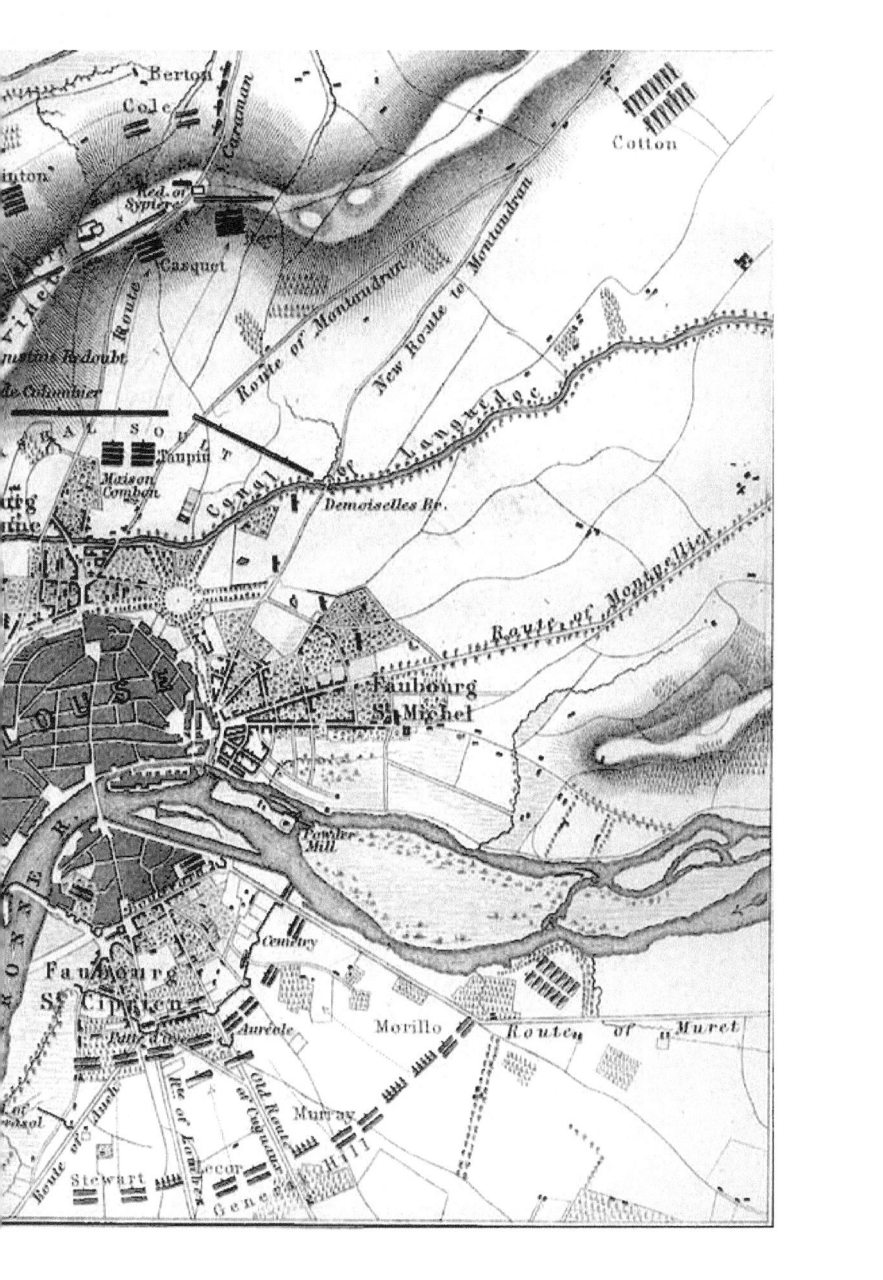

piece, and are scraping together our own fired in the field yesterday, as well as those of the enemy. A couple of hours ago, we began by telling the fellows how necessary it was for their own sakes to find shot; you might as well have talked Greek; but the sixpences have produced a pile, not so large as those probably in Toulouse, but a very jolly-looking one Good day for a while; all is yet quiet.

I am quite well; my yesterday's mishaps having been confined to a good roll on the road with my black Spaniard, who, because his countrymen had misbehaved in the morning, must needs follow their example as we were going home to St. Jory in the evening.

Letter 137

St. Auban: April 12, half-past 4 a.m.

I did not get home till an hour after dark last night, and was too tired to write. Yesterday was passed I know not how: in riding over the field of the previous day's action, in ascertaining how our ammunition held out, and in getting all put again in order. We expected to have had orders to attack some intrenchments between the left of our centre and Toulouse, but all was quiet. About two o'clock, we imagined the enemy was coming to attack us: a column assembled, but we afterwards-found it was a funeral party performing the last rites probably to some officer of rank; they fired over what we supposed to have been the grave.

I have been called away to go to the left to inquire about some boats stopped on the canal with ammunition and wounded on the day of the action. We are in great want of ammunition, and sent at daybreak yesterday Lieutenant Newland to ride post to Aire and Orthes, to order up the gun ammunition to Audi. We have already sent our empty waggons to Auch; our small-arm reserves are well up at the pontoon bridge at Blagnac—*Adieu*, I must manage today to give you an account of the action of the 10th, which was one of the sharpest I have seen.

In none have I seen Lord Wellington so animated; generally quiet, and even apparently indifferent, the moment of danger arouses him, and shows at once the great man.—*Adieu*.

Letter 138

Toulouse: April 12.

I little thought when I left St. Auban this morning, that I was bending my steps hither. On approaching the advanced posts, I met

Sir Henry Clinton, who told me the enemy had retreated during the night, that he had himself sent a few of the mounted staff corps into Toulouse, but had forbidden the entrance of troops. I told Sir Henry my errand, adding, that I thought I had better go and secure the arsenal; a moment sufficed to find me at the outposts in the town and in the midst of men, women, and children, crying, "*Vivent les Anglais!*" "*Vivent nos Libérateurs!*"—all were full of joy, and in passing through the streets, all were asking, "*Où est Wellington; où est ce heros?*"

I reached the arsenal, and was quitting it to pay a visit to the lady to whom I had promised protection, when Dickson arrived, so I left the arsenal under his auspices, and meeting a gentlemanly man, one of the city guard (composed of 2000 inhabitants well clothed and armed), I proceeded to the house of Madame de Finot, for such is the name of the sister of the Monsieur Cazalès mentioned in one of my late letters.

Nothing could exceed the attention with which I was received; tomorrow I am to repeat my visit, and you shall hear again. From the house of Madame de Finot, my conductor directed me to the foundry, formerly a fine one; latterly the founder has become a bankrupt, and four unfinished mortars and a couple of unfinished guns remain in a spacious and well-arranged foundry. During this time, Hill's corps filed through the street in which the foundry is; bands playing, the men with laurels in their hats, and the women sometimes cheering, at other times unable to speak.

7 p.m.

I had hardly written thus far, when I was invited to dinner with my host, a Monsieur de Davisard: he is married to a very pretty and very young lady; I never saw a more interesting one. We were four at table, and two nice children of five and three years—boy and girl—sat at a little table; I never passed a more pleasant hour. After dinner, arrived an invitation to a ball, to be given tonight by Lord Wellington, to which of course the lady will go; and I shall perhaps have the honour of dancing with her. We are going previously to the theatre, and I now wait for the lady's brother, with whom I have, since dinner, run all over the town, and the bridge, and the suburbs, and the cathedral, and I know not where.

Will you believe me that the lady is married to her uncle? so the brother told me, merely saying, "You see what love does." There seems no disparity of age. The husband is one of the proprietors of the celebrated canal, which, beginning near Toulouse, unites the Garonne with the Mediterranean. I shall tomorrow learn all the history of this canal. I seem today full of adventures; to whom should I be introduced on the bridge just now, but to a Monsieur de Medalle, son-in-law to Sterne? he speaks English perfectly well.

This is certainly a fine old town, and if some improvements projected before the revolution were carried into execution, would be finer still; but I am called away.——-*Adieu*, for this evening.

April 13, 8 a.m.

I know not what I have written, what I have told you, and what I have not; yesterday passed like a dream. On leaving off writing, I went with the brother-in-law of Monsieur de Davisard to the theatre; it is small, but not inelegant, and was crowded to excess. The play had been altered to *Richard Coeur de Lion*; it abounds with loyal passages and loyal songs, and was well timed; nothing could equal the cheering of these passages, except the burst of applause which broke out when Lord Wellington showed himself or moved. One must know the French character to be able to fancy their excessive joy; they shouted and wept, and shouted again.

Whilst all this was going on, I observed that most of the staff wore white cockades, and looking up at his lordship, who sat in an upper stage box, just over Monsieur de Davisard's, I was struck with the large white cockade which his lordship wore. In a moment an unusual tumult announced something new, and a person in black, attended by many candles, and having a paper in his hand, appeared in a side box struggling for room and utterance. After a quarter of an hour's roaring, silence was obtained, and he read at length the proclamation of King Louis XVIII., of which I could only hear part indistinctly. But he announced the abdication of Bonaparte, and all that you no doubt know. I cannot describe the scene which followed, you must fancy it.

From the theatre, we went to a ball at Lord Wellington's; many very pretty and even elegant women. I would have danced, as in duty bound, with Madame de Davisard, but with a sprained ankle and bruised hip and elbow from a violent fall I got from my horse two days ago, I really could not. I shall today make my apologies to *Madame*, whom I had not the gallantry to stay to hand last night into her carriage.

At the ball, I saw my friend Colonel Ponsonby of the 12th Dragoons, who had ridden post from Bordeaux, which he left the day before, coming through the enemy's lines. By the way Ponsonby met with no opposition, except at Montauban, where General Giradot hesitated about allowing him to pass; Colonel Cooke, who accompanied Ponsonby from Bordeaux, and who came direct from Paris, went on last night to communicate the intelligence to Soult. Although all these things are true, I can nevertheless scarcely believe their reality.

I have for the last two days intended to give you an account of the affair of the 10th instant, yet now whilst the hopes of an immediate peace occupy my mind, how shall I return to a relation of the horrors of war! Yet I shall endeavour, that you may know what really happened, and that you may join with me in thanks to the merciful Providence which has again preserved me in the field; I hope the last field in which I shall be called on to engage. Headquarters left St. Jory before daybreak on the 10th of April. Soult's army occupied a long rising ground to the east of Toulouse, and on the right bank of the Garonne, called Mont Eave, having their troops sheltered under the rise of the hill, so as to be hardly visible.

A brigade was stationed on a detached eminence on the left called Pujade, with three field-pieces on their left, on the road to Alby: a strong corps was stationed in front of the canal on the Montauban road, and another corps occupied redoubts and a chain of posts in front of the suburb of St. Cyprien. The enemy's artillery was posted in the redoubts on the rising ground to the east of the town; and there were some heavy guns (18-pounders) on the ramparts; there was also a battery at a fortified convent on the Montauban road, some guns in the redoubts in front of the suburb of St. Cyprien, and some heavy pieces near a bridge over the canal on the east of the Montpellier road.

The Allies were posted as follows: Hill's corps in front of St. Cyprien on the left of the Garonne. The third division with its right on the Garonne and its left stretching beyond the road to Montauban; Sir Thomas Picton commanded this division. On the left of the third division was General Alten's (the light) division, extending nearly to the road to Alby; by this road the Spanish Army of General Freyre advanced, having joined it about a mile and a half from Toulouse.

This army moved in two columns, and formed under a heavy fire beyond the hill Pujade, from which the enemy withdrew soon after the action commenced, and on which the Portuguese guns of Lieutenant-Colonel Arentschild were formed to fire on the redoubts of the enemy's position. The fourth and sixth divisions marching by Launaguet, also advanced by the Alby road, though more to the rear, turning off at the village of Croix Dorade to their left towards the village of Montblanc, nearly opposite the principal French redoubt, which was the key of the whole position.

In filing to their left the fourth and sixth divisions were necessarily exposed to a heavy though a distant cannonade from all the guns on the enemy's works; they had also some distance to march over a country apparently level, but extremely intersected with broad ditches and hollow roads. The artillery of these divisions was in the first instance posted in some low ground near the village of Montblanc, and fired with vivacity on the enemy's guns, which had the advantage of higher ground and were sheltered behind their works.

The affair commenced at 7 a.m. on our right, by the attack of our right or third division. By half-past 9 the affair became warm, and the enemy retiring from the Pujade, set fire to a very fine and large house with an avenue of cypress trees leading from it to the Alby road; the left of the light division, during the remainder of the action, rested on the ruins of this house. It was a little before this that the fourth and sixth divisions, under Marshal Beresford, moved to their left; at 11 the Spanish Army, which had been formed under cover of Arentschild's guns posted on the Pujade, advanced to assault the left redoubts of the enemy. They crossed the valley with great bravery, under a most galling and severe fire of cannon and musketry.

In their rear, and before they advanced, a brigade of their own troops, and a brigade of British heavy dragoons were formed as a reserve. The hussar brigade took the same route as the fourth and sixth divisions, but extended more to the left than the infantry; Gardiner's troop of horse artillery was also brought up to the left of the Spaniards to answer the enemy's fire of artillery, which became more and more vigorous throughout the day. The enemy's guns were served with admirable spirit and correctness. A heavy mortar from the town also played on the advancing columns. Soon after 11 the whole Spanish corps, which had for some time bravely sustained the fire from the enemy's left, suddenly gave way and fell back in great confusion.

In a moment Lord Wellington, who was on the Pujade, galloped to the spot, and by his personal exertions rallied about a company on the Alby road near the cypress trees. General Freyre was also very active. It should be mentioned to the honour of the Portuguese *caçadores* of the light division, that they boldly advanced through the flying Spaniards, drubbing them as they went on. A squadron or two of British heavy dragoons, sent still more in the rear of the routed Spaniards, rallied them by striking them with the flat side of their swords.

After some time (of which had the enemy profited the affair had been still more awkward) the Spanish troops rallied, and were

Colonel Sir Augustus Simon Frazer

again placed in position near the Pujade, from which they afterwards moved to their left in support of the sixth division, but were not again brought into serious action all the day. At a quarter before 12 Marshal Beresford's troops had gained the bridge to the right of the enemy's position, and the enemy's troops were seen moving in force towards that point. At this time a Portuguese *aide-de-camp* arrived from the marshal, requesting more infantry; none, however, was sent. The admirable alacrity and coolness of the marquis was eminently conspicuous during the trying and wholly unexpected circumstance of the failure of the Spanish attack, which, had a less gallant or less ready general commanded, might have been fatal to the success of the day.

The marshal's troops soon gained two redoubts near the centre of the enemy's position, and the fourth division gained without much opposition those of the enemy's extreme right.

The whole face of the hill is exceedingly intersected with deep hollow roads; the soil is a stiff heavy clay, in which with difficulty horses could move out of a walk. Aware of this, the enemy had judiciously made roads of planks, as communications for his artillery from one work to another; about this time there was a momentary cessation of firing. On looking round, the steeples and roofs of Toulouse were seen covered with spectators.

At 1 p.m. the enemy began to withdraw the artillery from his left, moving some guns about to keep us in check on that side, no longer the real point of attack. The affair in the centre now became more serious, and the marquis galloped thither. A little before two the marshal's artillery of the fourth and sixth divisions and Gardiner's troop opened, and the infantry of the sixth division, becoming warmly engaged, succeeded, with severe loss, in taking the central redoubts. It was, however, yet a couple of hours before the enemy was forced from the works still more to his left, which he quitted gradually, withdrawing his artillery by the hollow roads, across the bridge over the canal: but by 4 p.m. the day was decidedly ours, and his troops could be distinctly seen in full march, retiring on the road towards Montpellier.

The hussars, who had been exposed to a severe cannonade from heavy field-guns, had suffered a good deal; they had arrived at an unlucky moment; had they been sooner, they would have taken many prisoners, the enemy there having given way in confusion, at least equal to that of the Spaniards on our right. The brunt of the action fell on the sixth division, which had 13 officers killed, and 88 wounded; 123 men killed, and 1209 wounded; the returns of other divisions I

THE SORTIE FROM BAYONNE.

have not seen; the only artillery officer killed, was Lieutenant Blumenbach of the German artillery.

The efforts of Sir Rowland Hill's corps during the day were confined to driving the enemy from his more advanced position in front of St. Cyprien, and forcing him to abandon some redoubts there; this attack, however, was not intended to be real, but had the desired effect of distracting the enemy. The fruits of the affair of the 10th, were the retreat of Soult's whole force from the neighbourhood of Toulouse on the evening and during the night of the 11th. Had he remained, it would have been necessary to have invested the place; an obstinate defence of Toulouse would have at least occasioned great misery to the inhabitants, and might have unavoidably obliged us to rain this celebrated city. From these horrors Toulouse is fortunately delivered.

The enemy's loss during the action probably equalled our own; on the side of the hills opposite the city, the enemy's dead lay thickly strewed, many of them literally boys. As these dead lay in full view of the city, the enemy may have been politic in requesting (as he did on the 11th) leave to bury the dead. The funeral I have somewhere mentioned, proves to have been that of General Taupin: report says that four other generals were wounded in the affair, of whom Generals D'Armagnac and Harispe are here, the latter has lost a foot; to the humanity of the former, and to his advice that the French Army should not obstinately remain in a position which might lead to ultimate ruin, Toulouse owes its deliverance from the yoke of Soult's command, of which all bitterly complain. He is openly accused of extortion and robbery, and, whether justly or otherwise (though I believe the former), is execrated here. As heavy guns were fired from the ramparts, the enemy consider our having forborne to fire in return on the town as generous.

So much is this the prevailing idea, that all sorts of handsome things are said by almost everyone whom we meet. I should mention that, during the affair, the hussars took a convoy of boats on the canal, containing 200 wounded men, and a considerable quantity of ammunition; this was as early as 1 p.m., and was a league above the town; so that early in the day the enemy's loss had been severe. I do not, in the hurry we have been in, recollect the number of prisoners taken in the affair *Adieu*, awhile.

Letter 139

Toulouse: April 23.

How will your "hatred" of the siege of Bayonne have been in-

creased by the late sortie; how unlucky to all the unfortunates who suffered in it! The French loss was greater in this sortie than our own, yet ours, I think, was 800. As events have turned out, my not remaining at Bayonne has been most fortunate. I should not have been present at the Battle of Toulouse, one of the most remarkable, and decidedly the most interesting, I have seen.

Don't betray me, and I'll tell you all about Bayonne, and the investment, and the gun taken on February 27th. About 4 p. m. on that day, I passed the bridge of boats near Boucaut, and observing a more than usually animated fire near the citadel, galloped thither. My object was, under cover of this fire, to reconnoitre the place. After passing a brigade of guards, then halted in the road out of the range of musketry, we pushed on (Ord and myself) to the German battalions under General Hinüber, then warmly engaged.

There was a good deal of firing, both of musketry and cannon, from the citadel. We found the howitzer of Cairnes's troop in the road. The men, except those required to fire the howitzer occasionally, were ordered to lie down in the ditch on each side of the road, which was a paved one. To the right of the howitzer was a house filled with Hinüber's men, firing from the windows; to the left, and a little in advance of the Jews' burying-ground, the road in the immediate front of the howitzer was broken up, and a traverse had been made across it. Just beyond this traverse was a French fieldpiece, which formed the bone of contention, each party disputing the ground on which it stood.

General Hinüber was very desirous of securing this gun, and I smiled at his eagerness, believing it to be of no value whatever, and in reply to his wishing our artillerymen to drag it off with ropes, observed, that we had no ropes, nor in truth artillerymen to spare, having already half the number wounded; but that I would go with half a dozen of his men, if he would spare them, and bring the little gun (a 4-pounder) from behind the traverse. Accordingly, I ran forward, turned the gun round, and with the assistance of a few of the Germans, the gun was brought in. In this, several poor fellows lost their lives. The enemy about this time made several attempts to charge our howitzer: the opposite sides were about 100 yards asunder, each side screamed, as is common in these confusions; all fired, and all forgot to charge, so that, as I predicted, the affair came to nothing.

There are moments in which one is careless; such were those at this time, and I was standing in the middle of the road, before our own howitzer, when I received the trifling wound which has occasioned this long round-about story. General Hinüber and his Brigade Major were both wounded at the same time. The latter, I regret to hear, was killed in the late sortie. All this is pure egotism, and I should be ashamed to write it.

LETTER 140

Toulouse: April 28, 10 a.m.

Yesterday passed in a confusion of joy from which I have, even now, hardly recovered sufficiently to give you a description. From the earliest hour in the morning all had been preparation, the military lined the streets and the whole population was abroad: the houses were all adorned with laurel, and with variegated lamps and lanthorns intended for the night's illumination. It seems here, as in Spain, the custom to hang up tapestry, carpets, &c., as marks of joy: added to these, flags with patriotic devices were displayed at every window.

About 2, Lord Wellington, attended by his general officers and all headquarters in their gayest costume, rode out to meet the Duc d'Angoulême; the meeting took place about two leagues from Toulouse on the Audi road, a little beyond the village of St. Martin du Touch. On going out one could hardly get along; it was impossible, in passing the crowds, not to contemplate the passing scene, and to contrast it with the far different ones of which almost every step reminded us. Near St. Martin was to have been our field of action had Soult attacked us before we crossed the Garonne.

I had quitted the suite to examine some batteries, and a butt for practice, thrown up in the plain at a little distance from the road, so that on rejoining the cavalcade I found that the duke had arrived. His royal highness was preceded by a squadron of the British Royal Dragoons. At the moment of my meeting the procession, the corps of *Gardes Royales* (raised within a few days at Toulouse) saluted the duke, who received it very graciously, and it took its place immediately behind the squadron of the Royals. Lord Wellington rode on the left of the duke, mounted on a white horse beautifully caparisoned. The duke was also on a white, or rather grey, horse, and was dressed in green, with the Cordon Bleu (a royal order) of France over his shoulder.

The duke looked uncommonly well, and returned with politeness and animation the salutations on all sides. Women ran out of the crowd to present him with nosegays, others gazed at him unable to speak. In this manner, with frequent stoppages from the pressure of the multitude, we reached, at length, the suburb of St. Cyprien. Here the streets are wide and the houses handsome; every window crowded with women, the bands of the British and Portuguese troops playing at once, and a royal salute fired from an English battery of artillery, joined to the acclamations of the multitude, formed a scene impossible to be described. Even here we witnessed, as was frequent afterwards, women fainting for joy.

In this manner we reached the bridge on which part of Sir William Stewart's troops were posted. The Garde Urbaine (or national troops of Toulouse), which had been formed on the esplanade near the Porte de St^e. Catherine, at the entrance of the suburb, filed after the procession, keeping abreast of the duke. One could not but smile as their bayonets crossed, but not in strife, with those of the English troops. I should have mentioned that at the Porte de St^e. Catherine, the municipality waited on the duke, and that a canopy was offered to be borne over his head, which his royal highness declined.

Instead of going direct to the Place St. Etienne, where the cathedral is situated, the cavalcade moved slowly through the best streets. To describe the enthusiasm is impossible, the silent gaze of many, the wild tumultuous joy of others, and the cheers of acclamation which occasionally burst from all—"*Vive le Roi!*" "*Vivent les Anglais!*" "*Vivent nos Libérateurs!*" "*Vive Lord Wellington!*" and then, as if the duke had been for a moment forgotten, "*Vive le Duc d'Angoulême!*" "*Vive le Fils de Henri Quatre!*" Shakespeare would describe such a scene: I cannot.

In this manner we reached the cathedral, before which the 92nd Highlanders were drawn up. Knowing what a squeeze there would be, I had stationed a man to take my horse; and fortunately got in, though almost suffocated. I followed close after the few generals who were able to get in after Lord Wellington. His lordship was immediately behind the canopy carried over the heads of the duke and of the Archbishop of Toulouse. Forced forwards by the crowd entering the cathedral, I found myself within the railing of the altar, and within a few yards of the duke. A single row of the *Gardes Urbaines* were before me, and prevented my feeling myself too forward.

The duke stood by a throne placed on the right of the altar. On each side of his royal highness an officer held a standard of France. Opposite to the duke, and to the left of the altar, stood the Archbishop under a beautiful canopy, and in full robes. To the immediate right of the duke and rather nearer the altar, stood Lord Wellington with Generals Pakenham and Murray and one or two others behind him. In front of the altar and between the duke and the archbishop, a double row of priests and judges in full robes. The *Te Deum* began, chanted by all the choir, and accompanied by the organ and the whole orchestra of the city. From the acclamations of the crowds, both in the body of the cathedral and without, the music, which I believe was fine, was indistinctly heard.

At a particular part of the ceremony all knelt down, but the noise of the soldiers presenting arms as they knelt, and the drums beating, drowned all other sounds. I could only then observe that the Archbishop advanced and made his obeisance to the duke, and that the standards were twice waved over the head of His Royal Highness, who was immediately conducted to the front of the altar, where he knelt for a moment on a crimson velvet cushion, previously placed there; and then, escorted by the Archbishop on one side and Lord Wellington on the other, left the cathedral and gained the Palais Royal (lately the prefecture and headquarters), which is close by. I stayed a few moments wondering and musing at all I had witnessed, and then following the stream of the retiring crowd, found I had got out of the cathedral by a side-door leading to a narrow lane.

After strolling about for a little I went home: it was past 6, and I felt jaded with all I had heard and seen, and fatigued from the feelings which had been excited. A finer sight cannot be imagined: never was more enthusiastic joy shown; the day, too, was auspicious, from a cloudy, cold morning, the weather after 2 became mild, and the sun shone bright upon the festival, which will long be remembered in Toulouse.

I had promised to dine with some of our people "*Au Grand Soleil;*" accordingly, about eight o'clock we sat down to dinner, and were talking over the events of the day, over a few bottles of the best wines of the talkative landlady, when the old lady appeared.

"Would *Messieurs les Anglais,*—since her house was so full,—would they permit a French officer who was decorated with several orders, and looked like a colonel, to dine in their room."

To this we readily agreed, and a gentlemanly man appeared, and supped in the room; we soon got into conversation, and after drinking the health of the King of France, and saying some civil things, the officer rose up, and announced himself as M. de Kerboux, *aide-de-camp* of the minister of war (Dupont), and the bearer of despatches from Paris to Suchet. M. de Kerboux left Paris on Saturday, showed us his passports in French and Russian, and said that the purport of his despatches was to direct Suchet to assume the chief command of Soult's army as well as of his own, and to order Soult to Paris to give an account of his conduct. He further added, that two days before he had quitted Paris, Bonaparte had left Fontainebleau. M. de Kerboux said he had waited on the Duc d'Angoulême, but had not conceived himself as authorised to call at Lord Wellington's, though he wished his lordship to be apprised of so important a piece of intelligence.

This officer, after sitting with us a few minutes, and giving his name and residence at Paris, and offering to carry any one of us there when he should return in a few days, set off for Suchet's headquarters, believed to be at Narbonne. We did not go to the theatre last night, but the duke, after dining with Lord Wellington, went there, and was of course received in the most enthusiastic manner.

Upon inquiry I find that all that M. de Kerboux told us is strictly the case: he added that he was convinced that Soult, previous to the action of the 10th inst., was aware of what had passed in Paris on the 3rd; and from many little circumstances at the outposts, not regarded at the moment, it does seem more than probable. If so, he has indeed played an unworthy part. M. de Kerboux more than once asked if we were sure that Lord Wellington did not know what had happened at Paris; to this we replied we were convinced his lordship did not; it was impossible. *Adieu,* I write with a headache from yesterday's doings. By the way, I should mention that the only French general who waited yesterday upon the Duc d'Angoulême, was Count Clauzel, a pleasing-looking man; the count had previously paid his visit to Lord Wellington,

I have no news and cannot write; little Armandine seems resolved to prevent my doing so. The little girl will make me play with a skipjack I gave her yesterday. She was born on Bonaparte's birthday; how one hates his name, which should be forgotten! Let us turn to something else; let us hope never to see such scenes again. May future days be passed in quiet, and our attention be given to more pleasing duties.

I wrote a few lines yesterday to Henry Blachley's father, and sent also a letter announcing the particulars of Blachley's wound, as far as I knew them. A musket ball grazed his head and has carried away part of an ear, but he is doing well and no fears are entertained. I repeat this, lest my letter of yesterday should not reach you so soon as this: in this case it would be friendly towards the father to acquaint him with the particulars about his son, who is one of the most gallant fellows I ever saw. I am a little proud of all the Woodbridge boys, for they are all remarkable, and have been remarked, for their cheerfulness and zeal.

But now let us look to other scenes, and more peaceful employments.—*Adieu.*

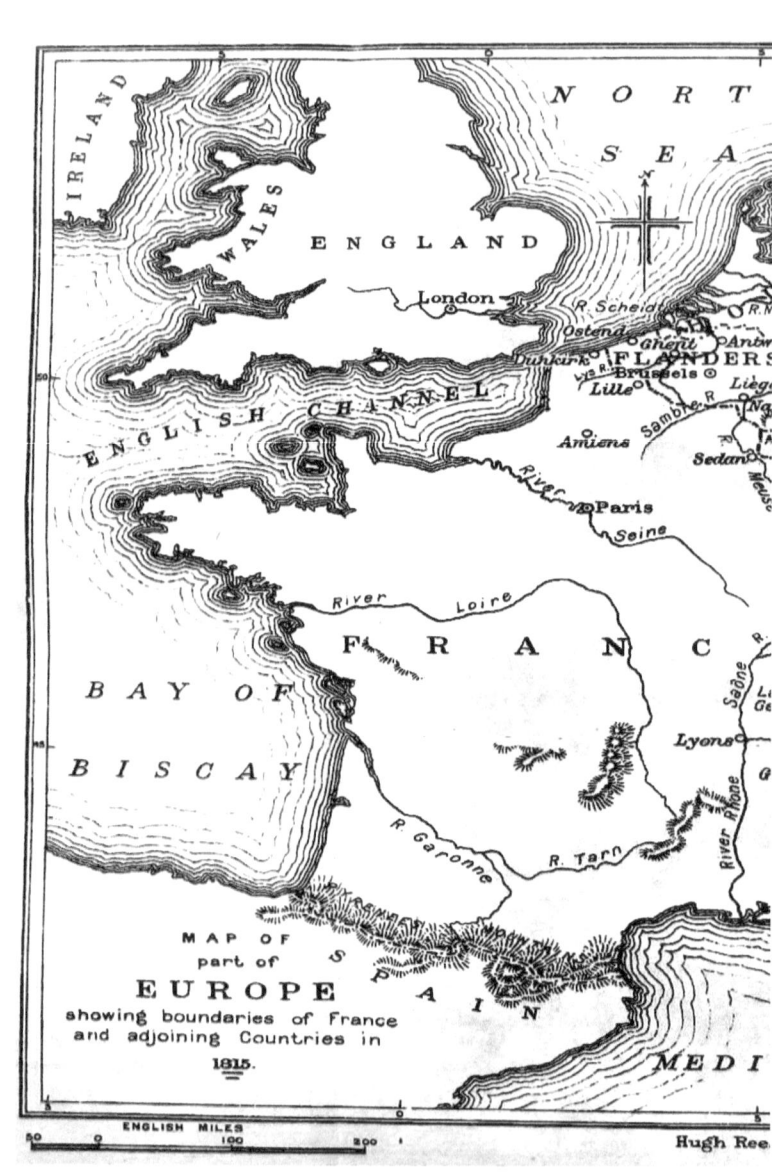

Letters During the Waterloo Campaign

1815

Letter 1

Ostend: April 17, 1815.

I landed a couple of miles from hence, about 10 this morning. We left Ramsgate at 3 p. m. yesterday, with a fresh though not a very favourable gale. During the passage the wind blew from every point of the compass, and for a while from none. The calm did not last long. At 9 the packet cast anchor about a mile from shore; and, impatient of the confinement of ship-board. General Vivian, Captain Harris, and I took the packet's boat, and got on shore without much wetting, though there was some surf. The packet will not be in the harbour till 6 this evening, and I hope to leave Ostend, or rather the village of Sas (a mile from hence), in the canal boat going hence to Ghent, at 5 tomorrow morning. My troop quitted Ostend two days ago, marching the first day to Gistel, six miles from hence, the next day to Bruges, and reaching Ghent today, where I hope to join my servant and horses.

I have seen the Duke of Wellington, who reviewed the garrison this morning; but I saw His Grace only at a distance, and he was on horseback. Having alighted from his carriage, he mounted the horse of Colonel Adye of the Artillery, and then rode to see the works.

The duke then continued his route to Nieuport, and was going to Ypres. The country round Nieuport has been laid under water, as a precaution against the enemy, who is said to have 7000 troops under Vandamme, in Dunkirk. The works here are repairing, and will be soon in a good state of defence. There are a couple of hundred pieces mounted, including mortars and howitzers. Among the mortars are four Napoleons, of the Seville long-shooting kind; they are 12-inch mortars. The garrison consists of the 44th (first battalion) British, and three Hanoverian battalions, with three companies of Artillery, and some scattered detachments of all corps finding their way to the army.

Since my arrival I have run over the works, and walked to Fort Imperial, a beautiful sunk fort, a mile to the eastward of Ostend; it is uncommonly strong; a pentagon, with three rows of loop-holes, having a dozen heavy guns on the top. Caponiers defend the ditch, which is deep, dry, and wide. The harbour is full of vessels all gaily dressed with colours, on account of the Duke's visit.—*Adieu*, I will write again from Ghent.

Letter 2

Ghent: April 19.

My last was written from Ostend, which I reached on the morning of the 17th, and quitted before daybreak yesterday, walking about a mile to the little village of Sas de Gard, where the Bruges canal approaches Ostend. At Sas I got into the canal boat, which was drawn by a couple of horses at a merry pace, and we reached Bruges about 9. A hackney-coach here carried myself and baggage to the other end of the city, and I embarked in a second and better boat, which reached Ghent about 5 in the afternoon. On getting to the quay, I found my servants waiting for me, and that a good billet had been provided, so that in a quarter of an hour I made myself clean and comfortable.

From Ostend to Bruges by water is about twelve miles, and from Bruges to Ghent by water about twenty-one; by land the journey is two or three leagues longer. Nothing can be pleasanter than travelling in these canal boats, which are large and commodious vessels. At either end is a cabin, nicely fitted up. In the middle is a kind of public-house; on one side an excellent kitchen, on the other, larders and store-rooms for all manner of eatables. The stern cabin, which is considered the best, is fitted up with looking-glasses, sofas, and chairs; and the sides, as well as ceiling, very prettily painted. There were six windows in the cabin of the boat yesterday; and at 1 p.m. we sat down to an excellent dinner, well put on the table. For this excellent dinner and carriage from Bruges, the price is five *francs*, that is, 4*s*. 2*d*. Wine, coffee, and liqueurs are paid for separately.

We were fifteen in the stern cabin; there might be twenty people in the middle part of the boat; and there were eighteen in the fore cabin; yet there seemed no difficulty in providing good cheer for all. There were several pretty and very agreeable women, and altogether no journey could be more pleasant. The country through which we passed is rich, and in all the fresh beauty of spring. Four horses drew the boat, and were changed about half way between this and Bruges.

The day was very cold, and I stayed below most part of the way.

Today I rode, after breakfast, to the end of the city, and inspected Colonel Macdonald's and Captain Mercer's troops of Horse Artillery. Besides these two troops, Drummond's and Brome's batteries have been here for some little while; and Rogers's marched in today. There are no regular troops in the city except the Artillery, which accordingly furnishes a guard of honour for Louis XVIII., who is here, and much afflicted with the gout. I had the honour of leaving a card for his majesty this morning.

There are (besides the king) the Duc de Feltre, Marshals Victor and Marmont (the latter with both his arms), and the Comte d'Artois. (It had been supposed that Marshal Marmont had had an arm amputated in consequence of a wound). The Duc de Grammont is also here, and many others of the royalist officers. There are, however, no royalist soldiers, if I may use the term royalist, though a corps of them is said to be at Alost, through which I shall pass tomorrow on my way to Brussels, for which I set off at 6 in the morning, with Macdonald and Hawker.

Soon after I rose this morning, I received a message from *Madame*, my hostess, that breakfast was ready, but declining the intended civility, one of the sons waited upon me to hope that I would dine with his mother, which I accordingly did, at 1 o'clock, the dinner lasting till half-past 3. I passed a very pleasant time with Madame Hamelin, for so is the lady called. Her husband, who is a banker, is at a country-house. The party consisted of *Madame*, her daughter, of five-and-twenty, and two sons, of eighteen and twenty. Never were folks more hospitable, and I am again engaged to sup with them this evening, which, however, I shall not be able to do.

My object in going to Brussels tomorrow is to see Sir George Wood, and to arrange my destination with him. He has been at Antwerp, but he is to return this evening to Brussels. I shall have no objection to coming back here for a day or two, just to look about, since there are several things well worth seeing. About 3000 of the inhabitants are daily at work near the gate leading to Courtray, throwing up some redoubts; but the city is too large to be fortified. Hawker tells me that in digging today, the workmen have found a couple of bottles of wine in an old vault on which they stumbled, and that they have found several pieces of Spanish money—perhaps buried in the Duke of Alva's time.—*Adieu*, for this day.

LETTER 3

Brussels: April 21.

I arrived here yesterday, and am off this morning for Ostend, to arrange and to hasten the landing of ordnance and stores; this will occupy a few days. The army cannot move for three weeks; our corps and every other is yet inefficient; we have here a couple of hundred horses, but no drivers; we pick up fellows in the streets to look after the horses. Our deficiency at this time is about 3000 men, and 5000 horses, but all these we may readily have, and I have written home on the subject. We are to have in all, 17 batteries, and 8 troops of artillery with the army.

There has been a small affair near Ancona, in which the Austrians claim the advantage, and accordingly, though somewhat inconsequentially, retire. The country here is very luxuriant, and very forward—so are the young ladies, troops of whom of a dozen years old turn round like wheels upon the road, singing "*Orange Boven!*"—*Adieu*, I have not time to write more.

LETTER 4

Ostend: April 24.

I left Brussels on the 21st and rode to Ghent, where after making some arrangements, I rode on to Bruges, and the rain was so heavy that I stopped and slept there. I proceeded at daybreak on the 22nd, and reached Ostend at 7 a. m., having travelled through as dirty roads as I ever remember to have seen; but in general, the roads from hence to Brussels are excellent. On Saturday, I began with Colonel Adye to arrange what could be done: we have both a good deal to do, and ample means to employ; therefore, I trust we shall get on. We are sending ordnance at once to Nieuport, Ypres, Ghent, and Antwerp; this, with issuing ammunition to all corps arriving, and landing and passing our artillery horses and detachments, affords good room for exertion.

We have, besides, to unload and place in the arsenals and magazines here more stores than are intended to remain; the object being to send back the ships to England, that they may return with fresh cargoes. It rained incessantly the whole of Saturday. Yesterday, after setting all hands to work, I rode with Colonel May to Nieuport, to see how all was going on there. Nieuport is nine miles from Ostend, and eighteen from Dunkirk. Much has been done, and much continues to be done to the works, which are already in a respectable state of defence. The garrison consists of the 78th British, and the Kalembourg Hanoverian regiments, with an invalid company of German artillery. They are not, however, above 700 effective men; 84 pieces of artillery are mounted on the works, and we are sending about 90 more. The approaches to Nieuport have been inundated, so that already, an attack can be made only on two points. The inundations extend nearly to Dunkirk on the one side, and to Dixmunde on the other. Nothing can more truly depict the wretchedness of war, than these inundations. Nothing is to be seen but houses standing like islands in the midst of the waters, and the unfortunate owners, now deprived of their fields, idling about.

All the ships off Ostend got into the harbour yesterday; among them the one with the guns and part of the carriages of Colonel Gardiner's troop, which is still here.

Since I began writing, we have additional orders to send away, in Schuyts, the following ordnance. The Schuyts are to go to Ghent, and to be forwarded from thence to their respective destinations.

	No.		Total.
For Mons - -	12	18-pounders	12
For Oudenarde -	4 16	24-pounders 12-pounders	20
For Tournay -	10 6	9-pounders 5½-in. howitzers	16
For Ghent - -	20 14 30 6 5 5	24-pounders 18-pounders 12-pounders 9-pounders 10-in. howitzers 8-in. howitzers	80
			128

Four hundred rounds per gun.
The Tournay guns have travelling carriages, the rest garrison.

The ordnance sending to Nieuport are:—

- 3   24-pounders.
- 22 18-pounders.
- 25 12-pounders.
- 15   9-pounders.
- 3   68-pounder carronades.
- 5   13-in. mortars.
- 5   10-in. mortars.
- 5   8-in. mortars.

10 $4^{2/5}$-in. mortars.

—

93

—

About seven hundred rounds per gun.

For Ypres:—

38 18-pounders.
50 12-pounders.
20 9-pounders.
 5 68-pounder carronades.
 5 10-in. howitzers.
 7 13-in. howitzers.
 7 10-in. howitzers.
 9 8-in. howitzers.
17 $4^{2/5}$-in. howitzers.

—

158

—

About seven hundred rounds per gun.

To return to Nieuport,—the weak part, or rather that exposed to be attacked, is on the north-west, between the mouth of the Isere on the right (looking from the town) and the inundation. The ground here cannot be laid under water, and is 500 yards wide. On the opposite side, *viz.* the south-east, the ground cannot be wholly laid under water. Altogether the place should make a good defence, but would require a garrison of 3000 infantry.

The River Isere is banked up, and becomes the Ypres canal—it receives at six leagues from Nieuport towards Ypres, the little river called Ypenlee. The canal is navigable to Ypres. From Nieuport to Ostend is eighteen miles by the canal, which makes a detour. Nieuport was originally called Sandhoost, which name it changed in 1168, when the harbour was built by Philip Alsace, Earl of Flanders. The last siege was in 1793, when the Hanoverian commandant surrendered the place after a slight bombardment. The town is surrounded with a rampart with round towers: three bastions have been added, but its strength is in its outworks, which are good.—*Adieu*, I am interrupted.

April 25.

I could not resume my pen yesterday; Gardiner's troop marched this morning towards Ghent, which Mercer's and Macdonald's troops, with Drummond's and Rogers's batteries leave this morning for Termonde (called also by us Dendermonde); Brome's battery has also quitted Ghent for Grammont. I have just seen Lord Uxbridge, who has set off for Brussels; he looks well. I rode some little way with Gardiner, and afterwards went to see the foundations of a pentagon fort, 1000 yards to the westward of the town. It is on a similar construction to the sunk pentagon, lately called Fort Imperial, and now Fort William. I do not know the reason of the movement of the troops and artillery from Ghent: probably to make room. Perhaps headquarters may be established there.

April 26, 6 a.m.

Yesterday was a most boisterous day. Two vessels were wrecked at the entrance of the harbour, one belonging to the mayor of this town. They were from Bayonne, and laden with wine, hundreds of casks of which were all day floating about the harbour; one vessel drove on the piles, and went to pieces. Many troops got on shore yesterday, and amongst other people, to my great joy, our Commissary-General Stace, to whom I had been writing in the morning about many deficiencies in his department, which his presence will supply. He is accompanied, or will be followed, by a dozen officers of his department, who are the very people we want. Since he is here, I shall of course leave Ostend in a day or two. No man I have ever seen equals Stace in arrangement and distribution of stores.

If possible, I shall this morning ride to Blankenberg, a little town on the sea coast, eight miles to the north east of Ostend. This is the point to which Sir Eyre Coote should have directed his retreat, when the surf prevented his re-embarkation, and it may be useful to examine the localities. I learn from Stace that Younghusband's and Foster's companies are coming here, and he believes Campbell's: besides the companies coming from America. We have ample employment for them all *Adieu*, for this day.

Letter 5

Ostend: April 27, 7 a. m.

I was going to Sas to select horses for the four English and two German troops of horse artillery, but Adye, from whose charge I am to receive them, wishes to delay our going for an hour; so, I sit down to write. Yesterday at 3 o'clock, Adye, Lloyd, and I, rode to Blankenberg, which is ten miles from hence to the north-east, a very neat fishing town, only separated from the town by sandhills. The streets, except one at each end, are all parallel to the sea, probably to prevent the inconvenience of the sand drifting, as it must do when the wind blows fresh from the sea. The town is very neat and clean, the inhabitants are all fishermen, and the streets were filled with fish laid on the ground, so much so, that we could not pass through some of them. To the east of the town, and close to it on the sand-hills, is a little square fort or tower of brickwork, with a ditch and three rows of loopholes. The top of the little fort, which might hold fifty men, is a very few feet above the level of the sand-hill; it is unfinished.

Having looked at the point where Sir Eyre Coote landed in 1797 to destroy the flood-gates of the Sas canal, or more properly speaking, the Bruges canal, it would seem that if instead of laying down his arms to the force sent from Bruges, which force surrounded him at the point where he landed, he had marched to Blankenberg, he might have held that town until the weather had so moderated as to have enabled him to re-embark his troops. At Blankenberg the shore is bolder, and there are plenty of stout fishing-boats fit to meet the surf, and to have held the troops. But it may be hardly fair to criticise what passed so many years ago, and Blankenberg being as near Bruges as Ostend, it would have been necessary that Sir Eyre Coote should have formed without the least hesitation the resolution to which I allude.

In the morning of yesterday I looked at the works here, and if I stay beyond tomorrow, will send you a plan of them. There is a very beautiful piece of work in the back water, retained to clear out the harbour. This water was formerly of very much greater extent than at present, but Bonaparte recovered and sold a great part of the overflowed land; and, as some imagine, has scarcely left a body of water sufficient for the purpose intended. The new work being hardly finished, a fair trial has not been given. The flood gates are very well constructed, and the masonry, in slabs of granite of six yards long, very beautiful.

In looking yesterday at the regulations of the Belgian king for raising 25,000 national militia, which regulations are dated the 15th inst, I observe the population of Ostend to be 10,550, of Bruges 34,245, Ypres 25,291, and Courtray 13,982; the scale of militia being the one-hundredth part of the population, gives 2½ millions for Belgium. The exceptions from the militia seem sensible and humane. Little fellows under 5 feet at 23 years are exempted, so are (but provisionally) diminutives under that size who may not be 23. The only sons of families are exempted; as are brothers who support sisters, both being orphans, &c. &c.

5 p.m.

I have been to Sas to select the men and horses for the six troops of horse artillery, and have sent off the detachments. I have since been to the fort at the entrance of the harbour. It is built on piles, and is a miserable place. Another vessel was wrecked in the harbour last night. Today it blows fresh, but the weather is milder. Seventeen of our ordnance ships will be discharged tomorrow, and by tomorrow all the ordnance and stores for the fortresses will be sent off; fifteen more vessels will be discharged by the end of the week. This is Stace's doing.—*Adieu*, I am called away.

April 28, 1 p.m.

Nothing new today. I anticipate orders to leave Ostend tomorrow. I have just returned from going round all the ships with Stace. All are busily employed, and in the midst of boats rowing to and fro the fishermen pull up their nets with a little windlass and catch flat fish and other small fry. At this moment we have twenty-six ordnance vessels here, but I think after this week we shall unload as fast as they can arrive, so that there will be no delay. I believe 10,000 Portuguese troops are coming; the agent of transports here talks of having orders to send part of his vessels for them. I am going at two o'clock to the top of a pillar, on which is a lighthouse, the key of which will be furnished by the mayor, who is very civil and obliging.

8 p.m.

We made our lighthouse visit, and had a good view of the sea front. I afterwards walked round the works.—*Adieu*: no news.

Letter 6

Brussels: May 3.

My last letter of the 28th April was from Ostend, which I quitted with Sir George Wood in his cabriolet. The road being very heavy owing to the previous rain (for we kept the road by the canal, which is shorter than that by the *pavé*), we did not reach Bruges till 4, nor Ghent till after 8 o'clock, meeting with nothing remarkable. At Ghent we drove to the Hôtel de Vienne, and after a good supper went to bed, with directions to be called a little after 5. However, it was past 7 before we sallied forth to look at the citadel and works erecting near the Courtray Gate. I am called away for a moment.—*Adieu*.

May 4, 10 a.m.

Yesterday was passed in one occupation or other, so that I could not resume my pen: and today I am quite disinclined to do so, but one must not be idle: so,—to return to Ghent. There are 4.000 peasants employed on the works. The idea is to have strong redoubts where the country cannot be inundated, and the ramparts of the city have also been repaired. The chief point of defence is in front of the Courtray Gate, on a rising ground about 300 yards from the rampart.

The citadel is a miserable work. Twenty-four guns and eight mortars are intended to be placed on it. This leaves forty-eight for redoubts and ramparts. But, altogether, Ghent is too large to be defended, except against a surprise. The Rivers Lys and Scheldt run under the walls of Ghent. At 11 we had seen all, and had learned that three troops and two batteries of artillery had quitted Termonde for cantonments on the right of the Dender, near Ninhove: however, our relay horses being at Termonde, we went thither. It is eighteen or twenty miles from Ghent, the country beautiful, and in the highest state of cultivation: the rye in ear—peas, in some places, in blossom.

From Termonde we came through Assche to Brussels, which we reached by 6. At 8 we found ourselves in the Salle des Nobles at a concert, and Catalani singing in her exquisite manner; but we arrived late, and the concert seemed over almost the moment we got there.

Yesterday morning I left my card at headquarters. The duke had gone to Tirlemont to see Blücher, but returned in the evening. . . . I have been employed in selecting and approving horses for the artillery. I passed eleven yesterday at 28*l*. per horse; forty-three yesterday, and twenty-five today, for which the price is to be arranged by His Grace. We expect also 1000 horses, purchased in this country, and some 500 from England. Drivers are chiefly wanting.

After seeing the horses, I went to the museum, where there are some bad paintings, much inferior to our exhibition at Somerset House. No less than four pictures on the subject of Baucis and Philemon. Among the natural and other curiosities (generally very inferior to Bullock's museum) are two whispering orbs, a coat worn by the Pretender Charles Stuart, a horse of the Infanta Isabel of Spain, another horse rode by Duke Albert at the siege of Ostend in 1500, where it was killed under the duke (the two wounds are visible in the neck), and some curious optical deceptions, which finished our amusement at the museum.

We afterwards visited the cathedral, a fine old building, where the painted windows, and especially one of Charlemagne receiving the benediction of the Pope Adrian, are chiefly remarkable. They are upwards of 400 years old. The pulpit is a chaste and beautiful piece of carved work—Adam and Eve; the angel driving them out of Paradise; Death attending; Eve with the apple in her hand; the serpent in the background. The serpent wreathes his many folds till his head, on the upper part of the sounding-board, is crushed by the heel of our Saviour. It is altogether very fine. *Adieu.*

Half-past 11 p.m.

Just returned from another concert at the Salle des Nobles. The duke and all the *grandees* there, except the king and queen, who were both there two nights ago, when I had a full view of their majesties.

Letter 7

Brussels: May 5.

I have only time to give you five lines by this mail. There is no news. Colonel Webber Smith writes me word that his troop reached Ghent yesterday, and that the *commandant* of that place had showed him a letter from Sir Charles Stuart saying that the Duke of Ragusa (Marshal Marmont) wished to see a troop of artillery:

"He accordingly saw us this morning, and was much pleased. He examined the *matériel* most minutely, and asked every question you can suppose an *Inspecteur Général d'Artillerie* could ask, and finished by saying our equipment in every respect was very far superior to anything he had ever seen. I breakfasted with him, and I will give you our conversation &c. &c. when I see you; 'tis nearly impossible to send it to you in writing, the questions were so numerous and minute."

I hope to go to Antwerp tomorrow, and do not despair of visiting Vienna before we take the field, which there is every reason to suppose we shall not do for three or four weeks.

Major Whinyates' rocket troop has received guns instead of the arm à *la Congrève*, of which it retains 800.—*Adieu*: I shall scarcely save the mail.

Letter 8

Brussels: May 7, 9 p.m.

My last hurried letter of the 5th spoke of my intention of going to Antwerp, for which place I shall start tomorrow; I much wish to see it, and another opportunity may not occur. On Friday, after closing my mail, I dined at the Café Bellevue at 3, and afterwards rode to the Palace of Lacken, a couple of miles from the city. The palace is on a rising ground, and is now fitting up for the king and queen, who intend residing there during the summer.

The apartments are fine, and altogether the palace is worth seeing. There are no pictures, nor, as we thought, any books; but upon inquiry the person who took us round the palace said there was a library in one of the corridors, but not permitted to be seen. There is a beautiful second hall, lighted by a dome which crowns the top of the palace, from the outside of which there is a very fine view of Brussels and the adjoining country. In going to and returning from the palace one passes by the Allée Verte, which is the fashionable promenade of the city. I have just returned from it; it is about a mile long, and consists of a good broad carriage road and a double avenue of fine trees; on one side is the canal leading towards Antwerp, on the other beautiful meadows.

On either side of the carriage road is a broad walk shaded by trees, and filled with all the pedestrian beauty of the city. At the one end is a bridge, and seats and benches in the German style, where wine and beer are quaffed to the sound of the organ and the tabor. A little beyond, and on the other side of the canal, is a favourite kind of teagarden called "the island," a kind of moat surrounding the house to which the garden belongs. At the end of the Allée Verte towards the city is a triumphal arch, of painted wood but handsome enough, erected on the occasion of the king's entry into Brussels.

The king, of course means the King of the Netherlands, and I had the honour this evening to make my bow in passing his majesty, who was on horseback, in the Allée Verte. Her majesty was in a carriage. There was a court day yesterday, which I should have attended had I known of it in time. Etiquette, it seems, prescribes that the names of those who intend to go to court should be given in the day before, of which I was not aware.

I went yesterday with Sir George Wood to make inquiries and arrangements about sending ordnance up the River Dender to Ath, which I believe may be done.

I also accompanied Sir George to the houses of several artists. At one of them (a Mons. de Cels) we saw two fine pictures. One of the Muse Erato, the other of Antigone, daughter of Œdipus, rendering the last duties to the body of her brother Polynices by scattering ashes over it. We afterwards went to the museum and saw the ancient collection of paintings, several by Rubens, one or two by Raphael, and a few very fine ones by Philippe de Champagne. A picture generally much admired did not please me, though painted by Rubens; the subject is horrid; it is of the Archbishop of Ghent whose tongue has been torn out and thrown to dogs.

There are a few paintings by Vandyke, but the most pleasing has for its subject Simeon in the temple taking the Infant Saviour in his arms,—this picture is by Philippe de Champagne, and is admirable. There are also some good imitations of *basso relievos*, and a pretty statue or two of the Venus de Medicis, and a beautiful piece of sculpture representing a merman and a mermaid, with a sea horse surmounted by a marine Cupid, all of white marble, the water flowing from the mouth of the cupid, the nostrils of the horse, the head of the merman, and the bosom of the mermaid; the last figure is beautifully executed. I afterwards dined at the Cafe Bellevue at four o'clock, and at five I rode to the Allée Verte, which was filled with every *belle* and *beau* in the place.

Sir George Wood talks of accompanying us to Antwerp; our going tomorrow, therefore, will depend on the Duke of Wellington's having returned from Ghent, whither His Grace went yesterday to pay his respects to the King of France.

We have many reports here difficult to be credited. One very generally believed is, that Marshals Ney and Mortier are out of favour with Napoleon; that he himself has not yet quitted Paris, where there is considerable agitation.—*Adieu* for this evening.

May 8.

I have only time before the mail closes to give you five lines. The duke did not return from Ghent last night, so we shall not start for Antwerp till 5 a.m. tomorrow. For the present I have been obliged to give up my Vienna trip; this I am sorry for: it would have well occupied the time which must apparently elapse before the troops can take the field. We are still weak, but besides the troops from America, we expect six regiments from Ireland. We now are:—

1st Division	3783
2nd ,,	6442
3rd ,,	6260
4th ,,	5721
Total	22186

This is infantry only. I doubt our advance to Paris. One takes fancies. I think *we* shall remain near the sea, and that the chain of fortresses in this direction is not to be passed. We are getting a battering train of 160 pieces of heavy ordnance; this is exclusive of the ordnance in our garrisons.

I see the papers, but I know not how, time is wanting: time, that jewel which one squanders as if it were of no value; yet "an hour well spent condemns a whole life," as says a lady of great genius, Miss Smith. Time passes rapidly here in a succession of employments; Ostend, its harbour and quays, and holds of ships, and agents and screaming captains of ships, are all forgotten. So are the beauties of the Allée Verte of last night: thus, the world passes before one. I am now squabbling with the powers at home for men and horses; for men, those "*tools*," perchance to be "*the broken tools of ambition*." The shifts and sly evasions used at home, to parry arguments not to be controverted, are whimsical, and might amuse were one not too much in earnest, and too fully convinced of the importance of our being complete.—*Adieu*; I shall write from Antwerp.

Letter 9

Antwerp: May 10, 6 a.m.

I left Brussels yesterday morning at four, travelling with Maxwell in his tilbury. Wood and Percy Drummond came here rather before us. We preferred the road through Boom to that leading through Vilvorde and Malines, in order to see a bridge of boats thrown over the Scheldt at Boom, where the river is about 200 yards wide. There are but ten boats, which are wide and about a dozen yards asunder. The bridge is not complete, and we crossed the Scheldt in a ferry-boat. Between Brussels and Boom our road was by the side of the canal; but, owing to the late rains, rather heavy. Today we propose to return by Malines, keeping the pave. The country is very rich on both sides the canal.

Near Vilvorde we passed one of those houses of correction occasionally seen in this country, where murder alone is punished with death. The building is large and oblong. We counted 440 little apertures for light on the two sides visible as we passed; there may, accordingly, if the building be single, be 800 cells; if double, twice that number. Speaking of punishments, one sees here multitudes of fellows heavily ironed and at hard labour in the public works. A delicacy towards minor offenders, is whimsical enough: instead of "man traps and spring guns are set here," boards hint that "wolf traps" are here.

We got to Antwerp early yesterday, and after breakfast visited Monsieur van Bree, an artist of much celebrity. Two of his paintings are of uncommon merit, and arrested our attention for a couple of hours; they are very large, perhaps ten yards long, the figures as large as life. The subjects are most interesting; one is the choosing by lot the seven virgins and seven youths sent annually as a tribute from Athens to Crete to be devoured by the Minotaur, and the heroic self-devotion of Theseus, who offers to accompany them. The king (Egeus) has just drawn from an urn the name of Melita, and the beautiful girl on hearing the fatal sentence is sinking in an agony of fear. Melita is the last of the seven virgins whose fate is to be determined, and her misery is well contrasted with the joy, too strong to be concealed, of another no less beautiful girl, who has for that time escaped the fatal lot.

The subject of the other picture is perhaps more interesting still, since its truth can be less questioned than that of the fabulous Minotaur. It is of Regulus, who, unmoved by the entreaties of his wife, his children, his relations and friends, voluntarily returns to the certain torments and death prepared for him by the Carthaginians. This picture is exquisite. Regulus is on the point of getting into the boat which is to convey him from Rome; never was story better told, every feeling is excited.—But I should never have done were I to continue the description.

From van Bree's we visited another collection of paintings, among which some by Vandyke, and the death of Abel by Guido, were admirable. The latter I should think the finest painting I have ever seen.

From paintings we went to the cathedral, a fine and spacious building, remarkable for the number of its aisles, having three on either side the nave. There are two paintings by Rubens, one the descent from the cross; the other the assumption of the Virgin. These were hidden when the French were here, who took to Paris all the paintings of celebrity, of which there were many. At the cathedral we went to the top of the spire, which is 450 feet high; the view beautiful: Breda, Bergen op Zoom, &c. &c., visible in the distance, and the Scheldt, the basins, the dockyards, the city and the works presented to our view as in a plan.

The river is about 400 yards wide. Not the "lazy Scheldt," but the "rapid Scheldt's descending wave" seemed applicable to a river running with great rapidity. From the city to the Tête de Flandres, one of the redoubts on the left bank of the river, one passes by a flying bridge, which is of the kind usual on the Rhine and other rivers in this part of Europe. We should have crossed, but the tide was flowing, and the bridge is only available when the tide is ebbing.

We visited the basins, bombarded, but ineffectually, by the British, two years ago. There are two basins; the inner, which is the larger, will contain twenty-five sail of the line. At this moment there are but four, of which one (a 74-gun ship) is preparing to sail. Near the basin is the once flourishing, now deserted India house. In former days this city was rich, and was the seat of commerce; it is now the reverse, and one cannot avoid a feeling of regret at the aspect of departed greatness which is everywhere recalled to one's recollection. It is full of fine buildings, some streets noble. That in which I write, the Place de Mer, is the principal street, and is 150 feet wide. A canal once ran in the middle. The dockyards present nothing but piles of wood which lately were ships on the stocks, but have been taken to pieces. With the exception of the four ships I have mentioned, all the Dutch men-of-war have been removed to Flushing.

We next visited the citadel, which is very strong. At 6, Colonel Maxwell and I dined with Colonel Gold. Mrs. Gold is here and five of their children. Antwerp is more clean than Brussels, but yet not clean; there is a sad want of police in both, so far as attention to cleanliness goes. Beyond the Tête de Flandres on the other side of the river, and at perhaps 1000 yards from it, is an extensive intrenchment protected by a broad ditch; the country still further in front may be inundated.

It was Bonaparte's intention to have built a new city within the intrenchment: each Marshal of France was to have built himself a house there; so were each of the men of property of this arrondissement. Antwerp was to have become the great port, from which were to have issued the rival fleets which were to have ruined England. There are three British and three Hanoverian battalions here in garrison; two companies of British artillery, and 550 pieces of artillery mounted on the works.

As I was walking just now, a procession carrying the Host passed by; there might be sixty persons carrying tapers in front of the four priests who supported the canopy, under which walked the fifth, who carried the consecrated chalice; every one knelt down and the Green Market was silent (for it was in the bustle of the market that I met the procession), till it had passed.

Brussels: May 10, 9. p.m.

I have dined with Sir George Wood, where I saw Colonel Jenkinson, who brings a great deal of regimental news. Jenkinson is going on to Frankfort to meet Lord Stewart, and to remain as military correspondent at the imperial headquarters.

I forgot to say that I went this morning with Colonel Gold to a Mr. van Anker's, who has a very fine collection of paintings. Two pictures by Wouvermans inimitable, many others very fine. From this gentleman's we went to a Mr. van Havere's, a descendant of Rubens. We first called at the house in which Rubens had resided. The garden and summer-house are just as the great artist left them. At Mr. van Havere's we saw three celebrated portraits by Rubens; two, of his two wives, and the third known by connoisseurs by the name of the Chapeau de Paille, which is said to be the finest portrait in existence.

The praise may not be misapplied, for the portrait seems really to live. I believe it to be the portrait, when young, of the lady who was afterwards Rubens' second wife. We saw, too, a landscape painted by this celebrated artist. The scene is the church of Lacken, near the palace, a couple of miles from hence. From Mr. van Havere's we went to the church of St. Jacques, and saw Rubens' tomb. He was born at Cologne, but chiefly resided, and died, at Antwerp. We left that city at 2 p.m., and returning by Malines and Vilvorde, were here by 6.

On the other side of Malines was Walcheren. I recognised the scene of a very sharp affair, for looking at which I had nearly paid dear in 1794. How many things have occurred since that time! for how many have I not reason to be thankful!—*Adieu.*

Letter 10

Brussels: May 11.

I have only time to write a few lines. We hear that Bonaparte is between Condé and Valenciennes, and in force; greater than that of the Allies in artillery, less in cavalry and infantry. We shrewdly suspect his intention of attacking us; if so, the rencontre may take place in a few days. The duke's intention is to fight, which His Grace considers eligible, even if we should be beaten. We have two positions; one in front of Ath, from Leuze to Mons; the other near Hal. In the possible event of our being beaten from either, or both, Bonaparte could hardly advance, since the Prussians would menace, and indeed turn his right flank. So much for general speculation.

Should the enemy remain quiet, we shall remain so too for a while. We are not ready, and can hardly conceive that he is; but his reinforcements are nearer, and his arrangements less shackled than ours. The Saxon affair at Liège was unlucky, but I cannot get at the truth of it. The Saxons were to have been drafted into the Prussian regiments; this they resented; they murmured, and even, it is said, threatened

Blücher's life; in consequence 10,000 of them are to be disarmed, and sent prisoners to Stettin. These Saxons will appear again on the stage, mixed up in some new way.

I suspect that we shall not advance; that our game will be to lay siege to Lille and another fortress or two, and to furnish the necessary armies of observation, and that the Allies will make the push forward.

I am going with Sir George Wood to look at our depot, removed from Hal to Vilvorde.—*Adieu.*

Letter 11

Brussels: May 22.

We are still here, nor do I anticipate a movement at present. I have just returned from a review at Vilvorde of the Brunswick troops: they made a very fine appearance. The Duke of Brunswick was at their head. The troops consisted of a regiment of hussars, two squadrons of lancers, two corps of riflemen, seven battalions of infantry, a troop of horse artillery, and a battery of artillery; in all about 7000 men. The Duke of Wellington was in his field marshal's uniform, accompanied by Lord Uxbridge and all the staff. A guard of honour of a squadron of the Brunswick Hussars preceded His Grace, and the cortege galloped down the Allée Verte in great style.

The Duke of Richmond and one of the Ladies Lennox rode with the Duke of Wellington. The Brunswickers are all in black, the duke having, in 1809, when the duchess died, paid this tribute of respect to the memory of his wife. There is something romantic in this. They are to change their uniform when they shall have avenged themselves on the French for an insult offered to the remains of the duke's father. Is this chivalry, or barbarity?

I had much conversation at the review with Lord Uxbridge. The arrangement of our troops is to be changed again. So, the earl told me he had arranged with the duke, but I did not learn how. I am to wait on Lord Uxbridge in the course of the day and learn particulars. The sooner we put things in the order they are to remain, the better.

Not a syllable more of Bonaparte. We believe the interior of France to be in a very strange state. La Vendée ready to rise, the south full of royalists. What will be the end of all this?

We are waiting for more companies of artillery from England, and daily expect dismounted cavalry to act as drivers for the artillery.

A fifth and sixth division of the army have been formed. Generals Cole and Picton will have them.

Three batteries of 18-pounders (four guns each) will be ordered up immediately. The reserves of musket ball cartridge will be sent to join the several divisions immediately. The battering train, of 160 pieces, will be placed in *schuyts* at Antwerp. To inspect these, reject inefficient horses, supply their places, and send them to the several points, will be my occupation. On Monday the whole cavalry and horse artillery will be reviewed. The horse artillery is previously to be remodelled, for which purpose I am to breakfast with Lord Oxbridge on Thursday, at Ninhove.—*Adieu* for this day.

Letter 12.

Brussels: May 12.

My allusion to the "jewel" was meant generally to all the joys left behind, and not sufficiently prized when enjoyed: the thought is Cowper's, as I need not say. I was delighted with my visit to Antwerp. I wished, when there, to have pushed on to Amsterdam, which capital I have not yet seen. I saw a curious door in the drawing-room of Mynheer van Anker, at Antwerp; the door was what is called a folding-door, on opening or shutting one half, the other by sympathy followed the motion. Mr. van Anker explaining it, said it was managed by an iron Z under the floor, and added that it was the simplest thing imaginable; so, it may be, and no doubt is, but I could not comprehend it.

We daily expect to hear of Bull's troop having arrived. Today I go to Bierghes, between Hal and Enghiem, to inspect Whinyates' rocket troop. It has lately received guns, retaining only a portion of its rockets. We shall pass (we meaning Maxwell and myself) near Hal, a position in which we may have a contest: that is, should Napoleon, who is in force near Condé (out with your map), advance to attack us. We have two positions; one between Leuze and Mons, the other near Hal. Somewhere near the latter town, I think, Marlborough fought a battle.

I have told you of Jenkinson's arrival from England: he goes to Frankfort to remain as military correspondent at the imperial headquarters, and brings various accounts of troops, majorities, and lieut.-colonelcies of horse artillery given, and to be given away.

I have just breakfasted, and wait to be called for by a M. de Bel, who has 100 horses to afford for the service. We have already here about 700, and without more than half a dozen drivers. All this is simple enough; and so, should we be, to believe what we are told very gravely, that there are none in England to send to us. By the way, Jenkinson adds, that this necessary auxiliary to the corps of artillery is about to be remodelled. We are always *about* to do something good: to what may not the observation be applied? undoubtedly it may to every one of us, as each knows full well. But a truce to reflections either on oneself or others.

Have you not already set me down for a wild one in my scheme of running to Vienna. I was vexed when this bubble burst; and would even now gladly hail the permission to go thither. Accordingly, my expectations of Bonaparte's movements are not very strong: too much depends on the first blow for either side to move till decidedly ready; but I contemplate reverses at first, and then in due time ultimate success. But to turn from politics: I hope Edward is as busy as you suppose him: at his age application is everything; in truth it is so at every age, as I have gravely thought full many a time, when lounging on the lawn at Bealings. In the "magnanimity of thought what wonders do we not perform? and thus from hour to hour," &c. &c.

I heartily wish Moor would set out: he should find friends and horses at every stage, and should quaff the best Rhenish to the best healths, and should return full of admiration of the agricultural,—and if his wife would not be offended, of the rustic,—beauties: there are such to be seen. I wish I was a farmer, but I wish in vain: I have not one farming idea, and make daily mistakes about wheat and rye; such as I should scold my boys for if they imitate their father.

I honestly look for your assistance in sending Moor hither; is it right that an F. R. S., and one of the quorum too, should have traversed more than half the globe to visit distant continents, and never have seen that of Europe? Why, he would return "à la mode de Bruxelles," perhaps "de Paris," and become the Chesterfield of the age.

You owe this torrent of nonsense to the delay of M. de Bel and his horses; my own are waiting at the door to obey his summons. That duty over I must change my tone, and with the earnestness of conviction repeat the many-times-told tale (here's alliteration and juxtaposition for you) of our dismal wants in the personnel of war. All this I have told the authorities at Woolwich so often in a sober strain, that I must, I believe, adopt a merrier one than the subject demands.—*Adieu!* God bless you and yours.

LETTER 13

Brussels: May 25, 5 a, m.

I am now going to Ninhove to see Lord Uxbridge, and to settle about the guns, &c. &c., which our troops are to have; more on this subject when I return.

We have nothing very new. Yesterday the heavy cavalry was reviewed; today the hussar brigade will be seen by Lord Uxbridge, and on the 29th the whole of the cavalry and horse artillery will be reviewed by the Duke.

No change of quarters has taken place among the troops of horse artillery, but I have letters ready to send off after I shall have seen Lord Uxbridge, which will make them all move a little in the change of guns which will probably take place. We are sadly in want of men and horses now that we are going to have heavier guns. I am interrupted, so goodbye.

4 p.m.

I have had a busy day. All was soon arranged with Lord Uxbridge, his orders received in a moment, and almost as soon letters written to Whinyates, Webber Smith, and Bull, to march; the first to Osterzeele near Grammont, Bull to Sheenhuyse, and Smith to Erweheghem. All these places are between Ghent and Grammont. Near the latter all the cavalry and horse artillery will be reviewed on Monday. As Ross, Bull, Mercer, and Macdonald will have guns of a heavier nature than the other troops, I have been puzzled to find horses to increase their numbers; but by giving a different direction to about sixty horses coming from Ostend to replace that number which I meant to have cast, and by writing to Ghent, Ostend and Antwerp for saddles and bridles which Stace has given me from the Civil Department, I have been able to promise Lord Uxbridge that the six troops (Ross not having arrived) shall be new armed and equipped, and at the review on Monday.

So far so well. I perceive that I shall get on very well with Lord Uxbridge, who is quiet in business and very decided; this is the true way to do much in a little time.

This country gets more and more beautiful. Near Ninhove, where I have been today, the undulations of the ground add beauty to the richness of the scenery. Today is a *fête*, I know not of what saint, but all business is at a stand; the villagers are all playing at bowls; all gay, all smiling, one would never suspect that war was so near at hand.

There has been some trifling affair near Mons; I know not the particulars. The enemy provoked the thing we are told, and several have been wounded on both sides. I am called away, and probably shall not resume my pen today.

Letter 14

Brussels: May 30.

I can hardly tell you what I have been doing since my last letter, but I will try. On Friday (26th) was the duke's ball; nothing could be more splendid, and His Grace all affability and condescension. I saw there all the gay world. The dancing rooms were crowded to excess, but the dancers were persevering, and made out waltzes and French country dances with great glee. At the ball I saw the Prince of Orange, to whom I had not spoken before. The prince is always very kind, and shook hands with me in a very friendly way. I saw too my old friend, Lord Saltoun of the 1st Guards, who has been married since we parted in Spain.

Saturday passed in writing and in getting the troops ready for yesterday's review. On Sunday the British troops in garrison here attended divine service at the Augustin church. A division (the 5th) of British infantry marched in from Ghent and Alost. Blücher and several Prussian generals arrived from Namur. The Duke, Marshal Blücher, the Duke of Brunswick, and a splendid party dined with the King of the Netherlands; there was a gay promenade in the Allée Verte, and the duke gave Marshal Blücher a supper.

Yesterday we rose early, and having sent our horses the day before, drove to Schlendelbeke (a little to the north of Grammont). We found on our arrival fifteen regiments of British cavalry, with six troops of horse artillery, drawn up in three lines on a beautiful plain on the banks of the Dender. About 1 p.m. the duke, Marshal Blücher, &c. &c., arrived, having come from Brussels by way of Enghiem and Grammont. We received the duke with a salute of nineteen guns. After going down the lines and inspecting the cavalry generally, and the horse artillery very minutely, and repeatedly expressing his approbation of our appearance, the duke took his station in front of the centre of the first line, and the different corps passed in columns of half squadrons.

It is not possible to imagine a finer sight. The day was bright and hot, but with a gentle breeze. We were in meadows with grass up to the horses' knees, in a country fertile and rich, and well wooded. There were thousands of spectators, both of military men from all parts of the army, and of the people of the country for ten leagues round. The review passed off without a check, an error, or an accident; one could see the cavalry had fallen into the hands of a master.

Lord Uxbridge's headquarters are at Ninhove, some six miles from the ground of review. His lordship gave a dinner to the duke, Blücher, and all the generals and commanding officers of corps. Dinner was laid for a hundred. Never was anything better arranged. His lordship lives in an abbey, the large rooms of which were well calculated for the princely feast. The duke, the two Princes of Orange, the Duke of Brunswick, Marshal Blücher, General Gneisenau, Count Daumberg, Count Galty—but I had as well omit names, since many of the persons to whom they belong, though illustrious here, are little known in England.

Before dinner, the party met in a fine hall. The Prince of Orange again singled me out, and crossed the hall to shake hands with me, and with the duke and Lord Uxbridge spoke handsomely of the troops of artillery. Dinner was served about five: it was princely, consisting of many courses, all served on plate. An excellent dessert followed, and the finest wines of every kind flowed in such profusion that 'tis well if I can this morning write of anything but pink champagne. The moment dinner was over, folding doors behind the duke opened, and a band struck up "God save the King." The Prince Regent's and the Duke of York's healths followed that of their royal father; and then Lord Uxbridge gave the duke, which was drunk with three times three.

By this time, all the doors of the hall being open, the ladies and gentry of the place came to look at the feast. The duke gave Blücher's health, and success to the arms of Prussia,—three times three again. Blücher, in a neat speech, gave the Cavalry and Horse Artillery of England. The Prince of Orange and the House of Nassau. The Duke of Brunswick, with three times three. The Allied Sovereigns; preceded by the health of the Emperor Alexander; and last, and with louder cheers than ever, the Navy of Great Britain. This seemed highly to please Sir Sidney Smith, the only naval officer present. Coffee was then brought in for the duke and princes, and we rose and returned to the former hall, the lofty passages to which were lined with well-dressed people, eager to show their respect to the duke.

One cannot but mark, and this continually, that even where persons of higher rank are present, the duke is still, as it were by the consent of all, the greatest of the great. A triumphal arch had been erected at Ninhove in the morning, with very flattering devices; the whole town, adorned with branches of trees, looked like a grove, and our troops, wearing the oak-bough of the 29th of May, gave to the whole additional gaiety. After remaining some little time in the hall, during which coffee was served, the different carriages drove up, and the party separated. A guard of honour of the Life Guards was ready to receive the duke as he came out.

We left Ninhove about eight o'clock, highly pleased with a day such as cannot often, and may never, be seen again. Many feelings are excited on days and in sights like this, in which one sees all this world has to show of splendour and of luxury—all that is prepared for the gratification of this life,—and for the destruction of it. A thousand thoughts filled my mind as I sat at table, and every now and then removed me far from the objects before me to those with whom a few tranquil hours, passed in social intercourse, were preferable to all this world can afford without them. But one may moralise for ever.

Tomorrow, I believe, we shall have an infantry review here, and I hope in a day or two a review, somewhere near Namur, of the Prussians. This I shall certainly go to see, should it be at double the distance of Namur. We have no particular news. We know of Murat's discomfiture, and that the Emperor Alexander is at Munich. The greatcoats of the army are called in. This is a common preparation for a move.— *Adieu* for this day!

Letter 15

Brussels: May 30.

I have again been idle—have again delayed writing till too late. This comes of dukes, and princes, and balls, and suppers, and reviews, and dinners, and troops, and saddles, and horses, &c. &c., and all that passes and occupies and steals away one's time. How yesterday passed another letter will have told you. We got home by twelve o'clock, jaded with the joy and jollity of the day. I know not why, but a great mass of armed men always brings to my mind strange associations and reflections; and in the midst of all that the poet calls "*the pride and pomp of war*," the reflection, which we are told made Xerxes burst into tears when his myriads crossed the Hellespont, will intrude, that in a few years all these will have passed away.

But what nonsense is all this! I had better say that on our way home one of the carriage-horses fell; that, in picking him up, the driver got a blow on the chest which stunned him; that Percy Drummond ran to the nearest village for a cup of water; that Wood held the horses, and that your humble servant lugged the body of the said driver to the side of the road, to get off his neckcloth; that after a decent time the man revived; that Drummond and I returned with the cup to the village, where we found a couple of dozen Brunswickers waltzing and playing blind-man's buff, a sober party playing cards, another screaming songs, and a third dancing,— all in the same room. The occasion of all this jollity we could not discover; but the adventure cost us an hour.

All our movements are uncertain, and to myself, who have, as it were, no locality, immaterial. Why don't those who call themselves "Locals" come hither?

Richard is hoarse with daring Richmond to the field.

So, say to Moor, and let him make the application.

"Another such a day as yesterday," and we shall be ruined as soldiers—ruined with burgundy and champagne, and with all that, as the Duchess of Gordon says, carries a man off his legs. —*Adieu!*

Letter 16

Headquarters, Brussels: May 31.

Determined not to be cheated out of my letter again, I sit down, though it is neither post-day nor am I in my best writing mood. Soon after I had written yesterday, I had to gallop to Ninhove to see the cavalry peer, but his lordship had gone to dine with Lord Hill, so I had nothing for it but to get paper, pen, and ink, and write what I had rather have said. It rained yesterday all day, so I had a comfortable soaking which, strange as it may appear, always puts me in a good humour.

I dined at Loutecke, finding I could not get in time to dine at the paymaster-general's where I was engaged; but I went there to tea. So much for yesterday's excursion, which, on my return, I found to have been useless, and from a conversation which Wood had in the interim with the duke, had better have been left undone. My visit was, of course, about guns, and I cannot but smile at the changes, backwards and forwards, which have taken place about them, and have cost me I know not how much ink: and so, we'll leave them. (This is in allusion to the partial substitution of 9-pounders for 6-pounders for the horse artillery, which Sir Augustus Frazer, aware of its importance, was happily enabled to effect).

Is it well, think you, that Lord Castlereagh should coldly tell the House of Commons that the want of success at New Orleans does not justify the erection of a monument to Sir Edward Pakenham? Had all on that fatal day shown equal devotion to their country's service, that monument had not been wanted. *Adieu!* 'Tis well I am called away; a subject like this is apt to set me on fire, to rouse feelings to be allayed, if not subdued, by every means in my power.

Wood keeps open house; I keep none, and generally dine at the *table d'hôte* at the Café Bellevue. One meets at these places all kinds of people, and the scene is amusing. My chief companion there is a Baron Drièses, a Russian general, lately governor of Mittau, who is old, fond of children, and seems what the French call a "*bon papa*."

We have no particular news. We are putting ourselves in order to move. Individually, I am of course ready, and the troops of our corps are so too, though we yet want more men and more horses, and so we shall do as long as the contest lasts. But if either sober reasoning or merry joking will produce reinforcements, we shall have them, for I spare neither; nor do I despair of getting all I ask for,—which is *only* every man and every horse of the corps now in England.

Yesterday arrived a budget of papers three inches thick. There were three letters to the Secretary of the Board of Ordnance from a person signing himself Edward Spencer Curling, resident at Blackheath, and as many from the said secretary to Sir George Wood, and all relating to a "shameful and disgraceful waste of the public property by certain privates of the horse artillery at Ostend," which had so roused the indignation of the said Curling, that, in zeal for his country, he could do no less than report the same to the "Right Honourable and Honourable the Board of Ordnance," and send to their secretary, "carefully tied up, and marked 'private,'" the articles which the knaves had sold, and which he, to detect them, had purchased. These articles, as carefully noted in the margin of the secretary's letters, have, by the Honourable Board's order, been as carefully put into a wooden box, and shipped for Ostend or Antwerp. They are, oh, age of degeneracy! a currycomb, a brush, and a pair of scissors!!!

I have added my mite of wonder and indignation at this sad proof of the wickedness of the age in which we live; and have had, moreover, to express my sorrow that, as none of the horse artillery were at Ostend at the time the said Curling bought the articles there, it would not be in my power to hang up any one for the offence.

Goodnight! No gentlemen coming home. Wood's wine, I take it, is good, and we all know his hospitality.

Letter 17

Brussels: June 4.

There have been daily inspections of regiments since my last, but no review till yesterday, when there was a grand one. One may say so from the quality rather than the number of the troops, since there were but eight British and three Hanoverian battalions on the ground, with a battery of artillery of each nation. The review was in the Allée Verte. The ground admitted of nothing more than the ordinary inspection and marching past, but the sight was beautiful; and the ladies especially admired the costume of the Highland regiments.

There was a ball last night at Sir Charles Stuart's, which was most splendid. A guard of honour in the courtyard added to the imposing appearance of the whole. Sir Charles understands these things, and they have their uses. In one of the rooms was a superb canopy of state with a throne, and paintings of the king and queen on either side.

All the gayest of the gay were there: and, as usual, there was some dancing and much squeezing. The lower suite of rooms was appropriated for dancing, and the upper one for supper. There were three bands of music, and a profusion of diamonds and beauty. The duke wore six stars on his breast, besides an embroidered sword. He had given a dinner to sixty people, and seemed uncommonly joyous. The whole entertainment passed off remarkably well.

I thought of going tomorrow to a Prussian review at Namur, but the review is put off. There is no appearance today of its being the king's birthday; indeed, I believe the good old custom is wearing out even in England, since the poor king's illness. We have no news. The rumours here are idle and endless; and balls, not wars, engage our every thought.—*Adieu!*

Letter 18

Brussels: June 9, 6 a. m.

On Tuesday, after closing our mail, Colonel Maxwell and I drove to Ghent, in the heaviest rain I remember. On reaching Ghent, we found Ross's troop had marched through to Oostakes, the village in which I had previously seen Bull's troop. This somewhat disconcerted us; however, we established ourselves at the Cerf Inn, where we dined and slept. On the following morning, Sir George Wood and I drove to Oostakes, saw Ross's troop, and afterwards returned to Brussels. In the evening we attended the duke ball, which was more gay and more full than ever; it was almost impossible to move. Yesterday passed in getting horses and other things for Ross. We dined at the Bellevue, and rode in the evening to the Palace of Lacken, which, as the royal family is gone to The Hague, we were able to see; and very beautiful it is.

We hear nothing of moving; but of course, the time approaches.

The enemy is said to be concentrating near Maubeuge. This may or may not be true, and it is not of much consequence; he must concentrate somewhere, and the exact spot is of little importance. We have no very particular news. There is a report which is generally credited, that Berthier, who has for some time been at Bamberg (where, being known to be entirely in Bonaparte's interest, he has been under the surveillance of the police), a few days since threw himself out of a window, and was killed on the spot. Chagrin at the number of Russian troops whom he saw daily marching towards France is supposed to have led to the act.

It seems strange, but Mr. Dunmore, the commissary-general, on whom I waited yesterday on business, tells me there is a probability of our being shortly in want of corn. This is owing to the speculators, who buy up all they can find; moreover, the Russians have latterly purchased all they could. It seems strange to talk of wanting anything in this plentiful country; and want, indeed, can be but partial, and for a moment. Green forage is ready to be cut.—*Adieu!*

June 10.

Yesterday there was some firing in the front, supposed to have been a *feu-de-joie*—perhaps on account of the arrival of Bonaparte, who is said to be at Maubeuge. Biscuit for four days has been delivered to some of the troops. Ross is ordered hither from Oostakes. All expect to move soon; nevertheless, I do not imagine we shall quit Brussels for ten days or a fortnight. The Emperor of Russia did not reach Munich till the 28th of May; and I doubt the Russians being up so as to' enable us to move for ten days. I am called away, and may not be able to resume my pen again today.

Sunday, June 11.

I have been writing the whole day, except when at divine service, which was performed and an excellent sermon preached in the square before my house, by the Rev. Mr. Frith.

The Knight of Kerry and a friend of his (a Mr. Butler, I believe) breakfast with me tomorrow, and I take them to the review tomorrow at Welle. On returning, we dine with Sir Dennis Pack. We are South American friends: in that disastrous expedition I had the opportunity of showing him attention, which he has never forgotten. In taking an afternoon's ride in the Allée Verte, Lord George Lennox gave me a note from my friend Ramsay, who has arrived at Ghent, and I hope to see him at the head of his troop in the field tomorrow. Ramsay is adored by his men; kind, generous, and manly, he is more than the friend of his soldiers.—*Adieu!* I am to be up at four tomorrow, and it is now midnight.

June 12, 4 p.m.

At six this morning the Knight of Kerry and Mr. Butler breakfasted with me, as did Barnard of the 95th. The Knight and Mr. Butler accompanied me to Welle, where the six troops were reviewed, and made a noble appearance. Koss joined us on the ground; so, did Ramsay. We found, on arriving at Welle, the Duc de Berri, with four squadrons of the *maison du roi*, or household troops of the French king, almost entirely composed of French officers. Of course, I offered to cede the ground, (which was small) to the duke, which His Royal Highness declined, and the French troops retired.

We went by Streyhern, whither I had sent a relay of horses, both for the gig and for myself, who rode. Our review was at Welle, which is near Alost. The cross roads we found so bad that we determined to return by Alost, keeping the *pavé* to Brussels. I say we, but I mean myself, since a very heavy thunderstorm determined my friends and Bell to stop at Alost.

Bean has reached Ostend, and I have written to him to march to Ghent immediately.— *Adieu!*

Letter 19

Brussels: June 15, 10 p.m.

I have this moment returned from dining with Hawker to celebrate his promotion to a lieutenant-colonelcy. He lives in a very large and comfortable house at the village of Lenniche St. Quentin. You will see the neighbouring village of Lenniche St. Martin in the map. We were a jolly party of a dozen, the cheer was excellent, but the roads detestable. On returning I find Ross here, he has dined at General Kempt's, and has learned in the course of the evening that the enemy has moved upon Mons, and that in consequence we are to move during the night. Sir George Wood has just been here to say the same thing. He was one of the party at Hawker's, and has gone to headquarters to learn the news.

I never suffer myself to be disturbed by these alerts: there is nothing new in looking the enemy in the face, and tomorrow may be as good a day as any other; not that I think we shall move; however, Wood will soon return from the duke's, and then we shall know what is to be done. I find on my table an invitation to dine with Delancey tomorrow; his lady is here; this will be a pleasanter way of passing the day than marching to Mons. Of course, I have accepted the invitation. The day before yesterday I dined at headquarters.

Yesterday morning I went to see a beautiful collection of paintings at the house of a Mons. de Burtin. I went thither with Colonels May and Drummond. We introduced ourselves to a grave-looking housekeeper, said we had heard of the collection of pictures, and had taken the liberty of coming. After waiting a little we were admitted upstairs, where we found an elderly man sitting in his arm chair, in his night cap and bed gown. On a table was some small beer.

Mons. de Burtin showed us a large library, saying "All those books are on painting; they are worth nothing; but, gentlemen, have you seen my book on the art of judging of pictures, &c?"

We had not.

"That is strange," said he, "the book is a classic book, and known as such all over the continent; you should read my 20th chapter."

Nothing could give us more pleasure. In short, after being assured by Mons. de Burtin that he was member of all the scientific academies of Europe, and the wisest, or at least one of the wisest of the wise, we went to see his gallery of paintings, which certainly is very fine.

But I have not time to talk of paintings. I have just called Ross out of bed, and ordered him to his troop, which is at Perk near Vilvorde. There seems every probability of our moving in the morning.

It seems that Bonaparte is at Maubeuge, that he has about 120,000 men there, that he has advanced in the direction of Binch, leaving Mons to his left and rear; that Blücher with 80,000 Prussians has moved from Namur to Sombreffe (on the road from Namur to Nivelle), that we shall concentrate our force in front of Braine l'Aleud (near Hal). Admitting all this to be true, we may have a battle the day after tomorrow. The duke has gone to a ball at the Duchess of Richmond's, but all is ready to move at daybreak.

Of course, all depends on the news which may arrive in the night. By way of being ready, I shall go to bed, and get a few hours' sleep. It is now half-past 11. I hope you and the dear boys are enjoying peaceful slumbers in our happy England, safe from all the alarms and confusions which tomorrow may see here. We have just sent to Antwerp for Colonel Gold, and to Lenniche for Hawker, and have sent off Adye to Enghiem. He has just arrived from Ghent, where he has been on a court of inquiry about some misconduct of part of the driver corps. Poor devils! they embarked last year at Bordeaux, went to America, and have returned; and all the time without receiving their pay.—Goodnight.

June 16, 6 a.m.

I have been sleeping very sound. We have a beautiful morning. I have sent to Sir George Wood's to hear if we are to move, which I conclude we are of course to do. I sent Major Bean orders yesterday by express to march to Vilvorde, or any village in its neighbourhood in which he could establish his troop. The other troops are ready.

Sir Alexander Dickson arrived here yesterday, looking very well; he had been but ten days in England. Sir Thomas Picton has arrived.

I have just learned that the duke moves in half an hour. Wood thinks to Waterloo, which we cannot find on the map: this is the old story over again. I have sent Bell to Delancey's office, where we shall learn the real name, &c. The whole place is in a bustle. Such jostling of baggage, of guns, and of waggons. It is very useful to acquire a quietness and composure about all these matters; one does not mend things by being in a hurry.

Adieu! I almost wonder I can write so quietly. But nothing can be done today. My horse is ready when the signal for mounting shall be given.

Our batteries were yesterday arranged as follows:—

Lieut.-Colonel Sir A. W. Frazer to command British Horse Artillery, and to be attached to Head Quarters.

Lieut.-Colonel Sir Julius Hartmann to command King's German Horse, Foot, and Hanoverian Artillery, and to be attached to Head Quarters.

Lieut.-Colonel Macdonald, Six Troops of Horse Artillery, attached to Cavalry.

Commander	Troop/Battery	Division
Lt.-Col. Adye	{ Major Kühlman's Troop { Captain Sandham's Battery	1st Division of Infantry.
Lt.-Col. Gold	{ Major Sympher's Troop { Captain Bolton's Battery	2nd Division of Infantry.
Lt.-Col. Williamson	{ Major Lloyd's Battery { Captain Cleeve's Battery (German)	3rd Division of Infantry.
Lt.-Col. Hawker	{ Major Brome's Battery { Captain Rettbery's Battery (Hanoverian)	4th Division of Infantry.
Major Heisse, Hanoverian Artillery	{ Major Rogers's Battery { Captain Braun's (Hanoverian)	5th Division of Infantry.
Lt.-Col. Brinkman, Hanoverian Artillery	Major Unit's Battery	6th Division of Infantry.
Major Drummond	{ Lt.-Col. Ross's Troop { Major Bean's Troop { Captain Sinclair's Battery	Reserve.

Letter 20

Brussels: June 16.

My journal is apparently on the point of commencing with something more interesting, or at least less peaceable, than has hitherto filled its pages. Bonaparte has moved; and in consequence we are moving too. It may be hardly worthwhile to describe what I hardly yet understand, but today will unravel the mystery; tomorrow we may try the fate of arms. Our troops are concentrating. I suspect the scene of the struggle will be in the vicinity of Braine l'Aleud near Hal. Whilst I write I receive your letters: shall I continue to describe movements and battles, or shall I read the delicious pages of affection? can I hesitate?

I accept your challenge at Dutch billiards, and care not how soon I play with balls amusing and harmless: can one avoid making the contrast with those here? You say your travelling days are over; no, no, they are not, I hope. I trust you will yet travel, and in company with a brother. (This letter was to Major Moor, Sir A. S. Frazer's brother-in-law).

Ought a man who should think of nothing but Braine l'Aleud and Bonaparte to bestow one thought on Bealings and billiards? methinks he ought, and without doubt he will. Fancy will turn; the heart, you know, untraveled will turn. A flower girl has just brought me a parting bouquet of roses: was it possible to receive it and not think of the dear boys, and the flowers which *may*, nay which *must* wither? and to what, and to how many reflections does not the idea lead?

I have written you a shabby return for your letter; but when I wrote this late last night, I little thought of having so much time as I now expect to have today. I have never less to do than previous to an action; there are then no difficulties, no littlenesses to be plagued with; in truth, at present every preparation in my power has already been made, and I never felt lighter or easier.

Now for Bonaparte, the disturber of all the great, as well as of all the little folks of this lower world. He has advanced from Maubeuge, has passed Binch, leaving Mons to his left and rear. His line (of 120,000) last night extended from Roeulx towards Charleroi. Blücher with 82,000 had quitted Namur, and, moving in the direction of Genappe, had reached Sombreffe. Our army (84,000) is concentrating near Braine l'Aleud. Today Bonaparte attacks the Prussians, or we join our forces; this seems the alternative. But a day or two are easily passed, one may say lost, in manoeuvring, before two masses meet; and perhaps after all the movement may be but a demonstration. "*When Greek meets Greek*," &c.; now have we the two great captains fairly met.—*Adieu*. Say what you know I feel to you and yours, and let me hear that my boys and their mother are happy.

Letter 21

Quatre Bras: June 17, half-past 7 a.m.

We have had a sanguinary contest. Bonaparte partially attacked Blücher's corps on the day before yesterday, and yesterday the affair was general both with the Prussians and ourselves. Quatre Bras is a little to the south of Genappe, and at the point where the road from Genappe to Charleroi intersects that from Namur to Nivelle—the severity of our struggle was between Quatre Bras and Frasne. The affair ended only with the close of the day—there was even a good deal of firing by moonlight. The enemy, who behaved with admirable gallantry, was repulsed in all his attacks.

We had no British cavalry in the field. Vandeleur's brigade of cavalry came up at dusk, but too late to be employed. No British horse artillery, and only one German troop (which did great execution) in the field. The enemy's lancers and *cuirassiers* are the finest fellows I ever saw;—they made several bold charges, and repeatedly advanced in the very teeth of our infantry. They have severely paid for their spirit—most of them are now lying before me. Had we but had a couple of brigades of British cavalry, we should have gained a decided advantage. We had but one Belgian regiment of hussars, and some Brunswick hussars, and both felt their inferiority, and made weak efforts against the enemy's cavalry, who pursuing them amongst our very infantry, made a mingled mass of the whole.

I have never seen a hotter fire than at some times of yesterday, nor seen more of what is called a *mêlée* of troops. Our number of wounded at the close of last night was said by the adjutant-general to be 5000—of the killed I have heard no estimate, but the number must be great. Great part of the action having been fought in standing corn, the dead are not so visible, and many of the wounded will never be found. The Duke of Brunswick, I believe, is killed. I saw and spoke to him in the course of the day, but I did not see him fall. Of artillery people, I hear of no officers killed, and none but Lieutenant Grüben of the German artillery wounded. Rogers's and Lloyd's batteries, especially the latter, have suffered much. Two of Lloyd's guns were dismounted, and for a time lost. We have since regained and remounted them, and are pro-

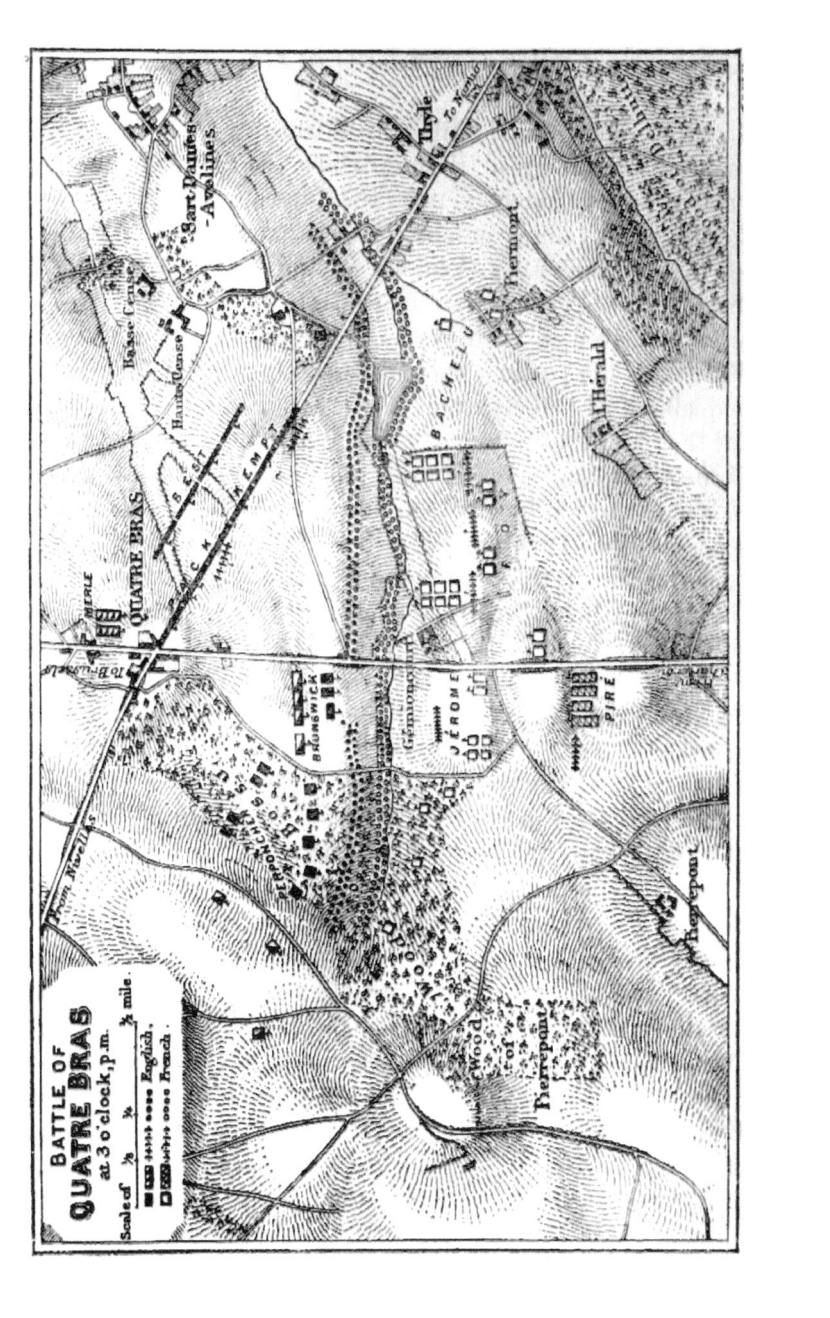

curing fresh horses to replace those which have been killed.

Our infantry behaved most admirably, setting good examples to our Belgian and German allies. Poor Cameron of the 92nd is severely, but, as I hope, not mortally, wounded by a musket ball in the groin. I helped him at the moment, and afterwards saw him put into a waggon and sent to the rear. I have his maps: and gave a sergeant his sword. I hope he may yet do well. Blücher fought obstinately, but lost ground; in consequence we shall retrograde a little, and I have sent off the ammunition carriages of the horse artillery to the front of Soignies, near Waterloo. Ross and Bean are known to be near Brussels. Bean has made a very forced march: in truth so have all the British cavalry which are at this moment in the field. Sir Henry Hardinge has lost his left hand by a cannon shot; his brother was with me last night, and I met him this morning returning with a surgeon towards Sombreffe, on the road from Namur to Nivelle, where was the brunt of the Prussian action.

The action seems now recommencing. We shall retire to make our communication with Blücher closer. I slept last night with Dickson, May and Hartmann, at Genappe. The house, and indeed all others, full of dying and dead. Henry Macleod is wounded: he has three stabs from the lancers. He is at Genappe: we have sent Baynes (his cousin) and our brigade major to him, and hope he will do well.

The country here is open, rich in corn, and having occasionally large and rather thick woods. It is undulating and deep, but without hedges or obstacles of any kind to the movements of all arms. Wood and I pointed out yesterday to the duke the bold advance of a French column, but it was seen too late to frustrate all its effects. However, the enemy was repulsed after severe loss on both sides. Tempted by the partial success of the bold manoeuvre, he repeated it, but without effect, a little before dusk.—*Adieu!* I am well and in good spirits.

Half-past 9.

Preparations making for withdrawing to the other side of Genappe. We are sending off spare carriages, &c. &c.

The *chef d'état major* of a French division deserted to us last night, bringing returns of the French force, which amounts to 130,000, of which 6,000 is cavalry. Artillery not specified. Ney was our opponent yesterday, with the 1st and 2nd corps under Reille and D'Erlon (Drouet, Count D'Erlon).

Bonaparte was opposed to Blücher, but is believed to have been opposite us about 4 p.m., when loud and continued cheerings among

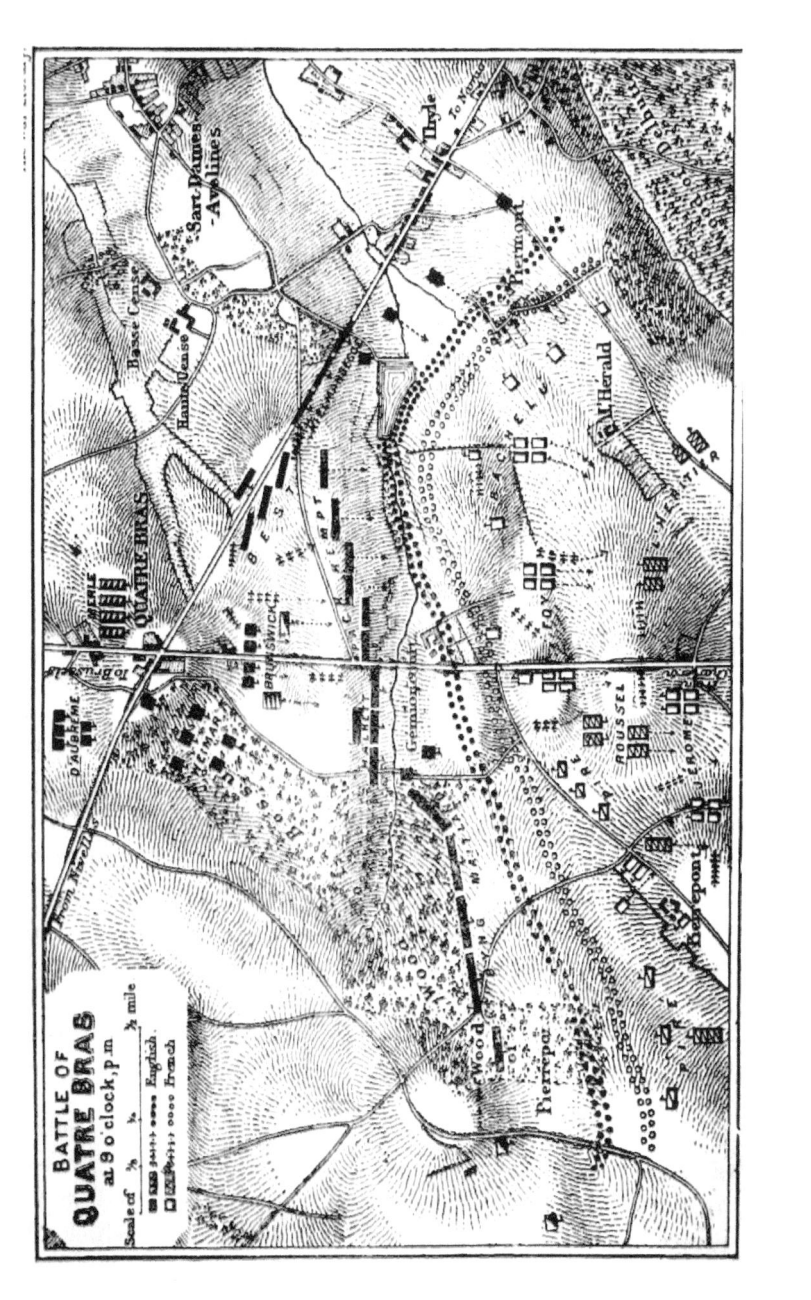

the French troops preceded one of their boldest attacks. The information brought by the *chef d'état major* I have from the Prince of Orange. An officer has just come from Blücher to the duke.

I have letters from Jenkinson, dated Frankfort, June 8th; of course, they contain nothing new. I think it probable that he may join Blücher, whose centre was pierced about eight last night by the French cavalry, who took sixteen pieces of cannon. The Prussians are retiring, so in consequence must we. These things are common enough in war.

Our Force.

	Infantry.	Cavalry.	Field Pieces.
King's German Legion	3,000	2,000	18
Hanoverian	22,500	1,800	12
Brunswick	7,000	800	16
British	25,000	6,000	120
Belgian	25,000	3,000	96
	82,500	13,600	262
Deduct Garrisons	10,000		
In the Field	72,500		

June 17, 11 p.m.

Just arrived from the front tired, jaded, dirty, and going to bed. I wrote this morning from Quatre Bras just to say I was safe and well; tomorrow I start before daybreak.—*Adieu.*

Letter 22

Waterloo: June 18, 3 a.m.

Quite refreshed after a comfortable night's rest. The British affair yesterday was merely the common skirmishing which naturally takes place on retiring in the face of the enemy. The French behave very well, and push us as much as they can. Our horse artillery yesterday were of much use; there were some trifling charges of cavalry on the *chaussée*, but nothing happened of any consequence.

We retired to a position previously selected, and we shall now make a stand; our right towards Braine l'Aleud, our left towards Limalle. Headquarters at Waterloo, and Genappe (now in the enemy's possession) in our front. In this position the forest of Soignies you will observe to be in our rear. Four *paves* run through it. The wood is open and practicable for infantry or cavalry. The trees are high, the roads and the whole wood very dark, and except in the paved part of the road, the ground is very deep. When I came this way last night the road was crowded and choked with carriages of every kind, many

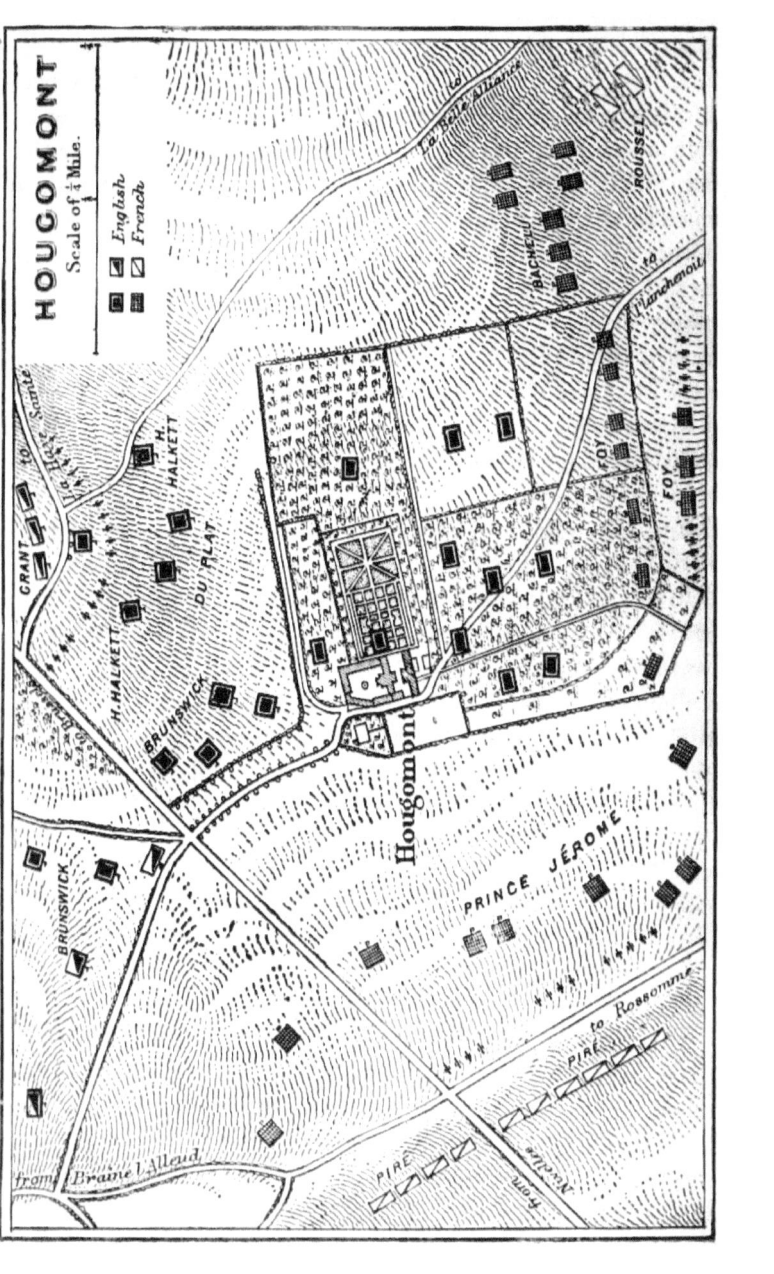

of them overturned. People get alarmed and confused, and lose their heads, and all about nothing.

Of Blücher's army I know nothing certain; but he was to retire on Wavre, and I have no doubt that our two armies are in perfect communication, and well placed. Our retiring at all was merely because Blücher had lost ground in the affair of the day before yesterday; in which, as I stated yesterday, he is said to have lost 14,000 men killed and wounded, and sixteen pieces of artillery. The enemy seems to have pierced his centre just about dusk, and to have taken *all* his reserve ammunition. These things will happen, and there will be jumblings just at first, but all will be very well. The enemy, taught by the day before, was very shy of attacking us yesterday.

Lloyd's two guns, which, from being dismounted and having the horses killed, were in the momentary possession of the enemy, were regained, placed on fresh carriages, and are again horsed. On our side, we left the enemy nothing but his own wounded, and the dead on both sides. Our own wounded we brought off on cavalry horses, except such as could not be found in the standing corn. Poor fellows! in these scenes, not in the actual rencontre, one sees the miseries of war. I saw Henry Macleod last night, free from fever and pain, and doing well. He has three pike stabs in the side, a graze in the head, and a contusion on the shoulder. Poor Cameron I hear is dead, but I am unwilling to believe it—*Adieu*. In all these strange scenes, ray mind is with you, but it is tranquil and composed, nor is there reason why it should be otherwise. All will be very well. God bless you.

June 18, quarter-past 9 a.m.

All quiet on both sides, all getting into order. Ammunition on ours, and doubtless on the enemy's side, coming up. The road from Brussels through the wood cleared. Finding it blocked up last night Dickson and I begged Captain Price, *aide-de-camp* to Sir Thomas Picton, whom we met coming up, to report to the adjutant-general the necessity of the road being cleared. In consequence, baggage has been removed, and the waggons which had been broken down have been burnt by General Lambert's brigade (four battalions of infantry and six Hanoverian field-pieces) from Ghent, who wanted fuel to cook their rations. Blücher's headquarters are at Wavre, and our left division (the 3rd) in full communication with us. The Russians will reach Metz in six days, so says General von Müffling, the Prussian general officer with the duke. The Austrians are expected to be at Metz at the same

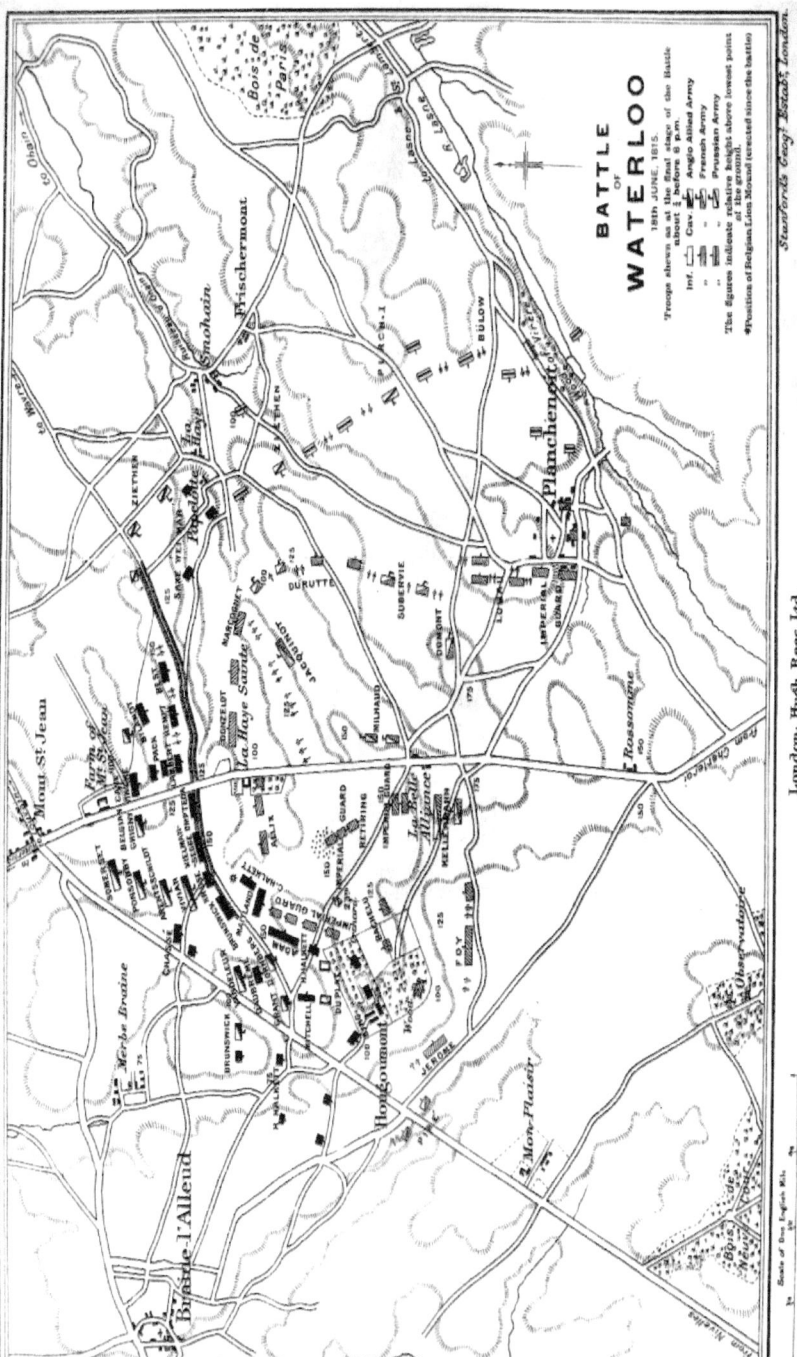

time. Admitting this, Bonaparte cannot afford to remain long in our front. He must take care that the Russians and the Austrians do not get into his rear. I expect we shall have some cannonading this afternoon.—*Adieu* for the present.

LETTER 23

June 18, 11 p.m.

How shall I describe the scenes through which I have passed since morning? I am now so tired that I can hardly hold my pen. We have gained a glorious victory, and against Napoleon himself. I know not yet the amount of killed, wounded, or prisoners, but all must be great. Never was there a more bloody affair, never so hot a fire. Bonaparte put in practice every device of war. He tried us with artillery, with cavalry, and last of all with infantry. The efforts of each were gigantic, but the admirable talents of our duke, seconded by such troops as he commands, baffled every attempt. For some hours the action was chiefly of artillery. We had 114 British, and some 16 Belgian guns, 6- and 9-pounders; the enemy upwards of 300, 8- and 12-pounders: never were guns better served on both sides.

After seven hours' cannonading, the French cavalry made some of the boldest charges I ever saw: they sounded the whole extent of our line, which was thrown into squares. Never did cavalry behave so nobly, or was received by infantry so firmly. Our guns were taken and retaken repeatedly. They were in masses, especially the horse artillery, which I placed and manoeuvred as I chose. Poor fellows! many of them—alas, how many!—lie on the bed of honour. Failing in his repeated attacks of cannonading and movements of cavalry, Napoleon at length pierced the left of our centre with the infantry of the Imperial Guard: the contest was severe beyond what I have seen, or could have fancied.

I cannot describe the scene of carnage. The struggle lasted even by moonlight. I know not the losses of other corps, nor hardly of our own; but Bean, Cairnes, and Ramsay, are among the horse artillery dead. Whinyates, Bull, Macdonald (junior), Webber, Strangways, Parker, Day, and, I am sorry to say, many others, including Robe, are among our wounded. Many of my troops are almost without officers, and almost all the guns were repeatedly in the enemy's hands; but we retired from them only to shelter ourselves under our squares of infantry, and instantly resumed our posts, the moment the cavalry were repulsed.

I have escaped very well. Maxwell's horse, on which I rode at first, received a ball in the neck, and I was afterwards rolled over by a round of case shot, which wounded my mare in several places, a ball grazing my right arm, just above the elbow, but without the slightest pain; and I now write without any inconvenience. In a momentary lull of the fire I buried my friend Ramsay, from whose body I took the portrait of his wife, which he always carried next his heart. Not a man assisted at the funeral who did not shed tears. Hardly had I cut from his head the hair which I enclose, and laid his yet warm body in the grave, when our convulsive sobs were stifled by the necessity of returning to renew the struggle.

Pray get me two mourning rings made; but I will describe them when I can write next. All now with me is confused recollection of scenes yet passing before me in idea: the noise, the groans of the dying, and all the horrid realities of the field are yet before me. In this very house are poor Lloyd (leg shot off but not yet amputated), Dumaresque (General Byng's *aide-de-camp*) shot through the lungs and dying; Macdonald, Robe, Whinyates, Strangways and Baynes, wounded. Sir Thomas Picton and Sir William Ponsonby are killed. So many wounded, that I dare not enumerate their names. Bolton of ours is killed, so is young Spearman.

What a strange letter is this, what a strange day has occasioned it! Today is Sunday! how often have I observed that actions are fought on Sundays. Alas! what three days have I passed, what days of glory, falsely so called; and what days of misery to thousands. The field of battle today is strewed with dead! never did I see so many. But let me turn from all that is distressing, even in description, and lay me down, which I shall do with a grateful sense of mercies vouchsafed.

I might have got a decoration for you, but the officer of the Imperial Guard who wore it, and who offered it as a prisoner, looked so wistfully at the reward of many a gallant day, that I could not think of taking it. I made an acquaintance in the field with a French lieut.-colonel of the 7th Dragoons, poor fellow, sadly wounded and prisoner. How misery makes friends of all. My friend Lord Saltoun is well. I hear he alone escaped of two companies of the Guards under his command. Lord Fitzroy Somerset has lost an arm. Lord Uxbridge has a ball in the knee. Delancey severely wounded.—*Adieu*: I will send you a more connected account of the battle when I am able.

LETTER 24

Nivelle: June 20.

All well. The victory was more complete than we at first supposed.

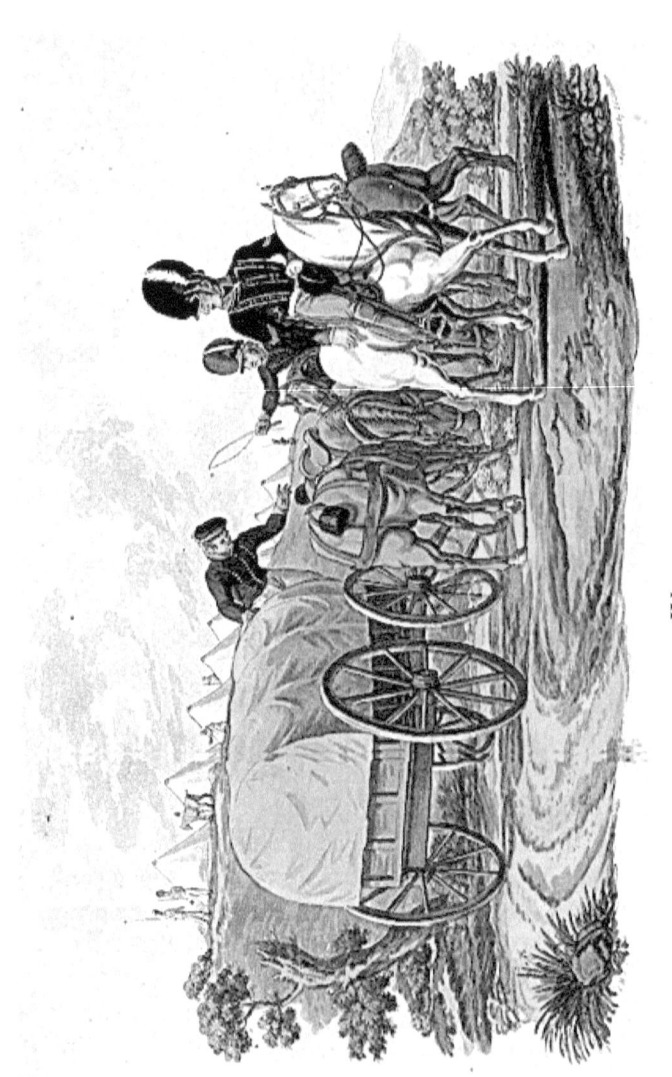

WATERLOO

I will give you in this letter a list of some of the fruits of the sanguinary contest of the day before yesterday. I cannot yet give you a connected account of the struggle. I wrote a few lines after the close of the day, and hope my letter was received before any reports could reach you. I would fain write, but am interrupted by all manner of demands to supply wants and repair casualties. In truth, now that the stern feelings of the day have given way to the return of better ones, I feel, with the bitterness of anguish not to be described, the loss of my friend Ramsay. Nor for this friend alone, but for many others, though less dear than poor Norman. Delancey is said to be dead: this is our greatest loss, none can be greater, public or private.

The troops are moving, the duke is still at Brussels; but Sir Charles Broke, now acting as quartermaster-general, has just sent a memorandum for our reserve artillery to move to Villers St. Ghislain, to the left of Mons. The duke forte is in pursuit of a beaten enemy. Where, indeed, and what is not his forte? Cold and indifferent, nay, apparently careless in the beginning of battles, when the moment of difficulty comes intelligence flashes from the eyes of this wonderful man; and he rises superior to all that can be imagined.—*Adieu* for a while. The following is the list I promised;—

Taken at Waterloo, June 18th 1815.

12-pounder guns	35
6-pounder guns	57
6-inch howitzers	13
24-pounder howitzers	17
Total cannon	122
12-pounder waggons	74
6-pounder waggons	71
Howitzer waggons	50
Total	195
Carry over	317
Brought over	317
Forge waggons	20
Waggons of Imperial Guard	52
Total	72
Spare gun carriages —	
12-pounder	6
Howitzer	6
6-pounder	8
Total	20
TOTAL	409

Letter 25

June 20, 9 a. m.

I leave off but to begin again; one ought to have twenty hands. I have just sent to Brussels a letter for you. Enclosed in it is a kind of rough sketch of our losses, that is, of part of them; but you shall have all the moment returns shall be sent. There are many poor artillery wives in your neighbourhood; happy will they be not to find their husbands' names in the fatal list.

I find my late troop (G) has lost ninety horses, but it behaved so well, so steadily, that I am highly and justly pleased. The English horse artillery did great execution, and I must be allowed to express my satisfaction, that *contrary to the opinion of most, I ventured to change (and under discouraging circumstances of partial want of means) the ordnance of the horse artillery.* (From 6-pounders to 9-pounders). Had the troops continued with light guns, I do not hesitate to say the day had been lost. The earlier hours of the battle were chiefly affairs of artillery; but kept down by the admirable and steadily-continued fire of our guns, the enemy's infantry could not come on *en masse*, and his cavalry, though bold, impetuous, and daring, was forced to try the flanks rather than the front of our position.

The steadiness of our infantry, too, became confirmed by the comparative repose afforded by our fire. Nevertheless, had Napoleon supported his first cavalry attacks on both flanks by masses of infantry, he had gained the day. His last attack, which was so supported, we were aware of: an officer of the Imperial Cuirassiers, whether a deserter or not I could not determine, apprised me of it, pointing to the side on which he said the attack would be made in a quarter of an hour. It was necessary to find the duke, from whom I had been for a little separated in assuring some guns which were about to be abandoned from a momentary want of ammunition; but finding my friend General Adam at the head of his brigade of infantry, I gave the *cuirassier* to him, and rode on to correct another mistake of the moment, and before I could rejoin the duke, Adam had reported the important information, so that the necessary dispositions were made.

With all these, however, this last struggle was nearly fatal to us; but our infantry remaining firm, and not only receiving the cavalry in squares, but, on their retiring, darting into line and charging the Imperial Infantry Guards, and again resuming their squares, the enemy was forced to give way. I have seen nothing like that moment, the sky literally darkened with smoke, the sun just going down, and which till then had not for some hours broken through the gloom of a dull day, the indescribable shouts of thousands, where it was impossible to distinguish between friend and foe. Every man's arm seemed to be raised against that of every other. Suddenly, after the mingled mass had ebbed and flowed, the enemy began to yield; and cheerings and English huzzas announced that the day must be ours.

Are you not tired of battles? Are you not sick of the sanguinary description? Judge then what must have been the reality. The duke himself said in the evening he had never seen such a battle, and hoped he never should again. To this hope we will all say: Amen.

Before the affair began, whilst riding towards the front, I met Thornhill, *aide-de-camp* to Lord Uxbridge, who was looking for the duke. He begged me to try and find the duke, and give His Grace a copy, which I wrote, of a report from Major Taylor of the 10th Hussars, who was on piquet at St. Lambert, that Bülow with 25,000 Prussians was arrived at Occey, three-quarters of a league from his post (we cannot find the name on any map); that Bülow had sent an officer to say so, and wished the duke to be acquainted with it. I trotted on with my copy, which I communicated to Sir Thomas Picton, whom I met by the way, and who was sending back to the bivouac men who were returning for provisions.

Sir Thomas told me the line was ordered under arms, and that we were to be attacked. I told him generally how the artillery were disposed, and to what points (principally the intersection of the paves, a little to the right of Braine l'Aleud) the reserves of musket ball cartridge carts were directed. Passing Sir Thomas, and riding to the left of the position, whither I understood the duke to have gone, the enemy's lancers were observed gaily stretching to their right; and the heads of their infantry columns just appearing. This was about 10 a.m. Whilst altering the position of some German guns. Wood came up. Sir Thomas Picton, with whose division we were, also came to the spot, and said something to us, but in the middle of his sentence, seeing some mistake in a Belgian battalion, rode to it and did not return. Sir Thomas has since fallen. Not finding the duke, we rode towards the centre. On telling Lord Fitzroy Somerset, whom with the duke we met near the centre, what I had learned, he said His Grace was aware of it.

To learn perfectly the position, I then galloped towards the right. Passing Sir Charles Alten, we learned that some little arrangement was necessary. Lloyd's battery, forming part of sixteen pieces placed for the defence of that part of the position, had, by some order of the Prince of Orange, been diverted to guard the point where our line was intersected by the *pavé* from Genappe to Brussels. This weakened Alten: both points required strengthening; and, by Wood's leave, Ross's troop was ordered from the reserve to guard the *pavé*, and I acquainted Alten that Lloyd would not be taken from him. Judge, however, of our surprise on learning that, by some misapprehension of orders, Lloyd's ammunition waggons had been sent to the rear. To be vexed was vain: *one* waggon was borrowed from Sandham's battery, and an officer sent to the rear for Lloyd's waggons.

Continuing (after placing Lloyd in position) towards the right, I rejoined the duke, and was rejoiced to hear that His Grace had determined not to lose a wood, (Hugoumont), 300 yards in front of that part of the line, which was in reality our weakest point. I had very hastily, on the preceding day, galloped to this wood, seen its importance, and determined that the heavy-howitzer troop should be brought to that point. Soon after, the duke came up, and the cortege walked up and down. I must more minutely explain this wood. It is close to where the extension of our line touched the pave leading to Nivelle from Waterloo.

From this *pavé* there is an avenue of 200 yards, leading to one large and a few smaller houses, enclosed, together with a large garden, within a wall. Beyond the wall, and embracing the whole front of the buildings and an orchard, and perhaps altogether three or four acres, is a thick wood. To the right, as viewed from our position, the wood was high; to the left, less high; and towards our position, thick, but low.

Whilst looking about, remarking again that the weak point of our line was on our right, and imagining that the enemy, making a demonstration on our centre and left, would forcibly seize the wood, and, interposing between us and Braine l'Aleud, would endeavour to turn the right flank of our second line, I met Lord Uxbridge, who very handsomely asked me what I thought of the position, and offered me the free use of the horse artillery. In a moment Bell was sent for the howitzer troop (Bull's), and I rode up and told the duke I had done so. By this time the enemy had forced a Belgian battalion out of the orchard to the left of the wood, and there was a hot fire on a battalion (or four companies, I forget which) of the Guards, stationed in the buildings and behind the walled garden.

The howitzer troop came up, and came up handsomely; their very appearance encouraged the remainder of the division of the Guards, then lying down to be sheltered from the fire. The duke said, "Colonel Frazer, you are going to do a delicate thing; can you depend upon the force of your howitzers? Part of the wood is held by our troops, part by the enemy," and His Grace calmly explained what I already knew.

I answered that I could perfectly depend upon the troop; and, after speaking to Major Bull and all his officers, and seeing that they, too, perfectly understood their orders, the troop commenced its fire, and in ten minutes the enemy was driven from the wood.

Pleased at this, I rode with Colonel Smyth (commanding Engineers) to the right of the second line, and again perceiving its weakness, ordered, by a written order, Mercer's and Ramsay's troops to the right of Sir Henry Clinton's division. In the way, I placed Webber Smith's troop to fire down the *pavé* leading from Nivelle towards Waterloo. By this time the enemy, stretching to his left, showed some squadrons of lancers and cuirassiers towards our right. There were several undulations and one hollow road by which he might advance rapidly to the attack, and I remained some time expecting to observe some indications of his approach, and in conversation on the subject with Sir Henry Clinton, whose division formed part of Lord Hill's corps; but the enemy not pressing, part of the 51st light battalion was pushed on beyond where the road in your map leads from the *pavé* to Braine l'Aleud.

I now returned to the first line, and the action becoming more general, the fire hotter, and nothing pressing on our right, I ordered Ramsay's troop to the centre of the second line. To this centre it became at one time necessary to send Bull's troop to refit and repair disabled carriages. The wood, from the front of which it went, was taken and retaken three times. At a quarter before three the large building burst out in a volume of flame, and formed a striking feature in the murderous scene. Imagining that this fire might oblige our troops to quit a post most material, and that it would have an effect, and possibly a great one, on the day, I remarked the time by my watch.

The Guards, however, held the post, and maintained themselves in the lesser buildings, from which the enemy could never dislodge them. To our right of the burning buildings, a troop of horse artillery, galled by the superior fire of the enemy's artillery, was forced to give way; but the point being essential, I ordered it up again at all hazards.

By this time the infantry were entirely formed into squares, the cavalry generally in solid columns, the crest of our position crowned with artillery. It was now that the French cavalry, advancing with an intrepidity unparalleled, attacked at once the right and centre of our position, their advance protected by a cannonade more violent than ever. Behind the crest of the position, the ground declined gradually to the easy valley in which the pave from Nivelle runs; by an equally gentle swell the ground rose beyond the pave to the position of the second line, perhaps half a mile from the first, but receding more towards the left.

This declination of ground was most favourable to the infantry, who, under a tremendous cannonade, were in a great measure sheltered by the nature of the ground—in great measure, too, by their lying down, by order. On the approach—the majestic approach—of the French cavalry, the squares rose, and, with a steadiness almost inconceivable, awaited, without firing, the rush of the cavalry, who, after making some fruitless efforts, sweeping the whole artillery of the line, and receiving the fire of the squares as they passed, retired, followed by, and pell-mell with our own cavalry, who, formed behind our squares, advanced on the first appearance (which was unexpected) of the enemy's squadrons.

The enemy rushed down the hill, forming again under its shelter, and in a great measure covered from the fire of our guns, which, by recoiling, had retired so as to lose their original and just position. But in a deep stiff soil, the fatigue of the horse artillerymen was great, and their best exertions were unable to move the guns again to the crest without horses; to employ horses was to ensure the loss of the animals.

The repeated charges of the enemy's noble cavalry were similar to the first: each was fruitless. Not an infantry soldier moved; and on each charge, abandoning their guns, our men sheltered themselves between the flanks of the squares. Twice, however, the enemy tried to charge in front; these attempts were entirely frustrated by the fire of the guns, wisely reserved till the hostile squadrons were within twenty yards of the muzzles. In this the cool and quiet steadiness of the troops of horse artillery was very creditable.

The obstinacy of these attacks made our situation critical: though never forced, our ranks were becoming thin. The second line, therefore, was chiefly ordered across the valley, and formed in masses behind the first, the broken intervals of which, where necessary, it filled up. Sometime before this the duke ordered me to bring up all the reserve horse artillery, which at that moment were Mercer's and Bull's troops, which advanced with an alacrity and rapidity most admirable.

It were tiresome to describe further. Somewhere or other I have mentioned the concluding struggle of this gigantic contest. The horror of the scene strikes me now; at the moment its magnificence alone filled my mind. Several times were critical; but confidence in the duke, I have no doubt, animated every breast. His Grace exposed his person, not unnecessarily but nobly: without his personal exertions, his continual presence wherever and whenever more than usual exertions were required, the day had been lost.

"Twice have I saved this day by perseverance," said His Grace before the last great struggle, and said so most justly.

Another saying of His Grace that evening to Lord Fitzroy deserves to be recorded:

"I have never fought such a battle, and I trust I never shall fight such another."

This was after the day was our own.

In the general action our cavalry behaved well. The Life Guards made some good charges, and overset the *cuirassiers*, searching with the coolness of experienced soldiers the unprotected parts of their opponents, and stabbing where the openings of the *cuirasse* would admit the points of their swords. The rockets were used, and were useful, as I am told. I did not see their application, the duke never having gone more to the left than the intersection of our centre by the *pavé*, which was in a ravine, and close by a large building occupied alternately by friend and foe; and a point more than ordinarily murderous.

The rocket troop was 200 yards to the left of this point. Ross and Bean were fifty yards in front of and to the right of it. The Belgian troops, though they yielded, yet returned to their posts. One corps of them, probably stragglers from all, galloped all the way to Brussels, spreading terror and dismay; and breaking open and plundering our spare carriages and store waggons, which, from prudence, were sent to the rear.

I may seem to have forgotten the Prussians in this battle. I saw none; but I believe that on our left they did advance; and the knowledge of their position might certainly induce Napoleon to withdraw, when his efforts against us were unavailing. We expected their cooperation early in the day, and earnestly looked for it; but it was not visible from any point where the duke was till dusk, when we had swept the enemy from the plain in our front. I was then separated from His Grace, whom I have not seen since.

Our present arrangements are that the troops (I speak now of horse artillery) have marched towards Mons as complete as they can;

all incomplete parts are assembling at Lillois, between Braine-l'Aleud and Nivelle, whither I have ordered equipments of all kinds to be sent, that we may put all again into an efficient state.

Adieu; the non-arrival of the duke from Brussels affords me the opportunity of writing to you today. Tomorrow may, nay must, bring its occupation with it, and soon, how soon! will all the day before yesterday presented, be utterly forgotten, unless arrested whilst yet fresh in recollection.

LETTER 26

Near Malplaquet: June 22, 8 a. m.

I reached Malplaquet last night at 12, after having ridden from Nivelle past the scene of the 18th to Genappe, back to Waterloo, again to Nivelle, and hither by Binch. Today we are moving on Cateau (near Cambray), the scene of a glorious victory at which I was present in 1794. All looks well. We have good news of victories, or at least advantages, in La Vendée. The duke has had communication with Paris. You will see that we have passed the frontier: tonight, if my geography does not fail me, (I have not my maps with me,) we shall be nearer Paris than Brussels.

I have written Moor an account of the battle; up to the 20th you will have my journal pretty exact. On the evening of that day, the duke being anxious that the captured guns should be parked, I offered, together with Colonel May, to our friend Sir George Wood to go and collect and park the captured guns and carriages during the night. It was feared that whilst our chief attention had been paid to re-equipping our troops and batteries, and sending them forward, and to getting up the battering-train and small arm and gun ammunition, the Prussians had run away with the trophies of our victory.

Pressing Close and Bell into the service, we rode to Lillois (between Waterloo and Nivelle), collected all the scattered artillerymen and horses, and proceeded by the burnt house (Hugoumont) and carefully rode over the ground of the action. Before we reached it, the air was tainted with the remains of the dead. It was a moonlight night, frequently dull, and with repeated flashes of lightning. We moved in silence, carefully looking over the ground, which I well knew; we soon reached poor Ramsay's grave; it stands close by a stone 800 yards from the wood, to the left of Hugoumont, and close, too, by a little road crossing from one *pavé* to the other; 400 yards to the right, as you look towards the wood, are three remarkable and isolated trees. I enter into this minuteness of detail, since, if I live, the grave of my friend shall have some stone, some mark, to record his worth. I had ordered a hole to be bored through the stone with a bayonet, but the order had been disregarded.

Passing by this, and carefully examining the field, we observed few guns; indeed, we already knew that most of them were blocked up in the road leading to Genappe, from which they had merely been thrown aside to clear the road. But anticipating that we should find in the field many wretched sufferers dying from neglect and want, I had taken all the spare horse-artillerymen whom I could find at Lillois, where all our broken parts of troops were sent to refit. Soon did we find full occupation for all; we found on every side poor fellows dying in every variety of wretchedness, and had repeatedly to enjoin the strictest silence that we might hear their scarcely audible groans.

After doing what we could, (and, thank God, before morning we collected several waggon loads of brave fellows, friends and foes,) we looked for the guns; but, except a few here and there, could observe none where we knew we had seen them in abundance the night before. We had our fears that we should not find them after all, but at last near Genappe we found 161 guns, with some hundreds of ammunition and other carriages. They were regularly parked with Prussian sentries. After much difficulty we found the Prussian officer, who was asleep under some straw, and evidently did not wish us to see him; however, after distinctly stating our errand, and showing our return of the guns taken by the British, (which return was made by Lieut.-Colonel Williamson of the artillery,) the officer assented readily to our receiving them, and we drew them and parked them near Waterloo.

Being so near Waterloo, I rode thither, and saw our wounded officers, who are all doing well. (337 killed and wounded, and 484 horses killed, of artillery in the last action of the 18th.) We are marching upon Laon, where we shall probably have another battle.

From Waterloo I returned to Nivelle. Headquarters were gone, so we pushed on to Malplaquet, turning a little out of our way to get refreshment at Binch, where we found the town in great confusion. Some parties of Prussians, we were told, but they proved Belgians, were stealing cows. By this time, I was so tired that, more asleep than awake, I hardly heard the appeal made to me by some unhappy women: "There go," said they, "the corporal and the men who are goading on the cows."

Away we scampered after them, seized the corporal, and brought him back. He pleaded orders; said he had authority from his officer and the mayor: so, said the officer himself, who came up; but insisting on his coming with me to the mayor, and resolutely ordering him instantly to return the cows, he acknowledged he was wrong; and we went to the Lion d'Or.

Before dinner was ready, I was awakened by more misery. One man had lost his cart; another, I know not what: there was nothing for it but to feign sleep; we could not assist, nor was I willing to interfere too much with the Belgian troops. However, before dinner was over, a Belgian officer came and offered excuses for what had happened; their troops, he said, had not had supplies of any kind for five days. This, too, reminds me that almost all the sufferers on the field complained that they had been *five* days in misery and want. Poor souls! The action was on the 18th; we saw them before daylight on the 21st—how misery prolongs time! how rapidity of idea and occupation prolongs, too, its recollection! It already seems an age since we were at Brussels; the very day of the 18th seems an age ago.

General orders just arrived. France to be considered a *friendly* country; no article to be taken without payment; vouchers and receipts to be given, and commissaries to account for all supplies in the same manner as in England.

The duke mounts.—*Adieu.*

Cateau: 6 p. m.

We reached Cateau, which is near Cambray, about 3 p.m., marching by Bavay. Bavay is a nice place. There are several remains there of antiquity, which I regret I could not see. We are making forced marches, and shall, as I hope and believe, march again tomorrow. We have no enemy in our front. Napoleon is on our left flank, or rather on the left flank of the Prussians, who are to our left; so that we are in the second line.

Avesnes, a little town to the south of Maubeuge, has surrendered. Lieutenant-Colonel Colquhoun Grant went to Maubeuge, and spoke to the governor yesterday evening. The governor said he would not surrender. Grant spoke to the National Guards and to the *Pensionnaires* or Invalids. The first said they would not leave the town; the others, that they would obey whoever were masters, that they might not lose their pensions.

The Austrians are said to be at Lyons. Blücher's headquarters are at Chatillon-sur-Sambre, just on our left. The bells here ring merrily, and the white flag is displayed from the steeple. Nothing but "*Vive*

Louis XVIII.!" shouted with as much energy as would have been "*Vive l'Empereur!*" had we been defeated. I trust we shall march rapidly on. I fully anticipate another battle, and hardly think it avoidable; but that our cause will prevail, I fully and confidently hope. We must neglect no precaution to insure it. Our march today has been through a beautiful country. I perfectly remember its features. How many former days are recalled, and how few companions of those days remain!

The duke today was in high glee. I had a long conversation with His Grace. I have since dined at an hotel crowded to excess. I hear many complaining: hitherto I have fared excellently. We halt here tomorrow; so much the better for our convenience, and of course the duke knows best as to the propriety.

Among the generals taken is, as report says, Lefebvre-Desnouettes; if so, he ought to be hanged. A Count Lobau, governor of these provinces, and well known to the duke, was also taken, and, with several generals, wished to see His Grace, on the score of former acquaintance; but the duke refused to see any of them, and drily added, that he associated only with gentlemen.

It is said and believed, that in Napoleon's carriage was taken, among other papers of consequence, a list of his spies and emissaries in all the countries of Europe. Quantities of crosses and decorations certainly were, as well as proclamations dated from *our Palace of Lacken*, so sure did Bonaparte make of beating us. How different in that case had been the situation of affairs!—*Adieu*, for today.

Letter 27

Headquarters, Cateau: June 23.

I have written almost daily; but you may be puzzled to make out the confused account.

All looks well. Headquarters and most of the army are halting. We who fly wish it were not; those who—tired with miry roads, and with knapsacks, and arms—can hardly get on, think otherwise. The duke, who knows best, judges it wise to halt for today, and to collect. The enemy moves on Laon; so, do we; so do the Prussians. Blücher's headquarters are, as I said before, at Chatillon-sur-Sambre. The Austrians are, we are told, at Lyons. The Russians should be at Metz in three days.

Laon, I should think, will be the scene of another battle. The position is strong. I know it well of old, and hope to know it better. We may perhaps try to turn the position, and, marching by St. Quentin or Ham, reach Noyon. For these ideas I have no manner of authority.

We have reports of all kinds. Cateau and the neighbouring towns were till yesterday morning filled with the enemy's troops, chiefly his *cuirassiers* (he had twelve regiments of them in the battle), accompanied by fugitives of all kinds; 8000 of his guards are supposed to have remained in a body, and to be firm and true to his cause. We must look at these gentry.

Avesnes surrendered the day before yesterday. The governor and garrison (National Guards and Invalids) of Maubeuge held a parley the evening before last with Lieutenant-Colonel Colquhoun Grant (chief of the secret-intelligence department), and declined surrendering their town; but the very parley proves their vacillating state, and it only remains for the star of Napoleon to be a little more set for them to turn sides.

Of our loss in the battle I can learn nothing certain. In continued movement ever since, and flying to all sides, I have been away from the adjutant-general's department, and to give reports without foundation were useless; but 8000 British may be about the number.

The more I reflect, the more I bless my stars that I had obstinacy enough to persist in changing the guns of the Horse Artillery, which, as it always should, stood (and so long as I can, always shall stand) the brunt of the day. Without their admirable fire, the enemy's masses might have carried the first position. "All this may be very true," you will say with Moses, in the *Vicar of Wakefield*, "but pray, sir, have I not heard all this before?" I really believe you may, so I cry you mercy, and must find something new for you.

Whilst I write I am ordered to Mons to make arrangements. Sir Charles Colville's division and the cavalry are moving on Cambray to invest it, and to offer terms to the governor; if he has spirit it will not surrender. We shall stay here a day or two *Adieu*.

Letter 28

Mons: June 24, 9 a. m,

I wrote yesterday from Cateau, galloped to Bavay, dined there, hired a cabriolet, and got here before dark. The roads from Bavay to Mons are execrable: much through woods and very deep. Roads blocked up too, by stragglers. Colonel Hartman (German Horse Artillery) is my fellow-traveller.

Hartman supplied the German and Hanoverian, and your friend the British wants. These are of all kinds, an officer or sergeant attending from every brigade in the country. We hope to arrange all, and to return to Gateau tonight. But horses, waggons, and ammunition of all kinds must arrive, as I have no doubt they will. Dickson is at Brussels, and is forwarding them.

We found the French king here; his majesty has just proceeded to the army. *Monsieur* has just gone too, and the French loyalists (2000) have marched from hence to Bavay. Sir C. Stuart is here, I shall wait on him, and write to Vienna.

Mons is a large town; its chief defences consist in the inundations which nearly surround it. On the south-east and on a high ground called the Montague de Peniselle, there is a Pentagon with bomb proofs for 400 men; eighteen guns are mounted on the fort, which was lately ordered to be defended to the last extremity. The ground is commanded (but at 1500 yards' distance, so that it is of no importance) by another and more rising ground. Mons has always been attacked on the Maubeuge side, on which a rising ground commands the town within 800 yards. There are three bombproof magazines, two of which have a double tier of bomb-proofs; they may in totality contain 3000 barrels of powder.

General Behr (Dutch) commands the garrison of four Dutch battalions (2000 men), and 206 Dutch artillery; fifty-seven pieces are mounted in the works, including those on Fort Peniselle, and in a small fort near the sluice of Genappe 1200 yards from the town; in that fort are five pieces.

The weak part of Mons is from La Porte du Parc, to the basin of the Condé canal. For 800 yards the rampart is only musket proof; the point of the Batterdeau is altogether weak. To the left (looking from the town) of this Batterdeau, the rampart has been quite thrown down to get earth to form the banks of the Condé canal: the heights of Genappe (where in 1792 was the great battle) are half a league from this spot. There are two basins for the canal, which basins, one on each side the rampart, are filled by the River Haine (whence Hainault takes its name). Formerly a fort stood here, called Fort de la Haine. There is now a small fort in front of the bridge. The sluice draws off the water from both basins, and from the ditches as far as the Batterdeau.

Near the Porte du Parc, where there is no inundation, water might be obtained, but without a dyke could not be retained, and a dyke of half a mile would be necessary, (its best position would be near the sluice of the Condé canal,) otherwise the water would run off towards Genappe: at the sluice the River Haine runs under the canal.

A very weak point, too, is at the Porte d'Eau (or de Genitte), half way between the Porte de France and the Porte de Havre. From the village of Eau (properly the village de la Haine) a dyke, leading to the Porte d'Eau cannot be inundated, and under its cover infantry might advance in safety. This dyke once cut, the inundation would be destroyed on that side.

11 a.m.

Talleyrand is here, so says Sir Charles Stuart, with whom I have had a long confab. Sir Charles has gone to Cateau after the French king. You know that we took (or rather the Prussians did) Bonaparte's carriage, the one in which he came from Elba. In it were his private papers, and lists of all his spies and emissaries in every country of Europe. This intelligence I know to be true; it comes from Count Gneisenau, Blücher's quartermaster-general, who adds, "there are many at Berlin implicated." It might be politic to burn this book, at least to announce that it was burnt. Did not Pompey do (or say) so when he had beat Sertorius in Spain? Talking of books and papers, the duke's red box containing his papers was lost in the field. The orderly who carried it was killed, which I well recollect, my own orderly's horse having been killed about the same time. Poor Canning then took the box, but he being also killed, his horse galloped off and was lost in the *mêlée*; and neither horse nor box has been found since.

Adieu.—I hope to be off for Bavay, and shall try hard to reach Cateau today.

Letter 29

Cateau: June 25, 7 a. m.

I got here last night by 12. Not a carriage of any kind being to be had at Mons, and learning that by some order (the origin of which I could not find out), the horses coming as remounts to Mons had been detained, or rather ordered back to Soignies, Hartman and I (after giving written orders to Captain Dewell and putting all at Mons under his direction,) stopped a country waggon, and were getting into it when a friend of Hartman's, M. Vanderbosche, who was accidently at Mons, offered his carriage, which we accepted, pressed four artillery horses, and took an artilleryman to reconduct the carriage to Mons, and to receive money for the artillerymen at Mons, who were without any.

We pushed on and reached Bavay at 9 p.m., found our orderlies and horses, rode on through the woods and bivouacs, and got there by 12. As we passed through the bivouacs the air resounded with music, the bands of almost all corps playing, and the troops sitting round blazing fires. In passing through that of the *maison du Roi*, where of course French alone was heard on all sides, it was impossible not to think oneself in the enemy's lines. I lost Hartman by the way; the road was blocked up with carriages of all sorts, and it required some scrambling and no fear to get on.

On reaching Cateau I found it illuminated; Louis XVIII. is here, the white flag waving from every house, the whole population is in the streets. My old landlady welcomed me back as if I had come from the antipodes. Could you but see the landlady, such a figure! Hogarth himself never pictured any more grotesque. I fear to attempt a description of a waist which commences at the neck, and the round-about of which must be some dozen metres.

The necessity for getting on the 18-pounders being urgent, I sent Bell back to Mons, with orders to stop, to park, and to take back the horses, of seventy-six waggons, which we sent in three convoys from Mons to Bavay last night. The town of Cambray is ours; the citadel still holds out. This place and Valenciennes would be important to us. A Prussian officer arrived last night from Blücher. It is said that he brought intelligence that a French general officer from Napoleon's troops had come in to Blücher's headquarters with an account that Bonaparte had abdicated. Landrecy is ours. The citadel of Cambray will surrender when the French king's order shall be received. All seems doing well. Headquarters move to Joucourt, five leagues from hence, and a little to the left of the road leading between Le Catelet and Bohain.

It rains in torrents today *Adieu.*

12 o'clock, and still at Cateau, and jollily wet: we have been in the street an hour or two. The duke not yet gone. Wood is with His Grace. We shall have fine work to get on our heavy ordnance. It will be necessary to write to have ships loaded with all we want—equipments of every kind,—ready to run for Dunkirk. I write in a house full of the *maison du Roi*; horses waiting in the street. Today, we have 112 guns with the army.

Adieu, off for Mons again; 'tis but forty miles. Stace goes with me.

LETTER 30

Mons: June 26, 5 a. m.

My last was from Cateau, whence headquarters moved yesterday to Joucourt, beyond and between Le Catelet and Bohain. The Duke is impatient, and wants ammunition, so off Stace and I scamper. We are to find, and to send to the army 4,000,000 musket ball-cartridges, and a double supply of gun ammunition for every piece (112) in the field. We got to Bavay by 4; road blocked up with troops and carriages. At Bavay we stopped to feed our horses, and get some bread; all else in the town eaten up. To increase the confusion, the hostess had just had an attack of apoplexy. Where do you come from? and where are you going? said a hundred voices; and where is the king? All these queries, and some dozen more, were made by some of the royal suite, more willing than able to get forward. Before I left headquarters, there were many reports, not to be traced, that Napoleon had abdicated: this is generally believed; and I saw a letter, which, if not a forgery, seems to confirm it; the news is most important.

Hurrying forward from Bavay, and reporting to Sir George Wood the artillery supplies of every kind which we met on the road, we galloped to Mons, that is, whenever the road, which is generally knee-deep, would permit. On arriving, behold, the 200 horses which ought to have been here, by a counter-order, and by a total misconception, after having been halted at Soignies, have been pushed to Nivelle, to join the army by the route of Binch. This was *mal-à-propos*—to lose a moment in regret, useless. Accordingly, we waited on the mayor, he was out; on the commissary-general, he, "good easy man!" had not a horse or a cart for us, and believed none were to be found in the country.

But the *intendant* of the province, on whom I waited, gave me an order for fifty waggons, which I secured; and Stace in the interim bustled and got fifteen more. They are now a league or two on their road, laden with musket ball-cartridges and gun ammunition. Having swept Mons clear of ammunition, we are going to Brussels. Stace has procured horses; I have found a carriage, and have found too, (don't be jealous,) a female companion. *Mademoiselle* is in the suite of the Duchesse de Levis, and is returning to Ghent. Young, very pretty, and in a little distress, how could I avoid offering the lady a seat in a carriage, which, I hope, is found!

We leave our own horses and orderlies here to refresh, and shall return from Brussels tomorrow. What curious lives we lead! Going last night to the *intendant*, I was beset by two dozen damsels, who insisted on money or on kissing me. In the sad alternative, I paid my *francs* to avoid the more dolorous evil. The money was to make a bonfire, or to increase one then made, in honour of some saint's day.

LETTER 31

Brussels: June 27, 5 a.m.

All well. Two batteries of 18-pounders marched,—seventy pieces of heavy cannon landed,—and the whole country scoured for more waggons and carts. Dickson is here. We have had a good laugh together; and pushing Stace to Vilvorde, and some dozen officers and commissaries in various directions for carts, horses, and waggons, had a good chat together about books and old stories. Major Jones is here: I saw him last evening, and his company having been broken up, I appointed him to the charge of the Horse Artillery detachment—that is, of 100 horses, which arrived yesterday from Ostend, and on which I seized.

I have seen nothing of my fair *protégée* from Mons, who was a nice girl. I hope she went to Ghent last night; if not, I shall see her off this morning. Madame Proft (hostess of the Bellevue) promised me yesterday to take care of her.

Lady Uxbridge is here. Fraser of the 7th Hussars went for and brought her ladyship, I saw Fraser and Lord Paget, to whom I gave my card and told my news from headquarters. Today I shall try to see Lord Uxbridge, Lord Fitzroy Somerset, and Frederick Ponsonby, who are all doing well. We have not good accounts of poor Delancey; I have great fears for him. I shall call, too, on the Prince of Orange, from whom I have just heard,

I have not yet had time to visit my old quarters, but shall before I leave the town. The beautiful park under my window is quite deserted; on every house as you enter the city is written in chalk, "Wounded," and by an ordonnance every medical man is obliged to make the round of some district; sensible printed medical regulations are everywhere distributed, teaching the inhabitants what treatment is best for the wounded where medical attendance cannot be procured.

The commanding engineer of the 2nd Prussian corps has demanded 100 pieces of heavy artillery from us, together with artillerymen, ammunition, and entrenching tools; and also transport for them. They are required, he says, for the sieges of Landrecy and Maubeuge. Of course, without the duke's order they cannot be given. Colonel Aster, Prussian Engineers, is the officer I allude to.

We stopped yesterday to water the horses at Hal, and sat down, the fair Maria too, at the *table-d'hôte*. Whom should we find descanting on his own feats and surprising escapes, but a lifeguardsman commonly called Joe Kelly. I never was more entertained in my life, and enjoyed leading him on to surprise the multitude.

I am anxious to be off, and to get to the front as soon as possible, but it was of importance to get Stace to Vilvorde, that the 200 horses coming from Antwerp might bring away as much as possible of the depot as they passed Vilvorde on their way thither.—*Adieu.*

LETTER 32

Mons: June 28, 8 a.m.

I wrote to you yesterday from Brussels, which Stace and myself left in our carriage about 3, and, dining at Hal, reached Mons about 11. The gates of course were shut, and it was only by alleging despatches for the duke that we persuaded the officer to permit them to be opened. After an excellent supper *la belle* Thérèse gave us good beds, and we slept till 4. We have since that sent our orderlies and horses to Bavay; and have secured horses to take our carriage so far. From Bavay I shall endeavour to ride to headquarters, which by this time must be well in advance.

Yesterday we pushed off from Brussels two 18-pounder batteries; today twenty pieces of heavy ordnance will set off; about half a million of musket ball-cartridges will come from Vilvorde to Brussels, and by tomorrow or next day we have every hope that our four millions of musket ball-cartridges, and a double proportion of gun ammunition for every piece in the field, will be on its route.

All goes on well. Lord Fitzroy told me the enemy had abandoned Laon; so much the better.

Did I tell you I had recovered poor Ramsay's snuff-boxes, which in the hurry of going for the captured guns had been left at Nivelle; Hincks has them, and I hope safe. Sir George Wood wishes to have one which he had given poor Ramsay; the other, through which a ball had passed in reaching his noble heart, I shall keep as a memento. How affectionately did he always speak of you and of our boys; and what a friend would you and they have found in him, had the fate of war reversed our dooms!—*Adieu.*

June 29, 5 a.m.

At a little cabaret near Vermande between Péronne and St. Quentin:—We arrived here about 12 o'clock last night, having left Mons at noon and dined at Bavay. Taught by experience we carried our dinner with us in the carriage; found the hostess recovering from her apoplectic attack, mounted our steeds, sent the carriage back to Mons in charge of a stray horse-artilleryman (who had quitted Mons without orders), and rode on to Cateau. On my way I met Lord Erskine, with whom I renewed my acquaintance. Lord Erskine is determined to follow the army even to Paris; as his lordship said, "I hope we are all going thither." Lord Erskine's son has lost one arm, and had the other bruised by a cannon shot; he is at Brussels. I had heard of Lord Erskine's being somewhere about from Hume the duke's surgeon, whom I met at Mons, and brought in the carriage to Bavay. Hume is travelling with Alava, but had missed the general, whom I tried to find, but without success, at Cateau, that I might learn the movements of headquarters.

We had a good ride of it last night, frequently losing the road but keeping the direction by the stars. Our adventures ended by our passing Vermande, embowered in trees and hardly visible, and my rapping at the window of a peasant's house, who very obligingly got out of bed and walked a mile to this little cabaret, where they received us very willingly, and we had a fricassee of turkey, and a jorum of water. No wine, no spirits, no beer to be got, so we agreed they were all unwholesome, and laid us down, and as you see by the date we have slept most soundly. Coffee is getting ready, and we shall soon start.

I was led to come here by seeing at Cateau Lieutenant Macbean, who has charge of our reserve convoys of ammunition, and who had received a note, dated Marets, 28th June (yesterday), to move as quickly as possible by Marets and Vermande to Nesle, whither we shall bend our steps and obtain further intelligence. Nesle is six leagues from hence. I trust at least to reach Roye today, should that prove to have been the route taken by headquarters, which left this place at noon on the 27th.

The inhabitants of this house, as well as of many others where we stopped to make inquiries on the road, complain a little of having been plundered by the followers and stragglers of the army. All however speak well of the English: "We had more trouble," said an old woman at Bavay, "to satisfy two Prussians who were in one house, than thirty English who were in another."

From a well-informed French spy, Napoleon's forces were:—

			General strength.		
1st Division	-	D'Erlon	22,800	3,600	
2nd "	-	Reille - -	29,400	5,400	cavalry: but included in the general strength.
3rd "	-	Vandamme	17,000		
4th "	-	Gerard -	20,200	1,800	
6th "	-	Lobau -	20,800	3,600	
Imperial Guards	-	-	25,000	1,800	
			135,200		

The cavalry regiments he estimated at 600 each; infantry 1200 each; about 400 pieces of artillery; of this number he was not sure. The fifth division (Rapp's) is near Strasburg. Clauzel's corps, not exceeding 8000 or 10,000, on the side of the Pyrenees. Grouchy, as is well known, commanded the cavalry in the late battle: The duke says he believes he saw him. The above statement of force is the one brought to the duke, and believed to be authentic. Part of His Grace's papers were found on the field by some of our artillerymen, and were sent to headquarters. They were part of the contents of the box lost when poor Canning was killed. We passed the great canal of St. Quentin last night near Bellicourt. Péronne surrendered yesterday, as we were told; St. Quentin had done so two days before.

I regret to state that poor Delancey is dead; so, Hume the duke's surgeon told me. He had opened the body; eight ribs were forced from the spine, one totally broke to pieces, and part of it in the lungs. Poor Delancey! he is our greatest loss; a noble fellow and an admirable officer.

Nesle: half-past 8 a.m.

The duke's headquarters were, at noon yesterday, at the house opposite the auberge from which I write. We have half an hour to breathe the horses, then off to Roye two leagues from hence, where we hope to hear certain accounts of headquarters. The Nassau troops are passing through, so that we are up with part of the army; but the front, not the rear, must be the point. Near Vermande we passed the village of Caulaincourt, where an estate and a magnificent *château*, give the title to that murderer Caulaincourt.

"What think you of that villain Caulaincourt?" said I to an old man.

"Sir," answered he, "I dare not think!"

Orville: 1p.m.

Orville is almost at the limits of your map. We have passed Roye, a good large town, very full. Near Tolloloy is a magnificent *château*, the property of Madame Latour-Maubeuge. *Madame* is at Paris, the villages seem deserted; a few women, and those generally crying, form the only inhabitants. The stragglers plunder, I believe, but I have as yet seen no English plundering, and the inhabitants speak well of them. At Nesle we had a barber to shave and cut our hair; such a vain, squinting, redheaded fellow I do not remember; were he but sixteen, he would go to England he said, and there he was sure to make a fortune! But he had a son of twelve years who, when sixteen, was certainly to go, and as certain to become rich and an ornament to his profession.

Headquarters are at Plessis-Longneau, which is some four leagues from hence, but in which direction I hardly know. The pontoons are hurrying forward, we have just passed forty; a bridge, I suppose will be thrown over the Oise. I presume we move on Compiègne. We have all manner of reports; a short time will develop their truth.—*Adieu.*

Letter 33

Wood near Pontarme (between Senlis and Louvres), eight or nine leagues from Paris: June 30, 11 a. m.

I reached headquarters at Plessis-Longneau about 8 last night, and glad was I to regain my post, and to find that I had not missed anything by my temporary absence. On reaching Plessis I learned that a deputation had already waited on the duke, consisting of Boissy d'Anglas, the Duc de Valence, Andréossy, Flaugergues, and Besnardière.

It cannot be supposed that what really passed can be fully known; but that the duke received the deputation very coldly is certain. (Heavy firing at this moment in the direction of Paris.

The Prussians are in front, having crossed our line of march.) It is said that Boissy d'Anglas offered to deliver Napoleon to the duke, observing—and I suppose in an offensive manner—that in delivering him to the English, France would get rid of him, and the British might destroy him if they pleased. To which the duke is understood to have replied, "Sir, I have never dishonoured myself; how do you dare to suppose I shall dishonour my Government?"

Much is believed to have passed to dissuade the duke from going to Paris; the position of Montmartre and its strength were insisted upon, and the misery it would occasion, intermixed with some scattered remarks that 24,000,000 of men were not yet to be conquered. To all this the duke coolly answered, that he was not there to receive a lesson, and, mounting his horse, left the deputies to return.

Something like a similar scene is believed to have taken place with Blücher, who is pushing his troops forward, and some of them may this evening reach Paris. The restitution of all taken at Berlin, an unconditional surrender of the town, and an indemnification to the King of Prussia for the expenses of the present war, are said to be the preliminaries insisted upon by Blücher previous to entering into any parley. Since the little affair of Péronne, which was taken by escalade two or three days ago, the British have not been engaged.

Yesterday the Prussians had an affair with Grouchy's corps near Compiègne. After taking the matter too lightly, and losing some men, the enemy were routed, leaving on the field fourteen pieces of artillery. This morning we crossed the Oise at Pont St^e. Maxence. The river is deep and rapid; the bridge, which was destroyed last year, has been repaired with planks. The little town is neat and elegant, and the pass on this side so strong that it would be most difficult to force. Luckily, it was not defended. Near Plessis-Longneau, and indeed where the duke slept last night, is a small but elegant *château*, said to have been built by Voltaire. The duke is gone to the front; His Grace went early this morning to confer with Blücher. Whilst I write, troops of every description are hurrying on. The heat is great, and the dust rises in clouds. The army will be today as follows:—

British cavalry	Near Louvres.
2nd Division infantry 4th „ „ Nassau troops	} Chantilly.
1st Corps Netherlands cavalry 1st Division British infantry 3rd „ Netherlands infantry	} Head of column at La Capelle. Rear at Senlis.
Brunswick cavalry 5th Division, British infantry 6th „ „ „ Brunswick infantry Reserve artillery	} Head of column, Flourines. The rear to rest on Pont St^e. Maxence.
Pontoon train	Senlis.
Hawser bridge	Senlis.
Reserve ammunition Civil Department	} Pont St^e. Maxence.

At Louvres today we shall be within seven leagues of Paris. The general opinion is that we shall enter it on Sunday. No further battle is expected; but we shall better understand probabilities tonight. I need not say that I earnestly hope there may not be more blood shed. The latter villages through which we have passed are deserted. The Prussians have gutted all the houses. The duke has hanged some Belgians detected in plundering. At Plessis, where the Prussians had been a night before us, the natives had fled; but returned on finding the English were there, and wept bitterly when we left them this morning. Scovel's *gendarmerie* are very active, and prevent much mischief.—*Adieu.*

I write on my knee, and am tired and thirsty; no water to be had. I will finish at Louvres.

LETTER 34

Louvres: July 1, 6. a.m.

We reached Louvres yesterday. There was a sharp affair with the Prussians near St. Denis. Today headquarters are some half a league nearer Paris. I have been up almost all night drawing a map. You shall have it; it will explain movements. Napoleon is in front of Paris, and has, by report, about 50,000 ragamuffins of all kinds. They fired yesterday on their own deputation; in consequence, Messrs. Boissy d'Anglas and Co. are still here. Our troops are come up, and the army will be in good shape, and tomorrow will be ready to measure its strength again.—*Adieu.*

Today the army will be as follows:—

Head-quarters - - -	Gonnesse (3 leagues from Paris).
2nd Corps, Baron Estorff's cavalry 2nd Division British infantry - 4th „ „ - Nassau troops - - -	Position between Pierrefitte and great road of Senlis.
1st Corps Netherlands cavalry - 1st Division Netherlands infantry 3rd „ „	Position with right on road at Le Bourget, its left on the Bois de Bondy.
Brunswick cavalry - - 1st Division Brunswick infantry - 6th „ „ - Reserve artillery - " -	Between Louvres and Vandeleau.
Reserve ammunition - -	Louvres.
Civil department - -	Senlis.
Pontoon train - - Hawser bridge - -	Road from Chntilly to Paris.

Cavalry encamped and cantoned about Le Haudouin, Vandeleau, and Boissy. Our infantry is passing, bands playing, &c.

LETTER 35

Headquarters, Gonnesse: July 1, 9 p.m.

I sent you a shabby letter this morning, accompanied by a plan of the country round Paris. It may assist in explaining the contest which tomorrow may see. The fate of the contending hosts now trembles in the balance. The sword tomorrow may determine that of Paris, unless the pen tonight shall prevent the struggle. That I wish it may, I need not say: who does not? Today we moved hither from Louvres. My hasty note will have explained our position. We have had today several flags of truce from the enemy, who unaccountably detained in the morning Captain Charmont (German Legion, and also in the Prussian service) and another officer. The duke, in consequence, has ordered an officer of Napoleon's Carabiniers de la Garde to be detained.

Napoleon has at Montmartre 36,000 troops of all sorts. Some cry, "*Vive le Roi!*" others, "*Vive l'Empereur!*" In Paris all is horror and dismay—the population in the streets ready to do any and every thing. Soult has been deprived of his office. Grouchy is disgraced by Napoleon; his crime is that of giving yesterday, at a council of war, his voice against further hostilities. At the duke's this morning were assembled in the same room, *Monsieur*, two of his *aides-de-camp*, Boissy d'Anglas and Andréossy, one of Napoleon's generals who had come in with a flag of truce, and a quondam *aide-de-camp* of the Duke of Ragusa who had come over to our side from Montmartre in the course of the night. General Hügel, who was in the room, says the wry faces the opposite factions made at each other were irresistibly ludicrous.

Napoleon is said to be furious, and to have exclaimed yesterday, "*Je montrerai au monde que la chûte d'un grand homme entrainera celle de beaucoup d'autres!*" (I will show the world that the fall of a great man will lead that of many others!) This is but gasconade; however, I shall not be surprised if, during the night, he should attempt something desperate. I sent Bell four hours ago with orders to the rocket troop to join Blücher's army at St. Germain, where the marshal's headquarters are. The Prussians have crossed the Seine at two points near St. Germain.

Lord Arthur Hill is now at the advanced posts with a flag of truce. Quesnoy has been taken, and in a gallant way, by Prince Frederick of Orange. So, Lord Apsley told me just now, but without particulars. Lord Apsley had just been informed of the circumstance by the duke. General Wrede (Bavarian) has beaten Rapp's corps. Wrede is believed to be by this time at Chalons sur-Marne. The Russian and Austrian Emperors will be at Nancy on the 5th instant. The Austrian General Frimont has beaten Suchet near the Lake of Geneva, at Thormon. Frimont had advanced by the Simplon Road.

Such is the news of the evening. A messenger from England has arrived today. I rejoice to find Colonel Smythe (our chief engineer) has been appointed *aide-de-camp* to the Prince Regent; this is a just attention, both to Smythe and to that invaluable corps.

What an eventful night is this! Tomorrow may see Paris in flames. I have as yet seen no violence, no disorder, on the part of our troops; but Blücher avows that he cannot be answerable for his people, who the day before yesterday, at Louvres, plundered the very quarters of Blücher himself, who could only say, "*Mes enfants, c'est trop.*" ("My children, it's too much"). Should then Paris be assaulted by these troops, what may not be expected! Goodnight; I shall lay me down quietly and compose myself.

Gonnesse: July 2, 7 a. m.

Contrary to expectation, the night has passed quietly. Napoleon has fled; he quitted his adherents the evening of the day before yesterday, and is supposed to have gone to Havre. This falsely called great man never fails to desert, when in extremity, those to whose exertions he owes his power. Davoust commands the mass on Montmartre: that mass is said to have proclaimed the son of Napoleon Emperor. The Bavarians are at Soissons. I hope Paris may surrender today; if not, and (if determined to play a desperate game) the Bonapartists *will* resist, the city may be taken,—but the contest will be most sanguinary. Such is the fury of the Prussians, that I am convinced that if they enter Paris by assault, it will be impossible to check them.

9 a.m.

Davoust has requested an armistice, which Blücher has refused. The one urges that Frimont (the Austrian) has granted an armistice to Rapp, the other, that the Austrian may be right, but that circumstances here are different. I have just been talking to General Washington (the Bavarian *Chargé d'Affaires*) who says that he thinks all will be arranged in the course of the day. I have been looking attentively at our line and at that of the enemy: it is wise to be prepared for all contingencies.

The duke is yet at home. The streets are crowded with troops, chiefly Prussians, hurrying forward: hundreds singing songs of triumph as they move on. At this moment pass the Brunswick Foresters: while they shout, reflexion will say, where is their leader? and where, in a few hours, may be those who seem to have already forgotten him? The inhabitants gaze with stupid unconcern. In not one person, since I entered France, have I yet discovered that indignation at the disgrace their country has suffered, which I hope with us would have burst from every bosom. I hope and expect the British will not be suffered to enter Paris by assault. Let us keep our hands free from rapine and plunder.,

1 p.m.

The reserve artillery (twenty-one pieces, of which four are 18-pounders), and the horse artillery 9-pounders, and the howitzer troop, are ordered to be placed on the great road leading to St. Denis, which is to be attacked. I am going forward to choose the position for the guns. The Jacobin faction seems desperate, if so, it must suffer. I imagine they are but gasconading,—however, we shall be in earnest,—and since they force us, let them take the consequences.—*Adieu.*

Headquarters, Gonnesse: July 3, 5 a. m.

We have been up these two hours. We were going to fight, and were quietly eating our breakfast when we learned that—

Général La Motte est chargé par l'armée de se rendre auprès du Roi, parceque l'armée a besoin de son Roi!!
(General La Motte is charged by the army to go to the king, because the army needs his king!!)
                Signé   Davoust, Duc d'Eckmuhl.

And thus, apparently ends this short, but bloody-war. That it may be so I most devoutly wish: the real state of the case will soon be known.

2 p.m.

It is true, thank God! all is over. Paris has surrendered, and a general officer gone to Roye (near Nesle) for the king, who may be here tonight and in Paris tomorrow. I passed yesterday in prowling at the outposts, and in selecting positions for more misery; today how different the employment! I rather hope that I have arranged to carry the duke's despatches to Vienna.—*Adieu,* I write to save the post. The enclosed little yellow tuft is my sole plunder. I took it, yesterday, from the ruined *château* of Jerome Bonaparte. I may return from Vienna in three weeks, and then I shall set my wits to work to visit England. God bless you.

LETTER 36

Headquarters, Neuilly, half a league from Paris:
July 6, 9 a. m.

I never wrote so much in my life; but times are interesting. As to my wound, you will have learned that it was trifling. When I supposed it otherwise, I refused to have my name inserted in the list already too long for the repose of thousands. On future occasions I should do the same. No man should be returned who can keep his place in the field. If his country loses for a time his exertions, it has a right to know the reason, otherwise the paltry vanity of seeing one's name in the list of wounded is unworthy of a soldier. Thinking in this way, I laughed some few more of our associates out of the list, and they have since thanked me. It is true enough that I have lost my bay mare. I gave fifty, and shall receive thirty-five guineas for the price of what is called a first charger. You may suppose few folks lose their second chargers, for which (by a law, I trust, not like those of the Medes and Persians) thirty guineas are allowed.

The duke *might* have mentioned the horse artillery, which really was of essential service. But my long, perhaps too long, and circumstantial account of the affair of the 18th June, sent to your lady, will have told more than all which need be said on the subject: *requiescat in pace*. May those, too, do so whom we regret.

I wrote a letter to Chapman yesterday, enclosing one relative to a claim for travelling expenses, which I found in the pocket of poor Ramsay. I had previously written to Chapman and Bloomfield, to urge their interest in favour of some remuneration to his sister. I cannot get Ramsay out of my head; such generosity, such romantic self-devotion as his are not common.

You know I contemplate a journey to Vienna; it would be doubly pleasing to me to see my mother and sister after what has happened. I have had a very flattering message from Lord Mulgrave, through Wood. So far so well. I am much flattered by the thanks I have received from my brother officers, for the change of their guns before the action.

I enclose some Paris papers. The French Army, I believe, quitted Paris yesterday. Major Stavely (staff corps) was wounded, I hear, in going to Montmartre yesterday, to receive possession of part of that strong position. Paris is in a ferment, as that city so often is, and has been. We have not yet heard of the proposed review and entry into Paris. Perhaps it is wise to wait a few hours. The "*Deux Chambres*" have produced another Constitution. I hardly know what to think on the subject; only whatever these gentry say, that, one may presume, they will *not* do. However, I doubt not in a few days all will be quiet. We shall have "*Vive Henri Quatre*," some *calembourgs* and loyal songs; and all that has passed will be forgotten. This is a beautiful place, close to the Seine. I suppose it is marked on the sketch I sent from Louvres. The bridge, within a hundred yards of my window, is beautiful, quite flat; some of the slabs of granite thirty-four feet long.—*Adieu*.

Letter 37

Neuilly: July 7, 8 a. m.

I wrote to you yesterday. I now send you the distribution of the army for today. You will see that the duke enters Paris this morning. I shall mount my horse and ride in too, but shall not have a house there till tomorrow. I rode within the barriers last night, or rather drove, having gone in the gig to see Montmartre; we took orderlies, and horses to ride where the ascent was too steep for a carriage. Montmartre is very strong: it would have cost much blood had we attempted to storm it. Work within work, strongly loopholed and palisadoed at every corner. We mounted the tower, on which is the telegraph, and beheld Paris at our feet. The Pantheon, the Tuileries, the Louvre, Notre-Dame, and all the well-known splendid buildings lay in gay confusion.

Our own troops, mixed with the National Guards, kept the barriers; the avenues filled with well-dressed people, walking about with apparent unconcern. The tricoloured flag was on the Tuileries; this, I imagine, will be removed today. General von Müffling (Prussian, and for some time attached to the duke's headquarters) is appointed governor of Paris. On our return we met an English carriage, perhaps Lord Castlereagh's. I have not yet been out, though I have been up for some hours. The day is cool, and we hope for rain. Yesterday was sultry, and the dust still blows in clouds.

That I may not omit mentioning what is really curious, I should tell you of my visiting the celebrated church of St. Denis on the 5th instant. It is a noble edifice: the Swiss who showed it pointed out the spot where, in 1792, he had assisted in burning and destroying the bodies of forty-two kings and queens. They were thrown into a hole and lime poured over them: that of Henri Quatre was first thrown in;—the idol of his people whilst alive, and the theme of history since, how little might such indignity have been expected!

A small mound of earth, encompassed by a few stone steps within a bower, marks the spot: some lilies grow on the mound. In the cathedral we were shown the place where, last year, the relics of Louis XVI. were deposited. The spot is a little to the right of the nave of the cathedral, and just before you mount a few steps leading to the altar.

From this solemn scene,—oh, sad transition!—we went to eat mutton-chops at a *traiteur's*. Had all the kings and queens above mentioned been there, or all the sovereigns of this world, there could not have been greater confusion. "But have you seen the institution for the daughters of officers of the Legion of Honour?"

"No," said everybody, and away we scampered. It is a noble building, originally a convent of Benedictines, with new galleries of Lutzen and of Friedland, and staircases of Jena and Madrid. 560 young ladies are there instructed by 120 governesses. Those whose parents pay anything give 1200 *francs* annually for their education; the rest are educated by the State. In the *salle de refectoire*, where the young ladies dine, is a noble picture representing Napoleon presenting, near Boulogne, the Imperial eagles to his army of England,—to that army which was to have destroyed all that you and I hold dear. With what emotions did we not view the picture! We then saw the school-rooms and sleeping-rooms: the beds are very neat, they are a yard asunder, have no curtains, and each has a little cupboard and drawer attached; the whole establishment (though the ladies had been removed into Paris since Sunday) was scrupulously clean.

There is a similar establishment for the education of the sons of members of the Legion of Honour. It is a superb building, on an eminence in full view from the bridge of Neuilly. The troops are filing past, crowned with laurel, and bands playing.—*Adieu.*

LETTER 38

Neuilly: July 8.

Just going to Paris, where I dined yesterday after seeing the Louvre and the Palais Royal. My billet is at No. 92, Rue de Richelieu. I think in former days (revolutionary ones) the street was called Rue de la Loi. The opera-house is in it. I was one of the first British officers in the Palais Royal: two or three others accompanied me. There was a good deal of crowding to see us, but no incivility. Altogether, Paris looks desolate; the streets look deserted. The Prussians were marching through the city; about 5000, *en masse*, halted in the Place de Carousel, in that spot where Napoleon reviewed his hosts previous to their issuing forth. How changed the scene! The gallery of the Louvre seems the same as to paintings, but there appear many more statues than there were. The king comes in at 3 o'clock. The two Chambers are dissolved; the tricoloured flag no longer waves on the Tuileries.— *Adieu.* I must send this off to save the post.

Paris: July 9.

Will you not wish us joy of being here, and of being here peaceably? The king arrived yesterday. The old government is replaced. The multitude shout "*Vive le Roi!*" and (but we are too wise, or at least too knowing, to trust to appearances) all are loyal, all sincerely desire peace.

I will not attempt to describe yesterday,—the scene baffles description. It was a strange day. Would you had witnessed it! This is a strange city: led away by every whim, the people shout for joy at anything, at nothing. The National Guards, who swore but the day before,—nay, whose printed declaration to support the tricoloured flag and cockade I read *after* I had seen them adopt the white ones,—absolutely danced, rather than marched past. But with their grenadiers' caps carried on the tops of their bayonets, one could not but recollect that a few years since they carried there with equal joy the heads of many a victim.

Our troops remain as mentioned in my letter of the 7th instant; my Vienna trip remains uncertain.—*Adieu.*

Letter 39

Hôtel du Nord, Rue de Richelieu, Paris: July 10.

With regard to poor Ramsay, I see no difficulty; there must be none where the wishes of his family are concerned. I have sent for Serjeant Livesay of Bull's troop, who knows the grave, and can do what is necessary; and Henegan, who is at Brussels, can also attend to the coffin. Let us quit this subject: it is a most painful one; and yet there is a mournful pleasure in attending to the memory of a friend. I have Purcell's inscription,—original,—and in that, and every other respect, better than mine, which is but an ill-managed composition of the thoughts of others. My only objection to Purcell's is the introduction of my own name: this looks like ostentation.

******

The following is the inscription on the tomb of Major Norman Ramsay, erected by Sir Augustus Frazer in the church at Waterloo.

Gulielmus Norman Ramsay
In Exercitu Britannico
Spectatâ Virtute Insignis,
Qui Honoris Illustrem Circulum
Per brevi Spatio Complevit,
Et Sibi satis Vixit
Sed non Patriæ;
Pro Liberatione Europæ
Et Gloriâ Angliæ,
Duce invicto Wellington
Fortissime Pugnans,
Pulcherrimam Mortem Hic Invenit
Die Octo Decima Junii MDCCCXV.
Æternæ Amici et Commilitonis Memoriæ
Hoc Marmor Sacrum Esse Voluit
Augustus Frazer.

******

I still think that, after the body shall have been removed, a stone should record the spot where he fell; and unless the family should object to it, I shall erect one.

I know not why, but I cannot write; this subject arrests me, yet I wish to leave it. I wish even to forget it: not that it is always before me, far from it; but in my gayest moments the recollection of all that passed at Waterloo will intrude, and I can then fancy such a scene of private distress! Alas! all that can be fancied is but too real.

You mention the brevet. I hope there may be one, and I should certainly be most glad that Wood were made a general officer. On some future occasion I should be glad, very glad, to be one of the Prince Regent's *aides-de-camp*. The step is worth a good deal, and the honour a good deal more:—all in good time. I certainly wish, on account of the boys, for several things which before never entered into my mind. But I shall ever make but a sorry courtier;—a natural quickness, best called impatience, will ever unfit me for a life of attendance. I had rather roll the lawn at Bealings than pass my time in any palace.

July 12, 8 p.m.

I began my letter in the morning; but this Paris is a vile place, and one runs about so of a morning; and so many folks assist in the loss of one's time, that the dinner-hour arrives, and then *adieu* to occupation. The Prussians have shown signs of discontent, and have exceedingly disquieted the Parisians, and that in a very tender point. One of the most beautiful bridges in Paris is the Bridge of Jena. It is at the bend of the Seine, opposite Chaillot, and takes its proud name from the defeat of the Prussians at Jena,—of those Prussians whom Napoleon then declared he would cause to beg their bread, and who have twice since that haughty speech entered his capital as conquerors!

This bridge the Prussians had begun to destroy. They had removed masses of masonry from two of the beautiful arches in order to blow it up; but they have been stopped, and the bridge is now the *Pont de l'École Militaire*, which at the farther end of the Champ-de-Mars is directly opposite the bridge. The Prussians, I am told, are packing up those paintings in the Louvre which formerly belonged to Berlin. This is fair, though I regret it; yet I hardly know why I do so, except that the assemblage of so many noble paintings in one place affords a facility to their inspection. But *adieu* for a while; I am going tomorrow to Malmaison, to St. Cloud, and to Sevres, and anticipate much amusement.

July 13.

And really a great deal have I had. We went by the Champs Elysees and Neuilly to Malmaison, late the property and residence of Josephine. The house is a good *château*, not remarkable for size or architecture, but elegantly furnished;—paintings, statues, vases, and pillars, all of great taste. In a beautiful gallery, among other statues, one particularly struck me as resembling Miss Ridout. It was of Josephine herself, of whom an old servant, who had lived with her fifteen years, and was present at her death, spoke in raptures,—said she was the kindest, the best soul that ever lived, the most humane, and attentive to the poor; and so everyone says.

Napoleon saw her twice after their divorce. The first time, the servant said, Josephine was visibly affected; the next, she received him as a stranger. Napoleon slept at Malmaison previous to quitting Paris the last time, but would not sleep in the room in which Josephine had died. This is a small circular room, hung with scarlet cloth; having a profusion of mirrors, and richly ornamented with gold. A circular table of mosaic stood in the middle. The *boudoir* we did not see, one of General Vandeleur's staff having possession of it, and being out. The general is quartered in the house.

The Prussians had torn away a little of the black velvet binding of some of the couches in the gallery, and had torn and carried away the richly ornamented cloth covering the kneeling-stool of a small chapel leading out of the antechamber of the gallery. In the gallery is a beautiful model of the pillar of the Place Vendôme. In another room were two exquisite water-colour drawings of the battles of Aboukir and the Pyramids; and on a most magnificent vase of porcelain, a very beautiful painting of the battle of Marengo. Malmaison is now the property of Eugène Beauharnois, who, after Josephine's death, divided the paintings with Pauline. Josephine lies buried in the church of the neighbouring village of Ruel.

The grounds about Malmaison are beautiful:—Marly in full view. From Malmaison we went to St. Cloud, about two leagues distant, but circling to the right, so as rather to decrease than increase the distance from Paris. St. Cloud is magnificent, but well known, so that I shall not attempt to describe it. A strong guard of Prussians, and equipages of all kinds, announced that was the headquarters of Blücher.

The Prussians have done much mischief, breaking mosaic tables from mere wantonness, and carrying off gilded ornaments, and even fringe and cornices of no value; and this, as the *concierge* told us, from apartments in which none but officers had been. He also told us he had been frequently beaten by the Prussians, though why he knew not. At St. Cloud we saw two celebrated paintings by David:—one of the death of General Dessaix, at Marengo; the other of Bonaparte passing the Alps. The latter picture has been taken from its place and frame, and stands in a passage, liable to injury from any passing knave. Near the painting of Dessaix are the busts of Dampière, Kleber, Hoche, and of an *aide-de-camp* of Kleber's,—Miron, I think. One of the best apartments had couches and chairs beautifully painted on silk. As we descended and were crossing the court-yard, Blücher arrived, and in a moment afterwards. Sir Sydney Smith, who had come to visit the prince.

Leaving St. Cloud, we turned to our right through the beautiful avenues on the banks of the Seine: under the shade we observed two of the royal carriages; Louis XVIII., we were told, was expected, and the carriages and horses were waiting as relays. Under the avenues were, *en bivouac*, a regiment of Prussian Hussars, who took us (we were not in uniform) for Frenchmen, and would hardly let us pass; but on satisfying them that we were English, they gave us three cheers, and we drove on to Sevres, the village celebrated for china. Here we dined and saw the king pass by; about two dozen of his guards attended his carriage, which was followed by another; both had eight horses; there was no cheering or "*Vive le Roi.*"

After dinner we walked to the porcelain manufactory, where we saw so many beautiful things that we were quite puzzled. I must visit Sevres again.—*Adieu.* We learn that we are to be presented to the king and to the Emperor of Austria tomorrow: you shall have an account of our reception.

Letter 40

July 15.

In consequence of a general order, we all attended yesterday at the duke's. All wore their gayest costume. After waiting some time, His Grace got into his state carriage, accompanied by General von Müffling, Lord Hill, and Sir Lowry Cole, and we followed, some on horseback, others in carriages, to the hotel in the Boulevards, where the Emperor of Austria resides. An Austrian guard under arms received His Grace, and we entered the house, and, in the furthest room of a magnificent suite, were presented to the Emperor Francis, who looks worn with care, and much older than when I last saw him, some fourteen years ago, at Vienna.

This ceremony over, we returned to the duke's; we there waited an hour till the appointed time should arrive for waiting on Louis XVIII. The duke retired to his own room, and pulled off his coat, and in that *dishabille* received Lord Cathcart, who had just arrived. I knew his lordship a little formerly, and made my bow as he passed, and was received by a very gracious shake of the hand. In due time we sallied forth as before, and went to the Tuileries. It was impossible in mounting the steps of the great staircase not to think of the massacre of the Swiss guards, and of all the horrors to which this palace had been witness.

We traversed some superb state apartments, and reached that in which is the throne of France: it is of blue velvet, surmounted by a crown with white plumes, and supported by the Imperial eagles, which have not been removed. In half an hour the king entered, attended by one person only, (Châteaubriand, I believe,) and the duke presented us as we severally moved past his majesty, who stood in the middle of the room. When all had been presented, and while we were moving slowly to retire, his majesty spoke in a very slow, dignified, and audible voice the following very pleasing address:—

Gentlemen,
I am very happy to see you here. I have wished to see you all together, to felicitate you on your valour, and to thank you for your humanity to my poor subjects. Many fathers and many children thank you for your humanity.

At concluding the address, his majesty's voice faltered a little, and he was visibly affected: so were all that heard him. I never witnessed a more interesting scene. On retiring, I went through several other apartments of the palace, looked at the theatre (the place, I believe, where Louis XVI. was tried and condemned), and at a noble painting by David of the battle of Austerlitz. This painting is on the ceiling. General Rapp, himself and horse wounded, is bringing, as prisoner, a general officer, whom Napoleon is receiving; Berthier is by the side of Napoleon, Duroc, Bessières, and Murat behind him: these are the principal figures, which are on horseback.

Previous to ascending a wing of the principal staircase leading to the apartment in which is this painting, I traversed one furnished with eighteen full-length figures of Marshals of France. I looked for the place where Ney's picture had stood, but there being no vacancy, began to doubt the report I had heard that the picture had been removed; Sir Charles Colville afterwards told me that Macdonald's picture had replaced Ney's. Macdonald's had previously been taken down. Napoleon having been displeased with him.—*Adieu* for this time.

LETTER 41

Paris: July 25.

Since my last letter little of public a nature has occurred worth relating; all is quite quiet here, and will be so. There has been some confusion on the Loire between the French and Austrians, Soult is taken at Meude, where he has been shut up in the Prefecture. Yesterday was a busy and splendid day of review of the British Army, by the Emperors of Russia and Austria and the King of Prussia. The review began a little before 10 a.m. when the sovereign appeared, and rode down the line. The dust was intolerable. The troops immediately began to march past; the emperors stood in the Place de Louis XV. It was near 5 o'clock before all had passed by: there were 65,000 men under arms, of whom about 10,000 were cavalry and 4000 artillery.

July 27.

I wrote to you the day before yesterday by the post. I have but little of novelty to communicate today. Yesterday I rode to the Hôtel des Invalides to see some beautiful models of fortresses; they far surpassed my expectations. I never saw anything so well executed. The Battle of Lodi (the celebrated passage of the bridge of Lodi in the first years of the Revolution) deserves a detailed account; but I hope you will soon be yourself a spectator of these interesting sights. From the models I went again to the cathedral church of Notre-Dame. I had been there before, but had then missed the chief inducement to a second visit,— the crowns of Napoleon, Maria-Louisa, and of Charlemagne. These crowns and their corresponding sceptres, these *"attributes to awe and majesty"* (as Shakespeare calls them; but where, alas! the *"mercy which is above this sceptred sway?"*) are well worth seeing; the crown of Napoleon is the most elegant, of simple gold, resembling a laurel wreath.

To be very impudent, and to the infinite horror of the grave man who showed the regalia, I put the laurel crown on my head. I had hardly time to run home and dress for S——'s dinner. I sat by a Doctor Marshal, a distinguished character who has long resided in Paris; and supported by strong interest, has lived there as an agent to the Bourbons even during Napoleon's late reign. I dined today with this Doctor Marshal at La Rapée half a mile above the bridge of Austerlitz.

I shall meet there some of those who chiefly contributed, within the walls, to Napoleon's overthrow. Much secret anecdote is picked up in these parties, and I like mixing in foreign society.—*Adieu.*

ALSO FROM LEONAUR
AVAILABLE IN SOFTCOVER OR HARDCOVER WITH DUST JACKET

THE FALL OF THE MOGHUL EMPIRE OF HINDUSTAN *by H. G. Keene*—By the beginning of the nineteenth century, as British and Indian armies under Lake and Wellesley dominated the scene, a little over half a century of conflict brought the Moghul Empire to its knees.

LADY SALE'S AFGHANISTAN *by Florentia Sale*—An Indomitable Victorian Lady's Account of the Retreat from Kabul During the First Afghan War.

THE CAMPAIGN OF MAGENTA AND SOLFERINO 1859 *by Harold Carmichael Wylly*—The Decisive Conflict for the Unification of Italy.

FRENCH'S CAVALRY CAMPAIGN *by J. G. Maydon*—A Special Correspondent's View of British Army Mounted Troops During the Boer War.

CAVALRY AT WATERLOO *by Sir Evelyn Wood*—British Mounted Troops During the Campaign of 1815.

THE SUBALTERN *by George Robert Gleig*—The Experiences of an Officer of the 85th Light Infantry During the Peninsular War.

NAPOLEON AT BAY, 1814 *by F. Loraine Petre*—The Campaigns to the Fall of the First Empire.

NAPOLEON AND THE CAMPAIGN OF 1806 *by Colonel Vachée*—The Napoleonic Method of Organisation and Command to the Battles of Jena & Auerstädt.

THE COMPLETE ADVENTURES IN THE CONNAUGHT RANGERS *by William Grattan*—The 88th Regiment during the Napoleonic Wars by a Serving Officer.

BUGLER AND OFFICER OF THE RIFLES *by William Green & Harry Smith*—With the 95th (Rifles) during the Peninsular & Waterloo Campaigns of the Napoleonic Wars.

NAPOLEONIC WAR STORIES *by Sir Arthur Quiller-Couch*—Tales of soldiers, spies, battles & sieges from the Peninsular & Waterloo campaingns.

CAPTAIN OF THE 95TH (RIFLES) *by Jonathan Leach*—An officer of Wellington's sharpshooters during the Peninsular, South of France and Waterloo campaigns of the Napoleonic wars.

RIFLEMAN COSTELLO *by Edward Costello*—The adventures of a soldier of the 95th (Rifles) in the Peninsular & Waterloo Campaigns of the Napoleonic wars.

AVAILABLE ONLINE AT **www.leonaur.com**
AND FROM ALL GOOD BOOK STORES

ALSO FROM LEONAUR
AVAILABLE IN SOFTCOVER OR HARDCOVER WITH DUST JACKET

OFFICERS & GENTLEMEN by Peter Hawker & William Graham—Two Accounts of British Officers During the Peninsula War: Officer of Light Dragoons by Peter Hawker & Campaign in Portugal and Spain by William Graham.

THE WALCHEREN EXPEDITION by Anonymous—The Experiences of a British Officer of the 81st Regt. During the Campaign in the Low Countries of 1809.

LADIES OF WATERLOO by Charlotte A. Eaton, Magdalene de Lancey & Juana Smith—The Experiences of Three Women During the Campaign of 1815: Waterloo Days by Charlotte A. Eaton, A Week at Waterloo by Magdalene de Lancey & Juana's Story by Juana Smith.

JOURNAL OF AN OFFICER IN THE KING'S GERMAN LEGION by John Frederick Hering—Recollections of Campaigning During the Napoleonic Wars.

JOURNAL OF AN ARMY SURGEON IN THE PENINSULAR WAR by Charles Boutflower—The Recollections of a British Army Medical Man on Campaign During the Napoleonic Wars.

ON CAMPAIGN WITH MOORE AND WELLINGTON by Anthony Hamilton—The Experiences of a Soldier of the 43rd Regiment During the Peninsular War.

THE ROAD TO AUSTERLITZ by R. G. Burton—Napoleon's Campaign of 1805.

SOLDIERS OF NAPOLEON by A. J. Doisy De Villargennes & Arthur Chuquet—The Experiences of the Men of the French First Empire: Under the Eagles by A. J. Doisy De Villargennes & Voices of 1812 by Arthur Chuquet.

INVASION OF FRANCE, 1814 by F. W. O. Maycock—The Final Battles of the Napoleonic First Empire.

LEIPZIG—A CONFLICT OF TITANS by Frederic Shoberl—A Personal Experience of the 'Battle of the Nations' During the Napoleonic Wars, October 14th-19th, 1813.

SLASHERS by Charles Cadell—The Campaigns of the 28th Regiment of Foot During the Napoleonic Wars by a Serving Officer.

BATTLE IMPERIAL by Charles William Vane—The Campaigns in Germany & France for the Defeat of Napoleon 1813-1814.

SWIFT & BOLD by Gibbes Rigaud—The 60th Rifles During the Peninsula War.

AVAILABLE ONLINE AT **www.leonaur.com**
AND FROM ALL GOOD BOOK STORES

www.ingramcontent.com/pod-product-compliance
Lightning Source LLC
Chambersburg PA
CBHW021957160426
43197CB00007B/156